ALSO BY DANIEL STASHOWER

The Adventure of the Ectoplasmic Man
Elephants in the Distance

TELLER OF TALES

TELLER OF TALES

The Life of Arthur Conan Doyle

☾ ☾ ☾

Daniel Stashower

Henry Holt and Company New York

Henry Holt and Company, Inc.
Publishers since 1866
115 West 18th Street
New York, New York 10011

Henry Holt is a registered
trademark of Henry Holt and Company, Inc.

Published in Canada by Fitzhenry & Whiteside Ltd.,
195 Allstate Parkway, Markham, Ontario L3R 4T8.

Library of Congress Cataloging-in-Publication Data
Stashower, Daniel.
Teller of tales : the life of Arthur Conan Doyle / by Daniel Stashower. — 1st ed.
p. cm.
Includes bibliographical references and index.
ISBN 0-8050-5074-4 (acid-free paper)
1. Doyle, Arthur Conan, Sir, 1859–1930. 2. Authors, Scottish—19th century—Biography. 3. Authors, Scottish—20th century—Biography. 4. Spiritualists—Great Britain—Biography. 5. Physicians—Great Britain—Biography. I. Title.
PR4623.S73 1999
823'.8—dc21 98-35059
[b] CIP

Henry Holt books are available for special
promotions and premiums. For details contact:
Director, Special Markets.

First Edition 1999

Designed by Paula Russell Szafranski

Printed in the United States of America
All first editions are printed on acid-free paper. ∞

1 3 5 7 9 10 8 6 4 2

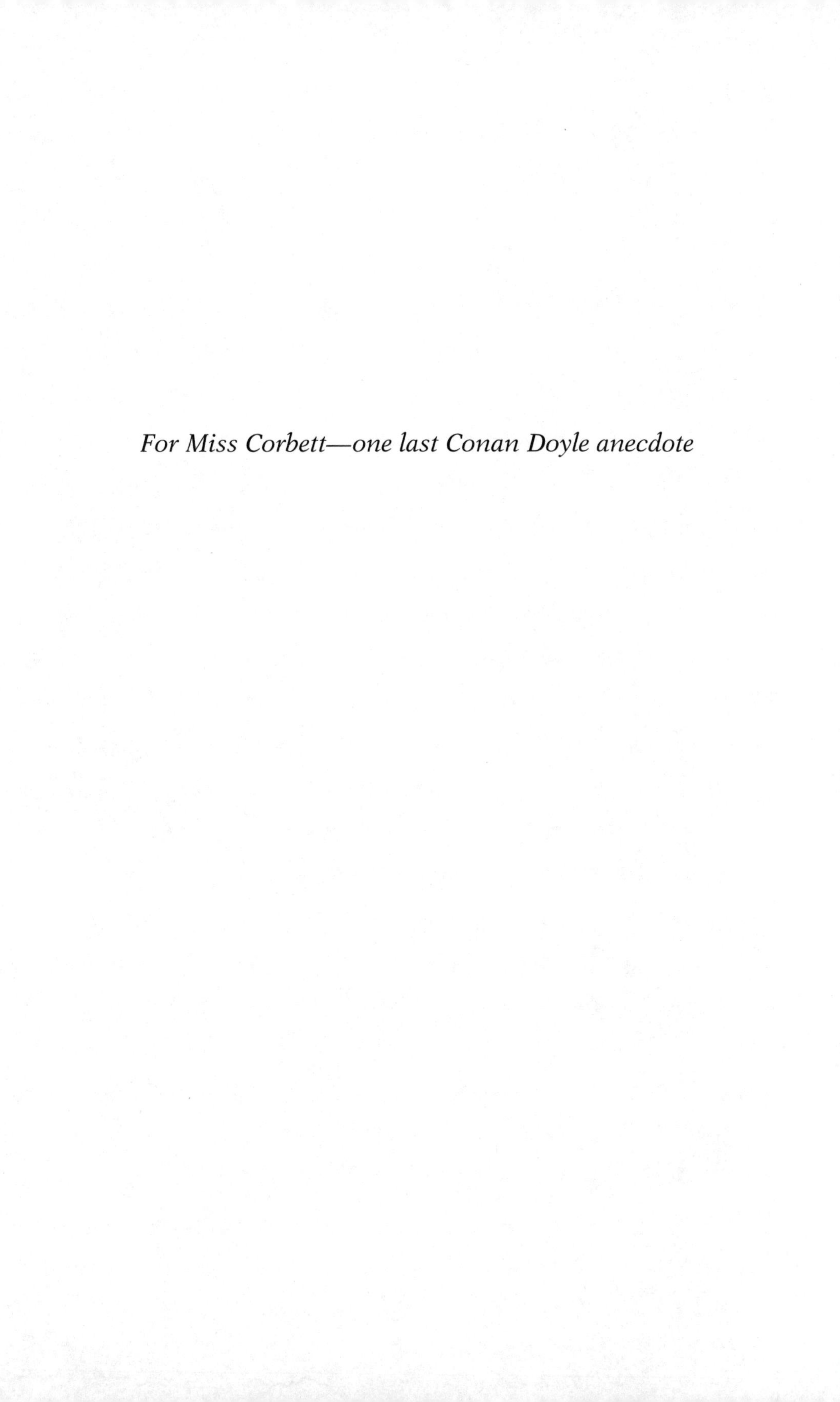

For Miss Corbett—one last Conan Doyle anecdote

Perhaps the greatest of the Sherlock Holmes mysteries is this: that when we talk of him we invariably fall into the fancy of his existence. Collins, after all, is more real to his readers than Cuff; Poe is more real than Dupin; but Sir A. Conan Doyle, the eminent spiritualist of whom we read in Sunday papers, the author of a number of exciting stories which we read years ago and have forgotten, what has he to do with Holmes?

—T. S. Eliot

CONTENTS

PREFACE

Not long ago, in the London showroom of a dealer in rare books, I asked to have a look at a first edition of *The Hound of the Baskervilles*. No price was posted, but I knew that a "bright and unrubbed" copy could go for £600, so my interest was largely theoretical. The assistant manager—an indulgent, friendly sort of person—opened the glass display case and waited patiently as I fingered the brittle volume. After a moment, when I handed it back, she mentioned that there might be some other Conan Doyle material in the back room. If I could wait a moment while she helped another customer, she would check with the manager. After five minutes or so, when my scan of the floor-to-ceiling bookshelves brought me as far as Thackeray, I happened to find myself outside the manager's open door. "There's a customer out front," I heard the assistant say. "He's interested in Conan Doyle."

"Oh, God," came the answer. "It must be an American."

I freely confess to being an American. But I'm not entirely sure why an interest in Conan Doyle should reveal this to a rare book dealer. Was it because only an American could afford the prices he was asking? Or was it, as his tone suggested, that only an American, with an American's suspect tastes in literature, would be interested in a second-rater like Conan Doyle?

It was not the first time I'd had this reaction. Many times over the past five years I've presented myself at British book shops and auction houses as a collector of Conan Doyle material—always taking care to look under *D* for Doyle, but also *C* for Conan Doyle, the compound surname he preferred. The response is invariably polite, but it generally carries a quiet note of sympathy, as though I'd just confessed some exotic intestinal complaint. "Conan Doyle? Well, Sherlock Holmes was brilliant, but Doyle went a bit potty at the end, didn't he? Fairies, ghosts, and that."

"Fairies, ghosts, and that" have been the millstone of Conan Doyle's reputation for the better part of a century. Toward the end of his life, Conan Doyle came to believe that communication with dead souls was possible. His efforts to spread this message, which he considered the most important work of his life, proved to be his undoing. The British public watched with growing incredulity as he made one foray after another into the spirit realm. On any given day he might pronounce upon a ghostly photograph of fallen World War I soldiers, or speculate on a possible literary collaboration with the late Charles Dickens. In America, where such reports were less frequent, it was possible to remain sympathetic, if bemused. In Britain, the general public's tolerance began to fray. "Poor Sherlock Holmes," ran one headline, "Hopelessly Crazy?"

The result was inevitable. Though Sherlock Holmes remains a colossus among cultural icons, Conan Doyle, once the most popular author of his generation, has been sharply downgraded. In Edinburgh, where Walter Scott is commemorated with a towering Gothic monument, Conan Doyle's birthplace is marked by a statue of his fictional detective. *The White Company* and *Sir Nigel*, the books Conan Doyle regarded as his finest work, are seldom read. Conan Doyle's portrait is not currently displayed at London's National Portrait Gallery. Though such decisions owe something to the quality of the portraits involved, it seems curious that Agatha

Christie, Dorothy Sayers, and Daphne du Maurier are all on view while Conan Doyle remains in storage.

Conan Doyle once declared that he would gladly sacrifice whatever literary reputation he enjoyed if it would bring about a greater acceptance of his spiritualist message. To a large extent, he made the sacrifice without achieving the objective. The critic Sherman Yellen, writing of Conan Doyle's spiritualist novel *The Land of Mist* in 1965, offered a view shared by many: "*The Land of Mist* demonstrates that Conan Doyle had made his greatest sacrifice to his Spiritualist beliefs; he had relinquished his literary power to it."

Any writer who would address this delicate topic must first declare a position on the paranormal. I should admit, then, that I have never had any traffic with the spirit realm, that I am a supporter of the Committee for Scientific Investigation of Claims of the Paranormal, and that it has been some years since I believed in fairies. At the same time, I also belong to the Society for Psychical Research, I once shook hands with Uri Geller, and some of my closest friends claim to be psychic. I consider myself, then, a cordial disbeliever.

None of which diminishes my regard for Conan Doyle in any way. Like most of his admirers, my introduction came through Sherlock Holmes. In fact, at the age of eleven I sported a deerstalker hat, carried a magnifying glass in my pocket, and was much given to declarations of "Brilliant deduction!" and "Elementary!"—which greatly endeared me to teachers, friends, and family. Some time later, as I was rereading *The Valley of Fear* for perhaps the ninth time, I noticed on the title page that the author had some twenty or thirty other books to his credit. I found a copy of *The Lost World* at my local library and never looked back.

Sooner or later, though, every Conan Doyle fan bumps up against *The Vital Message* or *The Edge of the Unknown* or one of the author's many other spiritualist works. Most readers simply shrug and look elsewhere, and only a very singular taste would prefer Conan Doyle's two-volume *History of Spiritualism* to *The Adventures of Sherlock Holmes*. In my own case, after dutifully slogging through *The Wanderings of a Spiritualist*, I found myself wondering about the author's state of mind. As John Dickson Carr wrote in 1949, echoing the popular attitude of Conan Doyle's contemporaries, "For a quarter of a century he had loomed thick-shouldered as the sturdy Briton, with no damned nonsense about him. What was wrong? What ailed the man?"

The answer, like the man himself, was far more complicated than it first appeared. Yes, Conan Doyle lost a son in the First World War and, like so many others, sought consolation in the séance room. This was not, however, where his involvement began. Conan Doyle's interest in the spirit realm took root some thirty years earlier, well before his son's birth. This interest was by no means unique; the Society of Psychical Research was already a going concern when Conan Doyle joined in 1893, and its members included prominent scientists, philosophers, members of Parliament, and a future prime minister. For many years Conan Doyle was a mere dabbler in psychic research. He experimented with table-tipping and automatic writing as possible methods of contacting the spirits, and had a short-lived interest in mesmerism and thought transference. Only later, when the testimony of those closest to him erased his lingering doubts, did he become a zealous crusader. For many, he became the living embodiment of the spiritualist craze, rather than its most vocal proponent. His outspokenness, weighed against the cool logic of Sherlock Holmes, seemed to invite public scorn.

"We who believe in the psychic revelation," he wrote near the end of his life, "and who appreciate that a perception of these things is of the utmost importance, certainly have hurled ourselves against the obstinacy of our time. Possibly we have allowed some of our lives to be gnawed away in what for the moment seemed a vain and thankless quest. Only the future can show whether the sacrifice was worth it."

"Personally," he added, "I think it was."

If Conan Doyle's generation was quick to dismiss his queer ideas, our own generation—with its power crystals, White House astrologers, and Area 51—must admit to harboring some queer ideas of its own. It is too much to say that Conan Doyle's vision of a spiritualist utopia has come to pass, nor is it likely that it ever will. The question is not whether we must accept Conan Doyle's beliefs to understand the man. The question is whether it is now possible, nearly seventy years after his death, to examine this aspect of his life with sympathy rather than derision.

Personally, I think it is.

TELLER
OF
TALES

INTRODUCTION

One morning in 1930, not long before his death, Sir Arthur Conan Doyle struggled to his writing desk and reached for pen and paper. He had done a great deal of writing in the previous months—mostly personal correspondence and letters to the press—but that morning he decided instead to try his hand at a sketch. He worked at it for some time, squinting intently over a troublesome detail or a tricky bit of lettering, gazing from the window when inspiration flagged. At length he set down his pen and pushed the drawing aside.

Today, a copy of the sketch hangs in London's Sherlock Holmes pub. It shows a flea-bitten workhorse pulling a heavy baggage cart. A tall pile of packing cases weighs the cart down, and each case bears the label of a different aspect of Conan Doyle's life and work. "Medical Practice" is piled alongside "Historical Novels." "Elections" rests on top of "Psychic Research." "Tales" and "Drama" prop up "Poems" and "The Great War." Perhaps the heaviest case in the pile is the one sandwiched in between "500 Lectures" and "Australia 1921." It reads: "Sherlock Holmes."

Self-pity played no part in Conan Doyle's character. Moreover, his heartfelt belief in spiritualism left him with no fear of death. But though his drawing strikes a lighthearted, self-deprecating tone, there is an unmistakable note of melancholy at its core. Conan Doyle came from a long line of artists—his grandfather was a pioneer of political caricature—and he knew the value of a well-chosen image. This was how he viewed himself as death approached: a draft animal hauling a cart. And Sherlock Holmes, his legendary fictional detective, was just another piece of heavy cargo.

Conan Doyle had lived long enough to realize that Sherlock Holmes would, in Watson's phrase, "eclipse and predominate" the rest of his work. Already the historical novels by which he hoped to be remembered had fallen out of fashion, and his poetry, plays, and wartime chronicles had largely disappeared from view. His dedication to spiritualism, and his vigorous campaign to spread his beliefs to others, had taken a heavy toll on his reputation as a serious man of letters. Many found it difficult to reconcile that the creator of Sherlock Holmes, the "perfect reasoning and observing machine," could have given himself so wholly to a cause that appeared to defy logic. A man who espoused such ideas, it seemed, could not be taken seriously as a writer.

In person, however, Conan Doyle seemed the very model of reason and sincerity. Interviewers were struck by his easy manner and lack of pretension. As he grew older, and thicker around the middle, Conan Doyle's heavy eyelids and drooping mustache made him look more and more like a genial walrus. "He was a great, burly, clumsy man," wrote one friend, "with an unwieldy-looking body that was meant for a farm bailiff, with hands like Westphalian hams, and a nervous halting voice whose burrs recalled the banks and braes of Scotland."

His looks were deceiving. Behind the placid, sleepy-eyed demeanor was a man of strong convictions, some of them absurd, all of them deeply felt. Conan Doyle's life had been a series of hard-fought crusades, of which spiritualism was only the latest. In 1890, he warned against an ill-tested cure for tuberculosis. In 1902, he defended the

British government against charges of misconduct in the Boer War. In 1906, he championed the cause of divorce law reform. In 1909, he spoke out against atrocities in the Congo. In 1910, he took up the case of Oscar Slater, a man falsely accused of murder. In 1914, he warned against the potentially devastating effects of a submarine blockade. In each case Conan Doyle fought his corner with skill and resourcefulness, marshaling whatever advantages could be wrought from his fame and natural eloquence. Many of his causes were unpopular, but Conan Doyle's private sense of honor mattered more to him than public opinion. "He seemed to us," his daughter Jean once wrote, "to be the very personification of the chivalry of the stories of King Arthur's Round Table."

It was probably not how he would have described himself. *The Strand* magazine, where the bulk of Conan Doyle's work first saw print, took a poll of its leading writers in 1927. Of all the characters of literature, the editors asked, which one would you most like to have created?

H. G. Wells put forward the name of Shakespeare's Falstaff, as did John Buchan. Compton Mackenzie expressed his preference for Don Quixote. The names of D'Artagnan, Don Juan, and Robinson Crusoe were raised by other prominent writers. Conan Doyle's answer, as the editors of *The Strand* were quick to point out, was "characteristic of him as a writer and a man." Conan Doyle gave the name of Colonel Newcome, a character from a Thackeray novel published shortly before his birth. The reason was simple. This character, Conan Doyle said, was "an ideal English gentleman."

Conan Doyle was not English—his family was Irish, and he himself had been born in Scotland—but he was very much a gentleman. In a sense his own character had been molded with greater care and ambition than that of Sherlock Holmes, Brigadier Gerard, Professor Challenger, or any of his other fictional heroes. It projected his natural decency, and expressed a wistful strain of nostalgia for the orderly values of a previous age. Of all his novels, he most prized the historical romances that celebrated the Regency period or the Napoleonic era. In later life, this insistence on old-fashioned values and propriety caused some to regard him as a quaint, if charming, old party, somewhat out of step with the times. Conan Doyle lived until 1930, but he remains fixed in the popular imagination as a figure of gaslight and hansom cabs. The final decade of his life saw the publication of *Lady Chatterley's Lover*, *A Farewell to Arms*, *The Great Gatsby*, *Ulysses*, and *To the Lighthouse*. Conan Doyle, by contrast, published a book in which undersea explorers travel to Atlantis.

And through it all, Sherlock Holmes, whose adventures he considered to be "on a different and humbler plane" from the rest of his books, continued to thrive. "I've written a good deal more about him than I ever intended to do," Conan Doyle said in 1927, forty years after Holmes first saw print, "but my hand has been rather forced by kind friends who continually wanted to know more. And so it is that this monstrous growth has come out, out of what was really a comparatively small seed."

Indeed, this "monstrous growth" had long since taken on a life of its own. "Sherlock Holmes and Dr. Watson are household words; both names have passed into the language," remarked H. Greenhough Smith, Conan Doyle's editor at *The Strand*. "This is a feat any author might feel proud of. Sherlock Holmes, without question, is the most familiar and most widely known character in English fiction." Even the *Times* of London, celebrating the great detective's longevity in 1930, felt compelled to offer a word of consolation to Conan Doyle's other creations: "Those who follow the fortunes of Rodney Stone, of the White Company, of the Brigadier Gerard, of Micah Clarke, and a crowd of others, share momentous events by the side of intimate friends, and this double gift of providing at once good company and stirring deeds is displayed by Conan Doyle in his short stories as well as his books. Seeing what perils they ran, and how nobly, it is easy to understand the resentment of the rest of the Conan Doyle characters that pride of place must always be yielded to a lean and somewhat inhuman scientific student of crime, living not in the brave and brutal fourteenth century or at the heart of the Napoleonic epic, but amid the hansom cabs and street urchins of the London of the later eighties."

Today, Sherlock Holmes has become a cultural archetype—like Robin Hood, Romeo and Juliet, or the Three Musketeers. Children in Zaire and Tibet recognize his image as easily as that of Santa Claus or Mickey Mouse. He has been featured in countless books, movies, television programs, musicals, stage plays—even a ballet. The familiar hawk-nosed profile appears on teapots, chess pieces, dinner plates, board games, computer programs, and chewing gum packages. He has acquired a cult of followers whose devotion borders on the mystical. Sherlockians, as they call themselves, can be found in every corner of the globe—and, increasingly, on the Internet—discussing such matters as the depth to which a sprig of parsley might sink in butter on a hot day or the true location of Dr. Watson's strangely transient war wound. Ask a Holmes buff for news of the giant rat of Sumatra and he or she will answer, gently, that it is a tale for which the world is not yet prepared.

"Every detective story writer makes mistakes," wrote Raymond Chandler, "and none will ever know as much as he should. Conan Doyle made mistakes which completely invalidated some of his stories, but he was a pioneer, and Sherlock Holmes is mostly an attitude and a few dozen lines of unforgettable dialogue."

Chandler's assessment, however cavalier, strikes at an essential truth. Sherlock Holmes can be read over and over again for the sheer joy of Conan Doyle's writing. It is not that we have forgotten who killed Sir Charles Baskerville or who stole the Bruce-Partington Plans. We return to Baker Street to watch a genius at work. Once heard, the call is never forgotten: The singular worm unknown to science. Wilson the notorious canary trainer. The curious incident of the dog in the nighttime. "Come, Watson, come. The game's afoot."

But in the rush to lionize Sherlock Holmes, Conan Doyle has been nudged aside. Too often Conan Doyle is dismissed as a figure who happened to be present when Holmes sprang into being—or, as some Sherlockians would have it, the "literary agent" who helped Dr. Watson's writings find their way into print. This would have been a great sadness to Conan Doyle. Though he played down his own achievement with Holmes, he understood that he had taken a little-known genre and pulled it into the light.

Conan Doyle is often portrayed as "the man who hated Sherlock Holmes," but this is only partially true. At times he sickened of his famous creation—as evidenced by the early attempt to kill him off—but in his final years he was able to strike a conciliatory note: "I have not in actual practice found that these lighter sketches have prevented me from exploring and finding my limitations in such varied branches of literature as history, poetry, historical novels, psychic research, and the drama. Had Holmes never existed I could not have done more, though he may perhaps have stood a little in the way of the recognition of my more serious literary work."

Perhaps. Though some would argue that these "lighter sketches" were the work of an innovative genius, breaking new ground and lighting the way for future generations of writers, while the more "serious" work remains hopelessly tethered to the past. Even so, Sherlock Holmes constitutes only a small part of Conan Doyle's total body of work, and if his admirers could be lured away from the bright lights of Baker Street for a few moments, they would find an interesting and rewarding writer waiting in the shadows. Conan Doyle gave the world a great deal of pleasure. He deserves, at least for a moment, to be taken on his own terms.

"I have had a life which, for variety and romance, could, I think, hardly be exceeded," he once wrote. "I have known what it was to be a poor man and I have known what it was to be fairly affluent. I have sampled every kind of human experience. I have known many of the most remarkable men of my time. I have had a long literary career after a medical training which gave me the M.D. of Edinburgh. I have tried my hand at very many sports, including boxing, cricket, billiards, motoring, football, aeronautics and skiing, having been the first to introduce the latter for long journeys into Switzerland. I have travelled as Doctor to a whaler for seven months in the Arctic and afterward in the West Coast of Africa. I have seen something of three wars, the Sudanese, the South African and the German. My life has been dotted with adventures of all kinds. Finally I have been constrained to devote my latter years to telling the world the final result of thirty-six years' study of the occult, and in endeavouring to make it realize the overwhelming importance of the question. In this mission I have already travelled more than 50,000 miles and addressed 300,000 people, besides writing seven books on the subject. Such is the life I have led."

And such is the story that follows.

1

The Empty Chair

I have learned never to ridicule any man's opinion, however strange it may seem.

—ARTHUR CONAN DOYLE,
"THE CAPTAIN OF THE POLE-STAR"

As many as six thousand people crowded into London's Royal Albert Hall that night, while hundreds more were turned away at the doors. Inside the great hall, men in evening dress and ladies in long gowns found their seats and whispered excitedly to one another. They had come to see and hear Sir Arthur Conan Doyle, perhaps the most beloved author of his generation, and he was expected to deliver startling news.

In most respects, the gathering was no different from the hundreds of lectures Conan Doyle had given in such places as Paris, New York, Melbourne, and Capetown. On this particular night, however, the sense of anticipation was especially intense. The reason was simple: Conan Doyle had died five days earlier at his home in Crowborough.

Even so, expectations remained high. Conan Doyle's death, according to the beliefs he himself passionately espoused, would not necessarily prohibit his appearance on the lecture platform that evening. At the time of his passing on July 8, 1930, Conan Doyle had long been established as the world's best-known and most outspoken proponent of spiritualism, the belief that the dead communicate with the living through an earthly conduit, or medium. For fourteen years Conan Doyle had devoted the better part of his time, energy, and resources to this cause, which he often described as "the most important thing in the world." For those who found comfort and meaning in his beliefs, he was "the Saint Paul of spiritualism." For those who did not, he was a sad and deluded old man who had squandered his greatness. The Albert Hall memorial, many believed, would settle the issue once and for all.

Sir Arthur's widow, Lady Jean Conan Doyle, entered the hall accompanied by her sons, Denis and Adrian, her daughter, Jean, and her stepdaughter, Mary. Denis and Adrian wore evening dress and carried top hats. Lady Conan Doyle, in keeping with the beliefs she shared with her husband, had chosen a dress of gray lace rather than traditional mourning garb, to signify that Sir Arthur's "translation" to the other side was not an occasion for sorrow. "I know perfectly well that I am going to have conversations with my father," Adrian Conan Doyle had told the press at his father's funeral. "We shall miss his footsteps and his physical presence, but that is all. Otherwise he might have only gone to Australia."

At the edge of the lecture platform, a row of chairs was set out for the family. A square of cardboard held one of them in reserve. It read: "Sir Arthur Conan Doyle." Lady Conan Doyle sat to the left of her husband's chair, just as she had for twenty-three years at nearly all of the many lectures, meetings, and other assemblies to which her husband lent his name and influence. This gathering, she had confided to a friend, would be the last public demonstration she would ever attend with her husband.

Conan Doyle's chair would have been the only empty seat in the house. Some accounts estimated the size of the crowd at ten thousand, though this would have seriously strained the hall's capacity. Extra seats had been set up to accommodate some of the overflow.

As the audience settled, Mr. George Craze of the Marylebone Spiritualist Association stepped to the microphone to open the proceedings. He offered a few words of welcome, then read out a written statement from Lady Conan Doyle. "I want in my children's, and my own and my beloved husband's name, to thank you all from my heart for the love for him which brought you here tonight," her message stated. However, she continued, she wished to correct an erroneous impression that Sir Arthur's materialized form was expected to appear in the empty chair. "At every meeting all over the world I have sat at my beloved husband's side, and at this great meeting, where people have come with respect and love in their hearts to do him honour, his chair is placed, as I know that in psychic presence he will be close to me, although our earthly eyes cannot see beyond the earth's vibration. Only those with the God-given extra sight, called clairvoyance, will be able to see the dear form in our midst."

Ernest Hunt, a spiritualist colleague of Conan Doyle's, added a forceful elaboration. Pointing to the vacant chair, Hunt warned that it would be "a very trifling thing if any people here with hectic imagination were to persuade themselves imaginatively that they could see Sir Arthur's form there. Nor would it be to me of surprising worth that some gifted clairvoyant could see the form. But it would be a great thing for you to see in the vacant chair a symbol of God's call to you to qualify for being Doyle's successors."

These words, however heartfelt, did little to quell the mood of charged expectancy. Since the first reports of Conan Doyle's death there had been a wave of heated speculation about his possible return. "Widow Indicates Hope of Message," declared a front-page headline in the *New York Times*. "Return of Sir Arthur Conan Doyle's Spirit Awaited by Widow and Sons," reported the *New York American*. London's *Daily Herald* gave details of a secret code word Conan Doyle had left with his wife, to prove the veracity of any spirit contact.

If Lady Conan Doyle clung to the hope of a message, however, she believed that such communication could only come through a "spirit sensitive." The notion that her husband's materialized form would suddenly pop into view arose from a series of ambiguous statements made by Conan Doyle's spiritualist colleagues. "I should imagine that he would be quite capable of demonstrating already," declared one of the organizers of the Albert Hall event. "He was quite prepared for his passing."

After five days of such statements, the attempt to inject a note of moderation had come too late. Throughout the hall eyes were kept trained on the empty chair beside Lady Conan Doyle, hoping for some telltale indication of an otherworldly presence.

For a time, the evening proceeded like any other memorial service. Friends and colleagues rose to pay tribute, hymns were sung, and passages of Scripture were read. A telegram from the prominent physicist Sir Oliver Lodge, who shared Conan Doyle's spiritualist beliefs, praised the author's unwavering dedication: "Our great-hearted champion will soon be continuing his campaign on the other side with added wisdom and knowledge," adding, *"Sursum corda!"*—lift up your hearts.

After nearly an hour, the more conventional portion of the service drew to a close. George Craze returned to the microphone and asked the audience to stand for two minutes of silent reflection. "The completeness of the silence," wrote one journalist, "was unforgettable."

As the congregants took their seats, Craze stepped forward once again. "This evening," he began, "we are going to make a very daring experiment with the courage implanted in us by our late leader. We have with us a spirit sensitive who is going to try to give impressions from this platform. One reason why we hesitate to do it in such a colossal meeting as this is that it is a terrific strain on the sensitive. In an assembly of ten thousand people a tremendous force is centered upon the medium. Tonight, Mrs. Roberts will try to describe some particular friends, but it will be the first time this has been attempted in such a tremendous gathering. You can help with your vibrations as you sing the next hymn, 'Open My Eyes.' "

Mrs. Estelle Roberts stepped to the front of the platform as the last notes of the hymn faded. A slimly built, fluttery woman with dark hair and large brown eyes, Mrs. Roberts stood at the microphone for several moments wringing her hands. Her anxious, dithery appearance belied a canny flair for the dramatic. She had been a favorite medium of Conan Doyle's before his departure for the spirit plane, and he had remarked more than once on her "mesmerizing presence."

In one sense, George Craze had been correct to call the evening a daring experiment. Mrs. Roberts had been called upon to make contact with departed souls—Conan Doyle's among them. In so doing, she would also attempt to make believers out of skeptics. Though spiritualism was by no means uncommon in 1930, it was generally practiced in the darkened confines of the séance room. There, under conditions set by the medium, one might expect to see tambourines floating in the air, or ghostly messages appearing on chalk slates, or any number of other discarnate effects taken to signify spirit contact. Under the bright lights of the Albert Hall, there would be no floating tambourines. Instead, Mrs. Roberts would be expected to stand before the microphone and pluck spirit messages out of the ether, apparently at random, and deliver them to individuals in the crowd. Any evidence of otherworldly phenomena, then, would show itself solely in the force of her spoken testimony.

The mesmerizing presence that had so impressed Conan Doyle was not immediately apparent. For some time, Mrs. Roberts did nothing more than rock back and forth on her heels, and soon the sounds of coughing and restless movement could be heard from the audience. At this, she appeared to gather her resolve. Shielding her eyes like a sailor on lookout, Mrs. Roberts swept her eyes over the gallery, tiers, and boxes. Her attention fixed not on the faces of the expectant crowd, but on the empty space above their heads. "There are vast numbers of spirits here with us," she announced. "They are pushing me like anything."

With that, she launched into a long unbroken monologue, apparently describing a series of spirits whom only she could see. "All around was a great concourse of spirit people anxious to communicate with their friends," she would later write. "For half an hour, by means of clairvoyance, I relayed their messages to individuals among the mass of people in the hall."

In fact, she did more than relay messages. She described the features of the departed spirits, along with their characteristics, their method of speech, and even their clothes. The audience sat in rapt attention as she related tales of whole families reunited in the spirit world, then pointed out their loved ones in the crowd. "There was something uncanny," one journalist noted, "in the sight of ten thousand people sitting in the Albert Hall, half afraid, yet half hoping that they might be singled out."

"There is a gentleman over there with hardly any hair," said Mrs.

Roberts, pointing to a man in the gallery. "Yes, there! That's right. I see standing there in front of you, a spirit form of a young soldier." She peered into the lights, as if for a better view.

"He looks to be about twenty-four. In khaki uniform. Upright. Well-built. Mouth droops a little at the corners. He passed suddenly." Mrs. Roberts angled her head, as though listening to a soft voice.

"He gives me 1916 as the year of passing. He distinctly calls you 'Uncle.' 'Uncle Fred.' "

The man in the gallery stiffened, and nodded that the details were correct.

"He speaks of a brother Charles," she continued. "Is that correct? He wants to know if you have Aunty Lillian with you. Do you understand?"

From his seat, the man nodded more vigorously.

"The boy tells me that there is a little anxiety going on, and wants me to tell you he is helping you. He—" Abruptly, as if pushed by unseen hands, Mrs. Roberts broke off her discourse and took a few lurching steps across the stage. She turned to an empty space on the platform behind her. "All right," she said, as though addressing a large and unruly knot of people. *"All right."*

She turned back to the audience and pointed to a woman seated in one of the boxes. "There is a gentleman here, John Martin. He says he is looking for his daughter Jane. Correct?"

The woman in the box confirmed that her name was Jane, and that her late father's name had been John Martin. Mrs. Roberts continued. "He has got her mother, Mary Martin, with him. Little Willie is with them. Also your sister Mary. Your sister-in-law Elizabeth is with him. You understand?" Mrs. Roberts opened her mouth to continue, then pitched forward as though shoved by invisible hands. "All right!" she said, glaring at the empty space behind her. "Just a minute!" She turned to the front of the platform, gathered herself, and carried on.

Then as now, opinions differed sharply as to whether such revelations were produced by psychic means or by more earthbound contrivances such as audience confederates and careful vetting of potential contacts. The crowd at the Albert Hall consisted mostly of those sympathetic to spiritualist phenomena, and at least one of those who received a message was himself a practicing medium. To a large extent, it seems fair to say, Mrs. Roberts was preaching to the converted.

But the audience also held a fair number of nonbelievers who had come only to pay tribute to Conan Doyle. "It was either an amazing proof of communication with the dead," said one skeptic, "or it was the most cold-blooded and cruel fraud." A reporter from the *Saturday Review* was more blunt: "I should like to have heard Sherlock Holmes examining the medium at the Albert Hall last Sunday, for the methods that were employed were hardly reminiscent of Baker Street. Indeed, far from satisfying Holmes, I doubt if the evidence would even have been good enough for Watson."

After half an hour or so, the nonbelievers could no longer suppress their irritation. From various parts of the hall, some forty or fifty people rose from their seats and headed for the exits. From the platform, Mrs. Roberts registered her distress: "I can't go on with all these people walking out," she announced. A blast of organ music rang out to cover the confusion, and for a few moments it appeared the memorial might come to a premature end.

At that moment, however, just as the meeting threatened to disband in an atmosphere of disarray, Sir Arthur Conan Doyle made his appearance. "He is here!" Mrs. Roberts shouted. "He is here!" The skeptics stopped in their tracks. All eyes locked on the empty chair.

Later, Mrs. Roberts would claim that Conan Doyle had been on the platform all along: "I saw him first during the two minutes' silence," she would recall. "Then when I was giving my messages I saw him again. He was wearing evening dress. He walked across the platform and sat in the empty chair. He was behind me, encouraging me while I was doing my work. I recognized once more that fine, clear voice of his, which could not be mistaken."

Whatever one's opinion of her psychic abilities, Mrs. Roberts's timing could not be faulted. Her announcement galvanized the audience. From the farthest reaches of the house, people strained for a better view of the empty chair.

A serene smile spread across Lady Conan Doyle's features. Mrs. Roberts stepped over to her side. "I have a message for you, dear, from Arthur," she said. Lady Conan Doyle gave a nod.

"Sir Arthur told me that one of you went into the hut this morning," Mrs. Roberts said, referring to a building on the family's Crowborough estate. "Is that correct?"

"Why, yes," said Lady Conan Doyle. "I did."

Mrs. Roberts nodded, and leaned forward. "The message is this: Tell Mary—"

Just then a second blast from the pipe organ drowned out the medium's voice, so that only those sitting nearby could hear. Mrs. Roberts spoke for some moments, while Conan Doyle's family listened intently. Occasionally one of his sons would lean forward to add a word of explanation or clarification. Lady Conan Doyle simply sat and listened.

For the rest of her life, Lady Conan Doyle would decline to discuss the contents of the message, saying only that she was perfectly convinced it had come from her husband. "I am as sure of that," she told a reporter that night, "and of the fact that he has been here, as I am that I am speaking to you."

Her sincerity was evident as she sat listening to the words of the medium. For several moments she sat perfectly still, her features radiant, her eyes fixed on a point at the far end of the hall. She held her gaze for several moments, then brushed her cheek and looked away.

2

The Cobbler's Lapstone

"I am a medical man, and observation is everything in my profession."
"I thought you were a detective at first."

—ARTHUR CONAN DOYLE,
"THE RECOLLECTIONS OF CAPTAIN WILKIE"

The students were pouring down the sloping street which led to the infirmary," wrote Conan Doyle in one of his earliest stories, "each with his little sheaf of note-books in hand. There were pale, frightened lads, fresh from the High Schools, and callous old chronics, whose generation had passed on and left them. They swept in an unbroken, tumultuous stream from the university gate to the hospital. The figures and gait of the men were young, but there was little youth in most of their faces. Some looked as if they ate too little—a few as if they drank too much. Tall and short, tweed coated and black, round-shouldered, bespectacled and slim, they crowded with clatter of feet and rattle of sticks through the hospital gate."

The story, called "His First Operation," takes place at the University of Edinburgh Medical School, where Conan Doyle went to study medicine in 1876. Centered on South Bridge in the "old town" section of Edinburgh, the university was a place of dark stone and winding keeps, vaguely sinister in appearance. "The old town," wrote Dorothy Wordsworth, sister of the poet, "with its irregular houses, stage above stage, seen as we saw it, in the obscurity of a rainy day, hardly resembles the work of man, it is more like a piling up of rocks."

By the time of Conan Doyle's arrival, the University of Edinburgh was already three hundred years old. Unlike the vastly wealthier Oxford and Cambridge, however, Edinburgh's only treasures of note were a jeweled mace and the skull of George Buchanan, an eminent scholar. Early students spoke Latin—so as not to soil their mouths with common Scots—and were forbidden to go to taverns or to funerals, both of which provided much of the city's entertainment at that time.

In Conan Doyle's day students no longer spoke Latin or wore academic gowns, though he might have welcomed an excuse to cover his threadbare clothing. In his first weeks, Conan Doyle would have been one of the "pale, frightened lads" making his way along the flagstone path toward the gloomy surgical amphitheater. But unlike the sensitive hero of his story, Conan Doyle probably did not faint away at the sight of a descending scalpel.

The Royal Infirmary's surgical amphitheater was a gaslit chamber lined with tiers of horseshoe benches, rising from floor to ceiling. The benches commanded a view of the solid wooden operating table at the center of the room, along with a long shelf of sturdy metal surgical instruments—forceps, tenacula, saws, and trocars. Below the table was a long tin tray filled with sawdust, for catching blood and debris.

Conan Doyle probably felt some relief, during an early surgery lecture, to see that the operating table had not been dressed for a demonstration. Instead, he and his classmates fixed their attention on the lecturer, an imposing figure in a swallowtail coat, who stood at the front of the table fingering a glass-stoppered vial.

Dr. Joseph Bell, author of *A Manual of the Operations of Surgery*, was only thirty-nine years old when Conan Doyle first saw him. He was a tall man with piercing gray eyes, sharp features, and an eagle-beak nose. His voice was high and strident, and like Conan Doyle he spoke in the richly accented tones of an Edinburgh native. Bell had a peculiar, jerky manner of walking, and gave off an aura of restless energy as he paced before the operating table. "He could be most impatient," recalled one student. "Woe to the young man whose preparation was found wanting."

Bell waited a moment while the young men settled themselves. Then he cleared his throat and began to speak. "This, gentlemen, contains a most potent drug," he said, holding the glass vial aloft. "It is *extremely* bitter to the taste. Now, I wish to see how many of you have developed the powers of observation that God granted you."

He folded his arms and surveyed the room. " 'But sair,' you will say. 'It can be analyzed chemically.' " Bell nodded, as if considering the point. "Aye, aye, but I want you to taste it—by smell and taste. What? You shrink back?" Bell pulled the stopper and waved the vial under his nose. Then he swirled the amber liquid with a finger. "As I don't ask anything of my students which I wouldn't do alone with myself, I will taste it before passing it around."

He brought his hand to his mouth and sucked his finger. Evidently the potion had a remarkably vile taste; Bell's features contorted as though he had sampled poison.

After a moment, he recovered himself. "Now," he said, handing the vial to a student in the first row, "you do likewise."

A murmur rose from the benches as the vial was passed from hand to hand. Conan Doyle's classmates would have been a varied and unusual group; Edinburgh's medical school was one of the finest in the world, drawing students from as far away as eastern Europe and America. Whatever one's background, Bell's lecture theater had a great leveling effect. Wealthy foreign students and scruffy local boys like Conan Doyle became equals; each had to pay his four guineas to the lecturer, and each had to sample the hideous amber liquid.

When the vial had completed its rounds, Bell looked out over the rows of students and gave a sad shake of his head. "Gentlemen," he said, "I am deeply grieved to find that not one of you has developed his power of perception, the faculty of observation which I speak so much of, for if you had truly observed me, you would have seen that, while I placed my *index* finger in the awful brew, it was my *middle* finger—aye—which somehow found its way into my mouth."

Bell sighed with satisfaction as a chorus of groans went up from the assembly. His point had been made.

Subsequent lectures would not be so frivolous. Having established the importance of developing one's powers of observation, Bell went on to give astonishing demonstrations. In one, a woman with a small child was shown into the amphitheater. Bell had never seen the woman before, and had no information about her case or her background. He greeted her politely, and she said good morning in reply.

"What sort of crossing did you have from Burntisland?" Bell asked.

"It was guid," came the answer.

"And had you a good walk up Inverleith Row?"

"Yes."

"And what did you do with the other wain?" Bell asked, indicating that the woman had only one child with her.

"I left him with my sister in Leith."

"And would you still be working at the linoleum factory?"

"Yes, I am."

It seemed a great deal of information to have extracted from a simple "good morning." "You see, gentlemen," said Bell, turning to his students, "when she said good morning to me I noted her Fife accent, and, as you know, the nearest town in Fife is Burntisland. You notice the red clay on the edges of the soles of her shoes, and the only such clay within twenty miles of Edinburgh is the Botanical Gardens. Inverleith Row borders the gardens and is her nearest way here from Leith. You observed that the coat she carried over her arm is too big for the child who is with her, and therefore she set out from home with two children. Finally she has dermatitis on the fingers of the right hand, which is peculiar to workers in the linoleum factory at Burntisland."

In the third row, Conan Doyle nodded slowly as he reviewed each link in the chain of reasoning. Then he opened his notebook and began to write.

Arthur Ignatius Conan Doyle was born on May 22, 1859, in a small flat at No. 11 Picardy Place, Edinburgh—about one mile from the university. He was the second of Charles and Mary Doyle's ten children, of whom seven survived. From his great-uncle Michael Conan, a distinguished journalist, Arthur and his elder sister, Annette, received the compound surname of Conan Doyle.

At the time of Arthur Conan Doyle's birth, his Irish-Catholic family enjoyed a prominent position in the world of art. John Doyle, Arthur's grandfather, had left Dublin at the age of twenty to become a celebrated portrait painter in London. Over the initials H.B., he also produced sketches of Regency notables that were thought to be "somewhat wicked." He is remembered today as a pioneer of political caricature.

John Doyle had four sons, three of whom also achieved notable success in the art world. (A fifth son, Francis, died at the age of fifteen.) James was a noted historian as well as an artist. Henry became director of the National Gallery of Ireland. Richard illustrated children's books and became well known for his work in the humor magazine *Punch*—one of his designs served as the magazine's cover for more than one hundred years.

Three of John Doyle's sons prospered; the fourth, Arthur Conan Doyle's father, did not. Charles Altamont Doyle had come to Edinburgh at the age of nineteen to become an assistant surveyor in Scotland's Board of Works. Initially, he met with some success—he is thought to have had a hand in the design of the fountain at Holyrood Palace, on Edinburgh's royal mile, and also a window at Glasgow Cathedral. At one stage in the 1860s, his talents were sought by the distinguished firm of George Waterston & Sons, which had recently expanded into lithographic printing. These were isolated accomplishments; Charles Doyle was a high-strung alcoholic and never advanced to any great degree from the position he took as a teenager.

In 1855, at the age of twenty-two, Charles Doyle had married seventeen-year-old Mary Foley, the granddaughter of his landlady. A lively, well-educated woman, Mary Doyle took a special interest in the traditions of chivalry, and captivated her children with tales of knights and their quests. Years later, in an autobiographical novel called *The Stark Munro Letters*, Conan Doyle drew on the memory of her "sweet face" and "general suggestion of a plump little hen" for his portrait of the title character's mother. "Ever since I can remember her," Mr. Stark Munro declared, "she has been the quaintest mixture of the housewife and the woman of letters, with the high-bred spirited lady as a basis for either character. Always a lady, whether she was bargaining with the butcher, or breaking in a skittish charwoman, or stirring the porridge, which I can see her doing with the porridge-stick in one hand, and the other holding her *Revie des deux Mondes* within two inches of her dear nose."

In truth, it is unlikely that Mary Doyle had many occasions to break in a skittish charwoman, but her love of books made a lasting impression on her son. She had, Conan Doyle would recall, a born storyteller's gift of "sinking her voice to a horror-stricken whisper" when she reached the crisis of a story. "In my early childhood," her son would write in his autobiography, "as far back as I can remember anything at all, the vivid stories which she would tell me stand out so clearly that they obscure the real facts of my life."

Perhaps this was just as well, as the real facts were none too happy. In later years, Conan Doyle would recall with characteristic cheer that he had been raised in "the hardy and bracing atmosphere of poverty." In truth, Charles Doyle gradually lost his struggle with alcohol, and as his behavior grew more and more erratic, the income from his surveyor's post could no longer be relied upon. The Doyle family changed addresses at least seven times by the time Arthur was ten, and on at least one occasion, it appears, the boy was sent to live with friends, possibly to shield him from his father's deterioration.

In 1868, when Arthur was nine years old, his wealthy uncles offered to send him to a Jesuit boarding school in England. Arthur boarded the train in Edinburgh by himself, and cried most of the way to the border. For the next seven years, he would see his family only during summer holidays. Through the long absences he remained devoted to his mother, whom he called "the Ma'am," and sent her letters almost continually—a habit that persisted for more than fifty years.

Conan Doyle spent two years at Hodder, in Lancashire, and another five years at its senior school, Stonyhurst. It was not a period he would recall with fondness. "Corporal punishment was severe," he wrote, "and I can speak with feeling as I think few, if any, boys of my time endured more of it. It was of a peculiar nature, imported, I fancy, from Holland. The instrument was a piece of india-rubber of the size and shape of a thick boot sole. One blow of this instrument, delivered with intent, would cause the palm of the hand to swell up and change color. When I say that the usual punishment was nine on each hand, and that nine on one hand was the absolute minimum, it will be understood that it was a severe ordeal, and that the sufferer could not, as a rule, turn the handle of the door to get out of the room in which he had suffered. To get twice nine on a cold day was about the extremity of human endurance."

The boys subsisted mainly on bread and hot milk, with a "joint" at lunchtime and fish on Fridays. In the afternoon a snack called "bread and beer" made its appearance—"a bit of dry bread and the most extraordinary drink," he recalled, "which was brown but had no other characteristic of beer."

Even so, Conan Doyle did not resent the Spartan lifestyle half so much as the soul-deadening quality of the education. Years later he wrote angrily of the "uncompromising bigotry" of his Jesuit masters and an educational system "calculated to leave a lasting abhorrence of the subjects."

His happiest hours were spent at sports, where his natural athleticism began to emerge. He enjoyed cricket above all, though he took a cricket ball to the knee at one match and had to be carried to the infirmary by the batsman. The experience failed to put him off; in time he became captain of the side at Stonyhurst.

The lonely student also came to realize that he had "some literary streak" that was not common to all. "There was my debut as a storyteller," he would tell an interviewer. "On a wet half-holiday I have been elevated onto a desk, and with an audience of little boys all squatting on the floor, with their chins upon their hands, I have talked myself husky over the misfortunes of my heroes. Week in and week out those unhappy men have battled and striven and groaned for the amusement of that little circle."

Those amusements came at a price. "I was bribed with pastry," he recalled. "Sometimes, too, I would stop dead in the very thrill of a crisis, and could only be set a-going again by apples. When I had got as far as 'With his left hand in her glossy locks, he was waving the blood-stained knife above her head, when—' I knew that I had my audience in my power."

Conan Doyle emerged from Stonyhurst at the age of sixteen. Too young to begin a course of professional training, he was packed off to Feldkirch, Austria, for another year of Jesuit schooling. This appears to have been a happier experience. He enjoyed the scenery and the sports, learned to play the tuba—possibly because he was the only student large enough to do it justice—and did a fair amount of reading for pleasure. One book he had with him was to exert a considerable influence: *Tales of Mystery and Imagination,* by Edgar Allan Poe.

On his return from Austria, the time had come to select a career. "I found that the family affairs were as straitened as ever," he wrote. "No promotion had come to my father, and two younger children, Innes, my only brother, and Ida, had arrived to add to the calls upon my mother. Another sister, Julia, followed shortly afterwards. But Annette, the eldest sister, had already gone out to Portugal to earn and send home a fair salary, while Lottie and Connie were about to do the same."

In fact, the circumstances were more dire than Conan Doyle let on. Far from receiving a promotion, Charles Doyle's alcoholism would soon bring his working life to a close. In 1876, when his son was only seventeen, Charles Doyle entered a nursing facility to receive treatment. Later, doctors diagnosed him as an epileptic. At the time, this dimly understood ailment carried a heavy stigma. In time, Charles Doyle would be transferred to a lunatic asylum.

In an early story called "The Surgeon of Gaster Fell," Conan Doyle offers a hint of the unhappy circumstances of his father's committal. In the story, a young surgeon is thought to have imprisoned an elderly man in a "sinister cage," possibly for the purpose of some cruel experiment. It is later revealed that the prisoner is the surgeon's own father, whose mental aberration has taken a "homicidal turn." The surgeon has resorted to drastic measures in order to keep his father from the lunatic asylum, a prospect that terrifies the old man. "It would weary you were I to describe the terrible experiences which his family have undergone," the surgeon declares. "Suffice it that, by the blessing of God, we have succeeded in keeping his poor crazed fingers clear of blood."

Conan Doyle waited more than twenty-five years before collecting this story in book form. When he did, the passage above had been stricken. Clearly the story is a dramatic exaggeration, but it suggests something of Conan Doyle's anguish over his father's confinement. It has been theorized, but never confirmed, that Conan Doyle himself was required to sign his father's committal papers.

Throughout his life, Conan Doyle kept silent about his father's unhappy decline, preferring instead to dwell on the artistic side of this "dreamy aesthetic figure." "The world," he was to write, "not the family, gets the fruits of genius." The remark reflects a generosity of spirit he probably did not feel at the time. At the age of seventeen, Conan Doyle felt a heavy pressure to assume at least some of his absent father's responsibilities. "Perhaps it was good for me that the times were hard," he wrote, "for I was wild, full-blooded, and a trifle reckless, but the situation called for energy and application so that one was bound to try to meet it. My mother had been so splendid that we could not fail her."

Full-blooded or not, Conan Doyle was keenly aware of the sacrifices his family had made, and would continue to make, so that he might receive a professional education. On his return from Austria, he found that his mother had begun taking in lodgers. This expedience, he would later write, "may have eased her in some ways, but was disastrous in others."

Why, exactly, this was disastrous is left unsaid. Conan Doyle was probably referring to a particular lodger, Dr. Bryan Charles Waller, who would come to assume a prominent role in the affairs of the Doyle family. Only six years older than Conan Doyle, Dr. Waller came into their lives as a lodger but soon took over paying the rent. Waller, who not only practiced medicine but also published poetry, made a powerful impression. Initially Conan Doyle warmed to the support and stability Waller offered, but his later silence is provocative. It has been suggested that Waller may have jilted one of Conan Doyle's sisters, but if this is true it cannot have caused too serious a breach. Mary Doyle was to spend more than thirty years living in a cottage on Waller's estate—long after her eldest son could easily have supported her.

If Waller remains an obscure figure, it is safe to speculate that he influenced Conan Doyle's choice of profession. Family tradition might have dictated an artistic pursuit, but instead a medical career was chosen. "It had been determined that I should become a doctor," Conan Doyle commented, "chiefly, I think, because Edinburgh was so famous a centre for medical learning." The fact that Waller had trained there, and could offer coaching for the entry examinations, must have had some bearing on the decision.

With Waller's assistance, Conan Doyle did well on his entrance examinations and won a bursary of £40, much to the relief of his hard-pressed mother. When he went to collect the money, however, he learned that the prize had been given to another student, as it was intended for study of the arts rather than the sciences. Worse yet, it was now too late to find a corresponding science prize. "It was manifest robbery," Conan Doyle recalled, and the unhappy incident colored his feelings as he began his studies.

"Edinburgh University," he would write in his early novel *The Firm of Girdlestone*, "may call herself, with grim jocoseness, the 'alma mater' of her students, but if she be a mother at all, she is one of a very stoic and Spartan cast, who conceals her maternal affection with remarkable success. The only signs of interest she ever deigns to evince towards her alumni are upon those not infrequent occasions when guineas are to be demanded from them. Then one is surprised to find how carefully the old hen has counted her chickens."

These are not, it seems fair to say, the words of a college booster, yet Conan Doyle never offered any criticism of the education he received. However grim and gray the buildings themselves may have been, the school itself bustled with energy. James Barrie and Robert Louis Stevenson were also students during Conan Doyle's years there. "Strange to think," he said, "that I probably brushed elbows with both of them in the crowded portal."

The medical faculty, too, boasted a number of famous names. These included Dr. James Young Simpson, a pioneer in the use of chloroform; Sir Charles Wyville Thomson, recently returned from his zoological expedition aboard the *Challenger*; and Baron Joseph Lister, of antiseptic fame, who held a chair of clinical surgery when Conan Doyle arrived on campus. Lister's theories were not universally accepted at the time, and Conan Doyle would write of the pointed rivalry between the supporters of Lister's antiseptic and those of the more established carbolic acid. "Shut the door," Lister's detractors were heard to say. "Ye'll let the germs oot!"

But it was Joseph Bell, the hawk-nosed master of deduction, who made the deepest impression. By the end of Conan Doyle's second year, Bell plucked him from the amphitheater benches to serve as an assistant in his ward, giving the young student a chance to observe his methods at close quarters. "A clerk's duties are to note down all the patients to be seen, and muster them together," Conan Doyle recalled. "Often I would have seventy or eighty. When everything was ready, I would show them in to Mr. Bell, who would have the students gathered round him. His intuitive powers were simply marvellous. Case No. 1 would step up. 'I see,' said Mr. Bell, 'you're suffering from drink. You even carry a flask in the inside breast pocket of your coat.' Another case would come forward. 'Cobbler, I see.' Then he would turn to the students, and point out to them that the inside of the knee of the man's trousers was worn. That was where the man had rested the lapstone—a peculiarity only found in cobblers."

A celebrated example of Bell's abilities—later recorded in Conan Doyle's autobiography—involved a patient who had given no information whatsoever before Conan Doyle brought him forward.

"Well, my man," Bell said, after a quick glance at the patient, "you've served in the army."

"Aye, sir," the patient replied.

"Not long discharged?"

"No, sir."

"A Highland regiment?"

"Aye, sir."

"A non-com officer?"

"Aye, sir."

"Stationed at Barbados?"

"Aye, sir."

Bell turned to his bewildered students. "You see, gentlemen," he explained, "the man was a respectful man but did not remove his hat. They do not in the army, but he would have learned civilian ways had he been long discharged. He has an air of authority and he is obviously Scottish. As to Barbados, his complaint is elephantiasis, which is West Indian and not British, and the Scottish regiments are at present in that particular island."

"To his audience of Watsons," Conan Doyle said, "it all seemed very miraculous—until it was explained, and then it became simple enough."

For Bell, this was far more than a parlor trick. "In teaching the treatment of disease and accident," he said, "all careful teachers have first to show the student how to recognize accurately the case. The recognition depends in great measure on the accurate and rapid appreciation of *small* points in which the diseased differs from the healthy state. In fact, the student must be taught to observe. To interest him in this kind of work we teachers find it useful to show the student how much a trained use of the observation can discover in ordinary matters such as the previous history, nationality, and occupation of a patient.

"The patient, too, is likely to be impressed by your ability to cure him in the future if he sees you, at a glance, know much of his past. And the whole trick is much easier than it appears at first. For instance, physiognomy helps you to nationality, accent to district, and, to an educated ear, almost to county. Nearly every handicraft writes its sign manual on the hands. The scars of the miner differ from those of the quarryman. The carpenter's callosities are not those of the mason. The shoemaker and the tailor are quite different.

"The soldier and the sailor differ in gait, though last month I had to tell a man who said he was a soldier that he had been a sailor in his boyhood. The subject is endless: the tattoo marks on his hand or arm will tell their own tale as to voyages; the ornaments on the watch chain of the successful settler will tell you where he made his money. A New Zealand squatter will not wear a gold mohur, nor an engineer on an Indian railway a Maori stone. Carry the same idea of using one's senses accurately and constantly, and you will see that many a surgical case will bring his past history, national, social, and medical, into the consulting room as he walks in."

Conan Doyle's own talents in this area were still far from developed. In fact, he often found himself struggling simply to understand what the patients were saying. An effective clerk, Bell had warned, must command a wide range of Scottish idioms. Would this be a problem? Conan Doyle assured him it would not. Shortly thereafter an elderly patient appeared complaining of a "bealin' in his oxter," which left the young clerk thoroughly baffled. "It seems," he admitted ruefully, "the words really mean an abscess in the armpit."

Though Joseph Bell remembered him as one of his brightest students, Conan Doyle considered himself a mediocre student. "I took my fences in my stride and balked at none of them," he said, "still I won no distinction in the race." This is hardly surprising, considering the punishing schedule he set for himself. Mindful of the financial pressures at home, Conan Doyle hit on a plan to compress each year's study into six months, leaving half the year free to work as a medical assistant. "When I first set forth to do this," he admitted, "my services were so obviously worth nothing that I had to put that valuation upon them. Even then it might have been a hard bargain for the doctor."

Even if he worked for free, Conan Doyle reasoned, there would still be something of a savings involved. If the assistantships provided room and board—and perhaps the possibility of some small stipend—the strain on his mother's pocketbook would be eased. With this modest goal in mind, Conan Doyle began advertising his services in a medical paper.

His first position, with a Dr. Richardson of Sheffield, did not bode well. They parted "by mutual consent" after only three weeks. He fared better with Dr. Elliot of Shropshire. His duties were not particularly taxing, so he spent much of his four-month tenure reading. On one occasion, though, when an old cannon exploded during a local celebration, the untried medical student had to step into the breach. Conan Doyle arrived on the scene to find a patient with a "lump of iron" protruding from his head. "I tried not to show the alarm which I felt," he recalled, "and I did the obvious thing by pulling out the iron." After satisfying himself that the brain had not been injured, he "pulled the gash together, staunched the bleeding, and finally bound it up, so that when the doctor did at last arrive he had little to add."

Conan Doyle's next position brought him two pounds a month with Dr. Reginald Hoare of Birmingham, whose "five-horse City practice" kept him on the go from morning to night. Hoare and his wife took a strong liking to the affable young Scot. "My position in the house," he claimed, "was soon rather that of a son than of an assistant."

In all, Conan Doyle would spend three clerkships with Dr. Hoare, cultivating not only his medical skills but also his growing passion for literature. "I used to be allowed twopence for my lunch," he wrote, "that being the price of a mutton pie, but near the pie shop was a secondhand book shop with a barrel full of old books and the legend 'Your choice for *2d*' stuck above it. Often the price of my luncheon used to be spent on some sample out of this barrel."

Any number of mutton pies gave way to Tacitus, Homer, and Swift during those months in Birmingham. Conan Doyle read with an indiscriminate passion, and many of the books he fished out of the bargain barrel remained on his shelves for the rest of his life. He often said that he wouldn't exchange his cheap edition of Macaulay for the finest leather-bound volume.

During his second stint with Dr. Hoare, inspired by the treasures of the bargain barrel, the nineteen-year-old medical assistant decided to try his own hand at fiction. "It was in this year that I first learned that shillings might be earned in other ways than by filling phials," he noted. "Some friend remarked to me that my letters were very vivid and surely I could write some things to sell."

Borrowing heavily from Poe and Bret Harte, two of his favorite writers at the time, Conan Doyle sat down and wrote a story called "The Mystery of Sasassa Valley," a treasure-hunt yarn set in South Africa. The story stands out among his early efforts for its polish and drive, with many of the Conan Doyle hallmarks already in evidence—a rich background, an engaging narrator, and a tight, neatly turned plot.

To Conan Doyle's delight, the story was accepted by a prominent

Edinburgh magazine called *Chambers's Journal,* which had published the debut of Thomas Hardy a few years earlier. Like most authors, he treasured his first publication—and the check for three guineas that came with it—and would always retain a warm feeling for the magazine. "After receiving that little cheque I was a beast that has once tasted blood," he would tell an interviewer, "for I knew that whatever rebuffs I might receive—and God knows I had plenty—I had once proved I could earn gold, and the spirit was in me to do it again."

Dozens of other stories followed, along with a somewhat larger collection of rejection notices. In later years, Conan Doyle would adopt an airy tone toward his early efforts, as though the whole thing had been something of a lark. In truth, his impulse to write was anything but lighthearted. It could not have been easy to find time for literary efforts on top of his accelerated calendar of studies, but Conan Doyle was already developing the ruthless self-discipline that would mark his entire career. He needed the money desperately—"My mother had been so splendid that we could not fail her"—and he was willing to try his hand at anything.

This sense of writing as a business, rather than a calling, never entirely left him. Like any young author, however, he took pride in his achievements. He felt a rush of satisfaction when James Hogg—who published his second story, "The American's Tale," in *London Society*—advised him to give up medicine in favor of literary pursuits. Hogg, Conan Doyle boasted in a letter to his mother, regarded him as "one of the coming men in literature."

Hogg's was a minority opinion. Though Conan Doyle's early stories showed a great deal of natural talent and imagination, most were derivative of the writers he admired—hardly a surprising trait in a writer not quite out of his teens. "Every writer is imitative at first," he later said. "I think that is an absolute rule; though sometimes he throws back on some model which is not easily traced. My early work, as I look back on it, was a sort of debased composite photograph in which five or six different styles were contending for the mastery." As he gained confidence, however, he began to draw on his own experiences as a medical student, rather than the exotic situations and locales he had read about in adventure tales.

As he turned inward for inspiration, the influence of Joseph Bell and his science of deduction began to assert itself. "I used to rather pride myself on being able to spot a man's trade or profession by a good look at his exterior," Conan Doyle wrote in a story called "The Recollections of Captain Wilkie," also published in *Chambers's Journal*. "I had the advantage of studying under a professor at Edinburgh who was a master of the art, and used to electrify both his patients and his clinical classes by long shots, sometimes at the most unlikely of pursuits, and never very far from the mark. 'Well, my man,' I have heard him say, 'I can see by your fingers that you play some musical instrument for your livelihood, but it is a rather curious one—something quite out of my line.' The man afterwards informed us that he earned a few coppers by blowing 'Rule Britannia' on a coffeepot, the spout of which was pierced to form a rough flute."

It would be some years yet before the Edinburgh professor evolved into the Baker Street detective, but in a small way the game was already afoot. Conan Doyle probably wrote this story as a student, but he would have to wait several years to see it in print. Other stories did not sell at all. As a means of generating extra shillings, he admitted, fiction left a great deal to be desired. His financial prospects were no brighter when he returned to Edinburgh for his third year of study. Every so often, though, he looked up from his medical texts and allowed his eyes to linger on the yellow-backed copy of *Chambers's Journal*.

One afternoon during Conan Doyle's third year, a fellow student named Currie broke in on his studies to make a strange proposition. "Would you care," Currie asked, "to start next week for a whaling cruise?" This "monstrous question," Conan Doyle recalled, made further study impossible.

Barely one week later, he sailed for the Arctic Circle.

3

The Great Northern Diver

First begin
Taking in.
Cargo stored,
All aboard,
Think about
Giving out.
Empty ship,
Useless trip!

—ARTHUR CONAN DOYLE,
"ADVICE TO A YOUNG AUTHOR"

The Greenland whaler *Hope* sailed from Peterhead on the afternoon of February 28, 1880, carrying a crew of twenty-five Scottish sailors. A throng of well-wishers cheered from shore as the four-hundred-ton ship sailed out of the harbor; the fortunes of the coastal fishing town depended heavily on the success of the voyage.

The *Hope* picked up twenty-five more sailors as it passed the Shetland islands, bringing the total complement of men to fifty. The crew would spend two months hunting seals off the coast of Greenland before heading farther north to track the bowhead, or "right," whale.

At the time, as whale oil gave way to petroleum products, the era of the great fleets of sailing whalers was drawing to a close. Whale oil was still used for soaps and lubricants, but the baleen—the long, bony plates in a whale's mouth—now had greater value. Strong and flexible, its uses ranged from kitchen utensils to corset stays.

Apart from its cannon-fired harpoon guns, the *Hope* employed hunting techniques in use for centuries. When a whale was sighted, seven of the ship's eight small whaling boats would be lowered into the water, and the crews would row silently toward the prey. When the boat pulled within range, the gunner fired a harpoon attached to a strong coil of rope, keeping the whale tethered as it sounded to as much as two hundred fathoms. The initial harpoon blast was seldom fatal; sperm whales were known to turn and ram the attacking boats, or even crush the vessels and crews in their powerful jaws. In most cases, however, the whale tired of being played on the line, allowing the lancers to finish the job. The carcass would then be towed back to the ship, lashed to the side, and stripped of its skin for processing. The blanket of blubber would be hacked into pieces and rendered in huge iron pots; the baleen was pried out, cleaned, and bundled.

Conan Doyle was a young man on the first real adventure of his life, and he soon found himself caught up in the thrill and camaraderie of the hunt. "To play a salmon is a royal game," he wrote, "but when your fish weighs more than a suburban villa . . . it dwarfs all other experience."

Even so, he would come to have qualms about this "murderous harvest," as he called it. "Yet amid all the excitement—and no one who has not held an oar in such a scene can tell how exciting it is—one's sympathies lie with the poor hunted creature. The whale has a small eye, little larger than that of a bullock, but I cannot easily forget the mute expostulation which I read in one, as it dimmed over in death within hand's touch of me."

Fresh from his third year of study, Conan Doyle knew nothing of whaling when he came aboard the *Hope*. He had signed on not as a crewman but as ship's surgeon. "I was only twenty years of age when I started," he recalled, "and as my knowledge of medicine was that of an average third year's student, I have often thought that it was as well that there was no very serious call upon my services."

The salary was "two pound ten a month and three shillings a ton oil money"—far more than he could hope to earn rolling pills for Dr. Hoare. Claud Currie, the student who offered him the berth, had arranged the adventure for himself, but found at the last minute that he could not go. He may have chosen Conan Doyle as his last-minute replacement because they were roughly the same size, and he could pass over the heavy clothing and leather boots he had purchased for himself. To Currie's Arctic kit, Conan Doyle added some books, a journal, and two pairs of boxing gloves.

The gloves caught the eye of Jack Lamb, the ship's steward, as Conan Doyle stowed his things under his bunk. Lamb examined the gloves while Conan Doyle explained that he had taken up boxing as a form of exercise at Edinburgh. Lamb, sizing up the tall recruit, seized on the chance to test his mettle. The steward pulled on the gloves and proposed a bout right then and there.

By all accounts Conan Doyle was a fine boxer, with a genuine appreciation for the rules and subtleties of the "manly art." Boxing would feature in several of his books—*The Croxley Master* would follow the adventures of a boxing medical student—and he was even to write a play with a boxing theme. Lamb, by contrast, was a street brawler. Conan Doyle had no sooner pulled on his gloves than the smaller, bandy-legged steward charged across the cramped cabin. Alarmed, the young ship's surgeon quickly put up his guard. For some time, Conan Doyle crouched behind his curled forearms in the best tradition of the Marquis of Queensberry. Lamb, meanwhile, flailed and thrashed as if trying to put out a grease fire with his fists. Every so often Conan Doyle ventured a sporting jab or a polite feint, then settled back, waiting for Lamb to play himself out like a whale on the line. In time, when Lamb showed no sign of tiring, Conan Doyle hauled off and flattened the smaller man with a thunderbolt to the head. Lamb was impressed. "So help me," he told the first mate, "he's the best surgeon we've had! He's blackened my e'e!"

"It was the first (and very nearly the last) testimonial that I ever received to my professional abilities," Conan Doyle said.

Having established his credentials, Conan Doyle quickly fell in with the rest of the ship's officers. It seemed odd that the captain had chosen a weak, spindly man as his first mate, while a brawny red-haired giant named Colin McLean worked as an assistant to the cook. All became clear when the ship left the harbor: McLean, who was illiterate, did not qualify for a Board of Trade certificate. Once the ship was safely under way, McLean and his counterpart switched places.

McLean, Conan Doyle soon learned, had a volcanic temper. "I have a vivid recollection of an evening which I spent dragging him off the steward, who had imprudently made some criticism upon his way of attacking a whale which had escaped. Both men had had some rum, which had made the one argumentative and the other violent, and as we were all three seated in a space of about seven by four, it took some hard work to prevent bloodshed. Every now and then, just as I thought all danger was past, the steward would begin again with his fatuous, 'No offense, Colin, but all I says is that if you had been a bit quicker on the fush—' I don't know how often this sentence was begun, but never once was it ended; for at the word 'fush' Colin always seized him by the throat, and I Colin round the waist, and we struggled until we were all panting and exhausted. Then when the steward had recovered a little breath he would start that miserable sentence once more, and the 'fush' would be the signal for another encounter. I really believe that if I had not been there the mate would have hurt him, for he was quite the angriest man that I have ever seen."

McLean's was not the only foul temper on the ship, and it often fell to the genial young surgeon to play peacemaker, as the captain would not have intervened in a case such as this. Ship's protocol kept him largely isolated from the rest of the officers and crew, and Conan Doyle soon found that his chief duty was to keep him company. "I should have found it intolerable if the captain had been a bad fellow," said Conan Doyle, "but John Gray of the *Hope* was a really splendid man, a grand seaman and a serious-minded Scot." One hopes that Captain Gray shared his young surgeon's fondness for the works of Thomas Babington Macaulay, whose historical and social essays were Conan Doyle's latest enthusiasm. For eight months he pressed Macaulay on everyone from the harpooner to the cook, at least some of whom were unacquainted with the works of this noted statesman-poet. "Honest Scotch harpooners have addled their brains over it," he wrote of his prized volume, "and you may still see the grease stains where the second engineer grappled with Frederick the Great."

Macaulay's influence faded somewhat as the ship progressed toward the Arctic ice fields. The vast white expanse seemed miraculous to the young surgeon, who had never set foot outside of Britain to that point. "I awoke one morning to hear the bump, bump of the floating pieces against the side of the ship," he wrote, "and I went on deck to see the whole sea covered with them to the horizon. They were none of them large, but they lay so thick that a man might travel far by springing from one to the other. Their dazzling whiteness made the sea seem bluer by contrast, and with a blue sky above, and that glorious Arctic air in one's nostrils, it was a morning to remember."

The *Hope* reached the open ice fields off the coast of Greenland by mid-March, but an agreement between Britain and Norway prohibited seal hunting until after the March breeding season. The crew used the time to track schools of seals to the main pack. "When you do come upon it, it is a wonderful sight," Conan Doyle wrote. "From the crow's nest at the top of the main mast, one can see no end of them. On the furthest visible ice one can still see that sprinkling of pepper grains."

On April 3, the date specified by the treaty, the crew fanned out across the ice with clubs in hand. Here, too, Conan Doyle felt the stirrings of conscience, though he soon fell back on the accepted rationale of the time. "It is brutal work," he admitted, "though not more brutal than that which goes on to supply every dinner table in the country. And yet those glaring crimson pools upon the dazzling white of the ice fields, under the peaceful silence of a blue Arctic sky, did seem a horrible intrusion. But an inexorable demand creates an inexorable supply, and the seals, by their death, help to give a living to the long line of seamen, dockers, tanners, curers, triers, chandlers, leather merchants, and oil-sellers, who stand between this annual butchery on the one hand, and the exquisite, with his soft leather boots, or the savant, using a delicate oil for his philosophical instruments, upon the other."

Conan Doyle's qualms about the brutality of the hunt did not stop him from volunteering to participate on the very first day. As he prepared to lower himself over the bulwarks, however, Captain Gray ordered him back—the ice was too dangerous for a novice. Annoyed, Conan Doyle sat down on an icy bulwark and promptly fell overboard. "The accident brought about what I had wished," he recalled, "for the captain remarked that as I was bound to fall into the ocean in any case, I might just as well be on the ice as on the ship."

Inexperienced on the ice, Conan Doyle fell in twice more and finished the day in bed while his clothes dried out in the engine room. "I had to answer to the name of 'the great northern diver' for a long time thereafter," he admitted.

Despite the inauspicious start, Conan Doyle soon became adept at hopping from one ice floe to another—so much so that he soon went off hunting by himself like any other member of the crew. One afternoon, while crouching over a freshly killed seal, he stood up to change position and slipped backward off the edge of the ice. Sheepishly, he reached up to pull himself out of the frigid water, but his hands slipped off the slick rim of ice. Fighting off panic, Conan Doyle tried another spot. He clawed frantically, but could not find a handhold on the smooth, glassy edge.

No one had seen him fall in, and Conan Doyle realized—as both a medical man and a sailor—that he would be dead in minutes if he could not get himself back on the ice. Worse, he could feel the frigid water doing its work—his limbs were growing numb and would soon be useless. He remembered the seal he had been skinning. With a desperate effort, he churned the water with his legs, extending his reach just enough to grab hold of the dead animal's hind flipper. Using the seal as leverage, he began hauling himself out of the water. To his horror, the dead seal's carcass began sliding toward him across the ice, yielding to his weight. Conan Doyle knew that if he dragged the animal over the edge of the ice, he would certainly die. For a few tense moments there was "a kind of nightmare tug-of-war," with Conan Doyle trying to ease himself over the rim before the animal came crashing down on top of him. At last he got one knee out of the water and flopped onto the ice beside the dead creature. Once again the great northern diver finished the day in bed.

This time, he had to spend a while thawing his clothes before he could even manage to remove them.

In June, the ship turned north and the whale hunt began. The *Hope* carried eight whaling boats, but it was usual to send out only seven while the so-called idlers, those who had not signed on as sailors, remained safely onboard. On Conan Doyle's voyage, the idlers felt themselves to be a particularly robust group. They volunteered to man the extra boat and made it, at least in Conan Doyle's estimation, one of the most efficient. "We were all young and strong and keen," he later told an interviewer, "and I think our boat was as good as any." Conan Doyle's willingness to pull his own oar would have made him extremely popular with his shipmates. Each man—Conan Doyle included—had a stake in the profits of the voyage. As an idler, he was mere baggage; in a boat, he became one of the crew.

For the young man, the whale hunt represented something more than money in his pocket. He had been raised on tales of knights and their quests. Now he himself was living a modern epic, pursuing a gigantic beast through a strange, otherworldly landscape. He may have felt misgivings about the slaughter—more than once he would be literally drenched in blood—but they gave way to the heady thrill of the hunt. The gloom of Edinburgh fell away under the brilliant midnight sun. His father's illness and his family's penury could not follow him here. His conscience was clear—the money he earned would go straight into his mother's purse—but a deeper strain of longing had begun to stir. The Arctic, he believed, had awakened "the soul of a born wanderer."

Conan Doyle became a seasoned whaler as the weeks passed, so much so that Captain Gray offered him double pay if he would serve as harpooner as well as surgeon on the next voyage. "It is well that I refused," he said, "for the life is dangerously fascinating."

In fact, it was dangerous in every way. On one hunt, Conan Doyle found himself in the lancing boat, charged with killing the whale once it had been harpooned and played. As the injured whale struggled, the rowers took up a safe position away from the thrashing tail. Suddenly, the wounded creature's enormous "side-flapper" rose out of the water and poised over the boat. For a moment the six men watched in mute horror as the huge fin arched over them, blocking out the sun. "One flap would have sent us to the bottom of the sea," Conan Doyle recalled, "and I can never forget how, as we pushed our way from under, each of us held one hand up to stave off that great, threatening fin—as if any strength of ours could have availed if the whale had meant it to descend." As the terrified men eased away, the dying whale rolled back away from the boat, and the fin slipped harmlessly below the waterline.

This brush with death only sharpened Conan Doyle's taste for the adventure. "It is exciting work pulling on to a whale," he would write. "Your own back is turned to him, and all you know about him is what you read upon the face of the boat-steerer. He is staring out over your head, watching the creature as it swims slowly through the water, raising his hand now and again as a signal to stop rowing when he sees that the eye is coming round, and then resuming the stealthy approach when the whale is end on. There are so many floating pieces of ice, that as long as the oars are quiet the boat alone will not cause the creature to dive. So you creep slowly up, and at last you are so near that the boat-steerer knows that you can get there before the creature has time to dive—for it takes some little time to get that huge body into motion. You see a sudden gleam in his eyes, and a flush in his cheeks, and it's 'Give way, boys! Give way, all! Hard!' Click goes the trigger of the big harpoon gun, and the foam flies from your oars. Six strokes, perhaps, and then with a dull greasy squelch the bows run upon something soft, and you and your oars are sent flying in every direction. But little you care for that, for as you touched the whale you heard the crash of the gun, and know that the harpoon has been fired point-blank into the huge, lead-coloured curve of its side. The creature sinks like a stone, the bows of the boat splash down in the water again, and there is the line whizzing swiftly under the seats and over the bows between your outstretched feet.

"And this is the great element of danger—for it is rarely indeed that the whale has spirit enough to turn upon its enemies. The line is very carefully coiled by a special man named the line-coiler, and it is warranted not to kink. If it should happen to do so, however, and if the loop catches the limbs of any one of the boat's crew, that man goes to his death so rapidly that his comrades hardly know that he has gone. It is a waste of fish to cut the line, for the victim is already hundreds of fathoms deep.

" 'Hold your hand, mon,' cried the harpooner, as a seaman raised his knife on such an occasion. 'The fish will be a fine thing for the widdey.' It sounds callous, but there was philosophy at the base of it."

By the time the *Hope* turned back toward Peterhead after many months at sea, the hunters had taken only four whales. Even so, the ship's hold carried sixty-six tons of cargo. For most of the crew, this fairly modest haul would have marked the voyage as uneventful, but Conan Doyle judged its success by a different measure. "I came of age," he was to tell an interviewer, "in 80 degrees north latitude."

Conan Doyle parted from his shipmates in Peterhead and made his way back to Edinburgh, where his reunion with his mother was made all the happier by his £50 share of the crew's profits. He threw himself back into his studies with his former diligence, but he was a changed man, something he attributed to the "peculiar other-world feeling" of the Arctic. "He who has once been within the borders of that mysterious region," he wrote, "which can be both the most lovely and the most repellent upon earth, must always retain something of its glamour."

Almost immediately, Conan Doyle's whaling experience found its way into his fiction. In the chilling "Captain of the Pole-Star," published in *Temple Bar* magazine in 1883, a distraught sea captain pursues the spirit of his lost love onto a treacherous ice floe, where he freezes to death. As the narrator and his shipmates discover the body, a strange gust of wind disturbs its covering of snow. "To my eyes," the narrator relates, "it seemed but a snow drift, but many of my companions averred that it started up in the shape of a woman, stooped over the corpse and kissed it, and then hurried away across the floe."

Like his contemporaries Jack London and Joseph Conrad, Conan Doyle would draw on his sailing adventures for the rest of his life, notably in a series of tales chronicling the adventures of a brutal pirate named Captain Sharkey. The experience also gave Conan Doyle a surprising appreciation for the writing of Herman Melville, whose work was largely unnoticed at the time. He also immersed himself in the tales of William Clark Russell, whose "fine sea stories" would one day find their way into the hands of Dr. Watson.

These influences were not immediately apparent as Conan Doyle returned to his studies in the autumn of 1880. What was obvious to all, however, was that Conan Doyle was no longer the gawky, uncertain teenager of old. "I went on board the whaler a big, straggling youth," he said. "I came off a powerful, well-grown man."

Edinburgh was no longer big enough to hold him.

4

A Man of Doubtful Antecedents

Wear flannel next to your skin, my dear boy, and never believe in eternal punishment.

—MR. STARK MUNRO'S MOTHER IN *THE STARK MUNRO LETTERS*

"I am beginning to see," Conan Doyle wrote to his mother during his medical training, "that I have certain advantages which, if properly directed and given a fair chance might lead to great success, but which it would be a thousand pities to nullify aboard ship or in a country practice. Let me once get my footing in a good hospital and my game is clear. Observe cases minutely, improve in my profession, write to the *Lancet*, supplement my income by literature, make friends and conciliate everyone I meet, wait ten years if need be, and then when my chance comes be prompt and decisive in stepping into an honorary surgeonship."

This measured, intensely practical view of his prospects grew out of Conan Doyle's impoverished background, but already his larger ambitions could scarcely be contained. "We'll aim high, old lady," he told the Ma'am, "and consider the success of a lifetime, rather than the difference of a fifty pound note in an annual screw."

In August of 1881, Conan Doyle received his Bachelor of Medicine and Master of Surgery qualifications. He came through without any great distinction—hardly surprising given his compressed schedule of studies—and the whaling adventure delayed his graduation by one year. Even so, he felt considerable elation over the achievement, and drew a giddy sketch of himself waving his diploma aloft. The caption read: "Licensed to Kill."

At home, matters had grown worse. Charles Doyle now resided in a nursing home called Fordoun House, which specialized in the treatment of alcoholism, placing yet another strain on the family resources. Bryan Waller, the Doyles' lodger, had taken on an ever larger share of the burden, and Conan Doyle's lifelong silence on the matter suggests that it was a painful memory. The only thing explicit in his writings was a profound longing to make something of himself.

Few avenues were open to him. The conventions of the day required him to gain experience in practice before he could claim the title of doctor. In order to do so, he would either have to buy into an existing practice or set up one of his own. Virtually penniless, Conan Doyle could do neither.

Restless, he visited his mother's relatives, applied for hospital posts, and served another brief apprenticeship with Dr. Hoare in Birmingham. He considered going out to India as a government doctor, or perhaps joining the navy. Either prospect would have brought a steady income, allowing him to send money home from abroad, just as his sisters had done.

For all the uncertainty about his future, Conan Doyle seemed well pleased with himself in the wake of his voyage aboard the *Hope*. Brimming with confidence, he turned his attentions toward the opposite sex, and began falling in love with a regularity that alarmed his mother. At one stage he confessed to being in love with five women at once—honorably, he insisted—though he eventually confined his attentions to a pretty, if slightly stout Irish girl named Elmore Welden. "Such a beauty!" he exclaimed. "We have been flirting hard for a week, so that things are about ripe."

The dark-eyed Miss Welden, whom he nicknamed "Elmo," would entrance him for some time to come. Conan Doyle recognized, however, that he had nothing to offer her, and must first secure some sort of future for himself before their relationship could progress. The hopeful suitor soon had his chance. A telegram arrived from the African Steam Navigation Company, offering a position as a shipboard medical officer at a salary of £12 per month. With this promise of steady income, Conan Doyle appears to have considered marrying Elmo and bringing her along on his travels. Whether the proposal was ever tendered is a matter for speculation. By the time Conan Doyle presented himself at the port of Liverpool in October of 1881, he and Elmo had temporarily parted company.

The steamer *Mayumba*, battered and creaky after twenty years in service, ran a regular route from Liverpool to the west coast of Africa. For the most part she carried passengers, general goods, and Royal Mail sacks on the outbound journey, and brought back palm oil, nuts, and ivory on her return. Conan Doyle had about thirty passengers under his care when the ship set sail at the end of October. The twenty-two-year-old doctor appeared to have found an ideal berth. Life aboard an African steamer would satisfy his taste for adventure, while providing a good income and medical seasoning. Conan Doyle had every reason to feel he had landed on his feet.

One day out of harbor, as the ship steamed south along the Irish coast in heavy fog, Conan Doyle noticed the faint glow of a lighthouse off the port side. "I could not imagine how any lighthouse could be on the port side," he recalled, so he tugged on the sleeve of the ship's mate and pointed toward the brightening light. Galvanized, the mate shouted to the wheelhouse and sent a frantic signal to the engine room. The ship pulled hard to port, narrowly avoiding a jagged reef.

Matters declined steadily from there. The ship headed into choppy waters as it crossed the Bay of Biscay, and Conan Doyle spent a week lurching across the rolling deck as he tended to seasick passengers. With his own cabin flooded, the young doctor found himself ankle-deep in water until the skies cleared. Eventually, he wrote, when "the angry sea changed into a long, greasy swell, there was a gradual divorce between our passengers and the basins. One of them even had the hardihood to appear upon deck with a sickly look of confidence upon his face, which, I regret to state, suddenly faded away, to give place to an earnest and all-absorbing interest in the appearance of the water alongside of the vessel."

The weather finally broke as the ship neared Madeira, where a number of passengers disembarked. Conan Doyle now had fewer patients under his care, but as the steamer made for Sierra Leone, he began to feel oppressed by the tropical climate. Dante, he suggested, might well have added another ring to the inferno if he had ever visited an African swamp. "When you feel your napkin at meals to be an intolerable thing," he wrote, "and when you find that it leaves a wet weal across your white duck trousers, then you know that you really have arrived."

The *Mayumba* put into numerous ports in Liberia and Nigeria, including Freetown, Monrovia, and Port Harcourt. Conan Doyle visited with various European colonials, but found little to recommend the expatriate lifestyle. Living under the constant threat of tropical disease, the colonials had a gloomy and fearful existence, and often turned to alcohol for solace. At one stage, Conan Doyle feared that he himself might be falling into bad habits. "I drank quite freely at this period of my life," he admitted, "having a head and a constitution which made me fairly immune, but my reason told me that the unbounded cocktails of West Africa were a danger, and with an effort I cut them out." Once again, Conan Doyle's remarks point to a significant omission. He may well have taken heed of the excesses of the colonials, but surely the example of his own father—tucked away in a treatment center for alcoholics—would have been a more significant factor in his decision. Conan Doyle abstained from alcohol for the remainder of the voyage. For the most part, he would be cautious with drink for the rest of his life.

Other local hazards proved more serious. Before long, several of Conan Doyle's charges aboard ship began to show symptoms of malaria, which he treated with doses of quinine—the best available treatment at the time. In mid-November, just three weeks out of Liverpool, Conan Doyle himself fell seriously ill. He barely managed to stagger to his bunk before collapsing in a delirium. "I lay for several days fighting it out with Death in a very small ring and without a second," he would write. "It must have been a close call, and I had scarcely sat up before I heard that another victim who got it at the same time was dead."

Writing of his experiences to a friend back home, Conan Doyle remarked that he had grown so weak that his pen felt heavy as an oar in his hand. After a week's convalescence, however, he felt well enough to resume his duties and join in a crocodile hunt. Some days later, he decided to refresh himself with a quick swim along the length of the ship. Drying off on deck, he noticed the dorsal fin of a shark rise from the murky water. "Several times in my life I have done utterly reckless things with so little motive that I have found it difficult to explain them to myself afterwards," he declared. "This was one of them."

In Liberia, a nation that had never known colonial rule, Conan Doyle spent considerable time with "the most intelligent and well-read man whom I met on the Coast." This was Henry Highland Garnet, the American consul in Liberia. The son of a slave, Garnet had been an influential spokesman of the abolition movement, and was near the end of his life when Conan Doyle met him. "This negro gentleman did me good," Conan Doyle admitted, and one begins to see the evidence in an article he published the following year. "With the exception of the natives," he wrote, "who have been demoralized by contact with the traders and by the brutality of the slave trade, the inhabitants of the dark continent are really a quiet and inoffensive race of men, whose whole ambition is to be allowed to lead an agricultural life, unmolested and in peace. That, at least, is the impression I have formed of them." He went on to express the opinion that a solitary man might travel in safety, but that a large party of heavily armed intruders would naturally be seen as a threat by certain of the warlike tribes. "This is why," he concluded, "they begin to get their stew-pans and sauce-bottles ready when they see a Stanley or any other modern explorer coming down on them." It is hardly a modern view, but there can be no doubt that Conan Doyle's respect for Henry Garnet expanded his horizons. He would spend considerable time in later life speaking out on behalf of oppressed races, and his fiction is largely free of the slurs and stereotypes that mar the work of his contemporaries.

At the island of Fernando Po, now Bioko, the *Mayumba* turned about and headed for home, stopping at various ports along the way to load the ship's hold with palm oil and other cargo. By now Conan Doyle had come to regard the unbroken stretches of African coastline as tedious, but the return trip would not be uneventful. As the ship steamed past Madeira, fire broke out in one of the coal bunkers. With nothing but a wooden partition to separate burning coal from flammable cargo, the captain faced a serious risk of losing the ship. For four days the crew battled to contain the "lurid glow" of burning coal, fearing a catastrophic explosion of oil and coal dust at any moment. At one stage a portion of the metal hull glowed red-hot, and choking smoke poured through the ventilators. Lifeboats were readied when it appeared the ship would go down, and the captain charged Conan Doyle with rousing the passengers from their bunks and keeping them calm. The crew's bravery averted the crisis, however, and the smoldering ship managed to continue her homeward voyage, sputtering into harbor at Liverpool in the middle of January 1882. "Just a line," Conan Doyle wrote upon arrival, "to say that I have turned up all safe after having had the African fever, been nearly eaten by a shark, and as a finale the *Mayumba* catching fire between Madeira and England."

For all of that, he had found the journey unbearably monotonous. Originally Conan Doyle planned to stay with the African Steam Navigation Company for a couple of years, putting money aside to launch his medical career. Three months on the *Mayumba* were sufficient to change his mind. In contrast to the wonders of the Arctic, he found Africa oppressive and demoralizing. "I don't intend to go to Africa again," he told his mother. "The pay is less than I could make by my pen in the same time, and the climate is atrocious. I trust you will not be disappointed by my leaving the ship, but this is not good enough."

The decision left him with few other prospects, as his pen had not proved quite as lucrative as he suggested. He had sold a modest handful of stories and articles, but seldom for as much as the three guineas he received for "The Mystery of Sasassa Valley." The African run, however unpleasant, carried a salary he could ill afford to lose.

As he considered his options—or the lack of them—an invitation arrived from his Aunt Annette, the sister of his father and his successful uncles Richard, Henry, and James. If he would come to London, Aunt Annette wrote, she and his uncles would be pleased to discuss his future.

This, Conan Doyle knew, could well be his "main chance." His uncles had money and influence. If they looked on him with favor, they could easily give him the start he needed. The London Doyles had long since washed their hands of Charles, the drunken wastrel, but his son Arthur had promise. Though they might have preferred that he follow in their footsteps by entering an artistic profession, they could see that Conan Doyle had become a hardworking, diligent young man—worthy, perhaps, of the family's patronage.

Conan Doyle traveled to London and presented himself at the stately house on Cambridge Terrace, near Hyde Park, that had once belonged to his grandfather John Doyle, the famous artist and family patriarch. For Conan Doyle, London brought happy memories. Eight years earlier, a visit to Uncle Richard provided a welcome release from Stonyhurst. Then as now, however, Conan Doyle felt conscious of his status as the poor relation and intimidated by the power and accomplishments of his uncles.

With his Scottish accent and threadbare clothes, Conan Doyle made a sharp contrast to his elegant, London-bred relatives. He may well have tried to puff himself up with stories of his seafaring adventures, which his straitlaced aunt and uncles would likely have found a trifle unseemly. After a decent interval, the conversation turned to business. The offer was plain enough: once Conan Doyle settled on an area where he would like to practice, the Doyle family would use its influence to put his name around among their social peers. Though no money would be forthcoming, the family prestige would be of greater value in the long term, enabling the young doctor to attract wealthy clients and build a profitable practice.

Conan Doyle listened intently and thanked his uncles for their confidence and generosity. There was, however, something of a problem. The Doyle family remained devoutly Catholic, and it was this connection that they intended to exercise on his behalf—with introductions to other prominent Catholic families and members of the clergy. To accept this sort of patronage, Conan Doyle felt, would be an act of hypocrisy. He had recently undergone what he called a "spiritual unfolding" and considered himself an agnostic.

"My head whirls," a client of Sherlock Holmes was to say. "Your words have dazed me." One imagines a similar reaction from the London Doyles, although the topic had already been broached in a letter. To Conan Doyle's uncles, this announcement would have seemed the worst possible ingratitude, seemingly calculated to give offense.

Many factors contributed to Conan Doyle's loss of faith—his unhappy religious schooling, his scientific training and turn of mind, and a careful reading of Darwin and his followers. At the University of Edinburgh, he joined in the general admiration of "Darwin's Bulldog," Professor Thomas Huxley, who coined the term "agnosticism" only a few years earlier. For Conan Doyle, though, this spiritual crisis was no mere fad. "I remember," he wrote, "that when, as a grown lad, I heard Father Murphy, a great fierce Irish priest, declare that there was sure damnation for everyone outside the church, I looked upon him with horror, and to that moment I trace the first rift which has grown into such a chasm between me and those who were my guides."

This chasm would grow wider over time. "Is religion the only domain of thought which is non-progressive," he would write in an early novel, "and to be referred forever to a standard set two thousand years ago? Can they not see as the human brain evolves it must take a wider outlook? A half-formed brain makes a half-formed God, and who shall say that our brains are even half-formed yet?"

Clearly Conan Doyle had thought deeply on the matter, but no matter how sincere his feelings, and no matter how passionately he expressed them, the London Doyles could not see past the perceived affront. The offer of patronage was withdrawn.

Conan Doyle's stand against his wealthy uncles—brave, headstrong, and more than a little reckless—set a pattern that would be repeated many times in his life. Another young doctor might have been more pliant, perhaps adjusting his beliefs to ensure his own comfort, but Conan Doyle had too much scruple and not enough guile for such a deception. His only real concern, as the first cracks appeared in his faith, was that his agnosticism might give pain to his mother. At this period of his life, Conan Doyle seldom formed a thought without expressing it to the Ma'am. Had she wished, Mary Doyle could very likely have persuaded her son to return to the fold and accept the support of his uncles. To her credit, she respected his convictions, and his principles in expressing them as he did. Within a few years she too would fall away from the Catholic Church to become an Anglican. Charles Doyle, meanwhile, remained as devout as ever within the confines of his institution. Charles Doyle's continued devotion—while everything else in his life had slipped away—can only have hastened the spiritual crisis of his son.

Richard Doyle, who had always been his nephew's favorite, made a final bid to change Conan Doyle's mind over lunch at the Athenaeum. The stately opulence of this gentlemen's club served to emphasize what the young doctor stood to lose by refusing his family's aid. Conan Doyle would not be swayed. When he left London, his relatives despaired of him.

The breach was never entirely forgotten, though Richard Doyle would make a gesture of reconciliation the following year. Shortly before succumbing to a fatal apoplectic fit, Richard sent his nephew letters of introduction to Catholic worthies. These came at a time when Conan Doyle badly needed a lifeline, but he destroyed them. His other two uncles lived another ten years, and therefore witnessed the dramatic early success of Sherlock Holmes, but they seldom acknowledged their recalcitrant nephew.

"When I first came out of the faith in which I had been reared," Conan Doyle would write in the autobiographical *The Stark Munro Letters*, "I certainly did feel for a time as if my life-belt had burst." This spiritual disorientation, and the attendant freedom of thought and deed, became the anvil upon which his personality was forged. Its effects would be felt immediately and forever. In the short term, he would have to rely on his own skill and cunning to make his way in the world. Once he had done so, his confidence in his own beliefs became absolute. Few men could claim the strength of their convictions with as much justice as Conan Doyle. Having succeeded so dramatically, he would never be troubled by any lack of self-assurance.

At the same time, his loss of faith created a hole he would spend the rest of his life trying to fill. "I had a very keen perception of the wonderful poise of the universe," he would write, "and the tremendous power of conception and sustenance which it implied. I was reverent in all my doubts and never ceased to think upon the matter, but the more I thought the more confirmed became my non-conformity."

This nonconformity would take him down some very strange paths. "Never will I accept anything which cannot be proved to me," he declared as a young man. "The evils of religion have all come from accepting things which cannot be proved." As he grew older, however, he would begin to substitute his own opinion for proof. As a result, many of the causes he took up—legal reform, defense of the falsely accused, and, finally, the so-called spirit revelation—were approached with what can only be called a religious fervor. In each case, he followed the example set by his younger self—the headstrong doctor with a burst life-belt.

Following the standoff at Cambridge Terrace, Conan Doyle was ready to jump at any chance that came along. In May of 1882, a strange telegram arrived from Plymouth, sent by an Edinburgh classmate named George Turnavine Budd. "Started here last June," the message ran. "Colossal success. Come down by next train if possible. Plenty of room for you. Splendid opening."

Conan Doyle did not catch the next train. He had reason to be wary of George Budd, whom he once described as "half genius and half quack." At Edinburgh, Budd had caused a scandal when he eloped with a girl who was not only underage but also a ward of the court. Anxious to mask his identity, he doused his blond hair with an inferior black dye, creating a two-tone effect that made him all the more conspicuous. Somehow the couple managed to escape detection long enough to exchange marriage vows, whereupon Budd set up housekeeping in Edinburgh under conditions of Dickensian poverty. "I have dined with them there on an apple dumpling," Conan Doyle wrote, "seated on a pile of thick volumes as there was no chair."

Upon leaving Edinburgh, Budd tried to establish a practice in Bristol, where his late father had made a huge success as a physician, lecturer, and town benefactor. Hoping to trade on this renown,

Budd assumed all the expensive accoutrements of his father's practice, including the lavish mansion his father had owned at the height of his success. Shortly before Conan Doyle's stint on the *Mayumba*, he had received a telegram from Budd asking him to come to Bristol. Budd, it emerged, had gone bankrupt trying to create the appearance of prosperity, and now turned to Conan Doyle for counsel. Conan Doyle advised him to assemble his creditors and ask that they defer his debts while he tried his luck elsewhere. Budd took the advice, bringing local tradesmen to the point of tears with an emotionally charged account of his struggles. Having secured a grace period, he packed his bags and moved on to Plymouth, where an uncle had enjoyed a successful practice.

Now, apparently, Budd had made such a success that he required a partner to cope with the flood of patients. Uncertain whether to accept the offer, Conan Doyle solicited advice from his three closest advisors—his mother, Bryan Waller, and Dr. Hoare. All of them advised against any further association with Budd. It was one thing to befriend such a person, the Ma'am declared, but quite another to join his medical practice. Still undecided, Conan Doyle wrote to Budd asking for clarification of the terms. Budd, indignant at the delay, sent a blistering reply. Thirty thousand patients had crossed his threshold in the past year, he insisted. Business was so good that he would not bestir himself to cross the street if Queen Victoria herself desired a consultation. Conan Doyle need only board a train to be guaranteed a salary of three hundred pounds. "This looked like business," Conan Doyle wrote, "so off I went."

What he found in Plymouth defied all expectations. Budd and his wife lived in an expensively furnished house at 6 Elliot Terrace, a fashionable neighborhood, but ran the surgery out of a large building on Durnford Street in the city's working-class district. Budd had hit on a surefire plan to attract patients: he offered consultations for free, but charged a hefty price for his prescriptions. He doled out medicines in a "heroic and indiscriminate manner," according to Conan Doyle, sometimes for no other reason than to earn a fee.

When Conan Doyle arrived on the scene, he found "something more like a cattle market than a medical practice." Well over a hundred patients spilled out of the consulting room onto the stairs and into the hallways of the surgery building. Budd claimed that he drew patients from fifty miles away, some of whom sat on his doorstep eating bread and treacle in the early hours of the morning, so as to be first in line when the doors opened.

Budd set his new partner up in a large consulting room with a simple table and two chairs. From there, Conan Doyle began to handle a small trickle of surgical cases, watching with growing wonder as Budd dealt with the majority of the patients. "His behavior to them was extraordinary," Conan Doyle wrote. "He roared and shouted, scolded them, joked them, pushed them about, and pursued them sometimes into the street, or addressed them collectively from the landing. A morning with him when the practice was in full blast was as funny as any pantomime and I was exhausted with laughter. He had a well-worn volume on Medical Jurisprudence which he pretended was the Bible, and he swore old women on it that they would drink no more tea." As to whether Budd's eccentric methods served any useful purpose, Conan Doyle offered a diplomatic assessment: "I have no doubt he did a great deal of good, for there was reason and knowledge behind all that he did, but his manner of doing it was unorthodox in the extreme."

This was not, as Conan Doyle well knew, a conventional medical practice. For the first time, however, he was earning money and practicing medicine on dry land. If working with Budd required a certain ethical flexibility, Conan Doyle briefly permitted himself this luxury to enjoy the rewards of an active practice.

Soon enough, his conscience began to bother him. It did not escape his notice that Budd showed no sign of paying off his creditors in Bristol, even though he could now well afford to do so. As always, Conan Doyle had been writing regularly to his mother, and reporting fully on the strange foibles of his new associate. Predictably, the Ma'am strongly disapproved of Budd and was not shy about saying so in her letters. In her view—as recorded in *The Stark Munro Letters*, where Conan Doyle presented a fictional treatment of these events—Budd was a man of "unscrupulous character and doubtful antecedents," and her son's association with him threatened to soil the family honor. Conan Doyle now found himself in the uneasy position of having to defend Budd's character, which provoked an even more outspoken stream of commentary from the Ma'am. Over the course of six weeks, a "serious breach" opened between Conan Doyle and his mother.

One day Budd began to complain that his profits had fallen sharply. Conan Doyle saw no cause for alarm, since the fine summer weather had cut down on sore throats and other cold weather ailments. The explanation did not satisfy Budd, who voiced an opinion that patients were being chased away by Conan Doyle's brass nameplate beside the door to the surgery. The patients wanted to see him, Budd reasoned, and would sooner turn away than risk having their cases fobbed off on Conan Doyle. If the account in *The Stark Munro Letters* is accurate, Conan Doyle promptly picked up a hammer, marched outside, and pried the offending nameplate off the wall.

Clearly, the partnership had reached its crisis. Somewhat contrite, Budd tried to calm Conan Doyle by advising him to go into practice for himself. Since Conan Doyle had no capital, Budd offered to provide him with a loan of one pound per week until he got himself established. Mollified, Conan Doyle accepted the offer, gathered his few belongings into his trunk, and parted with Budd on cordial terms.

After scouting the nearby town of Tavistock, Conan Doyle settled on Portsmouth as a likely spot for his new practice, being fairly "analogous" to Plymouth. He boarded an Irish steamer at the end of June 1882 and alighted at the Clarence Pier in Southsea, a residential suburb of Portsmouth that attracted visitors to its seafront in the summer months. Leaving his trunk at the pier, Conan Doyle made his way into town to find a rooming house. From there, he would study a plan of the town and try to find a suitable house for rent. With less than £10 to his name, Conan Doyle needed to get himself established as quickly as possible. If the prospect seemed intimidating, he could take comfort in the security of the weekly pound note from Budd.

Or so he thought. No sooner had Conan Doyle rented a house and purchased medical supplies on credit than Budd "hurled his thunderbolt" and withdrew his support. A curt letter informed Conan Doyle that one of his mother's letters had been discovered in the fireplace. It was unforgivable, Budd declared, that such a vicious attack on his character could have been tolerated beneath his own roof.

While it was certainly true that Mary Doyle had written such a letter—many, in fact—Budd could not have happened upon it as he claimed, since Conan Doyle had brought the offending correspondence with him to Portsmouth. Budd, Conan Doyle now realized, had been prying into his mail all along, and quietly plotting his revenge. By waiting until Conan Doyle had made financial commitments in Portsmouth, Budd had all but guaranteed his former partner's financial ruin.

"Well, I wrote him a little note," Conan Doyle declared in *The Stark Munro Letters*. "I said that his letter had been a source of gratification to me, as it removed the only cause for disagreement between my mother and myself. She had always thought him a blackguard, and I had always defended him; but I was forced now to confess that she had been right from the beginning."

Conan Doyle may well have wanted to put a brave face on the situation, but Budd's broken pledge left him in desperate straits. He knew no one in Portsmouth, and had no good reason to believe he could make a success there. As the full weight of Budd's connivance sank in, Conan Doyle must have felt a strong temptation to return to Edinburgh, or to throw himself on the mercy of Dr. Hoare, the benefactor of his student days. If so, his pride would have prevented any serious consideration of either option. He had joined Budd in Plymouth over the loud objections of his mother and his friends. He must now face the consequences on his own. "For a moment I was staggered," Conan Doyle recalled. "But my boats were burned and I must go forward."

In all, he had spent no more than two months in Plymouth, but the experience would make itself felt for years to come. Traces of George Budd can be found in every phase of Conan Doyle's literary career, from *The Stark Munro Letters* to the volatile Professor Challenger. Though the experience had been chastening—it would be some time before Conan Doyle rejected any further advice from the Ma'am—Conan Doyle could not bring himself to bear a grudge. "Even now," he admitted in his autobiography, "I can't help liking him."

George Budd died in 1889, in his early thirties, only seven years after the collapse of his partnership with Conan Doyle. At the time of his death an investigation into his unorthodox medical practices was under way, and he left his wife and four daughters in virtual poverty. In his autobiography, Conan Doyle disguised Budd as "Cullingworth," the name he adopted for *The Stark Munro Letters*, to spare Budd's widow any additional embarrassment. That account, written some forty-two years after the fact, offered a magnanimous view of their parting: "He had, of course, no real grievance," Conan Doyle wrote, "but I am quite willing to admit that he honestly thought he had."

Conan Doyle omitted one detail. Though Budd had attempted to engineer his financial ruin and social disgrace, Conan Doyle felt a debt of honor toward his widow. For years afterward, he quietly put up money for the support of Mrs. Budd and her daughters.

Publicly, Conan Doyle confined himself to an ambiguous final comment. "He was a remarkable man and narrowly escaped being a great one," Conan Doyle wrote in his autobiography. "I understand that an autopsy revealed some cerebral abnormality."

5

Three Pounds of Furniture and a Tin of Corned Beef

Dr. Doyle begs to notify that he has removed to 1, Bush Villas, Elm Grove, next to the Bush Hotel.

—NOTICE IN THE PORTSMOUTH *EVENING NEWS*, 1 JULY 1882

First of all," Conan Doyle wrote in *The Stark Munro Letters*, "I walked down to the post office and I bought a large shilling map of the town. Then back I came and pinned this out upon the lodging-house table. This done, I set to work to study it, and to arrange a series of walks by which I should pass through every street of the place. You have no idea what that means until you try to do it. I used to have breakfast, get out about ten, walk till one, have a cheap luncheon (I can do well on threepence), walk till four, get back and note results. On my map I put a cross for every empty house and a circle for every doctor. So at the end of that time I had a complete chart of the whole place, and could see at a glance where there was a possible opening, and what opposition there was at each point."

Conan Doyle's first days in Portsmouth almost certainly resembled those of his fictional hero, and like Munro he also found himself skirting the edge of financial ruin. His acrimonious parting with Budd—and the subsequent withdrawal of the promised £1 per week—left him gasping "like a cod on a sand-bank." He tried to adopt a cheery insouciance over his situation, but with less than £10 in his pocket, his outlook could not have been entirely lighthearted. Worse, he had championed Budd's character in defiance of his mother. "I knew, of course," wrote Munro, "that my mother would have sold everything down to her gold eye-glasses to help me, and that no thought of our recent disagreement would have weighed with her for an instant; but still a man has his feelings, you know, and I did not propose to act against her judgment and then run howling for help." In fact, Conan Doyle did run howling for help, and somehow the Ma'am managed to provide the weekly pound denied by Budd from her own resources.

Conan Doyle still faced a formidable task in setting up a practice with almost no capital. However poor he might be, he understood that he would have to create an impression of prosperity if he hoped to attract patients. His wanderings through Portsmouth and neighboring Southsea led him to an unoccupied, three-story brick house at 1 Bush Villas, Elm Grove, Southsea. The eight-room house had stood empty for some time, and Conan Doyle was able to rent it for £40 a year. Despite his recent falling out with his uncles, he was not above dangling their names before the leasing agent in lieu of an actual cash deposit.

The house came unfurnished, and Conan Doyle went scavenging for chairs and a table—"possibly tenth-hand"—at a mark-down sale, coming away with just enough to fill his consulting room. Even these modest purchases placed a serious drain on his cash reserves, but he had resolved, he told a friend, "to make a spoon or spoil a horn." He returned to Bush Villas with "three pounds' worth of furniture for the consulting room, a bed, a tin of corned beef and two enormous brass plates with my name on it."

The young doctor lavished attention on his front room, the only area of the house his patients would see. Had any of them pushed back the curtain leading to the rest of the house, they would have seen that the consulting room was little more than a stage set. The other seven rooms were almost entirely bare, leaving Conan Doyle to camp out with the few remaining sticks of furniture he owned. His trunk served as both a food locker and a dining table, while he perched unsteadily on a small stool. To save the expense of gas for the stove, he learned to cook over the flame of a gas illumination jet, becoming expert at frying up thin slices of bacon so as to stretch his rations. At times his supplies dwindled to plain bread and water, and his burly frame shrank by more than ten pounds in the first months of practice.

Conan Doyle hung out a red lamp—purchased on credit—to signal that a doctor was in residence, and spent his days waiting at the front window for patients to arrive. He did his shopping and housework at night, so that he would not be seen polishing his own nameplate or sweeping his own front stoop. He also took his exercise at night, for fear of missing a potential client during the day. In the early months he spent hours walking through the city, soaking up the historical resonances of the port where Nelson's *Victory* lay at anchor. "There is a great glamour there to anyone with the historic sense," he wrote of Southsea, "a sense which I drank in with my mother's milk."

In truth, the nearby naval dockyard gave the town a seedier character than Conan Doyle may have wished to remember. On his first night in town he came upon a "burly brute" threatening a distraught young woman. Conan Doyle stepped in to intercede while a large crowd gathered, hoping for blood sport. He now found himself, as he recorded in *The Stark Munro Letters*, "within a few hours of my entrance into this town, with my top-hat down to my ears, my highly professional frock-coat, and my kid gloves, fighting some low bruiser on a pedestal in one of the most public places, in the heart of a yelling and hostile mob! I ask whether that was cruel luck or not?" Conan Doyle landed a single blow before the jostling of the crowd threw him clear of the fight. He picked up his fallen walking stick and made for home, counting himself lucky to have escaped arrest.

This same "low bruiser" appeared at Conan Doyle's door a few days later, wanting to know if he needed any scissors sharpened. He did not recognize Conan Doyle as his top-hatted assailant. Only a small group of other visitors crossed his threshold in the early days of his practice. One, a "horse-faced old lady" of regal bearing, could be found sailing china plates at the heads of passersby when a certain mood came over her. Only Conan Doyle, it seemed, had the power to calm her when the plate-hurling impulse was felt. Whenever new patients appeared, Conan Doyle attempted to apply the diagnostic methods of Joseph Bell. Once, when a well-dressed man entered the consulting room amid much coughing and throat clearing, the young doctor hazarded a guess of bronchial trouble. "No," answered the visitor. "There's a small sum due on the gas meter."

Conan Doyle soon realized that a brass plaque and a red lamp offered no guarantee of success. "Do not think that practice will come to you," he wrote in *The Stark Munro Letters*. "You must go to it. You may sit upon your consulting-room chair until it breaks under you, but without purchase or partnership you will make little or no progress. The way to do it is to go out, to mix everywhere with men, to let them know you. You will come back many a time and be told by a reproachful housekeeper that someone has been for you in your absence. Never mind! Go out again. A noisy smoking concert where you will meet eighty men is better for you than the patient or two you might have seen at home. It took me some time to realise, but I speak now as one who knows."

In these earliest days, with no reproachful housekeeper to trouble him, Conan Doyle went out and pumped the flesh whenever possible. His love of sports offered a natural entrée. He joined the Southsea Bowling Club—which played outdoor lawn bowling, as opposed to tenpins—and took home a silver cigar case from a tournament. He also signed up with the Portsmouth Cricket Club, eventually becoming its captain. Since the town had no official English football matches, he helped to organize a Portsmouth Football Club. Fearing that the image of brawling footballer might compromise his professional dignity, Conan Doyle occasionally played under an assumed name. When foul weather drove him indoors, he shot billiards at the Bush Hotel, two doors down from his house.

There was one piece of Stark Munro's advice that Conan Doyle did not follow. "Above everything, beware of drink!" his fictional counterpart warned. Conan Doyle appears to have been somewhat lax on this point, despite his temporary injunction aboard the *Mayumba*. "I went to a ball the other night," he confided to his sister Lottie, "and by some mischance got drunk as an owl. I have a dim recollection that I proposed to half the women in the room—

married and single. I got one letter next day signed, 'Ruby,' and saying the writer had said 'yes' when she meant 'no'; but who the deuce she was or what she had said 'yes' about I can't conceive."

Conan Doyle may well have embroidered the scene for his sister's amusement, but if a drunken blackout really occurred, it is fortunate that such "mischances" did not occur often. Stark Munro understood, as his creator apparently did not, that a hard-drinking doctor had little hope of establishing a successful practice.

In more sober moments, Conan Doyle renewed his interest in Elmo Welden, the young woman he courted before his African voyage. Their relationship proceeded at a stately pace; they toured the Isle of Wight, and traveled to London to see Gilbert and Sullivan's *Patience*. The romance soon ran its course, but Conan Doyle, who complained of loneliness in his first weeks at Southsea, now had his brother Innes for company. The arrival of the "little knickerbockered fellow," then ten years old, appears to have been a practical measure for the Doyle family. The arrangement, which may have been a condition of the weekly pound note from Edinburgh, reduced Mary Doyle's burden to the care of her two youngest daughters, Ida and Dodo. Conan Doyle, meanwhile, gained a companion to break the solitude of his eight-room house. Innes enrolled in a local school, and soon took over the plaque-polishing and step-brushing duties at Bush Villas. Having grown accustomed to his family's straitened circumstances in Edinburgh, Innes had no difficulty adjusting to life in Southsea. He wrote cheerful letters to his mother describing a typical day of answering the door, running errands, and cooking up their meager ration of potatoes—"the only six we had in the world."

More than once, Conan Doyle's funds dipped low enough to send him to the pawn shop with his watch. He tried bartering with local tradesmen, exchanging his medical services for goods, and struck up a relationship with an epileptic grocer, which provided butter and tea. Like George Budd, he was not above seizing opportunities for self-promotion. When a riding accident occurred at his doorstep, Conan Doyle not only treated the victim but also placed a self-flattering account in the local *Evening News*. Sometimes his compassion overcame his business instincts, as when he treated a baby for measles and then handed over his pocket change to the indigent family.

By the end of 1882, Conan Doyle hit on the idea of letting out rooms in exchange for housekeeping services. The young doctor's admittedly "Bohemian" establishment now took on a more civilized air. Mary Doyle and Aunt Annette sent decorative odds and ends—including a formidable bust of John Doyle—to offset the effect of Conan Doyle's sale-price furniture.

Patients began to arrive more regularly, but with first-year earnings of only £154, the practice was off to a rocky start. When Conan Doyle filed his tax return to show that he wasn't liable, the assessors returned his form marked "Most unsatisfactory." Conan Doyle added the words "I entirely agree" and sent it back again. The revenue officers, failing to appreciate the joke, called him in to explain himself. "They could make nothing, however, out of me or my ledger," he wrote, "and we parted with mutual laughter and compliments."

No laughter and compliments were needed the following year, when Conan Doyle's income rose to £250. By the end of the third year the practice was bringing in £300 annually—the amount George Budd had promised in Plymouth. Though hardly munificent, this comfortable income marked Conan Doyle as a successful practitioner; he had overcome his early misadventure in a remarkably short time. Conan Doyle is often dismissed as a poor or disinterested medical man, owing to his early struggles, his modest performance at Edinburgh, and the subsequent abandonment of his career. In fact he was a hardworking, compassionate doctor, who kept up with the advances of medicine long after he had ceased to practice. If his competence failed to manifest itself in monetary rewards, this owed less to his abilities than to his rejection of the family patronage, his involvement with Budd, and his decision to settle in an area already well supplied with doctors. Only a doctor of considerable skill and dedication could have succeeded to the extent that he did.

While waiting for patients to arrive, Conan Doyle sat in his consulting room and wrote stories. "There was a time in my life which I divided among my patients and literature," he once remarked. "It is hard to say which suffered most." This sort of self-effacing humor served to enhance the impression that his doctoring cannot have been up to par, but actually Conan Doyle had energy for both. When he decided not to continue aboard the *Mayumba,* Conan Doyle told his mother he could easily make up the salary of £12 a month through his writing. It would take several years to make good on the claim, but an early effort called "My Friend the Murderer" brought a much-needed £10 from James Hogg, the editor of *London Society,* which settled his first quarter's rent.

The eerie "Captain of the Pole-Star," which drew on his whaling experiences, brought him a further ten guineas—or ten and a half pounds—from *Temple Bar* at the end of 1882. The greatest success of those early years came the following year, when the prestigious *Cornhill Magazine* paid an impressive 29 guineas (more than 30 pounds) for "J. Habakuk Jephson's Statement." Inspired by the real-life mystery of the *Marie Celeste,* a ship discovered abandoned off the west coast of Africa, the story appeared anonymously, as did all contributions to *Cornhill,* with the result that hundreds of readers wrote in to identify Robert Louis Stevenson as the author. Conan Doyle found the comparison flattering, but the confusion suggests the degree to which his immature work derived from other writers. Like Stevenson, Conan Doyle made canny use of known facts in his story, prompting a handful of British and American officials to mistake his fiction for a factual account. Conan Doyle expressed delight that any characters of his should be taken for living figures. This was to happen many times over the course of his career, and he would not always be so amused.

These early successes proved difficult to repeat. "Fifty little cylinders of manuscript did I send out during eight years," he wrote, referring to the mailing tubes in which he made his submissions. Unhappily, most of these literary parcels "described irregular orbits among publishers, and usually came back like paper boomerangs to the place that they had started from." Conan Doyle had high hopes for a story called "The Actor's Duel," which he considered the most powerful thing he had written to that point. When it drew rejections from the more prestigious magazines, he sent it to the less estimable *Boy's Own Paper,* his journal of last resort. They, too, gave it a miss, but later published "Crabbe's Practice," about a brilliant but unscrupulous doctor, not unlike George Budd, who was prone to reckless experimentation.

In later years, Conan Doyle would try to suppress many of these early efforts—some of which, he complained, had been written when he was "little more than a boy." He found it especially galling when his early stories began to appear in pirated anthologies in America, where copyright laws did not yet protect foreign authors. "It is rough on me," he was to tell a newspaper interviewer, "having these youthful effusions brought out in this catchpenny fashion, but I have no legal redress." In his autobiography, he offered a piece of hard-won advice to writers just starting out: "Have a care, young authors, have a care, or your own worst enemy will be your early self."

In these early days, Conan Doyle had few literary ambitions apart from supplementing his income. The process of building his practice absorbed most of his attention, and he constantly sought out opportunities to raise his profile in the Southsea community. In November of 1883 Conan Doyle became a member of the Portsmouth Literary and Scientific Society, which met on alternate Tuesdays during the cold winter months to discuss matters of intellectual interest. The following month, he gave an address on "The Arctic Seas" before an audience of two hundred and fifty people. To illustrate his lecture Conan Doyle borrowed numerous animal specimens from a local taxidermist, some of which, technically speaking, may not have been indigenous to the Arctic Circle. The mounted animals made an impressive display nonetheless, and when the audience concluded that Conan Doyle had bagged them all himself, he suddenly found himself with an enviable reputation as a hunter.

The Society became the cornerstone of Conan Doyle's social life. He contributed further lectures on some of his favorite authors—Edward Gibbon, Thomas Carlyle, and George Meredith—and listened to talks on subjects ranging from astronomy to military history. Intriguingly, on one occasion Conan Doyle entertained the society by devising an ending for Charles Dickens's unfinished *Mystery of Edwin Drood*. On another occasion, Arthur Balfour, the future prime minister, traveled down from London to give a speech on Ireland. A pair of "notorious partisans of the other side" waited outside the meeting hall to jeer at the politician, so Conan Doyle made it his business to greet the visitor as his carriage drew up. "However, the moment Balfour appeared one of them opened a huge mouth with the intention of emitting a howl of execration," Conan Doyle recalled. "But it never got out, for I clapped my hand pretty forcibly over the orifice." The other heckler promptly smashed Conan Doyle's hat with his walking stick, but Balfour passed unmolested.

At this stage, Conan Doyle preferred sidewalk scuffles to speechmaking. He had no natural facility for public speaking—his manner of speech is said to have been clipped and hesitant—and had to overcome a serious case of nerves whenever he addressed the Society. "I have been told," he wrote, "that the signal that I was about to join in the discussion was that the whole long bench on which I sat, with everyone on it, used to shake with my emotion."

Over time, Conan Doyle's dogged self-promotion began to bear fruit. Dr. William Royston Pike, a fellow member of the Southsea Bowling Club, began referring patients to him, and Conan Doyle became a consultant to the Gresham Life Insurance Company, whose local manager was also a fellow bowler. In March of 1885, Dr. Pike sought Conan Doyle's advice on a case involving a young man named Jack Hawkins, who suffered from a series of increasingly violent seizures. Conan Doyle confirmed his colleague's grim diagnosis—Hawkins had contracted cerebral meningitis, an inflammation of the brain lining for which there was then no cure. The unhappy news placed Hawkins in a seemingly hopeless situation, as he had arrived in town only a few months earlier with his widowed mother and elder sister. No hotel or lodging would keep them once the illness reached its final stages, and Mrs. Hawkins and her daughter could not provide the care required. Motivated by compassion rather than self-interest, Conan Doyle offered a solution; he would fix up a room in his house and take Jack Hawkins on as a resident patient.

No sooner had Conan Doyle brought Hawkins to Bush Villas than the patient's condition took a downward turn. Conan Doyle did what he could to ease the young man's suffering, but Hawkins died within a few days. Fortunately, Dr. Pike had seen the patient shortly before his death, and could confirm that Conan Doyle had done everything possible. Otherwise, Conan Doyle would likely have come under official scrutiny. As matters stood, the sight of a coffin emerging from the house did little to bolster the young doctor's practice, but Conan Doyle's concern now rested with Mrs. Hawkins and her daughter, Louisa. He rode with them in the modest funeral procession that conveyed the dead man from Bush Villas to the local cemetery. "There is great promise, I think, in the faces of the dead," Conan Doyle wrote. "They say it is but the post-mortem relaxation of the muscles, but it is one of the points on which I would like to see science wrong."

By all accounts, Louisa Hawkins, the sister of Conan Doyle's unfortunate patient, was a sweet-natured young woman with a pleasant, open face and captivating blue-green eyes. Her plight aroused protective feelings in Conan Doyle, who, even under the difficult circumstances, had not failed to note her attractions. Miss Hawkins, for her part, greatly admired the young doctor's decency and compassion, and regretted the professional distress her brother's condition had caused. After a decent interval, Conan Doyle asked for permission to call at the rooming house where she and her mother remained after the funeral. "Touie," as he came to call her, joined him on his evening walks and listened with undisguised admiration as he told stories of his travels and interests.

As the relationship progressed, Mary Doyle traveled to Southsea to meet the new young woman in her son's life. For the timid Louisa, the prospect of meeting this formidable figure must have suggested something on the order of a military tribunal. To everyone's relief, the Ma'am found nothing objectionable in her prospective daughter-in-law, noting with evident satisfaction that the kindly, round-faced Louisa bore a passing resemblance to herself. Once the Ma'am's approval had been secured, no further obstacles remained. It was agreed that the wedding would take place in August.

In his autobiography, written nearly forty years later, Conan Doyle dispenses with his courtship and wedding in the space of a single page. He twice describes his bride as "gentle and amiable," but fails to mention her first name—leaving a lasting confusion as to whether it was Louise or Louisa. By that time he had long since remarried, and it is possible that his reticence stemmed from consideration for his second wife's feelings. Another possibility suggests itself, however. Three years earlier, Mary Doyle and her two youngest daughters left Edinburgh to take up residence at Masongill Cottage, near Yorkshire, on an estate belonging to Bryan Waller, the Doyle family's longtime benefactor. Waller himself also took up residence at Masongill that year, in the family manor house he inherited at the time of his father's death five years earlier. The reasons for the move remain obscure. For Waller, it meant abandoning a none too prosperous medical career for the life of a country squire, which may well have been reason enough. Mary Doyle's presence is more difficult to explain. Waller charged her no rent for the use of Masongill Cottage, and must also have contributed to the family's support. His generosity surpassed all reasonable expectations of a well-meaning tenant toward his kindly landlady. The move separated Mary Doyle from her husband, which may also have been a motivation for the change of scene. Just a few months before his son's wedding, Charles Doyle smashed out a window in an attempt to break free of Fordoun House. For the next few years, he would be held under a detention order at the Montrose Royal Lunatic Asylum.

Mary Doyle would remain on Waller's estate for more than three decades. In time Waller would marry a local governess, but he remained devoted to his former landlady and often took his meals with her at Masongill Cottage, to the reported distress of his wife. Clearly Bryan Waller and Mary Doyle enjoyed each other's company and had forged an enduring bond during the Spartan years when he lodged with the family in Edinburgh. The exact nature of that bond has excited considerable speculation over the years. Inevitably, it has been implied that at some stage their relationship progressed beyond mere friendship. There have also been suggestions that Mary Doyle's youngest daughter, whose given name was Bryan Mary Julia Josephine, was in fact the child of Bryan Waller rather than Charles Doyle. While not impossible, the surmise is highly improbable. Though Waller had a grave, self-important manner that made him appear older than his years, he was in fact fifteen years younger than Mary Doyle—and only six years older than Conan Doyle. If this objection could conceivably have been overcome, Mary Doyle's nature could not. Such a liaison would have been an affront to the strong sense of family honor she had so successfully instilled in her son. In later years, Conan Doyle would come to know the frustrations of being bound to an infirm spouse. His sense of probity, learned from his mother, precluded any possibility of violating his marriage vows.

It seems more plausible, then, that Mary Doyle's feelings for Bryan Waller were maternal, rather than romantic, which could well have inspired resentment on the part of Conan Doyle. As a boy, he promised her a life of comfort in her old age: "When you are old," young Arthur had said, "you shall have a velvet dress and gold glasses and sit in comfort by the fire." He grew up to be a rich man and was able to shower his mother with gifts and finery, but she remained at Bryan Waller's fireside.

Conan Doyle's writings shed no light on the matter. Perhaps he felt embarrassment over his family's enormous debt to Waller. Possibly he avoided the subject to avoid dredging up any appearance of impropriety. Whatever his motivation, in order to preserve his silence he would have had to omit any detail of his wedding to Louisa Hawkins, which took place at Masongill on August 5, 1885, with Waller himself serving as best man.

Bryan Waller would have been the de facto host of the wedding festivities, as Louisa's father was dead and Charles Doyle remained in custodial care in Edinburgh. The demands on Waller's hospitality were considerable; he not only welcomed Louisa and Mrs. Hawkins to his estate for the wedding preparations, but also must have defrayed some if not all of the expenses. In the face of such benevolence, Conan Doyle's public silence must have been galling, especially in later life. Waller would outlive Conan Doyle by two years.

Following the wedding, Conan Doyle took his bride to Dublin for their honeymoon. Little is known of the trip, though in all likelihood Conan Doyle took the occasion to call on some of the Doyle relations who remained in Ireland. He also found time to play in two cricket matches for Stonyhurst, his old school.

The new Mrs. Conan Doyle would soon grow accustomed to

her husband's athletic interests. On their return to Bush Villas, Conan Doyle resumed his calendar of sporting events with undiminished vigor, while she took over the running of the household. Mrs. Hawkins, Louisa's mother, came to live with the Conan Doyles while Innes went off to a boarding school in Yorkshire.

Another change at Bush Villas could be found on the brass nameplate outside, which now read "A. Conan Doyle, M.D." In the months prior to his wedding, Conan Doyle completed a medical thesis entitled "An Essay upon the vasometer changes in tabes dorsalis and on the influence which is exerted by the sympathetic nervous system in that disease, being a thesis presented in the hope of obtaining a degree of the Doctorship of Medicine of the University of Edinburgh, by A. Conan Doyle, MB, CM." It was not the catchiest title he ever devised, nor was the content—on the problem of constricted blood flow to the spinal column—likely to attract a wide readership. Fortunately, it found favor with the medical faculty. Conan Doyle went to Edinburgh in July 1885 for his oral examination, and returned to Southsea with his doctorate.

To a large extent, the days of struggle were behind him. Louisa received an annual income of £100 from her late father's estate, which added a comfortable margin to Conan Doyle's medical earnings. The marriage also conferred a certain social respectability on him, and made him a more suitable physician for female patients than he had been as a bachelor.

Against this backdrop of modest prosperity, Conan Doyle's literary output began to increase. A common misapprehension, bolstered by the author's own testimony, holds that he wrote out of desperation, grinding out stories in the solitary fastness of his consulting room while bill collectors hammered at the door. "I should like to say that I was led into the field of letters by a cheering ambition," he once told a gathering at the Author's Club, "but I fear it is more correct to say that I was chased into it by a howling creditor." Actually, he produced most of his memorable early work in relative comfort, dashing off a few lines in between patients or in the evening after the doors of the surgery had closed. "After my marriage," he wrote, "my brain seems to have quickened and both my imagination and my range of expression were greatly improved." His work now appeared with greater regularity, and magazines that had been closed to him began to welcome his submissions.

A story called "The Fate of Evangeline," written earlier but published toward the end of that year, gave a glimpse of the road ahead. "It would be well," ran a notable passage, "if those who express opinions upon such subjects would bear in mind those simple rules as to the analysis of evidence laid down by Auguste Dupin. 'Exclude the impossible,' he remarks in one of Poe's immortal stories, 'and what is left, however improbable, *must* be the truth.' "

The pronouncement made a lasting impression on Conan Doyle, and he recycled it to great effect in a story he wrote a short time later. "How often have I said to you," he wrote, paraphrasing Poe's original remark, "that when you have eliminated the impossible, whatever remains, *however improbable,* must be the truth?"

This time, however, Monsieur Dupin would be dismissed as "a very inferior fellow," and the maxim would be claimed by Mr. Sherlock Holmes.

6

"You Have Been in Afghanistan, I Perceive"

"He was a concoction, a myth, an isolated strand from my bundle of personalities."

—SHERLOCK HOLMES IN "HIS LAST BOW"

It was about a year after my marriage that I realized that I could go on doing short stories forever and never make headway," Conan Doyle wrote in his autobiography. "What is necessary is that your name should be on the back of a volume. Only so do you assert your individuality, and get the full credit or discredit of your achievement."

Short fiction had provided a pleasant supplement to his income, but Conan Doyle now regretted the anonymous and transient nature of its rewards. Like most young writers, he longed for a book of his own. Marriage may have sharpened the edge of his ambition, but Conan Doyle had been striving toward book publication for some time. He began work on a novel called *The Narrative of John Smith* soon after his arrival in Southsea. Like *The Stark Munro Letters*, this early effort probably took its inspiration from the George Budd fiasco, though Conan Doyle described it as having a "personal-social-political complexion." His satisfaction at completing the manuscript soon gave way to feelings of horror when his only copy went missing in the mail. "The publishers never received it," he wrote, "the post office sent countless blue forms to say that they knew nothing about it, and from that day to this no word has ever been heard of it. Of course it was the best thing I ever wrote. Who ever lost a manuscript that wasn't? But I must in all honesty confess that my shock at its disappearance would be as nothing to my horror if it were suddenly to appear again—in print."

With this first effort "safely lost," Conan Doyle settled in to work on a new book, which eventually came to be called *The Firm of Girdlestone*. Still in his early twenties, Conan Doyle had not yet found a voice of his own. He tried instead to duplicate the effects of two of his literary heroes, Dickens and Thackeray, with predictably uneven results. Not surprisingly, Conan Doyle seemed most comfortable with the character of Thomas Dimsdale, a medical student at the University of Edinburgh, who finds employment aboard an African trading vessel. His story, Conan Doyle admitted, "interested me extremely at the time, though I have never heard that it had the same effect upon anyone else afterwards."

As his practice grew, Conan Doyle found it harder to balance the demands of fiction and medicine. With his short stories, he could make good use of the lulls between patients. A novel required a more sustained effort, which suffered from the frequent interruptions of the consulting room. Years later, Conan Doyle outlined his difficulties for an American magazine:

> How often have I rejoiced to find a clear morning before me, and settled down to my task, or rather, dashed ferociously at it, as knowing how precious were those hours of quiet. Then to me enters my housekeeper, with tidings of dismay.
>
> "Mrs. Thurston's little boy wants to see you, doctor."
>
> "Show him in," say I, striving to fix my scene in my mind that I may splice it when this trouble is over. "Well, my boy?"
>
> "Please, doctor, mother wants to know if she is to add water to that medicine?"
>
> "Certainly, certainly." Not that it matters in the least,

> but it is well to answer with decision. Exit the little boy, and the splice is about half accomplished when he suddenly bursts into the room again.
>
> "Please, doctor, when I got back mother had taken the medicine without the water."
>
> "Tut, tut!" I answer. "It really doesn't matter in the least." The youth withdraws with a suspicious glance, and one more paragraph has been written when the husband puts in an appearance.
>
> "There seems to have been some misunderstanding about that medicine," he remarks coldly.
>
> "Not at all," I say, "it really didn't matter."
>
> "Well, then, why did you tell the boy it should be taken with water?" And then I try to disentangle the business, and the husband shakes his head gloomily at me. "She feels very queer," says he, "we should all be easier in our minds if you came and looked at her." So I leave my heroine in the four-foot way with an express thundering towards her, and trudge sadly off, with the feeling that another morning has been wasted, and another seam left visible to the critic's eye in my unhappy novel.

Conan Doyle hoped the anecdote would explain the deficiencies of his novel, but the portrait of an easily distracted practitioner contrasts sharply with the recollection of others. "He would sit at a small desk in a corner of his own drawing room, writing a story, while a dozen people round about him were talking and laughing," a fellow writer would recall. "He preferred it to being alone in his study. Sometimes, without looking up from his work, he would make a remark, showing that he must have been listening to our conversation; but his pen never ceased moving."

Distracted or not, Conan Doyle took nearly two years to complete *The Firm of Girdlestone*. Even then, he had reservations about the book—and would later dismiss it as largely worthless—so he cannot have been entirely surprised when the publishers sent it circling back with "the precision of a homing pigeon." Eventually he decided to let the manuscript settle at the back of a drawer, and would not attempt to revive it for another four years.

With his usual resilience, Conan Doyle poured his energy into a new project, called *A Tangled Skein*, which introduced a character named Ormond Sacker and a "sleepy-eyed young man" variously called Sheridan Hope and Sherrinford Holmes. He began writing on March 8, 1886, and by the time he finished in April the title had been changed to *A Study in Scarlet* and the characters had become Sherlock Holmes and Dr. Watson.

In later years, Conan Doyle would often claim that he did not recall how he chanced upon those names, and the subject has long been a source of cheery debate among Baker Street aficionados. In his autobiography, Conan Doyle raised an objection to the "elementary art" of revealing personality traits through a character's name. The common-sounding "Holmes," then, seemed preferable to something on the order of "Mr. Sharps" or "Mr. Ferrets." Conan Doyle underscored the theme in a speech given in 1921. "In those old days," he said, "there was a reaction against what I look upon as the one blot in Charles Dickens, and I give way to no one in my admiration for that great man. But I think that if he had dropped all the Turveydrops and the Tittletits and the other extraordinary names he gave to people, he would have made his work more realistic."

Strong words from the author of *The Firm of Girdlestone*, which contained a Major Tobias Clutterbuck. But if Conan Doyle came to prefer a less flamboyant sound, his remarks do nothing to pinpoint the specific origin of the names. Over the years, various cricketers have been put forward as the likely source of "Sherlock," and Conan Doyle himself once endorsed this train of thought as "the most productive line to follow." He also had a classmate at Stonyhurst named Patrick Sherlock, and the name William Sherlock appears in his beloved Macaulay's *History of England*.

The name of "Holmes," though Conan Doyle used it once before in an early essay, almost certainly derived from Oliver Wendell Holmes, the American physician and man of letters. "Never," Conan Doyle once wrote, "have I so known and loved a man whom I have never seen." As fate would have it, Oliver Wendell Holmes spent three months in Britain in 1886—the year Conan Doyle composed *A Study in Scarlet*—and received an honorary degree from Conan Doyle's own University of Edinburgh. Though Conan Doyle never mentioned him in connection with Sherlock Holmes, he often acknowledged the American scholar as one of his own literary inspirations. "The gentle laughing philosopher whether as autocrat, poet, or professor, made a very deep mark upon my young mind," he wrote in later years. "Glorious fellow, so tolerant, so witty, so worldly-wise."

The naming of Dr. Watson also opens a rich field for speculation. There was a Dr. James Watson among the members of the Portsmouth Literary and Scientific Society, and a Dr. Patrick Heron Watson assisted Joseph Bell at the Edinburgh Royal Infirmary. One hesitates to invest too heavily in any one explanation, as Conan Doyle himself took a fairly relaxed view of the matter. In a later Holmes adventure, "The Man with the Twisted Lip," Watson's own wife adds to the confusion—calling her husband "James" though his name is actually "John."

Names aside, Conan Doyle's inspiration for his famous detective is more certain. "I thought of my old teacher Joe Bell," he wrote, "of his eagle face, of his curious ways, of his eerie trick of spotting details. If he were a detective he would surely reduce this fascinating but unorganized business to something nearer to an exact science."

With his sharp features and aquiline nose, Sherlock Holmes bore an obvious physical resemblance to Dr. Bell. The similarity grew more pronounced as soon as Holmes opened his mouth. "How are you?" asked Sherlock Holmes, upon meeting Dr. Watson. "You have been in Afghanistan, I perceive."

Just as Bell had inferred a Highland officer's background from his failure to remove his hat, Sherlock Holmes found enormous significance in Dr. Watson's stiff left arm and pale wrist:

> Here is a gentleman of a medical type, but with the air of a military man. Clearly an army doctor then. He has just come from the tropics, for his face is dark, and that is not the natural tint of his skin, for his wrists are fair. He has

> undergone hardship and sickness, as his haggard face says clearly. His left arm has been injured. He holds it in a stiff and unnatural manner. Where in the tropics could an English army doctor have seen much hardship and got his arm wounded? Clearly in Afghanistan.

This early display of the "science of deduction" set a pattern for every subsequent Holmes adventure. The detective's seemingly magical ability to conjure case histories from apparent trifles became his trademark, and remains the most engaging aspect of the stories. Later, when an interviewer expressed wonder that such a character had sprung from Conan Doyle's inner consciousness, the author gave an emphatic nod to his old teacher. "Oh!" he exclaimed. "But, if you please, he is not evolved out of anyone's inner consciousness. Sherlock Holmes is the literary embodiment, if I may so express it, of my memory of a professor of medicine at Edinburgh University."

In a letter to Bell himself, Conan Doyle made the point even more forcefully. "It is most certainly to you that I owe Sherlock Holmes," he wrote, "and though in the stories I have the advantage of being able to place him in all sorts of dramatic positions, I do not think that his analytical work is in the least an exaggeration of some of the effects which I have seen you produce in the out-patient ward."

Dr. Bell would come to relish his identification with Sherlock Holmes, but he was always quick to reflect due credit back onto Conan Doyle. "Dr. Conan Doyle has, by his imaginative genius, made a great deal out of very little," Bell would tell a journalist, "and his warm remembrance of one of his old teachers has coloured the picture." This becoming display of modesty invites the reader to disagree with Bell, but his reading was accurate—Conan Doyle had sold himself short. As with his disparaging remarks about his own medical skills, the young Conan Doyle seemed eager to play down his achievement with Sherlock Holmes.

That achievement was considerable. With *A Study in Scarlet*, Conan Doyle no longer contented himself to walk in the footsteps of other writers. He now had greater confidence in his own talent and imagination, which freed his mind for the series of inspirations that became Sherlock Holmes.

The first of these inspirations was to apply Bell's lecture room techniques to detective fiction. This decision would not have been an obvious one at the time. The genre—and the very word *detective*—had existed for barely forty years, and offered few worthwhile literary models. "The great defect in the detective of fiction is that he obtains results without any obvious reason," Conan Doyle told an early interviewer. "That is not fair, it is not art." With Sherlock Holmes, Conan Doyle resolved to play fair with his audience. He would not withhold vital evidence from the reader, as was common at the time, nor would he rely on outlandish coincidences or dim-witted criminals to drive his plots and make his hero look good. Instead, Conan Doyle aspired to create "a scientific detective, who solved cases on his own merits and not through the folly of the criminal."

Having made this decision, Conan Doyle sought inspiration from the master of the form, Edgar Allan Poe. Sherlock Holmes might dismiss Poe's Dupin as "very inferior," but Conan Doyle revered both the author and his creation, and *Tales of Mystery and Imagination* had been a favorite book of his boyhood. "I read it young when my mind was plastic," he later wrote. "It stimulated my imagination and set before me a supreme example of dignity and force in the methods of telling a story."

Poe's reputation as the father of modern detective fiction rests on five short stories written between the years of 1841 and 1844. In these stories, three of which feature C. Auguste Dupin, Poe anticipated virtually every convention of the classic detective story—the brooding, eccentric sleuth; the comparatively dense sidekick; the wrongfully accused client; the unlikely villain; the secret code; the false clue; and the impossible crime.

When Conan Doyle took up his pen to write *A Study in Scarlet*, Poe had not yet achieved his current renown, and would not have been an obvious model. Conan Doyle understood Poe's achievement as few others did, and saw a clear line between Poe's innovations and his own ambitions. That said, *A Study in Scarlet* is far less derivative than any of Conan Doyle's work to this point. Sherlock Holmes owed much to Dupin's fascination with "the infinity of mental excitement," but Poe's stories served as a catalyst rather than a template. At twenty-six, Conan Doyle was ready to work without a net.

Sherlock Holmes often chided Dr. Watson for attempting to inject color and life into what should have been, he felt, a dry and factual "course of lectures." In a sense, Conan Doyle did the same to Poe. "Murders in the Rue Morgue," Poe's first detective story, begins in a dry, clinical fashion:

> The mental features discoursed of as the analytical, are, in themselves, but little susceptible of analysis. We appreciate them only in their effects. We know of them, among other things, that they are always to their possessor, when inordinately possessed, a source of the liveliest enjoyment.

The contrast to "A Scandal in Bohemia," the first of the Sherlock Holmes short stories, could hardly be more pronounced:

> To Sherlock Holmes she is always *the* woman. I have seldom heard him mention her under any other name. In his eyes she eclipses and predominates the whole of her sex. It was not that he felt any emotion akin to love for Irene Adler. All emotions, and that one particularly, were abhorrent to his cold, precise, but admirably balanced mind. . . . Grit in a sensitive instrument, or a crack in one of his own high-power lenses, would not be more disturbing than a strong emotion in a nature such as his. And yet there was but one woman to him, and that woman was the late Irene Adler, of dubious and questionable memory.

Sherlock Holmes would undoubtedly have derided Conan Doyle for "pandering to popular taste," but the young author shrewdly recognized that he must make his character accessible to his contemporaries. The early readers of "A Scandal in Bohemia," for whom Sherlock Holmes was not yet a household name, would have recognized the comfortable conventions of romantic fiction, rather than the clinical chill of the unfamiliar detective genre.

Though Conan Doyle regarded Poe as the "master of all," a second, largely forgotten detective writer also exerted a strong influence on *A Study in Scarlet*. The French novelist Emile Gaboriau, whose sensationalist novels were hugely popular at the time, appealed to Conan Doyle for the "neat dovetailing of his plots." Gaboriau's detective, Monsieur Lecoq, possessed many of the traits and skills that came to be associated with Sherlock Holmes. Lecoq was not only a master of disguise but also employed scientific techniques, such as the use of a plaster cast to take impressions of footprints. Lecoq's disdain for Gevrol, the head of the Sureté, clearly anticipates the relationship between Sherlock Holmes and Inspector Lestrade of Scotland Yard, and the good-hearted but slow-witted Father Absinthe, Lecoq's admiring companion, suggests a prototype of Dr. Watson.

Conan Doyle finished *A Study in Scarlet* toward the end of April 1886. He had no way of knowing, as he rolled the manuscript into a tube and sent it to *Cornhill Magazine*, that he had created one of the most indelible characters of modern fiction. Today, a statue of Sherlock Holmes stands near Conan Doyle's birthplace in Edinburgh. The detective's likeness has adorned a series of British postage stamps. The Baker Street stop of the London Underground, near the famous lodgings at 221B, features scenes from his adventures. Few who read the manuscript in 1886 could have imagined such tributes. Though the characters of Sherlock Holmes and Dr. Watson are fully drawn, the young novelist had not quite found his stroke. After a strong investigative sequence, in which Holmes examines the corpse of Enoch J. Drebber of Cleveland, the story deteriorates with an extended flashback centered on the Mormons of Utah. Though such expository techniques were a familiar convention of the day, the lengthy digression kept Sherlock Holmes offstage for much of the narrative and exposed Conan Doyle's poor grasp of American idiom and geography. Later stories were distinguished by Conan Doyle's plotting skills and originality of thought. The *Study in Scarlet* flashback, by contrast, finds him drawing heavily on Robert Louis Stevenson's *The Dynamiter*, published the previous year.

Conan Doyle's decision to wedge a Mormon subplot into the middle of a Sherlock Holmes tale might strike the modern reader as curious. At the time, strange to say, this was Conan Doyle's hook. The Mormons' "life of immorality"—and especially the practice of polygamy—had been very much in the news as Conan Doyle sat down to write. Even the Portsmouth Literary and Scientific Society had addressed the subject, in a lecture given the previous year. Conan Doyle seems to have done extensive background reading, but he might also have done well to consult an atlas, as Utah and the Rio Grande appear to have wandered off from their usual positions in *A Study in Scarlet*. This was to be a recurring problem. Earlier, in a story set in New Zealand, he took great care in placing a thriving farm twenty miles out to sea. "These little things will happen," Conan Doyle admitted.

Even so, Conan Doyle held out great hope for *A Study in Scarlet* and considered it a better piece of work than *The Firm of Girdlestone*. "We rather fancy," Louisa confided in a letter, "that *A Study in Scarlet* may find its way into print before its elder brother." Soon, however, the first Sherlock Holmes story began to make the familiar "circular tour," with three publishers issuing prompt rejections. "Verily," Conan Doyle wrote to his mother, "literature is a difficult oyster to open."

In September, Conan Doyle rolled the manuscript into another tube and sent it to a fourth publisher—Ward, Lock and Company of London. At the end of October, a letter arrived to say that the editors were pleased with the story. "We could not publish it this year," they added, "as the market is flooded at present with cheap fiction." If Conan Doyle would not object to waiting until the following year, the publishers would offer £25 to purchase the copyright.

"It was not a very tempting offer," Conan Doyle wrote, "and even I, poor as I was, hesitated to accept it." He had good reason to hesitate. The money was rotten—he had earned better for "J. Habakuk Jephson's Statement," a far shorter piece—and he did not want to wait twelve months for publication. He wrote asking if a small royalty might be granted, but the publisher turned him down on the grounds that "it might give rise to some confusion." Reluctantly, Conan Doyle agreed to the terms. "I never at any time received another penny for it," he declared in his autobiography.

Conan Doyle hoped that Ward, Lock would bring out *A Study in Scarlet* as a separate volume, so that he would at last fulfill his ambition of seeing his name on the spine of a book. Instead, the story appeared in November of 1887 as the main feature of *Beeton's Christmas Annual,* a collection of fiction and short occasionals founded twenty years earlier by Samuel Orchart Beeton—whose wife had been the renowned Mrs. Beeton of cookbook and household management fame.

Priced at one shilling, the annual had a red, white, and yellow cover that featured Conan Doyle's villain apparently warming a syringe by the flame of a hanging lamp. Two "original drawing room plays" gave ballast to the volume, along with several pages of advertising for such items as a "lung invigorator," recommended for cases of incipient consumption, and "Steiner's Vermin Paste," said to be "A Sure and Certain Destroyer of Rats, Cockroaches, Mice and Black Beetles."

The annual sold out within two weeks, although this owed more to the Beeton reputation than to *A Study in Scarlet*. The story itself caused no great stir, but received enough favorable notice to justify a separate edition the following year. Touted as "a story of thrilling interest," the new edition featured six pen-and-ink drawings by Conan Doyle's father. It is not known whether Conan Doyle himself put his father's name forward as a possible illustrator, or whether the publisher sought an interesting novelty in the father-and-son collaboration. Charles Doyle fulfilled the commission from Edinburgh, where he remained in an institution. His illustrations are strangely tranquil and uninteresting, but the bearded figure of Holmes—who strongly resembles the artist—suggests that the elder Doyle recognized some of his own characteristics in his son's creation.

By the time *A Study in Scarlet* finally appeared in book form, Conan Doyle's attention had moved elsewhere. During the long waiting period he took up several other projects, hoping to find a smoother path to publication. Not all of these efforts were pitched at literary immortality. When the *Gas and Water Gazette* asked him to translate a German submission, Conan Doyle drew on his shaky schoolboy German to produce an article entitled "Testing Gas Pipes for Leakage." Years later, in a speech to the Author's Club, he would claim that this had been the great breakthrough of his career—rather than *A Study in Scarlet*, as one might have supposed. For the first time, he noted dryly, a publisher had asked for his services, rather than the other way around.

Having exhausted the potential of leaky gas pipes, Conan Doyle launched into a new novel in July of 1887. "I now determined to test my powers to the full," he wrote, "and I chose a historical novel for this end, because it seemed to me the one way of combining a certain amount of literary dignity with those scenes of action and adventure which were natural to my young and ardent mind."

Set in the late seventeenth century, *Micah Clarke* told the story of a group of English Puritans against the backdrop of the Monmouth Rebellion, James Scott's doomed campaign to usurp King James II. Conan Doyle established the habit of a lifetime with this novel, researching his background for several months so that every full-bottomed periwig and white berdash cravat could be rendered with loving detail. Though the novel occasionally bogs down in aimless window dressing, *Micah Clarke* displays all of the strengths that distinguished Conan Doyle's later historical fiction—a strong narrative voice, powerful battle scenes, and a lively period flavor.

"When it was finished early in 1888 my hopes ran high," the author wrote, "and out it went on its travels." Once again, Conan Doyle found the publishers to be strangely resistant to his charms. The editor of *Cornhill Magazine* wanted to know why he would waste his time and talent on historical novels. Bentley and Company advised him that the novel lacked "the one great necessary point for fiction, i.e. interest." Several other publishers returned equally depressing verdicts. "I remember smoking over my dog-eared manuscript when it returned for a whiff of country air after one of its descents upon town," Conan Doyle recalled, "and wondering what I should do if some sporting, reckless kind of publisher were suddenly to stride in and make me a bid of forty shillings or so for the lot."

Before it could come to that, Conan Doyle sent the manuscript to Longmans publishers, where it caught the attention of Andrew Lang, an influential Scottish editor and historian. Lang advised the firm to accept Conan Doyle's manuscript, and the following February *Micah Clarke* appeared in book form. Conan Doyle would always consider *Micah Clarke* his "first real opening," rather than *A Study in Scarlet*, which had appeared more than a year earlier. The novel received extremely good reviews, mixed with a few cavils about the author's historical liberties, and went through three printings in the first year. "*Micah Clarke* is a noticeable book," wrote one reviewer, comparing it favorably with R. D. Blackmore's *Lorna Doone*, "because it carries the reader out of the beaten track; it makes him now and then hold his breath with excitement; it presents a series of vivid pictures . . . and it leaves upon the mind the impression of well-rounded symmetry and completeness."

Coming so soon on the heels of *A Study in Scarlet*, *Micah Clarke* established a conflict that would prove to be the central dilemma of Conan Doyle's career. On the one side was Sherlock Holmes, who belonged to that "different and humbler plane" of literature that Conan Doyle visited now and then while making his way in the world. On the other side were the historical novels, plays, poems, and other works through which he hoped to gain a place in the literary pantheon. Only a few years later, when asked to write a preface for a new edition of *A Study in Scarlet*, Conan Doyle declared that "so elementary a form of fiction as the detective story hardly deserves the dignity of a Preface." With *Micah Clarke*, on the other hand, he had taken the high road. "I thought," he declared a short time later, "I had a tool in my hands that would cut a path for me."

For the moment, Conan Doyle had no further plans for Sherlock Holmes. He was enjoying what Dr. Watson was to call the "complete happiness, and the home-centered interests which rise up around the man who first finds himself the master of his own establishment." His medical practice had reached a comfortable level, his literary career was finally beginning to flourish, and he enjoyed an active social life in Southsea—throwing himself into local sporting events with such energy that he frequently came away with bruised ribs or a broken finger. As he did not own a horse and buggy, the young doctor could often be seen peddling around town on a sturdy-looking cycle, which resembled a reversed tricycle with oversized wheels. Occasionally Louisa rode along with him, awkwardly perched on a seat and footrest at the front.

When Louisa gave birth to their first child, Mary, on January 28, 1889, Conan Doyle had every reason to feel satisfied with life in Southsea. "She is fat and plump, blue eyes, bandy legs and a fat body," Conan Doyle told the Ma'am. "Any other points will be answered on inquiry. I have had no great practice in describing babies." Though happy at home, Conan Doyle continued to feel adrift spiritually in the wake of his break from the Catholic Church. His daughter would not be baptized for another eighteen months, and only then at the insistence of the Ma'am. This was no casual omission on Conan Doyle's part. Three of his nine siblings had died in childhood, so his initial refusal to baptize his daughter must be taken as a sign that his agnosticism had reached a fairly advanced state. "I had ceased to butt my head incessantly against what seemed to be an impenetrable wall," he wrote. "I had laid aside the old charts as useless, and had quite despaired of ever finding a new one which would enable me to steer an intelligible course." Yet he was already moving toward a new, unorthodox system of belief. "A dim light of dawn was to come to me soon in an uncertain way which was destined in time to spread and grow brighter."

In those early days, this dawning light took some peculiar forms. Up to this point, Conan Doyle's attitude toward the spirit world had been lighthearted. In a story called "Selecting a Ghost," published in 1883, a wealthy grocer hires a medium to audition prospective ghosts for his mansion. "I am the great ethereal sigh-heaver," intones one. "I kill dogs. Mortal, wilt thou choose me?"

Soon, however, the tone grew more serious. When discussing his early writing career, Conan Doyle generally neglected to mention a short novel called *The Mystery of Cloomber*, which appeared a few months before *Micah Clarke* and then sank into profound obscurity. This strange, confusing tale features a trio of Buddhist monks, apparently returned from the dead, who seek revenge against an English army officer for a crime committed forty years previously. Nearly every chapter introduces some weird new manifestation of the paranormal: astral projection, precognition, extrasensory perception, and even matter transmission—described as the "power of resolving an object into its chemical atoms" and then "compelling them to retake their original form."

Most reviewers didn't know what to make of it. One newspaper, noting the novel's Scottish setting, expressed relief that the author had not ventured to write in dialect. Clearly the reviewer had bailed out before reaching chapter eight, which begins, "Maister Fothergill West and the meenister say that I maun tell all I can aboot General Heatherstone and his hoose, but that I maunna say muckle aboot mysel' because the readers wouldna care to hear."

Years later, when Conan Doyle's interest in the spirit realm had become a matter of public record, critics never tired of pointing out the contrast between the author's beliefs and those of the clear-thinking, intensely logical Sherlock Holmes. The prevailing view at the time, which persists today, held that Conan Doyle underwent some softening of the brain in later life. In fact, this strange tension between the material and the spirit worlds is evident in all phases of Conan Doyle's career. Though *The Mystery of Cloomber* hardly qualifies as a neglected masterpiece, it clearly illustrates that the young novelist had already begun to question the received wisdom of science. "For what is science?" Conan Doyle asked in the book's final pages. "Science is the consensus of opinion of scientific men, and history has shown that it is slow to accept a truth. Science sneered at Newton for twenty years. Science proved mathematically that an iron ship could not swim, and science declared that a steamship could not cross the Atlantic."

From there, it was only a short step to the séance room.

7

A Traveler from Slattenmere

I am, I think, one of the most unsuspicious men upon earth, and through a certain easy-going indolence of disposition I never even think of the possibility of those with whom I am brought into contact trying to deceive me. It does not occur to me.

—MR. STARK MUNRO IN *THE STARK MUNRO LETTERS*

In February 1889, a Professor Milo de Meyer visited Southsea from Italy to give an exhibition of his "mesmeric force," more familiar today as hypnotism. In the audience were some two dozen men of science and medicine, including Dr. Conan Doyle. Speaking through an interpreter, Professor de Meyer explained that the art of mesmerism had its roots in the mysterious electrical force emanating from magnets, and that "its practice would be beneficial in the case of many surgical operations." His experiments, according to an account in the Portsmouth *Evening News*, had "lately attracted much attention on the Continent and in London and Brighton."

Conan Doyle had a long-standing interest in the subject, having studied the works of Franz Anton Mesmer, the eighteenth-century Austrian physician from whom mesmerism drew its name. Also known as "animal magnetism," mesmerism achieved a considerable vogue in the 1770s, with society patients coming to Mesmer for magnetized pills, magnetized clothing, and magnetized dinnerware. In time, when Marie Antoinette came under Mesmer's influence, a French royal commission concluded that the physician's success owed more to a patient's suggestibility than to any invisible force. As a result, though Mesmer himself is generally dismissed as a charlatan, his so-called mesmeric power is the acknowledged forerunner of modern hypnotism and its medical applications.

As a medical man with a predisposition toward the paranormal, Conan Doyle was naturally intrigued by Mesmer's theories. For a time, mesmerists became a feature of his fiction. In a story called "John Barrington Cowles," published in 1884, a character called "Dr. Messinger" sounded a cautionary note: "A strong will can, simply by virtue of its strength, take possession of a weaker one, even at a distance, and can regulate the impulses and the actions of the owner of it. If there was one man in the world who had a very much more highly developed will than any of the rest of the human family, there is no reason why he should not be able to rule over them all, and to reduce his fellow-creatures to the condition of automatons." Needless to say, by the end of the tale such a creature did emerge, but in a characteristic Conan Doyle touch, the superior will was found in a woman rather than a man.

It is hardly surprising, then, that Conan Doyle should have wanted to see the "eminent and renowned" Professor de Meyer. If he hoped for a sober discussion of mesmerism and its surgical applications, he was to be disappointed. As outlined in the Portsmouth *Evening News*, the demonstration unfolded more along the lines of a vaudeville act. Ten young men had been selected and hypnotized beforehand—"in order to save time"—as the professor had found that only one of every four people was susceptible to mesmerism on the first attempt. As these volunteers were brought out from the wings, Conan Doyle stepped forward to join them, "having volunteered to swell the number of would-be subjects." Professor de Meyer put his subjects through several demonstrations of his "animal magnetism." Some of the young volunteers, when asked to open their mouths, found they could not close them again. Others fell to their knees and could not rise, and another pair of volunteers were compelled to act out an "amusing scene" as a dentist and patient.

"An attempt to magnetise Dr. Doyle in a similar manner failed," the newspaper reported, "the Professor remarking, after making the attempt, that the process would take too long." One can only speculate as to whether a longer program might have found Conan Doyle peeling off his clothes or quacking like a duck. He had approached the evening in the spirit of scientific inquiry. What he did not know was that it had become common practice to dress up routine entertainments as scientific lectures. In the eighteenth century, rudimentary displays of electricity and magnetism were passed off as "Philosophical Experiments" so as to attract an upper-class audience. Even Edgar Allan Poe had been baffled by the celebrated Kempelen Chess Player, said to be a miracle of the clockmaker's art, but actually controlled by a concealed human player. In Conan Doyle's day, hypnotism and flashy chemical stunts took the place of automatons and electrical tricks.

One cannot say for certain if Professor de Meyer's subjects were preselected confederates, as is often the case in displays of this sort. If he had time to locate and hypnotize a sufficient number of suggestible volunteers, the demonstration could well have been genuine. What is notable is that Conan Doyle himself did not submit to the hypnotist's influence, and apparently did not feel constrained to "play along," as many people in his situation would have done. In years to come Conan Doyle would develop a reputation for intense credulity. At this stage, at least, he was not so easily led.

From his researches, Conan Doyle knew that people in the thrall of mesmerism occasionally produced random, disjointed snatches of conversation, believed by some observers to signify contact with the souls of the dead. For this reason, Conan Doyle's early fascination with mesmerism may well have shaped his budding interest in spiritualism. In later life, however, when he had occasion to trace his early influences, Conan Doyle had little to say about Mesmer. Instead, he focused his attention on what he called "The Hydesville Episode," the story of Margaretta and Katherine Fox, the weird sisters of the modern spiritualist movement.

In 1848, eleven years before Conan Doyle's birth, the Fox sisters lived with their parents in a two-room farmhouse in the town of Hydesville, in upstate New York. One night, strange and inexplicable noises roused the family from their beds. The sounds—described as "a shower of bumps and raps"—persisted over several nights, always in the vicinity of Maggie, age fourteen, and Katie, age eleven. Mrs. Fox, the girls' mother, discovered that some sort of intelligence lay behind the disturbance. If she snapped her fingers once or twice, she received the same number of raps in reply. The unseen force even responded to simple questions—with one rap for a "no" answer and two for "yes." On this evidence, Mrs. Fox attributed the phenomenon to spirit agencies.

By 1850, the Fox sisters and their mother were giving public demonstrations of their abilities. Soon they came to the attention of Horace Greeley, editor of the *New York Tribune*, who arranged to have them brought to New York City. In an open letter published in his newspaper, Greeley attested to the honesty of the girls and the wholly convincing nature of their spirit manifestations.

By this time, the notoriety of the Fox sisters had inspired dozens of imitators. Most prominent of these were Ira and William Davenport, a pair of brothers from Buffalo, who took the Fox sisters' simple effects and made them suitable for the stage. Their act began with an enormous wooden cabinet set on a raised platform at center stage. Inside was a long wooden bench. The brothers, tied hand and foot, were placed inside the cabinet, facing each other. Tambourines, trumpets, and other noisemakers were placed on the floor. Large doors at the front swung shut as the stage lights were extinguished. Instantly the air filled with the sound of jangling tambourines, strumming guitars, and other ghostly music. Ethereal hands appeared through openings in the cabinet and musical instruments were seen to float through space. At regular intervals during the demonstration, assistants threw open the doors. Inside, the brothers remained securely fastened, heads bowed, eyes closed in concentration. When the doors swung shut, the mysterious happenings resumed. Audiences were quick to credit the brothers with supernatural powers, an impression the Davenports did nothing to dispel. Not everyone was fooled. Occasionally a spectator would strike a match in the darkened theater. The brothers, their hands free, could plainly be seen ringing bells and waving instruments in the air. Still the crowds flocked to see them. One audience member, a thirteen-year-old named Ehrich Weiss, needed no match to illuminate their secrets. He realized at once that the brothers had discovered a means of slipping in and out of their bonds. Years later, as Harry Houdini, he would put the knowledge to good use.

Some forty years after the first raps were heard in Hydesville, Maggie Fox would confess that the entire affair had been a childish hoax. She and her sister initiated the prank with an apple tied to a string, she admitted, and later refined their noise-making ability by snapping their toes against hard surfaces. "We were led on unintentionally by my good mother," she explained. "She used to say when we were sitting in a dark circle at home: 'Is this a disembodied spirit that has taken possession of my dear children?' And then we would 'rap' just for the fun of the thing, you know, and mother would declare that it was the spirits that were speaking."

This confession, which Maggie Fox later withdrew, had no effect whatever on the spiritualist movement, which had long since passed beyond the influence of the Fox sisters. At the time of Conan Doyle's birth in 1859, more than ten million Americans admitted to being spiritualists. Hundreds of spiritualist churches had sprung up across the country, and more than twenty-five thousand self-professed mediums worked their trade in darkened séance rooms. Here, the floating trumpets and ghostly music of the Davenport show were duplicated on a smaller scale, and chalk messages—often written in a wavering, spectral hand—appeared on blank slates. Mediums claimed that these messages were written by spirit visitors. If the spirits seemed unresponsive, however, other avenues were available. Specially gaffed chalk slates—featuring a hidden flap that popped open to reveal a message—could be had from mail-order novelty houses.

As the craze spread through Europe and Asia, it found an especially fertile breeding ground in Britain. By 1869, London had no fewer than four monthly spiritualist journals, all dedicated to "the progress of the science and ethics of spiritualism." By this time Britain had produced a number of mediums to rival the Fox sisters, the most prominent of whom, Daniel Dunglas Home, won many converts. Home, who Conan Doyle was to describe as a "truly great man," was said to have the ability to float in the air, travel vast distances in the blink of an eye, and raise heavy objects without touching them. This last talent sparked a note of wonder in the poet Elizabeth Barrett Browning, an avowed believer in Home's powers. Writing to her sister on the occasion of Home's marriage, Mrs. Browning remarked, "Think of the conjugal furniture floating about the room at night, Henrietta."

Against this background, Conan Doyle's early flirtation with spiritualism cannot seem entirely surprising. As early as 1881, when he was only twenty-one years old, Conan Doyle attended a lecture in Birmingham entitled "Does Death End All?" He described his attitude as that of a "respectful materialist"; he felt willing to listen, but inclined toward disbelief. "I had at that time the usual contempt which the young educated man feels towards the whole subject which has been covered by the clumsy name of spiritualism," he later wrote. "I had read of mediums being convicted of fraud, I had heard of phenomena which were opposed to every known scientific law, and I had deplored the simplicity and credulity which could deceive good, earnest people into believing that such bogus happenings were signs of intelligence outside our own existence."

He could not fail to be impressed, however, by the number of prominent scientists who admitted their belief publicly. Earlier, the views of Thomas Huxley, Darwin's staunchest supporter, helped to shape Conan Doyle's agnosticism. Now, the writings of Alfred Russel Wallace, Darwin's fellow theorist of natural selection, suggested that science and spiritualism could be reconciled. Wallace, author of the groundbreaking *On the Law Which Has Regulated the Introduction of New Species*, also produced a book called *Miracles and Modern Spiritualism*, in which he suggested that natural selection explained only the physical aspect of human development, while the "spiritual essence . . . can only find an explanation in the unseen universe of Spirit." Conan Doyle was further impressed that William Crookes, inventor of the radiometer and the early "Crookes" evacuated tube, had personally tested and endorsed both Daniel Dunglas Home and Katie Fox, along with such up-and-coming mediums as Florrie Cook and Anna Eva Fay.

Wallace and Crookes were the exceptions among men of science, as Conan Doyle well knew. On the other side of the spectrum was Oliver Wendell Holmes, the man Conan Doyle so passionately admired, who regarded spiritualism as nothing less than a "plague." "While some," Holmes wrote in 1859, "are crying out against it as a delusion of the Devil, and some are getting angry with it as a mere trick of interested or mischievous persons, Spiritualism is quietly undermining the traditional ideas of the future state which have been and are still accepted."

For Conan Doyle, those traditional ideas had already been sufficiently undermined, but he understood how a trained physician such as Holmes might recoil from psychic double-talk. "I saw, as a medical man, how a spicule of bone or a tumour pressing on the brain would cause what seemed an alteration of the soul," Conan Doyle wrote. "I saw also how drugs or alcohol would turn on fleeting phases of virtue or vice." He had also seen more of death than most young men of his time, and had little reason to believe that the souls of patients such as Jack Hawkins survived their bodily death. "When the candle burns out," he wrote of his attitude at the time, "the light disappears."

Nonetheless, Conan Doyle remained fascinated by the uncharted potential of the mind. He read reports of a new phenomenon called mental telepathy, soon to be the subject of an influential book by F. W. H. Myers, and decided to see if he could duplicate some of the effects described. Working with a local architect named Henry Ball, Conan Doyle devised a simple test to see whether it might be possible to transmit unspoken thoughts. Both men sat with a pen and a notebook. Conan Doyle would then make a sketch while Ball, who faced in the opposite direction, attempted to duplicate the image. "Again and again," Conan Doyle wrote, "sitting behind him, I have drawn diagrams, and he in turn has made approximately the same figure. I showed beyond any doubt whatever that I could convey my thoughts without words."

Conan Doyle's account sounds intriguing as far as it goes, but he gives precious little detail—a problem that was to grow more pronounced over the years. Who initiated the experiments? What sort of person was Ball? Were the drawings complex designs or simple geometric shapes? Did Ball guess accurately every single time, or were a certain number of failures recorded? If so, what was the ratio of "hits" to "misses"? Without these particulars, it is difficult to distinguish a psychic event from a parlor trick. "Data! Data! Data!" as Sherlock Holmes was to say. "I can't make bricks without clay."

In any case, the apparent success of these experiments convinced Conan Doyle that his earlier resistance to psychic phenomena had been too rigid. "I had compared the thought-excretion of the brain to the bile excretion of the liver," he wrote. "Clearly this was untenable." If it were possible to transmit thoughts independently of the human body, he reasoned, then perhaps some form of human consciousness could also survive bodily death.

Up to this point, Conan Doyle had limited experience of the séance room, and his earliest results offered little in the way of encouragement. Soon after his marriage, a group of friends invited him to come and observe their attempts at "table-turning," a rudimentary form of mediumship not unlike a Ouija board. The participants, Conan Doyle explained, "sat round a dining-room table which after a time, their hands being upon it, began to sway and finally got sufficient motion to tap with one leg. They then asked questions and received answers, more or less wise and more or less to the point. They were got by the tedious process of reciting the alphabet and writing down the letter which the tap indicated. It seemed to me that we were collectively pushing the table, and that our own wills were concerned in bringing down the leg at the right moment. I was interested but very skeptical."

In the wake of his mind-reading success, however, Conan Doyle decided to try table-turning in his own home. "It is to be remembered that I was working without a medium, which is like an astronomer working without a telescope," he recounted. "Among us we could just muster enough of the magnetic force, or whatever you will call it, to get the table movements with their suspicious and often stupid messages."

On the whole, Conan Doyle remained unimpressed. One evening, after several inconclusive sessions, an event occurred that left him both "puzzled and disgusted." "We had very good conditions," he recalled, "and an amount of movement which seemed quite independent of our pressure. Long and detailed messages came through, which purported to be from a spirit who gave his name and said he was a commercial traveller who had lost his life in a recent fire at a theatre at Exeter."

This was exactly what Conan Doyle had wanted. Unlike the vague platitudes to which he had grown accustomed, this message contained verifiable information. He eagerly took notes as the unseen presence, communicating through the tapping of the table leg, gave precise details of his own death. The message continued with a request that Conan Doyle and his friends contact the traveler's surviving family, who lived, he said, in a town called Slattenmere, in northwest England. "I did so," Conan Doyle reported, "but my letter came back, appropriately enough, through the dead letter office."

Disenchanted, Conan Doyle might have dropped the subject of spiritualism altogether but for the influence of Major General Alfred Drayson, a fellow member of the Portsmouth Literary and Scientific Society. Drayson had retired to Southsea after a distinguished military career in India, South Africa, and North America. A prolific writer, he produced several volumes of memoirs, a handbook on *The Art of Practical Whist*, another on billiards, and dozens of contributions to magazines and newspapers. Drayson, who had also taught mathematics for many years, achieved his greatest renown as a theoretical astronomer, having advanced a resolution concerning a "second rotation of the earth" that gradually gained acceptance in scientific circles. Conan Doyle once compared Drayson favorably to Copernicus, and when one recalls that Professor Moriarty, the archnemesis of Sherlock Holmes, also taught mathematics and was the author of *The Dynamics of an Asteroid*, it is clear that Drayson made a lasting impression.

When Conan Doyle learned that Drayson also had an abiding interest in spiritualism, he could not fail to be impressed. Following his unhappy experience with the commercial traveler from Slattenmere, Conan Doyle came to the older man with his doubts. "You have not got the fundamental truth into your head," Drayson told him. "That truth is, that every spirit in the flesh passes over to the next world exactly as it is, with no change whatever. This world is full of weak or foolish people. So is the next."

The problem, according to Drayson, was not one of deception or self-delusion, but rather that Conan Doyle had chosen his spirit companions unwisely. "But suppose," Drayson continued, "a man in this world, who had lived in his house alone and never mixed with his fellows, was at last to put his head out of the window to see what sort of place it was, what would happen? Some naughty boy would probably say something rude. Anyhow, he would see nothing of the wisdom or greatness of the world. He would draw his head in thinking it was a very poor place. This is just what you have done."

From Drayson's perspective, then, any spirit phenomenon that did not stand up to close examination could simply be put down to "naughty" behavior. Furthermore, because the spirit realm mirrored our own world, any blatant deception on the part of a medium must also be excused. This uniquely pallid rationalization would be restated and embroidered by Conan Doyle for the rest of his life, enabling him to overlook countless shams and inconsistencies on both sides of the spirit divide.

Not all spiritualists subscribed to Drayson's views. In later years he would draw a fair amount of ridicule over his accounting of a strange psychic "apport"—a term used to describe the materialization of solid objects during a séance. In Drayson's case, these apports took the form of eggs, fruit, and vegetables reputed to have arrived by way of Brooklyn, New York. This spirit produce appeared with such regularity, Drayson claimed, that "none had to be bought for the household." Such phenomena were regarded with extreme suspicion even by the most sympathetic researchers. No less an authority than Frank Podmore, a leading light of the Society for Psychical Research, was to declare that "the history of materialisation, as far as professional mediums are concerned, is practically one unbroken line of fraud."

There is no evidence that Conan Doyle ever witnessed an apport in Drayson's household, and when he learned of the claim he was frankly skeptical. "So amazing a phenomenon," he wrote, "and one so easily simulated, was too much for a beginner, and it retarded rather than helped progress."

By this time, however, Conan Doyle had achieved independent results that convinced him of the underlying justice of Drayson's beliefs, if not all of its manifestations. At Drayson's urging, he continued to attend table-turning séances whenever possible. At one of these, a spirit who identified herself as Dorothy Postlethwaite came through, telling of her death five years earlier in Melbourne, Australia, at the age of sixteen. Miss Postlethwaite claimed to have been at school with one of the female sitters present at the séance, and proved her claim by spelling out the name of the headmistress of the school. Conan Doyle found this evidence extremely persuasive. Unfortunately, he gave no information at all about the other sitters at this gathering, as it would never have occurred to him to question their truthfulness. Since Miss Postlethwaite went on to reveal that the planet Mars is inhabited by a race far more advanced than our own, her testimony must be regarded with some degree of suspicion.

At about this time, Conan Doyle had a second experience that he found even more convincing, since he could verify it personally. A pair of friends invited him to attend a demonstration with an elderly gentleman who was said to possess "considerable mediumistic power." This, he declared, was the first time he had ever been in the presence of an actual medium, rather than a group of novices like himself. "On sitting," Conan Doyle reported, "our medium came quickly under control, and delivered a trance address, containing much interesting and elevating matter. He then became clairvoyant, describing one or two scenes which we had no opportunity of testing. So far, the meeting had been very interesting, but not above the possibility of deception. We then proposed writing. The medium took up a pencil, and after a few convulsive movements, he wrote a message to each of us. Mine ran: 'This gentleman is a healer. Tell him from me not to read Leigh Hunt's book.' "

It may seem odd that a spirit would manifest such concern over a sitter's reading habits, but Conan Doyle attached remarkable importance to this message. For some days he had been debating with himself whether or not he should acquire a copy of *Comic Dramatists of the Restoration*, by the controversial essayist Leigh Hunt, which he would undoubtedly have seen as a source of background material for *Micah Clarke*. The fact that a medium he had never before met could make reference to his private thoughts, no matter how trivial those thoughts may have been, seemed to him to be a final, incontrovertible proof of spirit intervention.

The incident so impressed Conan Doyle that he wrote a long account of the matter and sent it to *Light*, the journal of the London Spiritualistic Alliance. "I can swear that no one knew I had contemplated reading that book," he wrote, "and, moreover, it was no case of thought-reading, for I had never referred to the matter all day. I can only say that if I had had to devise a test message I could not have hit upon one which was so absolutely inexplicable on any hypothesis except that held by Spiritualists."

He had now declared, publicly and without equivocation, that "it was absolutely certain that intelligence could exist apart from the body." Having reached this conclusion, Conan Doyle found himself moved to new heights. "Let me conclude," he wrote, "by exhorting any other searcher never to despair of receiving personal testimony, but to persevere through any number of failures until at last conviction comes to him, as come it will. . . . Above all, let every inquirer bear in mind that phenomena are only a means to an end, of no value at all of themselves, and simply useful for giving us assurance of an after-existence for which we are to prepare by refining away our grosser animal feelings and cultivating our higher, nobler impulses."

It may seem a dramatic leap from Leigh Hunt to the redemption of humankind, but this was precisely the leap Conan Doyle was preparing to take. He had abandoned the Catholic Church because he could not accept, as he said at the time, anything that could not be proved to him. Now, a two-line message from an unnamed medium gave him a form of proof he could accept. "After weighing the evidence," he told the readers of *Light*, "I could no more doubt the existence of the phenomena than I could doubt the existence of lions in Africa, though I have been to that continent and have never chanced to see one."

Was this message really as definitive as Conan Doyle seemed to think? It is not possible to know how much digging the medium may have done in anticipation of the séance, or what sort of unconscious cues Conan Doyle may have given. Poe's Monsieur Dupin had a similar knack of breaking in on private thoughts, and the year before, in *A Study in Scarlet*, Sherlock Holmes dismissed this talent as "showy and superficial." Could Holmes have explained away the Leigh Hunt warning? Possibly.

As for the medium's other revelation—that Conan Doyle was a healer—Sherlock Holmes would have made short work of it. Not four years later, the detective was able to tell at a glance that Dr. Watson had returned to active practice: "[I]f a gentleman walks into my rooms smelling of iodoform, with a black mark of nitrate of silver upon his right forefinger, and a bulge on the right side of his top hat to show where he has secreted his stethoscope, I must be dull indeed if I do not pronounce him to be an active member of the medical profession."

"When I hear you give your reasons," Watson remarked on that occasion, "the thing always appears to me to be so remarkably simple that I could easily do it myself."

8

A Singularly Deep Young Man

There's money in ears, but the eye is a gold mine.

—JAMES CULLINGWORTH IN
THE STARK MUNRO LETTERS

Sherlock Holmes took his bottle from the corner of the mantelpiece, and his hypodermic syringe from its neat morocco case. With his long, white, nervous fingers he adjusted the delicate needle, and rolled back his left shirtcuff. For some little time his eyes rested thoughtfully upon the sinewy forearm and wrist, all dotted and scarred with innumerable puncture marks. Finally, he thrust the sharp point home, pressed down the tiny piston, and sank back into the velvet-lined armchair with a long sigh of satisfaction."

With these words, perhaps the most notorious in all of detective fiction, Conan Doyle revived the career of Sherlock Holmes and touched off an enduring controversy. Was Sherlock Holmes a drug addict, as the opening passage of *The Sign of the Four* appears to suggest? If so, to what extent were his abuses based on those of Conan Doyle himself?

Much has been written about Sherlock Holmes and his seven-percent solution of cocaine diluted in water. The subject has been raised in the pages of *The Lancet* and the *American Journal of*

Surgery, and no less a critic than George Bernard Shaw was moved to dismiss the detective—albeit privately—as "a drug addict without a single admirable trait."

Perhaps the most vocal commentator was Dr. Watson himself, who never missed an opportunity to offer a rebuke to his friend. "Surely the game is hardly worth the candle," Watson would declare in *The Sign of the Four*. "Why should you, for a mere passing pleasure, risk the loss of those great powers with which you have been endowed?"

In several of the early stories, Conan Doyle makes it clear that Holmes requires artificial stimulants to combat the "dull routine of existence." So long as he has a case to occupy his mind, all is well. During idle periods, he falls into a black depression or a lengthy period of lethargy. "My mind is like a racing engine," Holmes declares at one point, "tearing itself to pieces because it is not connected up with the work for which it was built." At such times, at least in the early stages of his career, Holmes required the "mental exaltation" of cocaine. His creator, whether by accident or design, never allowed these abuses to descend into actual addiction, as evidenced by the fact that Holmes could easily dispense with the drug when absorbed in a new problem. Once the case had ended, however, Holmes soon returned to the drug, as the final lines of *The Sign of the Four* remind us: " 'For me,' said Sherlock Holmes, 'there still remains the cocaine-bottle.' And he stretched his long white hand up for it."

Conan Doyle wrote *The Sign of the Four* in 1889, at a time when cocaine was the subject of intense interest in the medical community. A leading researcher was Professor Robert Christison of Conan Doyle's own University of Edinburgh, who had obtained a supply of coca leaves by way of Professor Thomson's famous *Challenger* expedition. Commonly used as an anesthetic, especially in eye surgery, cocaine also came highly recommended as a "nerve tonic." Easily and legally obtainable, the drug and its derivatives could be found in lozenges, sherrys, and gargles.

To Conan Doyle's original readers, then, the use of cocaine would not have seemed as jarring, or as worthy of reproach, as it does today. In fact, though Dr. Watson's censorious warnings about the drug may have struck some readers as priggish, the admonitions suggest that Conan Doyle regarded cocaine with greater suspicion than did the general public. By the end of the century, as the drug's addictive nature became more widely acknowledged, Conan Doyle communicated this information to his readers in a pointed fashion. "For years," Watson declared in a later adventure, "I gradually weaned him from that drug mania which had threatened once to check his remarkable career. Now I knew that under ordinary conditions he no longer craved for this artificial stimulus; but I was well aware that the fiend was not dead, but sleeping."

The question remains, did Conan Doyle himself ever experiment with cocaine? We know that he was not averse to testing medications upon himself. In 1879, before he had even finished his medical training, he reported to the *British Medical Journal* on the effects of a drug called gelseminum, an extract of jasmine root. Conan Doyle had been using gelseminum to treat a persistent neuralgia and decided to use himself as a guinea pig to "ascertain how far one might go in taking the drug, and what the primary symptoms of an overdose might be."

However reckless this type of self-experimentation may appear, it was an accepted practice at the time. Conan Doyle knew that Professor Christison had charted the effects of coca leaves by chewing them himself under controlled conditions. For the twenty-one-year-old medical student, the methods of a much-admired professor would have provided a clear model. For several days, then, Conan Doyle took increasing doses of gelseminum, and offered a candid account of the "extreme giddiness and weakness of the limbs" he experienced under its influence. The experiment ceased, he reported, only when a "persistent and prostrating" diarrhea made further doses undesirable.

Clearly, then, Conan Doyle had no objection to self-experimentation with the drugs he used in practice. It does not follow, however, that he did so with every medication available to him, nor do we have any evidence that he ever prescribed cocaine to a patient. It is not possible to say definitely that Conan Doyle never used cocaine or any of its derivatives. However, his long life and robust health offer some assurance that he did not indulge liberally, if at all. The high-minded young man who turned his back on the "unbounded cocktails" of colonial Africa seems unlikely to have gratified himself with narcotics.

Why, then, should he have wanted to make his detective a drug user? For the modern reader, the image of Sherlock Holmes plunging a needle into his arm comes as an unpleasant shock. To Conan Doyle's way of thinking, however, the syringe would have been very much of a piece with the violin, the purple dressing gown, and the interest in such abstruse subjects as the motets of Lassus. With Sherlock Holmes, Conan Doyle intended to elevate the science of criminal investigation to an art form. To do so, he needed to cast his detective as an artist rather than a simple policeman. Conan Doyle himself, with his broad shoulders, muscular frame, and ruddy complexion, could easily have passed for a stolid London patrolman. Holmes offered a striking contrast. He was thin, languid, and aesthetic. He easily fit the pattern of a bohemian artist, with all of the accompanying eccentricities and evil habits—one of which, sad to say, was cocaine. "Art in the blood," as Holmes was to say, "is liable to take the strangest forms."

The image of the Victorian habitué would have been very fresh in Conan Doyle's mind as he sat down to write *The Sign of the Four*. Only a few days earlier, he had met a young man he regarded as the very "champion of aestheticism." In August of 1889, Conan Doyle found himself invited up to London for a literary soiree. The editor Joseph Marshall Stoddart, of Philadelphia's *Lippincott's Monthly Magazine*, had come to London to arrange for an English edition of his publication. While in Britain, he hoped to commission work from some of the country's promising young writers. At the time, Conan Doyle's work was receiving far greater exposure in America than in Britain, owing to the lack of American copyright protection for foreign authors. Several of Conan Doyle's stories had appeared in pirated anthologies, which, he noted with dismay, "might have been printed on the paper that shopmen use for parcels."

Conan Doyle may have regretted the lost profits from these unauthorized printings, but they brought him a substantial American readership at a time when his name was less well known in Britain. Now, with Joseph Stoddart anxious for a meeting, Conan Doyle had reason to feel warmly toward his American audience. "Needless to say," he later wrote, "I gave my patients a rest for a day and eagerly kept the appointment."

The dinner was held in the West End at the prestigious Langham Hotel, a setting that would feature in three future Sherlock Holmes adventures. Two other guests enjoyed Stoddart's hospitality that night. The first was Thomas Patrick Gill, a former magazine editor who had gone on to become a member of Parliament. The second was Oscar Wilde.

At thirty-five, Oscar Wilde was already a notorious figure in London society. Though his great plays were still ahead of him, he had made his reputation with his early poetry and with essays such as "The Decay of Lying" and "The Truth of Masks." From the first, however, his true fame owed less to his literary output than to his celebrated wit and flamboyant personality.

It would be difficult to imagine two men more unlike each other than Oscar Wilde and Conan Doyle, and their first meeting must have produced raised eyebrows on both sides. The hale and hearty provincial doctor, with his bone-crushing handshake and earnest, direct manner of speaking, had traveled up from Portsmouth in his best professional suit. The world-weary, languorous Wilde cut a rather different figure. "He dressed as probably no grown man in the world was ever dressed before," the actress Lillie Langtry once wrote of him. "His hat was of brown cloth not less than six inches high; his coat was of black velvet; his overcoat was of green cloth, heavily trimmed with fur; his trousers matched his hat; his tie was gaudy and his shirtfront very open, displaying a large expanse of manly chest." One assumes that such attire was not a familiar sight in Southsea.

The two men also differed in their literary views. Conan Doyle, the champion of historical realism, was a born storyteller, and took pride in his clear, unadorned prose style. Wilde, by contrast, had set himself up as the leader of a movement dedicated to "art for art's sake."

Even so, the two writers got along famously. "It was indeed a golden evening for me," Conan Doyle said of his meeting with Wilde. "His conversation left an indelible impression upon my mind. He towered above us all, and yet had the art of seeming to be interested in all that we could say. He had delicacy of feeling and tact, for the monologue man, however clever, can never be a gentleman at heart." Only eight years earlier, Conan Doyle had gone up to London to see Gilbert and Sullivan's *Patience*, which featured a thinly disguised parody of Wilde in the character of Bunthorne, the "fleshy poet." Now he found himself sitting beside the "singularly deep young man" himself, while the pair of them basked in the attentions of a renowned American publisher.

Wilde impressed Conan Doyle with his "curious precision of statement," as when he described how a war of the future might be waged: "A chemist on each side will approach the frontier with a bottle." Not all of Wilde's remarks showcased his famous wit. To Conan Doyle's surprise, Wilde had not only read *Micah Clarke* but expressed enthusiasm for it. One must treat this report with caution. It is frankly difficult to conjure an image of Oscar Wilde, the archetype of Victorian aestheticism, with a lily in one hand and Conan Doyle's robust epic in the other. In *The Importance of Being Earnest*, Lady Bracknell expresses her disdain for the "three-volume novel of more than usually revolting sentimentality" that she has found in a perambulator. One imagines that *Micah Clarke* would have brought a similar reaction from Wilde, though he may not have wished to say so to the author.

The evening ended with both men agreeing to produce a short novel for *Lippincott's*. A few days later, Conan Doyle wrote to Stoddart to propose an idea. "I shall give Sherlock Holmes of *A Study in Scarlet* something else to unravel," he declared. "I notice that everyone who has read the book wants to know more of that young man." The author went on to suggest that *Lippincott's* should reprint *A Study in Scarlet* and "give me some dollars for it." Though *Lippincott's* did take up the suggestion, Conan Doyle may have been pressing his luck, as Stoddart had already offered him a handsome £100 for the new story. The terms seemed all the more generous because *Lippincott's* retained only the magazine serial rights; the book rights remained with Conan Doyle. Considering that he had signed away the entire copyright of *A Study in Scarlet* for a meager £25, Conan Doyle had reason to feel satisfied with his new terms.

Conan Doyle's contract called for a short novel of not less than forty thousand words, and he completed the commission within a month. Stoddart had wanted a "spicy title," and Conan Doyle eventually settled on *The Sign of Four*, though in America, the book came to be published as *The Sign of the Four*. "Holmes, I am glad to say, is in capital form all through," the author told Stoddart. "I think it is pretty fair, though I am not usually satisfied with my own things."

The novella appeared in *Lippincott's* on both sides of the Atlantic in February of 1890. It received extremely good notices—"This is the best story I ever read in my life," said one reviewer—and fully justified Stoddart's confidence. Conan Doyle gave the American editor his money's worth, including a "locked room" puzzle based on Poe's "Murders in the Rue Morgue," a missing treasure, a romance for Dr. Watson, a villainous dwarf with a blow gun, and a climactic boat chase on the Thames. As Conan Doyle had only a passing familiarity with London at this time, he had to use a post office map to chart out the action of the story. He came onto firmer ground with the romance between Dr. Watson and Mary Morstan, Holmes's client, whose "sweet and amiable" expression suggests that of Louisa. "In an experience of women which extends over many nations and three separate continents," Watson remarks, "I have never looked upon a face which gave a clearer promise of a refined and sensitive nature."

With *The Sign of the Four*, Conan Doyle consolidated the innovations of *A Study in Scarlet* and fleshed out the character of Sherlock Holmes. For all its strengths, however, the story's hasty composition led to several clumsy mistakes, creating endless difficulties for future generations of Sherlockians. The most prominent of these, as any Holmes fan can attest, is the bothersome matter of Dr. Watson's war wound. In *A Study in Scarlet* we are told that a Jezail bullet left the doctor with a shoulder injury. In *The Sign of the Four*, the wound has somehow migrated to Watson's leg. Already, Conan Doyle's readers were beginning to notice such things.

Oscar Wilde also did well out of his association with *Lippincott's*. His contribution was *The Picture of Dorian Gray*, one of the finest novels of the age. Upon publication, however, Wilde's book came under attack for its perceived immorality. "There is no such thing as a moral or an immoral book," Wilde declared, by way of defending himself. "Books are well written, or badly written. That is all." Conan Doyle, who came to regard some of his own stories as a trifle risqué, would not have endorsed this sentiment. Nonetheless, he thought Wilde's book was excellent and sent a letter saying so. "I am really delighted that you think my treatment subtle and artistically good," Wilde wrote in reply. "The newspapers seem to me to be written by the prurient for the Philistine."

Conan Doyle's respect for Wilde never dimmed, even after the "monstrous development" that sent Wilde to prison five years later. "[N]ever in Wilde's conversation did I observe one trace of coarseness of thought," Conan Doyle wrote, long after Wilde's death, "nor could one at that time associate him with such an idea." Needless to say, Wilde's difficulties arose from something more than coarseness of thought, and Conan Doyle's sympathy for Wilde should not be confused with a tolerance of homosexuality. In later years, Conan Doyle would demonstrate that he did not share in the loathing of homosexuals expressed by some of his contemporaries, but one cannot claim a modern sensibility for him. He believed that Wilde's homosexuality was "pathological" in nature, and that "a hospital rather than a police court was the place for its consideration."

With *The Sign of the Four* behind him, Conan Doyle returned to a project that had absorbed him for more than a year. Stoddart's commission had interrupted progress on a new historical novel, which Conan Doyle resolved to make "even bolder and more ambitious" than *Micah Clarke*. Once again, the Portsmouth Literary and Scientific Society played a role; when Conan Doyle attended a lecture entitled "Some Notes on Mediaeval Commerce," his mind turned toward the fourteenth century. Within a few months he started in on a new novel, called *The White Company*, which sprang from the tales of "gallant, pious knights" and the "valiant deeds of English chivalry" that had so thrilled him as a boy.

For several weeks in the summer of 1889, Conan Doyle sequestered himself in a small cottage in the New Forest of Hampshire—surrounded by more than a hundred books and research documents—while he drank in the historical resonances of the region. Apparently his medical practice, like Dr. Watson's, was not so absorbing that he could not put it aside now and then. Meanwhile the success of *Micah Clarke* gave a renewed priority to his literary pursuits.

"I devoted two years to the study of fourteenth-century life in England—Edward III's reign—when the country was at its height," he told an interviewer a short time later. "The period has hardly been treated in fiction at all, and I had to go back to early authorities for everything. I set myself to reconstruct the archer, who has always seemed to me to be the most striking figure in English history. . . . He was primarily a soldier, one of the finest that the world has ever seen—rough, hard-drinking, hard-swearing, but full of pluck and animal spirits."

The novel opened with the formation of the White Company, a band of "manly and true" bowmen commanded by Sir Nigel Loring, and followed their adventures across France and Spain. Along the way a young soldier named Alleyne Edricson faces many tests of courage and character, eventually winning a knighthood of his own along with the hand of Sir Nigel's daughter. Conan Doyle claimed to have grown so fond of these characters that it seemed he knew them in the flesh. "I feel," he wrote to his sister Lottie, "that the whole English-speaking race will come in time to be fond of them also."

Conan Doyle would always say that *The White Company* was the novel he most enjoyed writing. "I was young and full of the first joy of life and action," he told a journalist thirty years later, "and I think I got some of it into my pages. When I wrote the last line, I remember that I cried: 'Well, I'll never beat that,' and threw the inky pen at the opposite wall, which was papered with duck's-egg green. The black smudge was there for many a day."

It is not difficult to understand why Conan Doyle singled out this book as his sentimental favorite. He had given voice to the sense of chivalry and honor that guided his own life, and made an affectionate nod to its source. At one stage, Sir Nigel and his men sit spellbound as a French noblewoman—Lady Tiphaine, the wife of a famous soldier—spins a tale of knightly deeds. "The mind had gone out of them," Conan Doyle wrote, "and they could but look at this woman and listen to the words which fell from her lips—words which thrilled through their nerves and stirred their souls like the battle-call of a bugle . . . that sweet clear voice, with its high thrilling talk of the deathlessness of glory, of the worthlessness of life, of the pain of ignoble joy, and of the joy which lies in all pains which lead to a noble end. Still, as the shadows deepened, she spoke of valour and virtue, of loyalty, honour and fame, and still they sat drinking in her words while the fire burned down and the red ash turned to grey."

This was a son's loving tribute to his mother. Many years had passed since Conan Doyle sat at the hearth in Edinburgh listening to tales of long ago, but in every way that mattered, the fire had never burned down.

For all his enthusiasm about the new novel, Conan Doyle must have felt uneasy when it came time to run the gauntlet of publishers. Once again, he tried his luck with the prestigious *Cornhill Magazine*, whose editor, James Payn, had given such a high-handed dismissal of *Micah Clarke*. Now, after the success of that novel and *The Sign of the Four*, Payn reversed his field. *The White Company*, he declared, had "such 'go' and vigour in it that the reader is carried back by it through the centuries, and seems to live again the life of his forefathers." Payn ran the story in serial form throughout 1891, and at the end of the year it appeared as a three-volume novel. Oscar Wilde may have been dismissive of such works, but Conan Doyle's effort did wonders for him. He earned £200 for the serial, and an additional £350 for the initial book rights.

On publication, *The White Company* sold in vast numbers, and helped to put Conan Doyle's name forward as a "serious" novelist. "The novel," one reviewer declared, "commands our attention not only as a stirring evocation of our glorious past, but also as a gripping tale of adventure. Conan Doyle has balanced his twin aims with brilliant success." As stocks of the first edition dwindled, a new single-volume reissue replaced the three-decker version. The novel would go through more than fifty editions in Conan Doyle's lifetime, and soon found its way onto classroom reading lists, where Conan Doyle hoped it "would live and would illuminate our national traditions."

For all of this success, Conan Doyle remained disappointed with the verdict of the majority of the literary critics. "They treat it too much as a mere book of adventure," he wrote to the Ma'am, "as if it were an ordinary boy's book—whereas I have striven to draw the exact types of character of the folk then living and have spent much work and pains over it, which seems so far to be underappreciated by the critics." He returned to the theme in his autobiography. "I cultivate a simple style and avoid long words so far as possible," he explained, "and it may be that this surface of ease has sometimes caused the reader to underrate the amount of real research which lies in all my historical novels."

Conan Doyle insisted on this point again and again in the years to come. "*The White Company* is the best thing I have ever done," he told *The Bookman* in 1892. "I endeavored in that to reconstruct the whole of the fourteenth century. Indeed, I had to do it. Scott had always avoided it." His readers needed no reminding that he was working in the mode of Sir Walter Scott. James Payn had already assured the public that he had read "nothing of the kind so good since *Ivanhoe,* with which it has many points of resemblance." For Conan Doyle, this was an act of reverence, since he yielded to no one in his admiration for Scott, the master of historical fiction. In *Through the Magic Door,* his anecdotal survey of his favorite books, he would devote page after page to Scott. "But of all the sons of men," he concluded, "I don't think there are many greater than he who lies under the great slab at Dryburgh."

Having embraced the Scott tradition so fully and successfully, Conan Doyle could not understand why *The White Company* had not garnered a similar degree of respect. He came to believe that this book, taken together with *Sir Nigel,* a companion piece written fourteen years later, formed the most "complete, satisfying and ambitious" work of his career. "All things find their level," he wrote, "but I believe that if I had never touched Holmes, who has tended to obscure my higher work, my position in literature would at the present moment be a more commanding one."

The point is certainly open to debate. Sir Walter Scott had been dead for almost sixty years when *The White Company* appeared. Though Conan Doyle's novel achieved very considerable renown, the era of Scott and his sprawling historical novels had already passed—something Conan Doyle could never quite accept. In his so-called lesser work, Conan Doyle snatched up the inspirations of Poe and Gaboriau and transferred them to a vibrant present. With his historical novels, he celebrated the past masters at the expense of his own originality, creating an idealized and somewhat wooden view of the past. No one has ever denied that *The White Company* is a stirring yarn, but Conan Doyle's veneration of the era and its traditions occasionally has a sterilizing effect, while his characterizations usually take the form of a simple repetition of stock phrases. "By my hilt!" one character repeatedly exclaims. "By the black rood of Waltham!" shouts another.

To Conan Doyle's way of thinking, however, another triumph of serious literature had been undermined by Sherlock Holmes. He had interrupted two years of labor on *The White Company* to dash off *The Sign of the Four* in little more than a month. The success of Holmes, which would soon reach a fevered pitch, seemed entirely out of proportion.

If his historical novels failed to give a sufficient burnish to Conan Doyle's reputation, at least he no longer faced obstacles from the publishing community. After *Micah Clarke*, he told an interviewer, "I had no further difficulty in disposing of my manuscripts." A collection of ten short stories, entitled *The Captain of the Pole-Star*, appeared in March of 1890. The book carried a dedication reading: "To my friend Major-General A. W. Drayson as a slight token of my admiration of his great and as yet unrecognized services to astronomy." *The Firm of Girdlestone,* the novel he abandoned four years earlier, appeared the following month in a revised form.

"My life had been a pleasant one with my steadily increasing literary success, my practice, which was enough to keep me pleasantly occupied, and my sport," Conan Doyle remarked of this period. "Suddenly, however, there came a development which shook me out of my rut, and caused an absolute change in my life and plans."

Few men would regard a successful medical practice and thriving literary career as a "rut," but Conan Doyle had grown restless in Southsea. He was barely thirty years old, and had reached a professional and domestic plateau where he might well have remained for the rest of his life. "My mind rebels at stagnation," Sherlock Holmes had declared in *The Sign of the Four*. "I abhor the dull routine of existence."

With little thought to the consequences, Conan Doyle resolved to make a sudden and dramatic change of course. Trying to explain his foolhardy swim in the shark-infested waters of Africa, Conan Doyle had admitted to a tendency to do "utterly reckless things" that he had difficulty explaining afterward. Now, as he surveyed his life in Southsea, he prepared once again to take a flying leap into murky waters.

In August of 1890, the bacteriologist Robert Koch announced a bold new treatment for tuberculosis at the International Medical Congress of Berlin. Doctors from all over the world were traveling to Germany in huge numbers to see demonstrations of the new technique, which involved inoculation of the lymphatic system. Conan Doyle, who had recently defended the practice of compulsory smallpox vaccination in a letter to the press, could claim a legitimate medical interest in the topic. Even so, his abrupt decision to rush off to Berlin—literally at a few hours' notice—speaks more of a restive spirit than a desire for medical enlightenment. "I could give no clear reason for this," he admitted, "but it was an irresistible impulse and I at once determined to go. Had I been a well-known doctor or a specialist in consumption it would have been more intelligible, but I had, as a matter of fact, no great interest in the more recent developments of my own profession."

Nevertheless, Conan Doyle left Southsea with his coattails flying, determined that he should witness this breaking story firsthand. On the way, he passed through London and called on the influential newspaperman W. T. Stead, then the editor of the *Review of Reviews*. Stead, Conan Doyle reported, was "very amiable to this big unknown provincial doctor," and commissioned an article on Koch's cure.

Conan Doyle arrived in Berlin and found himself unable to get tickets for any of Koch's demonstrations. Undaunted, he went to the home of Koch himself, but got no farther than the doctor's front hall. There, he watched as a postal worker dumped out a huge sack of letters onto the floor of Koch's reception area. As he ran his eye over the letters, which bore stamps from all over Europe, Conan Doyle felt a sense of shock over "all the sad broken lives and wearied hearts which were turning in hope to Berlin." He knew that hundreds of stricken consumptives were struggling to reach Germany for the miracle cure, many of them so ill that they died en route. It seemed to him, given that Koch's findings had not yet been verified, that a "wave of madness had seized the world."

Having failed to get a ticket for one of the demonstrations, Conan Doyle had to satisfy himself with a set of lecture notes. These convinced him that the extravagant claims for Koch's new treatment were premature. In his view, countless victims of tuberculosis were clinging to a vain hope. He returned to his hotel and dashed off a letter to the *Daily Telegraph*. While praising the "noble modesty" of Koch himself, who remained at work in his laboratory while others demonstrated his technique, Conan Doyle attacked the Berlin findings as incomplete and inconclusive. "The sooner that this is recognized the less chance will there be of serious disappointment among those who are looking to Berlin for a panacea for their own or their friends' ill-health," he wrote. He amplified the point in his article for the *Review of Reviews*: "It would be an encouraging of false hopes to pretend that the result is in any way assured."

One may well question the authority by which Conan Doyle could make such a pronouncement. He was an unknown doctor with little experience of tuberculosis, and he had not even seen an official demonstration of the technique. Under the circumstances, he had little to gain in swimming against the tide of medical opinion. It pained him, however, to think of all the cases of suffering represented by that enormous sack of letters, and he felt a duty to express his reservations in the most public forum available to him. As it happened, subsequent events confirmed his doubts about Koch's findings, and Conan Doyle took great pride in the fact that his warnings had been justified. This was the first time he had taken up what might be called a public crusade, and he developed a taste for it.

"I came back a changed man," he declared. "I had spread my wings and had felt something of the powers within me." What changed him was not his time in Germany so much as a chance meeting he had during the journey. On the Continental Express to

Berlin, he fell into a conversation with a Harley Street specialist named Malcolm Morris. The two doctors sat up most of the night talking. Morris, a "very handsome and courteous" man, had been a provincial doctor like Conan Doyle, but soon realized that his practice had reached a dead end. He took himself to London and developed a specialty—dermatology—which brought success well beyond the scope of a small-town practice. Conan Doyle, Morris advised, must do the same if he hoped to get ahead. Otherwise, he was wasting his life.

For Conan Doyle, already grown so restless in Southsea, the advice carried a great deal of weight. Still, as he told Morris, he could not afford to be cavalier with his medical practice, which represented years of sacrifice on the part of his mother. When Morris persisted, Conan Doyle allowed that he had recently developed an interest in ophthalmology. For some time he had been writing to his sister Lottie about the possibility of training as an eye surgeon—"still, of course, keeping literature as my milk-cow." With this in mind, he had studied at the Portsmouth Eye Hospital under his friend Arthur Vernon Ford, an ophthalmic surgeon, and he had qualified to perform eye tests and prescribe eyeglasses. For Morris, this seemed to decide the matter. "Well," he said, "why not specialize upon the eye? Go to Vienna, put in six months' work, come back and start in London. Thus you will have a nice clean life with plenty of leisure for your literature."

By the time the Continental Express reached Berlin, Conan Doyle needed no further convincing, nor did he waste any time putting Morris's advice into effect. He returned to Southsea on November 22, and two days later he announced to a local newspaper that he would be leaving for the continent. As for the practice he had struggled so hard to build, it was too small to sell to another physician, so Conan Doyle simply closed it up and referred his patients elsewhere.

Louisa, Conan Doyle recalled, was "quite willing" to follow along with the new plans, though she cannot have had any choice in the matter. She undoubtedly trusted her husband's business sense, but she can't have been entirely sanguine about leaving her daughter behind while they trotted off to Vienna. Two-year-old Mary remained in England with Mrs. Hawkins, Louisa's mother, who now lived on the Isle of Wight.

The Portsmouth Literary and Scientific Society, which had been the center of so much of Conan Doyle's social life, threw a farewell banquet at the local Grosvenor Hotel. Dr. James Watson presided over the festivities, and General Drayson gave a warm tribute to his young friend. In response, Conan Doyle rose and recounted the story of his first night in Southsea, which found him scuffling with the unruly scissor-grinder in the public square. It made a remarkable contrast to this, his final night in the town, surrounded by his many friends and colleagues. He expressed regret over leaving such genial companions behind, but, as he intended eventually to settle in London, he consoled himself with the knowledge that "London nowadays was after all a suburb of Southsea, or vice versa." It pleased him to think that he left no enemy behind him—with the possible exception, he added, of the scissor-grinder.

With this, Dr. Conan Doyle took down his shingle, paid up the eight months remaining on his annual lease, put his belongings in storage, and quit Southsea forever. On mature consideration, he might have thought better of his new career plans, which required him to attend medical lectures in a language he barely understood. Translating an article on gas pipes was one thing; qualifying in ophthalmic surgery was quite another.

For the moment, such considerations did not trouble him. "We closed the door of Bush Villas behind us for the last time," he recalled. "Now it was with a sense of wonderful freedom and exhilarating adventure that we set forth upon the next phase of our lives."

9

Reams of Impossible Stuff

Good night, Mister Sherlock Holmes.

—IRENE ADLER IN "A SCANDAL IN BOHEMIA"

After spending the holidays with the Ma'am in Masongill, the Conan Doyles reached Vienna on January 5, 1891. A "gloomy, ominous reception" of bitter cold and swirling snow awaited them, but their spirits soon lifted as they settled in rented rooms at a cheery *pension*. Conan Doyle had a few hundred pounds in savings thanks to the initial sales of *The White Company*, which was just beginning its run in *Cornhill Magazine*, but he hoped he would not have to dip into them to finance the Vienna expedition. After closing the practice in Southsea, he had a belated inspiration to offset his expenses with a new book. With his growing status as a writer, he had no trouble drumming up interest. A magazine called *Answers* commissioned him to produce a novella.

It proved fortunate that Conan Doyle had something to occupy his time, as the folly of his intended course of study soon became apparent. "I attended eye lectures at the Krankenhaus," he recalled, "but could certainly have learned far more in London, for even if one has a fair knowledge of conversational German it is a very different thing from following accurately a rapid lecture filled with technical terms."

Indeed, the medical lectures left him so baffled that he soon abandoned his intended course of study—"if it can be said to have ever begun"—and turned the Vienna sojourn into something of an extended vacation. The Conan Doyles spent their days ice-skating, sipping coffee on the banks of the Danube, and enjoying "a little of gay Viennese society."

It cannot have all been steamed milk and pastries, as Conan Doyle completed his commission for *Answers* in just over three weeks. The result was a novella of nearly forty thousand words entitled *The Doings of Raffles Haw,* which even he admitted was "not a very notable achievement." The story centers on the unhappy fate of a chemist who discovers the secret of alchemy, the power of transmuting base metal into gold. "This is the great secret," the title character tells an admiring companion. "It is the secret which endows the man who knows it with such a universal power as no man has ever enjoyed since the world was made. This secret it is the dearest wish of my heart to use for good, and I swear to you, Robert McIntyre, that if I thought it would tend to anything but good I would have done with it forever."

Not surprisingly, Mr. Haw's charitable impulses soon miscarry, but in a manner that one reviewer dismissed as "unfortunate, but uninvolving." In recent years there has been a halfhearted effort to reclaim the book as an early work of science fiction, but it would probably be more accurate to view the effort as another homage to Poe, whose story "Von Kempelen and His Discovery" offers many suggestive parallels. *The Doings of Raffles Haw* appeared in 1892, and soon joined *The Mystery of Cloomber* on the list of Conan Doyle's most obscure works.

Conan Doyle originally intended to spend half a year in Vienna, but he cut this back to two months once he dropped his medical studies. Before returning to England, he and Louisa stopped in Venice and Milan, then made their way to Paris where the young doctor attempted to resurrect something of the journey's original purpose. He spent a few days observing Edmund Landolt, "the most famous French oculist of his time," who had written an influential treatise on diseases of the eye.

At the end of March, the Conan Doyles arrived in London and took a large flat at 23 Montague Place, directly behind the British Museum. Mrs. Hawkins brought the couple's daughter up from the Isle of Wight and was soon spending most of her time with the family in London.

Conan Doyle had brought back no official qualifications from Vienna, but he still declared himself ready to "put up my plate as an oculist." He signed a lease for £120 per year on a consulting room at 2 Upper Wimpole Street, a short distance from Harley Street, where the more established medical men plied their trade. "I was aware that many of the big men did not find time to work out refractions," he wrote. "I was capable in this work and liked it, so I hoped that some of it might drift my way."

For a time, Conan Doyle made a concerted effort to put his name around, just as he had in the early days in Southsea. He joined the Ophthalmologic Society of the United Kingdom and wrote to Dr. Hoare that he had "hooked on" with the Royal Westminster Eye Infirmary, around the corner from Montague Place. It soon became evident, however, that London would be even less congenial to an unknown, untested doctor than Southsea had been. His lease on Upper Wimpole Street entitled him to a consulting room and a share of a waiting room, but, as Conan Doyle ruefully admitted, "I was soon to find that they were both waiting rooms."

Once again, such remarks show that Conan Doyle was all too willing to disparage his own medical skills. This time, however, he had good reason. Although he had enjoyed reasonable success in Portsmouth for eight years, the London eye practice—which had been a rash undertaking from the first—never got off the ground. London already had plenty of eye specialists, and potential patients were unlikely to entrust their vision to an unknown practitioner who could demonstrate so few qualifications.

Undeterred, Conan Doyle set out each morning from Montague Place and walked the fifteen minutes or so to Upper Wimpole Street. There, he sat at his desk until late afternoon—"with never a ring to disturb my serenity." In contrast to his early days in Southsea, he could now afford to take a relaxed view. Installments of *The White Company* were still appearing each month in *Cornhill Magazine*, which gave him tremendous confidence in his literary prospects, if not his medical ones. Still, though he would often joke about the solitary fastness of his London consulting room, at the time he tried to give the opposite impression. In at least one interview, given to *The World* the following year, he presented himself as a man so torn between the demands of literature and a thriving practice that his health began to suffer. At length, he told his sympathetic interviewer, he resolved to "throw physic to the dogs" and give himself over entirely to the life of an author.

This seems to have been wishful thinking. The portrait he gave in his autobiography—in which he admitted that not a single patient ever crossed the threshold of Upper Wimpole Street—appears to be the truth. As far as his literary ambitions were concerned, this was just as well. Sitting alone in his consulting room, Conan Doyle hit on an idea that may well have been the single greatest inspiration of his career.

For some time, Conan Doyle had poured most of his energy into novels, because the disjointed collection of stories from his early days had done nothing to advance his career. Now, as he surveyed the publishing scene from his vantage on Wimpole Street, he changed direction once again. It struck him that there might be some benefit in writing a series of short stories featuring a single, continuing character. This offered an advantage over the more conventional serialized novel, because the reader would not lose interest if one installment or another was missed. Conan Doyle realized, of course, that the serialization of novels had done no harm to Charles Dickens, but there were now far more magazines on the stands, and a far greater number of literate people to read them, not all of whom would have the patience or the means to follow a continuing saga. "Looking round for my central character," he wrote, "I felt that Sherlock Holmes, whom I had already handled in two little books, would easily lend himself to a succession of short stories."

The importance of this decision cannot be overstated. Not only had Conan Doyle made a canny marketing decision, he had also found an especially good showcase for his own talents. "This I am sure of," he would write in *Through the Magic Door*, "that there are far fewer supremely good short stories than there are supremely good long books. It takes more exquisite skill to carve the cameo than the statue." Conan Doyle, as it happened, possessed this skill in abundance, and this was never more apparent than in the character of Sherlock Holmes. In the novellas and the later novels, the detective was obliged to trundle offstage for long, dull patches of exposition. The short story format offered a compact execution and brisk pace, and highlighted Conan Doyle's singular talent for puzzle plots. Of the sixty tales that compose the complete Sherlock Holmes adventures, fifty-six are short stories. Sherlock Holmes was a sprinter, not a distance runner.

Having decided on this new direction, Conan Doyle needed only to find a magazine receptive to the idea. For ten years, a magazine called *Tit-Bits* had been a fixture at every corner newsstand. Made up of nuggets, or "tit-bits," of informative material, humor, and stories, the magazine made a fortune for its founder, George Newnes, who parlayed the success into an entire stable of periodicals. The latest of these, as Conan Doyle set to work on his Sherlock Holmes short stories, was *The Strand* magazine, which began publication in January of that year under the editorship of Herbert Greenhough Smith.

In *The Strand*'s first issue, Greenhough Smith wrote an editor's letter setting forth his agenda. The new magazine, he announced, would "contain stories and articles by the best British writers, and special translations from the first foreign authors. These will be illustrated by eminent artists. . . . The past efforts of the Editor in supplying cheap, healthful literature have met with such generous favour from the public, that he ventures to hope that this new enterprise will prove a popular one."

The Strand was to justify its editor's ambitions for nearly sixty years, thanks in no small part to its long association with Conan Doyle. After a brief flirtation with crusading journalism in its first year, the magazine soon settled into a pattern largely inspired by the American *Harper's New Monthly Magazine*. Fiction, interviews, and fact pieces formed the bulk of its content, spelled off by topical filler material. The magazine had a particular weakness for celebrity reporting, as demonstrated by a long-running feature called "Portraits of Celebrities at Different Times of Their Lives." Interviews with the likes of Sarah Bernhardt alternated with somewhat fawning profiles of the royal family. One typical issue included articles on "Lord Rosebury's Turf Successes" and "A Visit to the Patent Office," along with a profile of a one-legged daredevil and a sampling of antique riddle books—"When is a jar not a door? When it's partly open." Another popular running feature showcased curiosities sent in by readers, such as a metal cigarette box that had stopped a bullet, and a portrait of President McKinley rendered in canceled postage stamps. The mixture of "healthful literature" and up-to-date happenings proved successful straight out of the starting gate, with the first issue selling in excess of 300,000 copies.

Conan Doyle had recently acquired a professional representative, A. P. Watt, to relieve him of the "hateful bargaining" associated with magazine and book publishing. Watt, who is credited with having coined the term "literary agent," was known to be a shrewd operator. Initially, Conan Doyle may have engaged Watt to tend his interests during the hiatus in Vienna, but the association continued for years to come. While Conan Doyle was still abroad, Watt had submitted a story called "The Voice of Science" to *The Strand*. Set in "Birchespool"—Conan Doyle's fictional name for Portsmouth—the story centers on a recording phonograph, intended to play some learned remarks on the "life history of the Medusiform Gonophore," which instead becomes instrumental in breaking off an unsuitable romance. Conan Doyle received payment of £4 per thousand words for this story, which appeared in the third issue of *The Strand* in March.

In April, Conan Doyle began sending the first of his Sherlock Holmes short stories to his agent. Two of these—probably "A Scandal in Bohemia" and "The Red-Headed League"—were forwarded to Greenhough Smith at *The Strand*. "The Voice of Science" seems not to have made much of an impression on the editor, but in later years Smith would often speak of the day when the first Holmes stories crossed his desk: "What a God-send to an editor jaded with wading through reams of impossible stuff! The ingenuity of plot, the limpid clearness of style, the perfect art of telling a story! The very hand-writing, full of character, and clear as print."

In years to come, Conan Doyle would speak of the many "kind friends" who continually pressed him for more Sherlock Holmes adventures. Of all of these, Greenhough Smith was by far the most prominent. Almost from the first, as Conan Doyle wearied of Sherlock Holmes, Greenhough Smith managed to draw ever more stories out of his reluctant author through a combination of encouragement, financial inducement, and appeals to loyalty. As for Conan Doyle, he would feel a debt to Smith for the rest of his life, and often refused higher fees in order to give preference to *The Strand*.

Educated at Cambridge, Greenhough Smith was a bookish but powerfully built man whose heavy eyeglasses and bushy mustache contributed to a somewhat melancholy demeanor—earning him the nickname of "Calamity Smith." Thirty-five years old when the magazine debuted, he remained in the editor's post for nearly forty years. His career had many highlights, but he ranked his introduction to Conan Doyle's work as the most memorable. "I realized at once that here was the greatest short story writer since Edgar Allan Poe," he recounted. "I can still remember rushing into Mr. Newnes' room and thrusting the stories before his eyes."

The publisher shared Smith's enthusiasm, and *The Strand* immediately commissioned four more Sherlock Holmes tales, for a total of six stories to run from July to December of that year. Along with the two originally submitted, Conan Doyle added "The Man with the Twisted Lip," "A Case of Identity," "The Boscombe Valley Mystery," and "The Five Orange Pips." He received £35 per story.

The first to appear was "A Scandal in Bohemia," perhaps the finest Sherlock Holmes story Conan Doyle would ever write. Though the central plot device recalls Poe's "The Purloined Letter," the story draws its energy from Conan Doyle's vivid prose, skillful pacing, and easy wit. The story opens as a heavily disguised client presents himself at Baker Street. Holmes recognizes him as no less a personage than the King of Bohemia, who has come to enlist the detective's aid in recovering an indiscreet photograph of himself in the company of a young opera singer—Irene Adler of New Jersey. Holmes attacks the problem with uncommon subtlety, but the plot machinations are secondary to the remarkable portrait of Miss Adler, the "well-known adventuress," who outmaneuvers Holmes in the end. The detective is so chastened and impressed by this outcome that he requests a photograph of Miss Adler instead of payment for his services. "He used to make merry over the cleverness of women," Watson writes in conclusion, "but I have not heard him do it of late. And when he speaks of Irene Adler, or when he refers to her photograph, it is always under the honourable title of *the* woman."

One must take it as extraordinary that Conan Doyle should have launched his series in this manner, allowing his detective to be bested by a woman. In fiction, if not always in life, Conan Doyle took great delight in strong, independent women. In a later, non-Holmesian story called "The Doctors of Hoyland," a Dr. James Ripley meets fierce competition from a lady doctor, whose very existence seems a "blasphemy" to him. Here Conan Doyle was drawing on the memory of Sophia Jex-Blake, whose pioneering effort to receive a medical education created an uproar at Edinburgh in the 1870s. In Conan Doyle's story, the female doctor is a far superior practitioner, and Dr. Ripley finds himself falling in love in spite of himself. In time, after she has saved his leg following a riding accident, Dr. Ripley proposes marriage. "What," exclaims the prospective bride, "and unite the practices?" A crestfallen Dr. Ripley sees his hopes dashed.

Such characters, it seems fair to say, were not typical of late Victorian literature. Though Sherlock Holmes had not proposed marriage, his defeat at the hands of Irene Adler made for a hugely entertaining story, and humanized a character who had previously been nothing more than a "perfect reasoning and observing machine." Sherlock Holmes, unlike Poe's Dupin, now had an interior life.

Ingeniously, Conan Doyle had dropped in a few titillating details that suggested real-life scandals. Many readers believed the story to be a thinly veiled account of actual events, and sought the true identities of the mysterious Irene Adler and her feckless admirer. One strong contender was a singer named Ludmilla Hubel, whose involvement with Archduke John Salvator of Tuscany—the nephew of Emperor Franz Joseph—would have inspired much gossip during

Conan Doyle's stay in Vienna. Other readers inclined toward Lola Montez, who had once been the mistress of Ludwig I of Bavaria. A few preferred to seek their scandals closer to home, observing certain parallels to the Prince of Wales, whose affair with the actress Lillie Langtry had been a subject of furious interest.

Whatever Conan Doyle's inspiration, the story created a considerable sensation when it appeared in July of 1891, and each subsequent Holmes adventure that year saw an increase in sales of *The Strand*. Readers became so eager to hear more about the detective that they lined up at newsstands on the day that a new issue was due. "Sherlock Holmes appears to have caught on," Conan Doyle told his mother in a rare moment of understatement. "It augurs well for the new book."

George Newnes had decreed that every page of *The Strand* must carry an illustration, and the initial success of Sherlock Holmes owed much to the magazine's evocative drawings, which fixed the image of the lean, pipe-smoking detective in the public's mind. While casting about for an artist, Greenhough Smith and art editor W. H. J. Boot had been impressed by the work of Walter Paget, who contributed regularly to the *Illustrated London News*. As fate would have it, neither of the editors could recall Paget's first name, so the commission went to Walter's brother Sidney by mistake. Walter served instead as Sidney's life model for the detective. Conan Doyle had imagined his detective as having "a thin, razor-like face, with a great hawk's-bill of a nose, and two small eyes, set close together on either side of it." Walter Paget, a strikingly handsome man, inspired a far more dashing incarnation of Holmes. Perhaps, Conan Doyle admitted, "from the point of view of my lady readers it was as well." Walter Paget would probably not have agreed. Not only had he missed out on a lucrative commission, but he would soon find himself being accosted in public by enthusiastic readers of *The Strand* who mistook him for the newly famous detective. One evening, a popular anecdote holds, his enjoyment of an event at the Covent Garden opera house was punctuated by shouts of "There goes Sherlock Holmes!"

Greenhough Smith recognized a literary phenomenon in the making. Four months after the stories began running, the editor asked for six more adventures. Conan Doyle, who had given no thought to extending the series, seems to have refused at first. "*The Strand* are simply imploring me to continue Sherlock Holmes," he wrote to the Ma'am. "I have written by this post to say that if they offer me £50 each, irrespective of length, I may be induced to reconsider my refusal." Smith agreed to the terms without hesitation, stating only that he would like to have the new batch as soon as possible.

Smith and his star author were to have negotiations of this sort many times over the next forty years, usually with A. P. Watt acting as intermediary. Within a few years, Conan Doyle's name carried such weight that it could add 100,000 copies to *The Strand*'s monthly circulation figures. On one occasion, after returning to England on a Channel ferry, Conan Doyle expressed wonder at the magazine's popularity. "Foreigners used to recognize the English by their check suits," he remarked. "I think they will soon learn to do it by their *Strand* magazines. Everyone on the Channel boat, except the man at the wheel, was clutching one." He knew full well that he had played a major role in that success.

Having agreed to Greenhough Smith's request, Conan Doyle produced five more stories in a matter of weeks. These included "The Engineer's Thumb," "The Noble Bachelor," "The Blue Carbuncle," "The Beryl Coronet," and—best of all—"The Speckled Band," a classic locked-room chiller. This astonishing rate of production, and Conan Doyle's ingenuity in dreaming up plots, drew almost as much interest as the stories themselves. "Dr. Doyle invariably conceives the end of his story first, and writes up to it," *The Strand* reported the following year. "He gets the climax, and his art lies in the ingenious way in which he conceals it from his readers. A story—similar to those which have appeared in these pages—occupies about a week in writing, and the ideas have come at all manner of times—when out walking, cricketing, tricycling, or playing tennis." Conan Doyle would often say that it struck him as incredible when readers asked if he knew the outcome of a story when he embarked on it. "Of course I do," he remarked in his autobiography. "One could not possibly steer a course if one did not know one's destination."

As 1891 drew to a close, Conan Doyle began steering a course toward a very unexpected destination. As he reported to his mother, he had now written five of the six new stories and he planned to make the final adventure especially memorable. "I think of slaying Holmes in the sixth and winding him up for good and all," Conan Doyle announced. "He takes my mind from better things."

Mary Doyle received this news with horror—"You won't!" she replied. "You can't! You mustn't!"—and went on to suggest an idea that would not involve violence to the detective. Moved by his mother's pleas, Conan Doyle granted a stay of execution. Instead, he wrote "The Copper Beeches," and credited the Ma'am with providing a crucial plot point. Having completed his commission, Conan Doyle now expected to say a "long farewell to Sherlock" while he turned to other matters. "He still lives," he told his mother, "thanks to your entreaties."

When "The Copper Beeches" appeared in the June 1892 issue of *The Strand*, the first dozen Holmes stories were gathered together in book form as *The Adventures of Sherlock Holmes*. Conan Doyle wrote to Joseph Bell, his old medical lecturer, to ask if he might dedicate the collection to him. "I am sure," Conan Doyle wrote, "that no other name has as good a right to the place."

Conan Doyle was to call this period of his life "The Great Break," and the greatest of the changes it brought involved his medical career. While writing the early Holmes stories, he continued to trudge off to his consulting room each day, still hoping to salvage something of his new specialization. On the morning of May 4, 1891, he had set off for Wimpole Street as usual when he felt an icy shiver pass over him. He turned back and barely managed to get through the door before his knees buckled under him. "It was a virulent attack of influenza," he recalled, "at a time when influenza was in its deadly prime."

The treatment for this disease, in the days before antibiotics, amounted to little more than bed rest. For several days Conan Doyle lay helpless on his back and there seemed a very real chance that he would die. He described himself as "weak as a child and as emotional," which was natural enough given his history with the illness. "Only three years before," he later explained, "my dear sister

Annette, after spending her whole life on the family needs, had died of it at Lisbon at the very moment when my success would have enabled me to recall her from her long servitude."

After a torturous week, he slowly began to recover. As his mind cleared, Conan Doyle realized that he was "once more at a cross-roads." Still too weak to move, he took stock of his life and career. It had been foolish, he now admitted to himself, to maintain an expensive consulting room in the increasingly vain hope of establishing an ophthalmic practice. For years, medicine had been Conan Doyle's main occupation, while literature served as a pleasant sideline. Now, in the wake of the Vienna interlude, his medical practice was completely stalled while his literary career had caught fire. Sherlock Holmes had made him a celebrity. *The White Company* promised a degree of respect from Britain's literary elite. Money poured in from all quarters, especially from the United States, which now submitted to international copyright laws.

With "a wild rush of joy," Conan Doyle decided that the time had come to cut his losses in Wimpole Street. He would abandon his medical career forever and give himself over entirely to his writing. "I remember in my delight taking the handkerchief which lay upon the coverlet in my enfeebled hand, and tossing it up to the ceiling in my exultation," he wrote. "I should at last be my own master."

In a few days, Conan Doyle was out of bed and hobbling around with the aid of a walking stick. With no more practice to concern him, he decided he no longer needed to live in the noisy heart of central London. He began calling on housing agents and soon found a sixteen-room redbrick house at 12 Tennison Road, in the comfortable middle-class suburb of South Norwood. In his large study on the ground floor, Conan Doyle would have peace and quiet to pursue his new projects, but could easily travel into central London by train whenever necessary.

It is not known what Louisa thought of this latest upheaval, though she must have had qualms about uprooting the household yet again. In all, the entire length of the family's stay in Montague Place amounted to no more than three months. Louisa must have hoped, as she saw her possessions crated up once more, that the new home would bring some measure of stability to their lives. In this, she would be sadly disappointed.

With his immediate family settled in South Norwood, Conan Doyle began sharing his new prosperity with his other relatives. When his sister Connie returned from her governess duties in Portugal, Conan Doyle brought her to live with the family in their new home. Later, his sister Lottie would also join them. There can be little doubt that he would also have extended an invitation to the Ma'am, but apparently she preferred to stay in Masongill. Conan Doyle began sending her a monthly allowance, which helped to send his brother Innes to a military academy.

Conan Doyle settled into a routine that found him retreating into his office each morning after breakfast and working through until lunchtime. In the afternoons he gave himself over to leisure pursuits—sports, photography, or long bicycle rides with Louisa—and then resumed writing each evening from five until eight. He had now entered the most productive stretch of his career, turning out an average of three thousand words a day when he found his stride, and, on one occasion, recording a mind-boggling ten thousand words in a single day. Although he owned a typewriter, Conan Doyle continued to work in longhand, writing out his manuscripts in the neat, precise hand that had so impressed Greenhough Smith.

Harry How, a journalist who visited South Norwood in August of 1892, noted that the walls of Conan Doyle's study featured several sketches by Charles Doyle, while oil paintings by the late Jack Hawkins brightened the dining room. Harpoons, a seal skull, and various sporting trophies attested to the varied interests of the occupant. "I found him totally different from the man I expected to see," How said of Conan Doyle. "There was nothing lynx-eyed, nothing 'detective' about him—not even the regulation walk of our modern solver of mysteries. He is just a happy, genial, homely man; tall, broad-shouldered, with a hand that grips you heartily, and, in its sincerity of welcome, hurts." (For How, the word "homely" would have meant comfortable and unpretentious, rather than unattractive.)

The first series of Sherlock Holmes stories was still running in *The Strand* as the family settled into its new life in South Norwood, but Conan Doyle resolved "to do some work which would certainly be less remunerative but would be more ambitious from a literary point of view." By this, of course, he meant that he would once again turn out a historical novel in the hope of luring the public away from the baser charms of detective fiction. In February 1892 he completed *The Refugees: A Tale of Two Continents*, centered on the suppression of the seventeenth-century Huguenots, the French Calvinist Protestants, and their flight to America. The novel appeared the following year in a three-volume edition, after serial publication in *The Strand* and in America in *Harper's New Monthly Magazine*. A commentator in *Harper's* found much to praise in Conan Doyle's portrait of Madame de Maintenon, the second wife of Louis XIV: "He has seen the slow blood mantle her cheek and her white hand tremble. He has felt the steady gaze of her luminous gray eyes. He has heard the thrill in her vibrant voice." Perhaps so, but Conan Doyle's readers did not demonstrate any great enthusiasm for the enterprise. *The Refugees* sold respectably and enjoyed many translations, but weighed against Sherlock Holmes, its success was modest.

As always, Conan Doyle had researched his subject exhaustively. A short time later, the Ma'am happened to be visiting the Chateau de Fontainebleau when a tour guide recommended *The Refugees* as a means of gaining an understanding of the court of Louis XIV. "I expect the guide would have been considerably astonished had he then and there been kissed by an elderly English lady," wrote a gratified Conan Doyle, "but it was an experience which he must have narrowly missed."

Two months after winding up *The Refugees*, Conan Doyle threw himself into *The Great Shadow*, another historical novel, for which he had received a commission from the Arrowsmith publishing firm. Focused on the Battle of Waterloo, the book's title referred to Napoleon Bonaparte himself, who had "scrawled his name in red letters across the map of Europe." The Napoleonic era had intrigued Conan Doyle since childhood, and he would make use of his vast knowledge of the period again and again throughout his career. Despite his enormous enthusiasm, however, *The Great Shadow* proved to be another disappointment. Though he handled the battle scenes with his usual skill, the novel lacked the insistent drive of *The*

White Company. Conan Doyle would shortly make better use of the material in his Brigadier Gerard stories.

Rounding out this astonishingly fruitful period, Conan Doyle produced a third book called *Beyond the City*, an uncharacteristic novel of domestic life and manners. Serialization began at the end of 1891 in a magazine called *Good Words*. The story features a Mrs. Westmacott—a sharp-tongued, heavy-smoking old party with a taste for stout—and her muscular young nephew Charles, who have just arrived in South Norwood as the story opens. "I am sorry that I have no tea to offer you," Mrs. Westmacott tells her new neighbors. "I look upon the subserviency of woman as largely due to her abandoning nutritious drinks and invigorating exercises to the male. I do neither." That said, she swings a pair of heavy dumbbells over her head. "You see what may be done on stout," she declares.

Apparently Conan Doyle was seeking comedic possibilities in the burgeoning women's suffrage movement, but the results were uneven. Though Mrs. Westmacott can be seen as another in his long line of strong female characters, his portrayal wavers between admiration and parody. If his humor occasionally fell flat, however, one can only marvel at the powerful opinions of Mrs. Westmacott, who seems at times to be picking a fight with Conan Doyle. "I say that a woman is a colossal monument to the selfishness of man," she states. "What is all this boasted chivalry—these fine words and vague phrases? Where is it when we wish to put it to the test? Man, in the abstract, will do anything to help a woman. Of course. How does it work when his pocket is touched? Where is his chivalry then?"

In later years, Conan Doyle would raise a strenuous objection to the violent behavior of some female suffragettes, but it is unfair to dismiss him as an opponent of women's rights. Unlike many men of his time, he made some attempt to understand the plight of women in a repressive society, and often addressed the issue in his fiction. In this case, his evident sympathy for his female protagonist gave rise to some confusion, at least in the eyes of one New York publisher, who rushed out a pirated edition before the new copyright laws came into full force. Instead of the usual author's photo, the cover featured an attractive young woman in Conan Doyle's place. "I still preserve a copy of this most flattering representation," Conan Doyle wrote.

With *Beyond the City*, *The Refugees*, and *The Great Shadow*, Conan Doyle had returned to the "better things" from which Sherlock Holmes had kept him, but the public's noisy enthusiasm for the detective had not abated. While he was writing *The Refugees*, Greenhough Smith had asked for another series of Holmes stories. Conan Doyle hesitated, not because he disliked the character but because he feared he would have trouble devising suitable plots. "The difficulty of the Holmes work was that every story needed as clear-cut and original a plot as a longish book would do," he wrote in his autobiography. "One cannot without effort spin plots at such a rate. They are apt to become thin or to break."

Conan Doyle let it be known that he would produce another dozen stories if *The Strand* agreed to pay £1,000 for the group. This was an unprecedented amount of money, and it appears that he would have been perfectly content if the figure had discouraged Smith from pressing the matter. Once again, however, *The Strand* agreed to the terms without protest, and Conan Doyle set to work on the stories that became *The Memoirs of Sherlock Holmes*.

Though the new series presented a challenge to his ingenuity, Conan Doyle still took enjoyment from his creation. "His reason for refraining from writing any more stories for a while is a candid one," *The Strand*'s interviewer would report. "He is fearful of spoiling a character of which he is particularly fond, but he declares that already he has enough material to carry him through another series, and merrily assures me that he thought the opening story of the next series of 'Sherlock Holmes,' to be published in this magazine, was of such an unsolvable character, that he had positively bet his wife a shilling that she would not guess the true solution of it until she got to the end of the chapter!"

It's likely that Conan Doyle kept his shilling, as the first of the new stories was "Silver Blaze," published in December 1892. The story marked another high point in the career of Sherlock Holmes. Though the plot, involving a missing racehorse, was especially good, Sherlockians cherish the story for a deathless patch of dialogue. This occurs as a local police inspector, sensing that the detective knows more than he is telling about the case, tries to draw him out:

> "Is there any other point to which you would wish to draw my attention?"
>
> "To the curious incident of the dog in the night-time."
>
> "The dog did nothing in the night-time."
>
> "That was the curious incident," remarked Sherlock Holmes.

Even before Greenhough Smith requested the new series, Conan Doyle must have realized that Holmes could not be abandoned so easily. Mail had been pouring in at an astonishing rate, much of it addressed to Holmes himself. "I get many letters from all over the country about Sherlock Holmes," Conan Doyle told *The Bookman*. "Sometimes from schoolboys, sometimes from commercial travellers who are great readers, sometimes from lawyers pointing out mistakes in my law. One letter actually contained a request for portraits of Sherlock at different periods of his life."

Requests for autographs were also a regular feature of the post bag—though Sherlock Holmes tended to get more requests than Conan Doyle. Occasionally, when a certain "pawky strain of humor" came over him, Conan Doyle would send a brief postcard in reply, expressing regret that the detective was not available.

The signature, however, was calculated to raise eyebrows. It was: "Dr. John Watson."

10

The Two Collaborators

"And you have been most intimately associated with someone whose initials were J.A., and whom you afterwards were eager to entirely forget."

—SHERLOCK HOLMES IN "THE GLORIA SCOTT"

In August of 1893, a letter arrived from Robert Louis Stevenson, one of Conan Doyle's literary heroes. Stevenson, who was then living in Samoa, wrote to compliment him on his vivid descriptions of Louis XIV's court in *The Refugees*. "Have you any document for the decapitation?" Stevenson went on to inquire. For Conan Doyle, praise and encouragement from Stevenson would have been very welcome—especially the words: "Do it again."

The two men corresponded for much of that year, and discovered that they shared an interest in spiritualism—Stevenson opened one letter with the salutation, "O! Frolic fellow Spookist!" Conan Doyle even toyed with the idea of visiting his new correspondent in Samoa, prompting Stevenson to inquire if he and his wife were "Great Eaters," as rations were often spare. No doubt Conan Doyle would have received an enthusiastic welcome in spite of his large appetite, as Stevenson made a point of reading the Sherlock Holmes tales aloud to his household. Stevenson, who had also attended the

University of Edinburgh, took a particular interest in the inspiration for Conan Doyle's detective. "Only one thing troubles me," he wrote, "can this be my old friend 'Joe' Bell?"

In these early years of his success, Conan Doyle liked to imagine himself at the center of a community of writers. "At that time I was practicing in a small way as a doctor," he was to say of his Southsea and London years, "and in a draper's shop close by H. G. Wells was an assistant. There was also a raw-boned Irishman rolling about London. His name was Bernard Shaw. There was another named Thomas Hardy, and there was a young journalist struggling for a living in Nottingham, whose name was Barrie."

Sherlock Holmes had made Conan Doyle's name, but *The White Company*, he believed, served to establish his credentials. Encouraged by its success, he made an effort to meet and befriend other men of letters. Not all of these meetings went well. Ralph David Blumenfeld, a journalist with the *Daily Express*, found the young writer to be a singularly grim figure.

"The Author's Club, just established in St. James' Place, used to have Monday evening sessions at which budding authors were wont to read from their manuscripts," Blumenfeld recalled.

> On one of these evenings I sat between Mr. F. Frankfort Moore, then a leading story writer, and Sir Walter Besant, the father of the Author's Club.
>
> Dr. Conan Doyle rose to read from a new story which he had just completed. It was all about obstetrics and the terror of a household in which a woman was about to become a mother; all about the husband's agonies, the doctor's embarrassments and professional distress—I forget the details, but my mind jumps across to that evening in St. James', with a hundred men in evening dress sitting uneasily under the monotonous flow of the Scottish-Northumbrian phrases, with not a sign of light, just a long, gloomy, ghastly dissertation which, if I remember rightly, made me feel unhappy and cold.
>
> Finally, the big man with the rough voice stopped talk-

> ing and sat down abruptly. Walter Besant turned to me and said, "Have you ever heard worse?" I had not.

The story, probably "The Curse of Eve," later published in *Round the Red Lamp,* may not have won any admirers at the Author's Club, but Conan Doyle would fare better elsewhere. A new magazine called *The Idler*—whose founders included Jerome K. Jerome of *Three Men in a Boat* fame—introduced the rising young author to a "jolly crew" of literary types. As *The Strand* could not absorb all of Conan Doyle's flood of manuscripts, he was glad to have an additional outlet for his work. *The Idler* purported to take a more humorous tone than *The Strand,* but one would not have guessed it from Conan Doyle's contributions. While Jerome offered bits of whimsy concerning fashion and sport, Conan Doyle weighed in with a series of grisly medical stories of the type that had so impressed the gentlemen of the Author's Club. Even so, *The Idler* staff welcomed Conan Doyle as one of their own. The stable of writers ranged from the Anglo-Jewish activist Israel Zangwill to the prolific Eden Phillpotts and the Canadian-born Gilbert Parker. All of them warmed to the affable, unpretentious Conan Doyle. Anthony Hope, author of *The Prisoner of Zenda,* remarked that the famous newcomer looked as if he'd never heard of a book, and from the point of view of *The Idler* crew, this was an asset. Conan Doyle enjoyed the surprisingly boisterous merriment of the magazine's afternoon teas, which often led to drinking of a more serious nature, and ended on one occasion with three of the magazine's leading lights asleep under the table.

Conan Doyle got along especially well with Jerome himself, who later dedicated a collection of essays to "Big-Hearted, Big-Souled, Big-Bodied Friend Conan Doyle." In the summer of 1892, Jerome joined the family on a brief excursion to Norway. The trip had been organized as a restful holiday for Louisa, who was pregnant again, but since the itinerary included long days on horse trails and a visit to a leper colony, it cannot have been entirely restorative. Jerome found the Conan Doyles to be a "vigorous family," and evinced a particular admiration for Conan Doyle's sister Connie, who spent much of the choppy crossing to Norway ministering to seasick companions. "A handsome girl," Jerome declared, "she might have posed as Brunhilda."

While Connie tended to the sick, Conan Doyle busied himself learning Norwegian. One day, he fell into a conversation with a young Norwegian military officer, offering what he took to be a series of comments on the weather. In fact, he had unwittingly surrendered his horse to his new acquaintance, a fact that did not become apparent until both the horse and the young officer were long gone. "For the rest of that trip," Jerome recalled, "Doyle talked less Norwegian."

In December 1892, Conan Doyle and Jerome took a tour of Scotland Yard's famed "Black Museum." Joining them was a young journalist named E. W. Hornung, who despite his poor eyesight and fragile health was an enthusiastic participant in *Idler* cricket matches. Willie, as he was known, became a frequent visitor in South Norwood, though his interest had less to do with Conan Doyle than with his sister Connie, whom Hornung was actively courting. "I like young Willie Hornung very much," Conan Doyle reported to the Ma'am. "He is one of the sweetest natured and most delicate-minded men I ever knew."

Hornung and Connie would marry the following year, and for a time Conan Doyle continued to give his sister an allowance to help the couple get started. The help would not be needed for very long, since Hornung went on to become a successful author in his own right. His most famous creations, the gentleman burglar A. J. Raffles and his sidekick "Bunny" Manders, were a kind of inverse Holmes and Watson. Hornung dedicated his best-selling *Raffles, the Amateur Cracksman*, which introduced the debonair thief, to Conan Doyle—"To A.C.D.," he wrote. "This form of flattery." It is thought that *The Doings of Raffles Haw* may have suggested the name of Hornung's famous character.

Conan Doyle expressed a somewhat priggish ambivalence over the "rather dangerous" device of casting a villain as the hero of an adventure tale, but this did not prevent him from writing a glowing foreword to a collection of Hornung's work in later years. Hornung, he claimed, had a finer wit than Samuel Johnson: "No one could say a neater thing, and his writings, good as they are, never adequately represented the powers of the man, nor the quickness of his brain." As proof of this, Conan Doyle was fond of repeating a Hornung quip about Sherlock Holmes: "Though he might be more humble, there is no police like Holmes."

Conan Doyle had an even greater regard for the wit of James Barrie, another new friend from *The Idler* crew. Though *Peter Pan* was still some years off, Barrie had already made his name with *A Window in Thrums*, *The Little Minister*, and the play *Richard Savage*. Conan Doyle took an immediate liking to the five-foot-one writer—"about whom," he wrote, "there is nothing small except his body."

The two men had much in common; both were Scots, and Barrie, like Stevenson, had also attended the University of Edinburgh. Conan Doyle's passion for cricket, the sport that gave him "more pleasure than any other," sealed their friendship. Barrie had organized a team called the "Allahakbarries"—a play on his own name and an Arabic phrase meaning "Lord help us"—largely composed of authors and theater people. Conan Doyle, the natural athlete, made a welcome addition. "A grand bowler," one teammate wrote. "Knows a batsman's weakness by the colour of the mud on his shoes."

"We played in the old style," Conan Doyle would recall, "caring little about the game and a good deal about a jolly time and pleasant scenery." Actually, this was true of Barrie, but Conan Doyle plowed into these friendly contests with his usual intensity, to the alarm of his more easygoing companions. After one typically energetic performance, a fellow author expressed relief over the "surprisingly low death rate."

Among friends Conan Doyle always downplayed his ability, but in his autobiography, written some thirty years later, he took pains to quote a newspaper account of one such "jolly time," which noted that the Allahakbarries' seventy-two runs were scored "chiefly, if not wholly" by Conan Doyle. Though he takes care to garland the account in modesty, claiming it "entirely exaggerates" his powers, he obviously took pleasure in his sporting reputation. He kept a mud-encrusted cricket bat in his study, a souvenir of a day in which he scored a century at the famed Lord's Cricket Ground, and he traveled abroad with British teams whenever possible. Once, while playing in Holland, Conan Doyle's stellar play averted a looming defeat, and his teammates swarmed around to bear him from the field in triumph. No sooner had the players hoisted the beefy champion onto their shoulders than their knees gave out. Somewhat embarrassed, Conan Doyle walked off under his own power. Despite his bulk, more than one spectator mistook Conan Doyle for a professional. After a particularly hard-fought test at Lord's, he was asked if he, like his companions, also claimed to be an author. Conan Doyle allowed as how he did a bit of writing now and then, when his cricket engagements allowed him some leisure.

Toward the end of 1892 Conan Doyle's cricket schedule eased sufficiently to allow a lecture tour of Scotland. There he paid a visit to Barrie at his boyhood home in Kirriemuir, which had provided the background for much of Barrie's early fiction. The locals, Conan Doyle discovered, could not quite come to grips with the achievements of their native son, even though tourists had begun to appear in the village, eager to see the setting of Barrie's books. "Some people here," Conan Doyle wrote, "think that Barrie's fame is due to the excellence of his handwriting. Others think that he prints the books himself and hawks them round London. When he goes for a walk they stalk him, and watch him from behind trees to find out how he does it."

Conan Doyle himself harbored no such misapprehensions, and even after Barrie had gone on to greater fame as a playwright, Conan Doyle maintained a preference for the early fiction. "Great as are Barrie's plays—and some of them I think are very great—I wish he had never written a line for the theatre. The glamour of it and the—to him—easy success have diverted from literature the man with the purest style of his age." This was meant kindly, but it can hardly be said that Barrie's success came easily, as Conan Doyle would learn to his sorrow.

Some weeks after the Scottish tour, Conan Doyle received a cryptic telegram to the effect that Barrie was ill and needed assistance. Like Watson answering a summons from Holmes—"Come at once if convenient—if inconvenient, come all the same"—Conan Doyle rushed to Barrie's home in Suffolk to learn the source of his friend's distress.

Barrie's difficulty, it emerged, lay in a commission he had

accepted from Richard D'Oyly Carte, the famed theatrical manager. D'Oyly Carte was best known for bringing the work of Gilbert and Sullivan to the English stage. His Savoy Theater and D'Oyly Carte Opera Company existed almost exclusively to showcase Gilbert and Sullivan operettas. Despite their success, relations between W. S. Gilbert, the lyricist, and Arthur Sullivan, the composer, had never been harmonious. Escalating tensions during the producing of *The Gondoliers* earlier that year had led to a temporary rift between the partners. This left D'Oyly Carte with a gaping hole in his production schedule, and he turned to James Barrie to fill it.

Initially, D'Oyly Carte had the idea of pairing Barrie, as lyricist, with Sir Arthur Sullivan himself. Sullivan begged off, recommending a former pupil named Ernest Ford as composer. By this time Barrie was hard at work on a comic libretto called *Jane Annie, or The Good Conduct Prize*, involving the goings-on at a seminary for "the little things that grow into women." Barrie began the work in high spirits, but soon realized he had bitten off more than he could chew. With D'Oyly Carte pressuring him for a final draft, Barrie called in Conan Doyle, his ringer from the Allahakbarries.

Ever discreet, Conan Doyle would attribute Barrie's ill health to a variety of afflictions ranging from a bronchial condition to family bereavement and heart trouble. In fact, Barrie had suffered a nervous collapse under the strain of pinch-hitting for Gilbert. In the circumstances, Conan Doyle felt he could not refuse his ailing friend. He put aside his own work and dedicated himself to helping to finish the libretto.

As he looked over what Barrie had already written, Conan Doyle felt a sense of gathering doom. "The only literary gift which Barrie has not got is the sense of poetic rhythm, and the instinct for what is permissible in verse," he wrote. "Ideas and wit were there in abundance. But the plot itself was not strong, though the dialogue and the situations also were occasionally excellent. I did my best and wrote the lyrics for the second act, and much of the dialogue, but it had to take the predestined shape."

This predestined shape, as one reviewer would note, was "hampered by no considerations of probability." In the first act, Jane Annie, the title character, reveals a strange mesmeric power that causes various mishaps and mistaken identities. In time, this expeditious talent enables her to elope under the watchful eye of her schoolmistress, to the astonishment of the chorus:

> Their conduct's praised, we are amazed,
> Miss Sims doth sympathize.
> Now let us sing of this wonderful thing,
> With a hyp-hyp-hypnotize!

"We have rarely seen such a childish device so lavishly employed," one reviewer would write, "and 'when in difficulty work it out by hypnotising' is a maxim that a very poor hack might invent and even a mediocre playwright would despise." Sad to say, this unhappy inspiration can only have been Conan Doyle's. His interest in mesmerism had carried over from his Southsea days, and his novella *The Parasite*, published the following year, would feature a character who shared Jane Annie's ability to "hyp-hyp-hypnotize."

W. S. Gilbert would have found little cause for alarm. Nevertheless, Conan Doyle enjoyed the "comradeship of production" as he and the recuperating Barrie struggled to get the libretto ready for opening night. Conan Doyle, Barrie would recall, "was so good-natured that if we lost him at rehearsals he was sure to be found in a shrouded box writing a new song for some obscure member of the company. They had only to plead with him, 'I have nothing to say, Mr. Doyle, except half a dozen lines in the first act,' when he would reply, 'Oh, my poor chap, too bad,' and retire into a box, from which he emerged almost instantly with a song."

Barrie also had problems in this area. He cultivated a particular liking for the character of a ten-year-old page boy named Caddie, played by an accomplished twelve-year-old actor named Henry Rignold. When Rignold distinguished himself in rehearsal, Barrie heaped additional lines of dialogue on him—far more, in the end, than the script would bear. In the final week of rehearsal, Barrie hit on a peculiar solution: he gathered up Rignold's extra lines and had them printed as marginal notes in the play's program book, to be read along by the audience as the production unfolded. "Miss Sims was the kind of mistress as is always making you turn out your pockets," one note reads. "Mine is a very difficult part," says another, "and I want the critics to say about it that it would be nothing in less experienced hands."

This was not an entirely happy brainstorm, since not everyone in the audience elected to purchase the program book. Worse yet, it required that the house lights be left up throughout the evening, so that those who did purchase the notes would be able to read them.

Not surprisingly, Richard D'Oyly Carte felt no great confidence in the emerging production. He pushed back the opening for five days to allow some frantic last-minute tinkering, but the curtain finally went up on May 13, 1893. Barrie and Conan Doyle received a loud ovation as they took their seats, but this enthusiasm dimmed noticeably as the evening wore on. "At the end a youthful friend came into our box," Barrie recalled, "and Doyle expressed my feelings in saying to him reprovingly, 'Why did you not cheer?' but I also sympathized with our visitor when he answered plaintively, 'I didn't like to, when no one else was doing it.' "

There seemed little point in waiting for the customary "Author! Author!" from the audience—indeed, one critic would note that "some dissentient noises" were heard at the final curtain. One of the female leads, Decima Moore, grew so distressed by the hostile mood of the audience that she refused to leave her dressing room for the curtain call. By this time, Barrie and Conan Doyle had quietly removed themselves to commiserate over dinner at the Athenaeum Club.

The reviews were not kind. Most expressed wonder that two such capable writers had stumbled so badly. "Messrs. Barrie and Conan Doyle have thoroughly exemplified how *not* to do it," noted the *Sporting Times*. "It is quite unworthy of the two eminent names," observed the *Pall Mall Gazette*.

More than one critic indicated that the play might have benefited from the presence of a certain Baker Street detective, a remark seemingly calculated to infuriate Conan Doyle. "The presence of this remarkable individual," the *Morning Post* offered, "would have been of great service to the spectators in helping them to unravel the tangled skein of the story."

Perhaps the loudest voice in the chorus of boos was that of

George Bernard Shaw, the "raw-boned Irishman" whom Conan Doyle had seen rolling about London. "It would ill become me, as a brother of the literary craft, to pretend to congratulate them seriously upon the most unblushing outburst of tomfoolery that two responsible citizens could conceivably indulge in publicly," Shaw wrote in *The World*. "The high privilege of joking in public should never be granted except to people who know thoroughly what they are joking about."

Other, more forgiving critics strained desperately to find some note of kindness among the wreckage. "The orchestra," observed one reviewer, "is never obstreperous." Another found the pretty girls in "dishabille" to be a pleasant compensation for the faults of the play. The London *Times*, in a surprisingly cordial review, voiced its expectation that the show would run until the girls had learned to handle their golf clubs a little less stiffly, and the college caps had lost their "very unrealistic condition of preternatural neatness."

Sadly, the college caps were still gleaming when *Jane Annie* folded seven weeks later. The production ran for fifty performances, but only because D'Oyly Carte had nothing ready to take its place. In that time no less than four versions of the libretto appeared, reflecting the feverish pace of revision. A modest tour extended its life a while longer, but by August *Jane Annie* was buried for good.

Strangely, the most forbearing of the critics may have been W. S. Gilbert and Arthur Sullivan, who had by now agreed to renew their partnership. Sullivan, who attended the opening night, is reported to have made a note in his diary: "Dialogue dull—music very pretty." Gilbert is thought to have allowed the influence of two of the characters to creep into the libretto of *Utopia, Limited*, which opened in October of that year.

This would have been a slender consolation, but both Conan Doyle and Barrie managed to be philosophical. Barrie, for his part, had recovered his health and good spirits. With *The Admirable Crichton* and *Peter Pan* still ahead of him, he could afford to laugh about *Jane Annie* in years to come.

Conan Doyle also had reasons for optimism. "There is indeed nothing more miserable than a theatrical failure," he wrote some years later, "for you feel how many others who have backed you have been affected by it. It was, I am glad to say, my only experience of it, and I have no doubt that Barrie could say the same."

Actually, this was by no means his only experience of theatrical failure—Conan Doyle would go on to produce several more box office duds—but none quite as leaden as *Jane Annie*. If his memory played false on the subject, perhaps it was clouded by the stunning success of his next play, *A Story of Waterloo,* which was to appear the following year. For the moment, however, Conan Doyle withdrew into the more familiar territory of historical fiction and Sherlock Holmes.

Some time later, a copy of Barrie's *A Window in Thrums* arrived at Conan Doyle's home in South Norwood. Written on the flyleaves in Barrie's hand was a short story called "The Adventure of the Two Collaborators," in which a pair of writers call on Sherlock Holmes to discover why their musical comedy has failed. The collaborators—one of whom is tall and brutish, the other small and "handsomer"—receive a cold reception at Baker Street: "I am not particular about the people I mix with for business purposes," Holmes declares, "but at literary characters I draw the line."

As Watson relates, the two men ("if such they can be called") are not long in coming to the point:

> "Let us cut the first four pages," said the big man, "and proceed to business. I want to know why—"
>
> "Allow me," said Mr. Holmes, with some of his old courage. "You want to know why the public does not go to your opera."
>
> "Exactly," said the other ironically, "as you perceive by my shirt stud." He added more gravely, "And as you can only find out in one way, I must insist on your witnessing an entire programme of the piece."
>
> It was an anxious moment for me. I shuddered, for I knew that if Holmes went, I should have to go with him. But my friend had a heart of gold. "Never," he cried fiercely. "I will do anything for you save that."

"Your continued existence depends on it," said the big man menacingly.

"I would rather melt into air," replied Holmes, proudly taking another chair. "But I can tell you why the public don't go to your piece without sitting the thing out myself."

"Why?"

"Because," replied Holmes calmly, "they prefer to stay away."

11

The Tremendous Abyss

After a glorious career, happily and decently dead.

—H. G. WELLS ON SHERLOCK HOLMES, 1896

I was certainly working hard," Conan Doyle said of his prolific days in South Norwood, but so far he had not succeeded in coaxing his readers away from Baker Street. "It was still the Sherlock Holmes stories for which the public clamoured," he admitted, "and these from time to time I endeavoured to supply. At last, after I had done two series of them I saw that I was in danger of having my hand forced, and of being entirely identified with what I regarded as a lower stratum of literary achievement. Therefore as a sign of my resolution I determined to end the life of my hero."

The decision had been brewing for some time, and only Greenhough Smith's checkbook and the Ma'am's remonstrances had kept the detective alive for a second collection of stories. Now, as he neared the end of this new series, Conan Doyle renewed his conviction that Holmes must die. As he had told his mother on more than one occasion: "I am weary of his name."

Conan Doyle discussed his plans with any number of friends and colleagues, most of whom tried to talk him out of it. "I sat with him on the seashore at Aldeburgh when he decided to kill Sherlock Holmes," James Barrie wrote, though in all likelihood Conan Doyle had long since made up his mind. The chief difficulty lay in finding an appropriately dramatic way of doing the deed. "A man like that mustn't die of a pin-prick or influenza," Conan Doyle explained to Frederic Villiers, a journalist and artist. "His end must be violent and intensely dramatic."

For the moment, Conan Doyle seemed content to wait for inspiration, as he had other things to occupy his mind. In November 1892, Louisa had given birth to a son, Alleyne, which the proud father called "the chief event" of their life in Norwood. Named for the young hero of *The White Company*, the boy would always be known to the family by his second name, Kingsley. The following month, as a special Christmas surprise, Conan Doyle dressed himself up as a scaly green monster and burst in on his family and friends as they gathered by the fireside. Panic broke out as the noisy intruder flailed about with its pointed claws, with the result that Conan Doyle sat up well into the night with his hysterical four-year-old daughter, reassuring her that the monster would not return. Only the baby appeared unperturbed.

The monster might have provided a novel means of doing away with Sherlock Holmes, but Conan Doyle elected to seek out a more traditional finale. A suitable method came to hand on a trip to Switzerland the following year. There is a difference of opinion as to when Conan Doyle made this visit, and some researchers, in attempting to piece together his hectic itinerary at this time, have concluded that he made more than one excursion. Problems of this sort have long troubled Conan Doyle's admirers; fans of Sherlock Holmes, in attempting to establish a chronology for the stories, have concluded that Dr. Watson must have married more than once—and possibly as many as six times. Only in this fashion, the reasoning holds, can we understand Watson's fitful habitation of the rooms in Baker Street.

It is fairly certain, however, that Conan Doyle brought Louisa to Switzerland in August of 1893 (just as *Jane Annie* was breathing her last) so that he could give a series of lectures in Lucerne. From there, they traveled on to the Rifel Alp Hotel in Zermatt, where

Conan Doyle fell into conversation with a pair of English clerics, Silas K. Hocking and Edward F. Benson, who also happened to be novelists. Anxious to see some of the local scenery, the three men hired a guide to help them climb a section of the nearby Findelen glacier. Their ascent was slow, as they had to follow in a line as the guide chopped steps into the ice with an ax, and soon enough the three writers began talking shop. By the time they reached the top, the conversation had turned to Sherlock Holmes. "Doyle confessed frankly that he was tired of his own creation," Hocking recalled in his memoirs. " 'The fact is,' he said, 'he has got to be an "old man of the sea" about my neck, and I intend to make an end of him. If I don't he'll make an end of me.' "

Both Hocking and Benson made some effort to change Conan Doyle's mind. Such a drastic action, Hocking declared, would be "rather rough on an old friend" who had brought his author such fame and fortune. Seeing that Conan Doyle would not be swayed, Hocking naturally wanted to know how he planned to dispose of the detective. Conan Doyle admitted that he did not yet know. "We reached at length a wide crevasse," Hocking continued, "and stood for some time on the brink looking down into its bluey-green depths. 'If you are determined on making an end of Holmes,' I said, 'why not bring him out to Switzerland and drop him down a crevasse? It would save funeral expenses.' "

Conan Doyle seems to have found the suggestion amusing. He laughed "in his hearty way," Hocking recalled, and said, "Not a bad idea."

Apparently the notion set Conan Doyle's mind turning. At another stage of the journey, when the Conan Doyles stopped in Meiringen, the intrepid hiker went out to see the famous Reichenbach Falls. Then as now, Reichenbach was a popular tourist destination—a "necessary and illuminating point of interest," according to a guidebook of the day. Here, Conan Doyle decided, was a place that would make a "worthy tomb for poor Sherlock, even if I buried my banking account along with him."

Having found a suitable venue, Conan Doyle took up his pen to write "The Final Problem," the story he sincerely believed would be the end of Sherlock Holmes. If the sinister Reichenbach Falls seemed appropriate to his intent, there still remained the difficulty of dropping Sherlock Holmes into the chasm. Rising to the challenge, Conan Doyle created one of the most memorable villains of all time. The notorious Professor Moriarty, who has since become such a fixture of stage and screen, appears only briefly in Conan Doyle's original work, but he made a formidable impression. "He is the Napoleon of crime, Watson," Holmes declared. "He is the organizer of half that is evil and of nearly all that is undetected in this great city. He is a genius, a philosopher, an abstract thinker. He has a brain of the first order. He sits motionless, like a spider in the centre of its web, but that web has a thousand radiations, and he knows well every quiver of each of them."

Conan Doyle took delight in presenting Moriarty as the dark mirror of Sherlock Holmes. By this time, his readers had come to expect showy displays of deduction from the detective—in the tradition of Joseph Bell and the cobbler's lapstone. When Holmes faces off with Moriarty in the rooms at Baker Street, however, Conan Doyle puts an evil spin on his established formula: "All that I have to say," the professor declares, "has already crossed your mind."

"Then possibly," answers Sherlock Holmes, "my answer has crossed yours."

"You stand fast?"

"Absolutely."

Clearly, Arthur had found his Mordred. "Your memoirs will draw to an end," Holmes tells Watson in a none-too-subtle piece of foreshadowing, "upon the day that I crown my career by the capture or extinction of the most dangerous and capable criminal in Europe." Extinction proved to be the only option, but at the cost of Holmes's own life. By the end of the story the two men—"the most dangerous criminal and the foremost champion of the law of their generation"—have apparently plunged to their deaths at Reichenbach.

This done, Conan Doyle made a laconic notation in his diary—"Killed Holmes"—and moved on to other matters.

"The Final Problem" appeared in the December 1893 edition of *The Strand*, and readers lost no time in making their displeasure known. "I was amazed," Conan Doyle admitted, "at the concern expressed by the public." The author had good reason to feel amazed, as much of this concern took the form of outright hostility. Angry letters poured in—"You Brute!" one of them began—and a popular anecdote of the time has Conan Doyle on the receiving end of a blow from an irate reader's handbag. At the offices of *The Strand,* where Greenhough Smith had quite literally pleaded for the detective's life, shareholders braced for the repercussions of what George Newnes called the "dreadful event." For Newnes and Smith, the initial dismay turned to genuine alarm as twenty thousand people canceled their subscriptions. Only eighteen months had elapsed since "A Scandal in Bohemia," but already the fate of the magazine had become entwined with that of Sherlock Holmes.

No one, least of all Conan Doyle, anticipated such a furor. In London, black mourning bands were seen. The detective's passing was discussed in language usually reserved for state funerals. Members of the royal family were said to be distraught. The general sentiment was later captured in a cartoon by H. T. Webster, which showed a boy sitting up in bed with the story, his face a study in heartbreak and shattered innocence. The caption read: "Life's Darkest Moment."

Even as the news traveled around the world—"Tragic Death of Mr. Sherlock Holmes," read one headline—commentators sifted through the evidence for any sign that Holmes might one day return from his watery grave. "There is no proof positive given by any eyewitness whose veracity is unimpeachable," noted the humor magazine *Punch*. "Where is the merry Swiss boy who delivered the note and disappeared?"

Conan Doyle did nothing to encourage this sort of speculation. Silas Hocking is supposed to have received a terse communication that read "Have dropped Sherlock Holmes down the Reichenbach Falls," which does not suggest an author overcome with remorse. The public uproar did nothing to soften his mood. "Poor Holmes is dead and damned," he was to say in 1896. "I have had such an overdose of him that I feel towards him as I do towards *paté de foie gras,* of which I once ate too much, so that the name of it gives me a sickly feeling to this day." He took up the theme again that year in a speech to the Author's Club: "I have been much blamed for doing that gentleman to death," he said, "but I hold that it was not murder, but justifiable homicide in self-defence, since, if I had not killed him, he would certainly have killed me."

In spite of such pronouncements from Conan Doyle, Holmes fans held fast to one immutable fact: Dr. Watson had not actually seen the detective fall to his death. The doctor had been called away at the critical moment to tend "an English lady" who was suffering through the last stage of consumption. "She had wintered at Davos Platz," the explanation ran, "and was journeying now to join her friends at Lucerne, when a sudden haemorrhage had overtaken her." In the story, the consumptive proved to be nothing more than a ruse. For Conan Doyle, however, the patient had become a bitter reality.

For some time, Louisa's health had been fragile. Her second pregnancy left her considerably weakened, and following the trip to Switzerland she developed a persistent cough and complained of pains in her side. Conan Doyle sent for a local doctor. "To my surprise and alarm," he wrote, "he told me when he descended from the bedroom that the lungs were very gravely affected, that there was every sign of rapid consumption and that he thought the case a most serious one with little hope." Conan Doyle brought in a Harley Street specialist to confirm the grim diagnosis: Louisa had contracted tuberculosis. Worse yet, he identified the strain as the particularly virulent form of the disease known as "galloping" consumption. His wife, Conan Doyle was told, would not live more than a few months.

Conan Doyle did not subscribe to the Victorian notion of consumptives as romantic, tragic figures. At the time, tuberculosis amounted to nothing less than a death sentence, and Conan Doyle knew this better than most. Moreover, he could not deny, once the diagnosis had been confirmed, that his own rugged pursuits—foul weather cycling, outdoor sports, travels to cold climates—must have played a role in undermining his wife's health. Now, as Louisa's cough grew worse, and traces of blood began to appear in her handkerchief, Conan Doyle must have felt a mixture of horror and self-recrimination.

Some commentators have called it "unfortunate" and "disagreeably ironical" that Conan Doyle failed to notice the onset of his wife's fatal illness. Only three years had passed since he visited Berlin to examine Robert Koch's findings on the illness, so one must regard this oversight as more than passing strange. There are several possible explanations for the lapse, and the one that springs most readily to mind is that Conan Doyle must have been a fairly shoddy medical man after all. On the face of it, the evidence appears overwhelming: not only had his London practice been a notable failure, but he remained blithely ignorant while his wife reached an advanced stage of consumption. If one acknowledges, however, that Conan Doyle's medical training was the best available, and that his struggles in practice owed more to poor decisions than inept doctoring, then one must look elsewhere to explain the missed diagnosis.

For nearly two years, ever since that fateful hour when Sherlock Holmes made him an instant sensation, Conan Doyle had been struggling to regain his balance. He had become suddenly, colossally famous, but famous for something he held in low esteem, and thought to be a poor reflection of his true aspirations as a writer. In his effort to climb out from under the burden of Sherlock Holmes, Conan Doyle imposed a punishing work schedule on himself, producing three novels and various other stories and pieces of journalism, along with two dozen Sherlock Holmes adventures. In this same stretch of time, he traveled to Norway and Switzerland, gave lectures in Scotland and elsewhere, and made room on his calendar for sporting junkets at home and abroad. Added to this were his rollicking times with *The Idler* crew, his hobnobbing at various other authors' societies and—for good measure—the ill-starred collaboration with James Barrie. For most authors, this roster of activities would fill a lifetime. Conan Doyle managed to pack it all into eighteen months. Not surprisingly, the strain began to show. He suffered from bouts of moodiness as his fame grew, which occasionally erupted into bursts of temper. He began to experience periods of insomnia, and complained to his mother that he was troubled by nerves "more than most people know." Something, amid all this frantic activity and the attendant sense of disorientation, had to fall through the cracks. That something, it appears, was his wife.

Not surprisingly, the diagnosis had a galvanizing effect on Conan Doyle. He abandoned his crowded slate of activities in order to devote all of his formidable energy and resources to attacking his wife's illness. His most urgent priority, at the end of 1893, was to get her away from the chill and fog of London. As a younger man, he had set great store in the "marvellous invigorating properties of the Arctic." With this in mind, he took Louisa to a famous sanatorium resort at Davos, a valley high in the Swiss Alps, where it was believed that a combination of altitude and crisp, clear air offered some hope of a cure. Institutions such as this one, intended for the improvement or maintenance of health, had become prominent over the previous twenty years as tuberculosis spread across Europe and America. They not only provided a healthful atmosphere but also segregated the afflicted from the rest of the population. Among such places, Davos was perhaps the most beautiful, a small community of picturesque chalets sheltered between two mountain ranges, with horse-drawn sleighs and carriages carrying visitors from the hotels to the restaurants, sporting facilities, and concert plaza. Robert Louis Stevenson had taken the cure there ten years earlier, and the view so impressed Thomas Mann, who would visit in 1912, that it suggested a resonant phrase—"The Magic Mountain." The charming scenery aside, Conan Doyle believed that Davos offered his wife "the best chance of killing the accursed microbe which was rapidly eating out her vitals."

The doctors had given Louisa only a few months to live. In fact, she would live another thirteen years, thanks in large part to Conan Doyle's aggressive course of treatment. "The invalid's life was happy too," he wrote, "for it was necessarily spent in glorious scenery. It was seldom marred by pain, and it was sustained by that optimism which is peculiar to the disease, and which came naturally to her quietly contented nature." One hopes that Louisa's final years were as happy as her husband claimed. For Conan Doyle, the onset of his wife's illness marked a deepening of his personal unhappiness. Louisa, as he had baldly stated, was now an invalid rather than a wife; a patient rather than a companion. Each fit of coughing can only have sharpened his distress, and reminded him of his culpability.

This unhappy turn of events signaled the beginning of a long, restless period of travel as Conan Doyle sought various restorative climates to keep Louisa's illness in check. For the moment, they were installed in Davos at the Curhaus Davos hotel, where Louisa spent much of her time reclining in the cold air beneath a pile of heavy blankets. According to a medical journal of the time, the clean, sharp air of Davos was expected to "purge and rejuvenate" the afflicted lung tissue.

In the first months, Conan Doyle spent much of his time at his wife's side. It is not entirely clear whether their two children joined them initially or stayed in South Norwood under the care of Louisa's mother and Conan Doyle's sisters. It seems probable that Conan Doyle and Louisa traveled to Davos alone, and were joined by other members of the family as her condition improved.

Just as Louisa's illness asserted itself, a second blow fell—Conan Doyle received word from Scotland that his father had died on October 10 at the Crighton Royal Institution, a mental hospital near Dumfries. His health had been weakened by years of alcohol abuse, and he appeared much older than his sixty years. The cause of death was given as epilepsy, though it has been variously reported that he suffered a heart attack or swallowed his tongue during a seizure. He died a lonely and pathetic man, heartsick for his family and believing himself to have been unjustly confined.

In his confinement, Charles Doyle had spent a great deal of time drawing and painting watercolors. One of his sketchbooks, published many decades later, affords a poignant visual diary of his final years. "Keep steadily in view," the artist warns in the opening pages, "that this Book is ascribed wholly to the produce of a MADMAN."

Charles Doyle began his sketchbook in 1889, the year his son dined with Oscar Wilde and wrote *The Sign of the Four*. The drawings range from delicate and wistful to dark and macabre, with strange but often self-mocking marginal notes. "Portrait of a gentleman," he writes beneath one sketch of himself, "and you'd require to be told so."

Like his famous brother Richard, Charles Doyle evinced a particular fascination with fairies and other woodland sprites, who can be seen cavorting with alarmingly large and detailed birds and insects. "His brush," Conan Doyle later wrote, "was concerned not only with fairies and delicate themes of the kind, but with wild and fearsome subjects, so that his work had a very peculiar style of its own, mitigated by great natural humor."

"I believe," the artist himself noted, "I am branded as mad solely from the narrow Scotch Misconception of Jokes."

Thoughts of his family run all through the pages, and it is clear that Charles Doyle followed his son's career with fatherly pride. He makes note of favorable reviews of *Micah Clarke* in the Scottish newspapers, and quotes at length from a critic's thoughts on *The Mystery of Cloomber*. At other times he expresses the forlorn hope of a reunion with his wife. A carefully rendered illustration features a placid Mary Doyle busy with her sewing while the bearded Charles gazes up longingly from a footstool. "Mary, my ideal home ruler," runs the caption, a sly allusion to the issue of Irish unity. "No repeal of the union proposed in this case."

The death of Charles Doyle, coming in tandem with the onset of Louisa's tuberculosis, left Conan Doyle even more despondent. The two events, he admitted to his mother, proved "a little overwhelming," and Conan Doyle may have felt that he had not done enough to ease his father's declining years. His late sister, Annette, had bequeathed her estate of some £400 to her father's care, but it is not known whether Conan Doyle also contributed to Charles Doyle's maintenance. The relationship between father and son had never been strong, and for Conan Doyle, his father's condition had become—in the words of Charles himself—"the dreadful secret." In a society that placed great emphasis on family background, the young Conan Doyle can only have felt at a great disadvantage. Even now, for all his robust health, Conan Doyle would likely have nursed a fear that his father's infirmities were hereditary.

With the passage of time Conan Doyle's feelings would soften, and he later made a concerted effort to restore his father's reputation as an artist. "My father, Charles Doyle, was in truth a great unrecognized genius," he would tell an interviewer in 1905. "His mind was on strange moonlight effects, done with extraordinary skill in water colours; dancing witches, drowning seamen, death coaches on lonely moors at night, and goblins chasing children across churchyards."

In his autobiography, Conan Doyle carried the sentiment even further, expressing the opinion that his father, though unrecognized, had been "far the greatest" artist of the distinguished family. The passing years allowed Conan Doyle to view his father with greater compassion, but he still took care to obscure the details. "My father's life was full of the tragedy of unfulfilled powers and of undeveloped gifts," he wrote. "He had his weaknesses, as all of us have ours, but he had also some very remarkable and outstanding virtues. . . . I am sure that Charles Doyle had no enemy in the world, and that those who knew him best sympathized most with the hard fate which had thrown him, a man of sensitive genius, into an environment which neither his age nor his nature were fitted to face." It was an affecting and sensitive tribute, but also somewhat misleading, as Conan Doyle had included it in a chapter entitled "Recollections of a Student," detailing the family's hardships during his years at Edinburgh, before the whaling expedition. Though Charles Doyle's death is truthfully noted as having occurred "a few years later," the reader is invited to think that the sad event took place while Conan Doyle was still a young unknown, rather than fourteen years later when he had become a world-renowned author. Even at this late stage, thirty years after the actual date of Charles Doyle's death, his son apparently did not wish to invite undue interest in the family's affairs.

For all his ambivalence toward his father, Conan Doyle regretted that he had not been able to travel to Scotland for the funeral, but his concern for Louisa and the arrangements for her care made the trip impractical. Now, in the enforced solitude of Switzerland, he had plenty of time to reflect on his father's passing. In his early story "The Surgeon of Gaster Fell," Conan Doyle gave a harrowing portrait of a son's struggles to contain the "morbid impulses" of a mentally unbalanced father. "He has an intense dread of madhouses," Conan Doyle wrote in a passage he later altered, "and in his sane intervals would beg and pray so piteously not to be condemned to one, that I could never find the heart to resist him." In life, however, Conan Doyle and his family had found this resolve. There can be no doubt that the circumstances of Charles Doyle's lonely death in Scotland weighed heavily on his son.

Against this background, one begins to understand Conan Doyle's feelings when, in December, the publication of "The Final Problem" announced the death of Sherlock Holmes to the world. Being away from England, the full force of the public's indignation did not reach him. Even at a remove, however, Conan Doyle could not help but feel a sense of disbelief. His father was dead and his wife was dying, but the public, oblivious to his personal tragedies, had sent up a howl of protest over the death of a fictional character. Charles Doyle's passing had not warranted an obituary in any of the London newspapers. The fate of Sherlock Holmes had made headlines around the world. In the circumstances, the Reichenbach backlash struck him as unseemly and entirely out of proportion, and Conan Doyle must be forgiven if some of his disgust came to rest with Sherlock Holmes. At one stage, he let it be known that the pressure of producing so many stories had caused him to neglect Louisa, and that this was a mistake he would not repeat. While this does not ring entirely true, given all the other work and social commitments he managed to fulfill in the same period, it does help to explain his increasingly frosty attitude toward Sherlock Holmes.

As the year turned, some of his gloom began to lift. To Conan Doyle's relief, Louisa's condition began to show improvement in Switzerland. "I think one more winter," he told his mother-in-law, "might really cure her permanently." Buoyed by the hopeful signs, he found fresh enthusiasm for his new projects. "I was able to devote myself to doing a good deal of work," he wrote of Davos, "and also to taking up with some energy the winter sports for which the place is famous."

One sport that Conan Doyle took up with unusual energy was skiing—or ski-running, as it was known at the time. He had tried the sport in Norway, and was intrigued by the Norwegian explorer Fridjot Nansen's account of crossing Greenland on skis. At the time, other snow sports such as sleigh-riding, tobogganing, and skating were already well established in Switzerland, but skiing, especially downhill skiing, was still largely unknown. As luck would have it, a local man named Tobias Branger, who ran a shop specializing in sporting equipment and "travelling utensils," was the nearest thing to a ski instructor in the whole of Switzerland. Together with his brother Johannes, Tobias Branger had been experimenting with ski techniques for a year or so. After months of diligent practice, the brothers had conquered the Furka Pass from Davos to nearby Arosa, a route previously impassable in the winter.

The Branger brothers were only too happy to instruct their famous British visitor on the rudiments of skiing. "There is nothing peculiarly malignant in the appearance of a pair of skis," Conan Doyle told the readers of *The Strand* later that year. "They are two slips of elm-wood, 8 ft. long, 4 in. broad, with a square heel, turned-up toes, and straps in the centre to secure your feet. No one to look at them would guess at the possibilities which lurk in them. But you put them on, and you turn with a smile to see whether your friends are looking at you, and then the next moment you are boring your head madly into a snow-bank, and kicking frantically with both feet, and half rising only to butt viciously into that snow-bank again, and your friends are getting more entertainment than they had ever thought you capable of giving."

He may have gotten off to a rocky start, but the Brangers recognized a born skier and invited Conan Doyle to join them in an assault on the Jacobshorn, a 7,700-foot mountain some two and a half miles distant. Though Conan Doyle managed to keep up with his more practiced companions, he spent much of the climb with his face in the snow and his skis in the air. "Whenever you think yourself absolutely secure it is all over with you," he commented. "Then, if your mouth is not full of snow, you find yourself muttering the names of a few Swiss villages to relieve your feelings. 'Ragatz!' is a very handy word, and may save a scandal."

No doubt the names of many Swiss villages were invoked before the Jacobshorn was conquered, but Conan Doyle persevered. Reaching the summit, he and the Brangers turned to see the flags of Davos dipped in tribute to their achievement. It is thought to be the first time an alpine mountain had been scaled on skis.

On March 23, 1894, the Branger brothers took Conan Doyle along as they retraced their treacherous route across the Furka Pass. The trio set off in the middle of the night, and did some hard climbing over rough terrain to reach the pass, which they crossed at an elevation of nearly nine thousand feet. On the descent into Arosa, they were able to ski for considerable distances, an experience Conan

Doyle wished to share with his readers in *The Strand*. "But now we had a pleasure which boots can never give," he wrote. "For a third of a mile we shot along over gently dipping curves, skimming down into the valley without a motion of our feet. In that great untrodden waste, with snow-fields bounding our vision on every side and no marks of life save the track of chamois and of foxes, it was glorious to whizz along in this easy fashion."

It wasn't all smooth powder. For the steeper slopes, the Brangers devised a method of lashing their skis together and making a seated descent, as if on a toboggan. As they approached one particularly sheer drop, the Brangers demonstrated the technique for the newcomer. Conan Doyle prepared to follow when his skis promptly "flew away like an arrow from a bow," leaving him stuck for a means of joining the Brangers, who were by now hundreds of feet below. "There was no possible choice as to what to do, so I did it," he recalled. "I let myself go over the edge, and came squatting down, with legs and arms extended to check the momentum. A minute later I was rolling covered with snow at the feet of my guides." As Conan Doyle had set out for the journey dressed in an author's tweed knickerbockers, he had to face the consequences of his undignified descent. "My tailor tells me that Harris tweed cannot wear out," he said. "This is a mere theory, and will not stand a thorough test. He will find samples of his wares on view from the Furka Pass to Arosa."

That afternoon in Arosa, a group of villagers turned out to witness the approach of the hardy trio. To their surprise, Conan Doyle and the Brangers had long since arrived, and were in fact finishing up a pleasant lunch as the crowd gathered. "I would not grudge them any innocent amusement," Conan Doyle wrote, "but, still, I was just as glad that my own little performance was over before they assembled with their opera-glasses." If Conan Doyle's dignity had been spared, the seat of his trousers had not. For the remainder of the day, he admitted, "I was happiest when nearest the wall."

Later, while signing a hotel register, Tobias Branger paid his new friend an apt tribute. Under the heading for "profession," he entered the German word *Sportesmann* after Conan Doyle's name. The gesture greatly pleased Conan Doyle, who had developed a sincere admiration for his rugged instructors. "They are both men of considerable endurance," he remarked in *The Strand*, "and even a long spell of my German did not appear to exhaust them."

Conan Doyle did not introduce the sport of skiing to Switzerland, as has often been reported, nor was he the first Briton to strap on a pair of skis in that country. He did, however, do more than any man of his time to popularize the sport. His account of his ski adventure, accompanied by eight photographs, would be reprinted many times in Britain and America. In it, he assured his readers that the thrill of skiing came "as near to flying as any earth-bound man can." He felt certain, he continued, that this new sport would soon find an enthusiastic following. "This is not appreciated yet," he admitted, "but I am convinced that the time will come when hundreds of Englishmen will come to Switzerland for the 'ski'-ing season, in March and April."

Within ten years, Conan Doyle's prediction would be borne out. With the founding of a Davos English Ski Club in 1903, the village was on its way to becoming an internationally renowned ski resort. As Tobias Branger would write, "Arthur Conan Doyle gave the impulse that led to the crossing of mountains and gave proof of the practical utility of ski."

Today, a plaque in Davos pays tribute to Conan Doyle's role in bringing the attractions of the Swiss Alps to the attention of the world. It concludes with a fitting testimonial to the man in the distressed knickerbockers. He was, to the citizens of Davos, "The pattern of a perfect gentleman."

Conan Doyle, *Sportesmann,* would have been pleased.

12

A Skeleton in the Garden

I shall not commit the fashionable stupidity of regarding everything I cannot explain as fraud.

—CARL JUNG, NOTE FOR AN ADDRESS TO THE SOCIETY FOR PSYCHICAL RESEARCH

In the early months of 1894, as Louisa's health continued to improve, Conan Doyle's work schedule accelerated. He had two novels in the pipeline—the autobiographical *Stark Munro Letters* and a "mesmeric and hypnotic mystery" called *The Parasite*. He also prepared a collection of medical stories, entitled *Round the Red Lamp*, and began crafting a new series character, Brigadier Gerard, drawing on his interest in the Napoleonic era.

As these projects advanced, business obligations began to call him back to London for periodic visits. Conan Doyle undoubtedly felt reluctant to abandon Louisa for any length of time, but he must also have welcomed these opportunities to renew his contacts in London and to escape, however briefly, the climate of sickliness in Davos.

Louisa herself must have enjoyed the respite when, in April, her doctors permitted her a trip to South Norwood to see the family. Within two months, however, she returned to Davos under the care of her sister-in-law, Lottie.

Though the chaos of the previous year seemed to be receding, Conan Doyle still felt an inner turbulence. "I had everything in those few years to make a man contented," he wrote, "save only the constant illness of my partner. And yet my soul was often troubled within me. I felt that I was born for something else, and yet I was not clear what that something might be. My mind felt out continually into the various religions of the world. I could no more get into the old ones, as commonly received, than a man could get into his boy's suit." It cannot be entirely coincidental that he chose this moment to join the Society for Psychical Research, a decision that marked a turning point of his life.

Conan Doyle made his application in November 1893, one month after the death of Charles Doyle. Six years had passed since he published his letter in *Light* declaring his interest in spiritualism. In the interim, Conan Doyle had corresponded with several of the Society's founding members, including F. W. H. Myers, whose study entitled *Human Personality and its Survival of Bodily Death* was to become a cornerstone of psychic research.

In the tumult of Vienna, London, and *The Strand*, Conan Doyle had had little time for the table-turning and mind-reading exercises of Southsea. Now, in Davos, surrounded by the sick and dying, it was natural that his thoughts should have returned to the subject of "life beyond the veil."

Conan Doyle's decision to join the Society for Psychical Research—thereby making a public declaration of his interest in spiritualism—has drawn much comment over the years. Unlike the obscure Southsea doctor who had stated his convictions to the readers of *Light*, Conan Doyle now had a global reputation as the creator of Sherlock Holmes, the embodiment of cold logic. Then as now, his detractors have considered it unseemly, and perhaps a trifle witless, that such a man should suddenly profess an interest in spirits.

Such attitudes are based in part on a false assumption—that Conan Doyle had allied himself with a group of cranks and social pariahs. In fact, the opposite is true. At the time that Conan Doyle joined the S.P.R., its leading lights were prominent in the world of science, and its newly elected president was no less a figure than Arthur Balfour, the future prime minister. Much had changed in

Conan Doyle's life since his first encounter with Balfour, when he defended the politician against hecklers at the Portsmouth Literary and Scientific Society. Now, in joining the S.P.R., he stood shoulder to shoulder not only with Balfour, but also with the philosopher William James, the naturalist Alfred Russel Wallace, and the scientists Oliver Lodge and William Crookes. Conan Doyle's long-established interest in spiritualism, on top of his recent misfortunes, made it natural enough that he should sign on when he did. If, however, his interest had been restricted to social climbing, he could have done worse than to join the S.P.R.

A Sherlock Holmes story called "The Naval Treaty," published in 1893, suggests that Conan Doyle took a keen interest in the career of Arthur Balfour. The story features a character named Percy "Tadpole" Phelps, an old school chum of Watson's, whose uncle is a Conservative party powerhouse named Lord Holdhurst. Contemporary readers would have noted the parallel to Balfour's own uncle, the Conservative Foreign Secretary Robert Cecil, to whom Balfour owed his early cabinet appointments. At the time of the story's publication, Robert Cecil's pattern of family patronage had become so prominent that it gave rise to the expression: "Bob's your uncle."

Like Conan Doyle, Balfour had compelling reasons to take an interest in spiritualism. As a young man, he had become engaged to a beautiful young woman named May Lyttelton, a niece of William Gladstone. A short time later, a violent attack of typhoid fever claimed her life. In his grief, Balfour sought to restore contact with his dead fiancée through séances, but he soon grew frustrated and disenchanted by a series of transparently fake mediums.

Though he despaired of ever communicating with Miss Lyttelton, Balfour remained interested in psychic research. His brother-in-law was Henry Sidgwick, another founding member of the S.P.R., and it was undoubtedly through him that Balfour became involved in the organization's affairs.

Conan Doyle admired Balfour enormously, and came to regard him as one of the "great ones of earth." A favorite anecdote of his later years involved their subsequent meeting at the home of Lord Burnham, of the prominent newspaper family, who had recently installed an elaborate Turkish bath. At his host's insistence, Conan

Doyle took a long steam, then withdrew to the drying room wearing nothing but a pair of towels, one knotted around his head and the other roughly approximating a toga. "Presently the door opened," he recalled, "and entered Arthur Balfour, Prime Minister of England. He knew nothing of the house or its ways, and I can remember the amazement with which he gazed at me. Lord Burnham following at his heels introduced me, and I raised the towel from my head. There were no explanations, and I felt that he went away with the impression that this was my usual costume."

Presumably Conan Doyle wore trousers at their later meetings, and the two men developed a strong mutual admiration over the years. Balfour's opinions carried a great deal of weight with Conan Doyle. Early in 1894, the journal of the S.P.R.—*Transactions of the Society for Psychical Research*—reprinted an address by Balfour on the subject of mesmerism. The young politician discoursed at length on "these half-seen phenomena" that might exist "outside the world, as we have, from the point of science, been in the habit of conceiving it." Paraphrasing Shakespeare, Balfour concluded that "there are things in heaven and earth not hitherto dreamed of in our scientific philosophy."

Balfour's address seems to have reawakened Conan Doyle's interest in the subject, inspiring the "mesmeric and hypnotic" story that became *The Parasite*. If Conan Doyle took inspiration from his new associates, there can be little doubt that the gentlemen of the S.P.R. saw great potential in having a world-famous novelist in their midst. Upon joining the Society, Conan Doyle began corresponding with the distinguished physicist Oliver Lodge, a pioneer of radio telegraphy. Today, their letters are preserved in the archives of Cambridge University. The envelope of one early letter bears a scrawled notation to Lodge from his associate and fellow spiritualist J. Arthur Hill: "He may be very useful," Hill said of Conan Doyle, "as a doctor & a Sherlock Holmes, his testimony will have great weight with the public or with a magistrate."

In those early days, Conan Doyle seemed perfectly happy to make himself useful in this way. Already, however, the seeds of his later extremism had been planted. Commenting on Lodge's account of a spirit séance, and its possible value as a proof of spiritualism, Conan

Doyle chided Lodge for his conservatism. "My only possible criticism was that you seemed to speak too guardedly," he wrote. "After all, it is, if established (and what more can be demanded to establish it) infinitely the most important thing in the history of the world."

Within months of joining the S.P.R., while on one of his visits to England from Davos, Conan Doyle was invited to lend his talents as a Sherlock Holmes. A man named Colonel Elmore, a veteran of the Second Afghan War, had written to the Society to complain of strange goings-on at his home in Dorset. Eerie noises were disturbing the household at night. The sound of chains dragging across a wooden floor could be heard in the small hours, along with the fearful moaning of a soul in torment. Colonel Elmore seemed inclined to attribute these happenings to rats, but his wife and their adult daughter were highly agitated. Most of their household staff had deserted them, and even the family dog could not be compelled to enter certain rooms of the house.

Colonel Elmore had signed a long-term lease on the property and could not afford to move. He had contacted the S.P.R. as a last resort. The idea of a ghost hunt greatly appealed to Conan Doyle, who set out from Paddington Station with two highly regarded members of the Society, Dr. Sydney Scott and Mr. Frank Podmore. Podmore, who produced a book called *Apparitions and Thought Transference* that year, had already established himself as an eminence in the field of psychic research. Together with F. W. H. Myers and Edmund Gurney, he had compiled a groundbreaking study of spirit phenomena called *Phantasms of the Living*, published in 1886. This monumental undertaking collected hundreds of reports of paranormal occurrences, many of them involving near-death experiences, and attempted to identify common elements that might yield to scientific analysis.

Podmore seems to have gathered a great deal of information concerning the Dorset case. "I remember," Conan Doyle said, "that it took us the whole railway journey from Paddington to read up the evidence as to the senseless noises which had made life unendurable for the occupants."

Arriving in Dorset, the three investigators noted that Colonel Elmore appeared to be a steady, no-nonsense sort of person, unlikely to be carried away by imaginative fancies. The old soldier had asked that his visitors conceal the true purpose of their visit, so as not to further alarm his wife and daughter. Accordingly, Conan Doyle and his companions pretended to be old army friends, and their dinnertime conversation was restricted to various military campaigns in Afghanistan.

After a rubber of whist in the cards room, the three investigators decided to turn in early, claiming that the country air had made them drowsy. As the household fell quiet, Conan Doyle, Podmore, and Scott made silent preparations for the night ahead. They fastened the windows, bolted the doors, and strung lengths of thread across to the stairs and passages to show if anyone passed during the night.

The three men took turns on watch through the night, but heard nothing unusual. Dr. Scott returned to London the following day, but Conan Doyle and Podmore remained. On the second night, a "fearsome uproar" broke the silence of the house. "It was like someone belabouring a resounding table with a heavy cudgel," Conan Doyle reported. "It was not an accidental creaking of wood, or anything of that sort, but a deafening row." Conan Doyle rushed from his bedroom carrying a lamp. He and Podmore hurried to the kitchen, where the sounds appeared to be centered, but they found nothing out of the ordinary. The doors were still bolted, the windows remained fastened, and the threads had not been disturbed.

By now Colonel Elmore and his wife and daughter had been roused, but they could add nothing to the puzzle. Conan Doyle and Podmore made a pretense of returning to bed, but instead sat up waiting for fresh outbreak of the tumult. The rest of the night passed without incident.

Here, Conan Doyle's account takes a strange turn. He left the house, he said, unsatisfied with the results and unable to shed any light on the mystery. He insisted that he felt uncertain about what he had heard, and could not rule out the possibility that he and his friends had not been the victims of some elaborate practical joke. "But there was a sequel to the story," he wrote in his autobiography. "Some years later the house was burned down, which may or may not have a bearing upon the sprite which seemed to haunt it, but a more suggestive thing is that the skeleton of a child about ten years old was dug up in the garden."

The child's skeleton, Conan Doyle believed, offered a possible explanation for the strange happenings. "There is a theory," he explained, "that a young life cut short in sudden and unnatural fashion may leave, as it were, a store of unused vitality which may be put to strange uses."

Conan Doyle's account, like most of his spiritualist writings, is fascinating as far as it goes. The details of his story are consistent with many other reports gathered by the S.P.R. over the years. The conclusion he posited, concerning the restless spirit of the girl buried in the garden, is familiar today as *poltergeist* phenomena—a word that literally means "noisy ghost." One could wish for amplification of certain details, but at first reading Conan Doyle appears to have made a sober and fair-minded assessment of the situation, without insisting too much on a spiritualist interpretation.

There was, however, another side to the story. Over the years, the episode of Colonel Elmore and his haunted house became enormously important to Conan Doyle. He gave an account of the experience in his autobiography, and offered variations on the tale in two of his spiritualist tracts—*The New Revelation* and *The Edge of the Unknown*. The story also featured in dozens of his spiritualist lectures in cities all over the world. It is not difficult to understand why he placed so much emphasis on this one incident. He liked to claim, in later life, that his fascination with spiritualism came as the result of decades of study, rather than a latter-day conversion. He had little evidence of this, however, apart from his youthful letter to *Light*, his early membership in the S.P.R., and this one quasi-official "investigation." Each time he repeated the tale, he reinforced his own credentials as a fair-minded investigator with a lifetime of experience.

In all those repetitions, however, Conan Doyle always withheld one crucial detail. For years, he insisted that he had uncovered no earthly explanation for the "fearsome uproar" that night. At the time, it seems, he told a different story. According to his friend Jerome K. Jerome, Conan Doyle returned from Dorset claiming to have discovered a more prosaic explanation for the odd noises. In this version of the tale, Conan Doyle not only solved the mystery, he also unmasked a human perpetrator—Colonel Elmore's daughter.

"Doyle always had a bent toward the occult," Jerome remarks in his autobiography. "He told me a curious story." In Jerome's rendition of the events, which he apparently had from Conan Doyle's own lips, the story took an unexpected twist. Although the events unfolded much as Conan Doyle had related, the Colonel's daughter—"an unmarried woman of about five and thirty"—behaved in a suspicious manner after the household had been roused. After insisting that she had heard nothing, and that the others had simply imagined the disturbance, she suddenly burst into a violent fit of weeping. According to Jerome, this stirred Conan Doyle's detective instincts, and inspired him to set a trap. "The next night they laid their plans," Jerome wrote, "and discovered, as Doyle had suspected, that the ghost was the daughter herself."

"She was not mad," Jerome continued. "She protested her love both for her father and her mother. She could offer no explanation. The thing seemed as unaccountable to her as it did to Doyle. On the understanding that the thing ended, secrecy was promised. The noises were never heard again."

If Jerome's account is true, it places a serious strain on Conan Doyle's credibility as a psychic researcher. For this reason, one must examine Jerome's motivations as carefully as those of Conan Doyle. Jerome's autobiography, *My Life and Times,* appeared in 1926. Two years earlier, Conan Doyle had published his own autobiography, in which he pronounced Jerome to be "hotheaded and intolerant in political matters"—a judgment that astonished Jerome. "It is precisely what I should have said myself concerning Doyle," he retorted.

It is also apparent that Jerome had a low opinion of his friend's interest in psychic research, as the two had disagreed publicly over the subject in the letters column of *Common Sense*. It does not necessarily follow, however, that Jerome decided to take his revenge by torpedoing one of Conan Doyle's most cherished tales of psychic adventure. Jerome's tone reveals a certain exasperation with his colleague, but he is hardly vindictive. To the contrary, it seems that

Jerome intended to present his friend in a flattering light—a sharp-eyed Sherlock Holmes, rather than a gullible ghost hunter.

If one takes Jerome at his word, it suggests that Conan Doyle deliberately obscured the facts of the case to support his own agenda. His motives for doing so are difficult to gauge, especially since he altered details of the story with each repetition. In one version, for instance, the family is comprised of an "elderly mother, a grown-up son and a married daughter." In another he speaks of the "young master of the house," a phrase unlikely to describe an officer of a war that ended fourteen years previously.

Possibly Conan Doyle's ancient promise of silence to Colonel Elmore's daughter inspired him to change the details and conceal her part in the incident. If so, it must be taken as rather disingenuous that he should have troubled to relate the story at all, much less attribute the events to the restless spirit of the unhappy ten-year-old. In his autobiography, Conan Doyle acknowledges that Frank Podmore filed a report attributing the noises to a "young man," but he goes on to say that this was not plausible since the young man was with them when the disturbances broke out. "I learned from this," he wrote, "what I have often confirmed since, that while we should be most critical of all psychic assertions, if we are to get at the truth, we should be equally critical of all negatives and especially so-called 'exposures' in this subject. Again and again I have probed them and found them to depend upon prejudice or upon imperfect acquaintance with psychic law."

Unfortunately, the prejudice in this instance seems to have been entirely on the part of Conan Doyle. Frank Podmore spent most of his life gathering accounts of psychic phenomena and examining their veracity. His reputation as a thorough and exacting researcher was one that Conan Doyle himself might have envied. This had not always been the case. In his early career, Podmore came in for many of the same charges of gullibility that were to plague Conan Doyle's later years. In 1894, the year of the haunted house episode, no less a figure than H. G. Wells published a review of Podmore's *Apparitions and Thought Transference*, and accused the author of being too credulous. Podmore's response, to the despair of some of his colleagues, was to become even more rigid in his standard of what constituted psychic evidence. In Conan Doyle's view, this made Podmore an adversary. One can chart the increasing vehemence of Conan Doyle's feelings in his descriptions of Podmore over the years. In Conan Doyle's autobiography, Podmore is described as "a man whose name was associated with such investigations." Only a few years later, Podmore had become, in Conan Doyle's view, "a determined and very unreasonable opponent of Spiritualism." Writing of Podmore's research in his two-volume *History of Spiritualism*, published in 1926, Conan Doyle was even more damning: "Mr. Frank Podmore brought together a large number of the facts, and, by ignoring those which did not suit his purpose, endeavoured to suggest the worthlessness of most of the rest, especially the physical phenomena, which in his view were mainly the result of fraud." By this time, unfortunately, Podmore could no longer defend himself or dispute Conan Doyle's version of the events in Dorset. Podmore had drowned in 1910, amid whispers of a homosexual scandal.

The events in Dorset marked the young Conan Doyle's first and perhaps only direct experience of what might be called a paranormal inquiry. Sad to say, he did not cover himself in glory. The disparity between his statements at the time—if Jerome's account can be trusted—and his later recollections points to a serious measure of self-delusion or outright deception. Moreover, he had harsh words for anyone—especially Frank Podmore—who disagreed with him. It is difficult to reconcile Conan Doyle's handling of this episode with his otherwise unblemished reputation for honor and probity. As Podmore himself once remarked of a different investigation, "It is easier to find the explanation in a fallacy of memory than in a fallacy of sense." Possibly Conan Doyle's memory played him false over the years. If so, such lapses were to prove remarkably persistent. One is forced to conclude that on some level—consciously or not—Conan Doyle manipulated the facts to support his own views. General Drayson, the mentor of Conan Doyle's early psychic experiences in Southsea, had spoken of the "naughty boys" who might pervert the course of a novice's belief. In this case, the naughty boy seems to have been Conan Doyle himself.

Unfortunately, it would not be the last time. On Jerome's evidence, the young Conan Doyle was a level-headed, open-minded investigator, and had been perfectly happy to admit that this particular case had contained no genuine psychic occurrence. In a few years hence, when his need to believe had overwhelmed his critical faculties, he would revise his earlier conclusions, and that cleareyed young man would disappear forever. Though it would not become apparent for some time, this contradiction in character would define his later years.

In time, Conan Doyle would also revise his early admiration for Arthur Balfour, whose interest in psychic research had made such a strong impression. In the early days of his infatuation with spiritualism, however, Conan Doyle considered Balfour's knowledge of the subject to be far greater than his own. In the January 1894 edition of *Transactions of the Society for Psychical Research,* Balfour gave a measured assessment of what he called the "recent provoking inquiries" into the subject of mesmerism. There can be little doubt that Balfour's thoughts were close at hand when Conan Doyle began work on *The Parasite,* his "mesmeric and hypnotic mystery," which appeared later that year.

As it happens, Conan Doyle's novel was not the only popular fiction to address the subject of mesmerism that year. In George du Maurier's *Trilby,* also published in 1894, a young singer rises to greatness under the mesmeric influence of a Hungarian musician named Svengali. Conan Doyle would certainly have been aware of du Maurier, whose long career as a caricaturist for *Punch* would have made him a colleague of Richard Doyle. In January, just as work on *The Parasite* began, serialized installments of *Trilby* began running in *Harper's New Monthly Magazine,* which had previously published work by Conan Doyle. It is probable, therefore, that Conan Doyle became aware of this influential book at some stage during the writing of *The Parasite*. Given Conan Doyle's speed of composition, however, it is unlikely that *Trilby* registered as anything more than a collateral influence. Both authors had a long-standing interest in mesmerism, and their books captured a contemporary enthusiasm for the subject.

While du Maurier's Svengali inhabited a bohemian society, Conan Doyle's book featured a cunning female mesmerist who worked her wiles against an academic backdrop. *The Parasite* concerns a skeptical professor named Austin Gilroy who reluctantly attends a demonstration given by a Miss Helen Penclosa, a mysterious visitor from Trinidad. Like Svengali, Miss Penclosa is presented as an older, slightly repellent figure. Gilroy describes her as furtive and sallow, with an infirm leg that emphasizes her physical frailty. In spite of his reservations, Professor Gilroy is forced to concede Miss Penclosa's odd power when his fiancée, while hypnotized, is briefly compelled to break off their engagement. Impressed, Gilroy expresses his feelings in terms that echo Conan Doyle's own pronouncements on the subject. "I had always looked upon spirit as a product of matter," Gilroy states. "The brain, I thought, secreted the mind, as the liver does the bile. But how can this be when I see mind working from a distance and playing upon matter as a musician might upon a violin? The body does not give rise to the soul, then, but is rather the rough instrument by which the spirit manifests itself. The windmill does not give rise to the wind, but only indicates it. It was opposed to my whole habit of thought, and yet it was undeniably possible and worthy of investigation."

Following this change of heart, Gilroy begins to submit to Miss Penclosa's mesmeric experiments, and gradually becomes an instrument of her will. In his brief moments of clarity, he conceives of her as a "monstrous parasite" who has insinuated herself into his mind as completely as the "hermit crab does into the whelk's shell." Matters take an even more sinister turn as the professor, helpless to resist Miss Penclosa's commands, attempts to rob the Bank of England. At the critical moment, as he menaces his fiancée with a vial of vitriol, Gilroy breaks free of the malign influence. The shock of severing the mesmeric link proves fatal to Miss Penclosa.

This was yet another novel written in haste and repented at leisure. *The Parasite* recorded only modest sales, with two limited reprintings in Britain and a single edition in the United States. Once again Conan Doyle had failed to sever the apparently mesmeric hold that Sherlock Holmes exerted on the public. In time, he would relegate the effort to a "very inferior plane" and have it removed from future listings of his collected works. Meanwhile, George du Maurier's *Trilby* had become a spectacular best-seller, inspiring what one newspaper described as a "maudlin mania" for its young heroine and her distressing tale. The novel's success inspired a flood of plays, songs, and dances, and created a market for *Trilby*-themed merchandise, which included jewelry, clothing, ice cream, a "Trilby sausage," and, finally, the "Trilby" hat. London had not seen a sensation on this scale since Sherlock Holmes burst onto the pages of *The Strand*, a fact that cannot have been lost on Conan Doyle.

At least part of the appeal of *Trilby* lay in the novel's rather daring portrayal of the heroine's bohemian lifestyle. As an artist's model, Trilby not only posed "in the altogether"—a phrase apparently coined by du Maurier—but also surrendered her virtue. Strange to say, the normally chaste Conan Doyle also explored sexual themes in *The Parasite*. At one stage, Professor Gilroy's "craving for the society" of Miss Penclosa grows so intense that he must lock himself away in his own bedroom.

Conan Doyle did not broach such topics lightly. When *The Memoirs of Sherlock Holmes* appeared the previous year, he withheld one of the stories—"The Adventure of the Cardboard Box"—on the grounds that it was "rather more sensational than I care for." The offending story contained "a gruesome packet" of two severed human ears and touched on the theme of adultery, which apparently served to give the author second thoughts. Having established this standard of decorum, his portrait of a character in the throes of sexual desire is worthy of attention.

It must be remembered that Conan Doyle's wife had now fallen victim to a terminal illness, and that medical wisdom of the day forbade any further sexual relations between them. Conan Doyle did not subscribe to the notion that all fiction is autobiographical, and one hesitates to assign literal meaning to a story that features evil hypnotists, bank robberies, and an aborted vitriol-throwing. Even so, it seems notable that the author's enforced celibacy should have been followed so closely by a scene in which a character claws his way out of a locked bedroom to hurry to the side of a potential lover.

The portrait of Gilroy's "monstrous temptation" is virtually unique among Conan Doyle's works. Though a period of illness had briefly relaxed Miss Penclosa's power, her recovery has apparently strengthened her hold over Gilroy. "A peculiar double consciousness possessed me," the professor relates. "There was the predominant alien will, which was bent upon drawing me to the side of its owner, and there was the feebler protesting personality, which I recognized as being myself, tugging feebly at the overmastering impulse as a led terrier might at its chain."

Irresistibly drawn to the mesmerist's boudoir, Gilroy finds her reclining on a sofa, covered in a tigerskin rug. Taking a seat on a low stool beside her, the professor seizes her hand and presses it to his lips: "She lay quietly looking down at me with imperious eyes and her provocative smile. Once I remember that she passed her hand over my hair as one caresses a dog; and it gave me pleasure—the caress. I thrilled under it. I was her slave, body and soul, and for the moment I rejoiced in my slavery."

Only then, as he stands at the "brink of perdition," does Gilroy experience a sudden deliverance. "As I looked up at her," Gilroy records, "I was conscious of a change in her. Her face, which had been pale before, was now ghastly. Her eyes were dull, and the lids drooped heavily over them. Above all, the look of serene confidence had gone from her features. Her mouth had weakened. Her forehead had puckered. She was frightened and undecided. And as I watched the change my own spirit fluttered and struggled, trying hard to tear itself from the grip which held it—a grip which, from moment to moment, grew less secure."

That said, Conan Doyle put down his pen and returned to his invalid wife.

13

Mr. Irving Takes Paregoric

"It is always a joy to me to meet an American."

—SHERLOCK HOLMES IN "THE NOBLE BACHELOR"

In September of 1894, at the Princes Theatre in Bristol, the curtain went up on a play that drew nearly universal praise as "a signal achievement in the history of the stage." The play came to light two and a half years earlier when Henry Irving, the most celebrated actor of his time, hurried into his office at the Lyceum Theater in a high state of excitement. "He was a little late," his business manager recalled. "As he came hurrying out to the stage, after putting on the brown soft broad-brimmed felt hat for which he usually exchanged his 'topper' during rehearsals, he stopped beside my table where I was writing, and laying a parcel on it said: 'I wish you would throw an eye over that during rehearsal. It came this morning. You can tell me what you think of it when I come off!' "

Inside the parcel was the manuscript of a play. "I read it with profound interest and was touched to my very heart's core by its humour and pathos," Irving's manager remarked. "It was very short, and before Irving came in again from the stage I had read it a second time."

"What did you think of it?" the actor asked when he returned to the office.

"I think this," came the reply, "that that play is never going to leave the Lyceum. You must own it—at any price. It is made for you."

"So I think, too!" Irving said. "You had better write to the author today and ask him what cheque we are to send. We had better buy the whole rights."

"Who is the author?"

"Conan Doyle!"

If the account sounds a bit mannered, it must be remembered that Henry Irving's business manager was none other than Bram Stoker, soon to be world famous as the author of *Dracula*. It is likely that some of Stoker's dramatic flair found its way into his *Personal Reminiscences of Henry Irving*. At the time, the forty-five-year-old Stoker had been in Irving's employ for many years, and never missed an opportunity to romanticize the life of the man he called "the finest actor who ever trod the boards."

Many shared Stoker's high opinion of Henry Irving. At fifty-four, Irving had become the dominant theatrical figure of the age. "His object was to realize his own perfection as an artist," wrote Oscar Wilde. "I often wonder, however, whether the public understands that that success is entirely due to the fact that he did not accept their standard, but realized his own."

Conan Doyle had been captivated by the actor since boyhood. He had seen Irving's legendary *Hamlet* on a visit to London from Stonyhurst, an experience that left him "quite transported." When Irving came to Edinburgh a few years later, Conan Doyle somehow found the money for a sixpence ticket night after night to sit in the gallery and marvel at the actor's skill.

To this point, Conan Doyle had shown no great promise as a playwright. *Jane Annie* would resound through the ages as a fiasco, and another early effort called *Angels of Darkness*, based on the Mormon episode of *A Study in Scarlet*, was never completed. In the remarkably fertile period that followed his withdrawal from medical practice, Conan Doyle summoned his courage for another attempt. The result was a one-act play called *A Story of Waterloo*, which concerned the reminiscences of the "gaunt, bent and doddering" Corporal

Gregory Brewster, age eighty-six, who had served under Wellington in the Napoleonic Wars. Conan Doyle adapted the play from a short story of his own called "A Straggler of '15," which had appeared in *Harper's New Monthly Magazine* three years earlier. The story, he wrote, "had seemed to me to be a moving picture of an old soldier and his ways. My own eyes were moist as I wrote it, and that is the surest way to moisten those of others."

Having transferred this emotion to the stage, the aspiring playwright, "greatly daring," sent it on to Irving, who cheerfully paid £100 for the rights. In spite of his initial enthusiasm for the play, Irving would not find occasion to perform it for more than two years. At one hour in length, Conan Doyle's play was too long to use as a curtain-raiser, but too short to stage on its own. Finally, in the summer of 1894, Irving decided to pair *A Story of Waterloo* with another one-act play, *The Bells,* which featured a murderer haunted by his crime.

The publicity for *A Story of Waterloo* made much of its being Conan Doyle's first venture into drama, as opposed to the light comedy of *Jane Annie*. The opening in Bristol, then, was a matter of "considerable importance in the dramatic world," Bram Stoker wrote. "The chief newspapers of London and some of the greater provincial cities wished to be represented on the occasion; the American press also wished to send its critical contingent. Accordingly we arranged for a special train to bring the critical force."

The judgment of this critical force was nearly unanimous: Irving had scored another triumph. "New play enormous success," Stoker wrote in his diary. "H. I. fine and great. All laughed and wept. Marvellous study of senility. Eight calls at end."

If Conan Doyle intended to tug at the heartstrings of his audience, he succeeded brilliantly. Irving brought a forlorn dignity to his portrayal of the aged Corporal Brewster, the last survivor of a regiment that had fought at Waterloo. The old soldier, whose health is failing rapidly as the curtain rises, spends much of the play reliving his former glories for a visiting sergeant. The audience soon learns of his uncommon bravery in driving a cart loaded with gunpowder through a flaming hedge to reach his stranded unit. "Why I sees it afore me, every time I shuts my eyes," he declares. "Lordy, sir, you wouldn't hardly believe how clear it is to me. There's our line right along from the paregoric bottle to the inhaler, d'ye see! Well then, the pill box is for Hougoumont on the right, where we was, and the thimble for Le Hay Saint . . . and over here, where the cough drops are, was the Proosians a comin' up on our left flank. Jimini, but it was a glad sight to see the smoke of their guns."

Finally, as his condition worsens, Brewster is lost to his visions of the past. "The Guards need powder!" he shouts, struggling to his feet. "The Guards need powder, and, by God, they shall have it!" That said, he falls back into his chair and expires. "I think," says the visiting sergeant gravely, "that the Third Guards have a full muster now."

However mawkish, Conan Doyle's play was perfectly suited to its times and to the skills of Henry Irving. The actor, according to one review, had created "one of the most remarkable stage pictures of our time, perfect in its verisimilitude, infinitely touching in its human pathos . . . a signal achievement even in Mr. Irving's long roll of dramatic triumphs." The critical consensus very nearly matched the lavish praises of Stoker himself, who found Irving's performance to be "the high-water mark of histrionic art."

Conan Doyle's role in the triumph was not so universally acknowledged. "Several critics went out of their way to explain that the merit lay entirely with the great actor and had nothing to do with the indifferent play," the author noted. In truth, the playwright appears to have been overly sensitive on this point. "Dr. Conan Doyle's little play," said London's *Daily News*, "carried all before it with its perfectly symmetrical and balanced art." Several other reviewers expressed pleasure that so renowned a literary figure should turn his energies to the stage.

There was, however, one voice of dissent. George Bernard Shaw, who had expressed himself so energetically on the subject of *Jane Annie*, addressed the new production with even greater venom. "Shaw was always a thorn in Irving's side," Conan Doyle admitted, "and was usually the one jarring note among the chorus of praise which greeted each fresh production. At a first night at the Lyceum—those wonderful first nights which have never been equalled—the lanky Irishman with his bloodless face, his red beard, and his sardonic expression must have been like the death's-head at the banquet to Irving."

Shaw's review, titled "Mr. Irving Takes Paregoric," appeared in *The Saturday Review* in May of the following year, after the play had transferred to London. For all of the scorn that followed, Conan Doyle must have derived some measure of satisfaction from the opening lines of Shaw's review: "Anyone who consults recent visitors to the Lyceum," Shaw began, "or who seeks for information in the Press as to the merits of Mr. Conan Doyle's *Story of Waterloo*, will in nineteen cases out of twenty learn that the piece is a trifle raised into importance by the marvellous acting of Mr. Irving as Corporal Gregory Brewster. As a matter of fact, the entire effect is contrived by the author, and is due to him alone. There is absolutely no acting in it—none whatever."

Shaw went on to fulminate about the makeup and "cheap and simple mimicry" that constituted Irving's performance, claiming that half of the work had been done in advance by the "suggestive effect" of sympathetic program notes, and the other half by Fuller Mellish and Annie Hughes in the supporting roles. In Shaw's view, so much had been done to rouse the expectations of the audience that it could hardly fail to go into raptures when the great man made his entrance:

"Enter Mr. Irving, in a dirty white wig, toothless, blear-eyed, palsied, shaky at the knees, stooping at the shoulders, incredibly aged and very poor, but respectable. He makes his way to his chair, and can only sit down, so stiff are his aged limbs, very slowly and creakily. This sitting down business is not acting: the callboy could do it; but we are so thoroughly primed by the playbill, the scene-painter, the stage-manager, Miss Hughes and Mr. Mellish, that we go off in enthusiastic whispers, 'What superb acting! How wonderfully he does it!' . . . He gets a bronchial attack and gasps for paregoric, which Miss Hughes administers with a spoon, whilst our faces glisten with tearful smiles. 'Is there another living actor who could take paregoric like that?' "

At the time, this degree of disdain seemed inconceivable to Conan Doyle, though in time he grew resigned to Shaw's obstinance. "Irving ascribed this animosity to Shaw's pique because his plays were not accepted," he wrote, "but in this I am sure that he did an injustice. It was simply that contrary twist in the man which makes him delight in opposing whatever anyone else approved."

Shaw's views aside, *A Story of Waterloo* quickly became a staple of Irving's repertoire, and a recurring feature of his twilight years. Within weeks of the play's London opening in May 1895, Irving received word that Queen Victoria was to confer a knighthood upon him, making him the first actor ever to be awarded this honor. Two years later, to mark Victoria's diamond jubilee, Irving performed the play—"with Royal Assent"—before an audience of two thousand colonial troops.

In all, Irving would perform *A Story of Waterloo* 343 times over the next decade, and Conan Doyle reported that he received a guinea from Irving after each performance. "It was a good bargain for him," Conan Doyle remarked, "for it is not too much to say that Corporal Gregory Brewster became one of his stock parts and it had the enormous advantage that the older he got the more naturally he played it."

The success of *A Story of Waterloo* did much to erase the memory of *Jane Annie*. Conan Doyle would see the production many times in the years to come, but as it happened, he was forced to miss the triumphant opening night in Bristol. A new series of lecturing commitments found him entertaining audiences of his own—in America.

Before the onset of Louisa's illness, Conan Doyle had gone out on a handful of small lecture tours in Britain and discovered that the "movement and bustle was not distasteful." Now, as he began spending more time back in England, he found himself "strongly pressed to go to America on the same errand."

Writing of these events thirty years later, Conan Doyle was careful to justify his decision to undertake an American lecture tour. The nursing skills of his sister Lottie, he wrote, and the steady improvement of Louisa's health had combined to give him "renewed liberty of action." Despite his assurances that "no sudden crisis was thought at all possible," Conan Doyle's readiness to leave his ailing wife's side for several months is surprising.

It is not too much to say that visiting America had been a lifelong dream, and one that, as a struggling doctor, he despaired of ever realizing. As a boy, Conan Doyle had been fascinated by the frontier tales of Fenimore Cooper and Mayne Reid, and as a young writer he drew inspiration from Poe, Mark Twain, and Bret Harte. Throughout his life he cherished a hope that the United States and Britain might one day merge to form a joint empire. In that spirit, the title page of *The White Company* bore the words: "To the Hope of the Future, the Reunion of the English Speaking Races, This Little Chronicle of Our Common Ancestry Is Inscribed." Sherlock Holmes also expressed a hope, in "The Noble Bachelor," that the two countries might one day join together "under a flag which shall be a quartering of the Union Jack with the Stars and Stripes."

It is also true that Louisa's illness—and the attendant worry, guilt, and sexual abstinence—had placed a huge strain on Conan Doyle. For the most part, he channeled this worry and nervous energy into his work, and for a time he returned to his prior schedule of literary gatherings and sporting events in London. Life could not go on as before, however; there would have been reminders of Louisa's condition at every turn. Possibly the trip to America, which he could justify to himself as a business obligation, offered a respite from his troubles and self-recriminations, though he would not have admitted as much to himself. "Work is the best antidote to sorrow, Watson," Sherlock Holmes once declared.

In any event, Conan Doyle allowed himself to be persuaded to undertake the tour, and sailed for New York aboard the German liner *Elbe* on September 23, 1894. His brother Innes, now a twenty-one-year-old subaltern in the Royal Artillery, joined him on the journey. "I needed some companion," Conan Doyle wrote, and "thought that the change would do him good."

On the ten-day crossing, the brothers got a taste of anti-British feeling among the vessel's predominantly German passengers and crew. At a dinner party given onboard, Conan Doyle noticed that the Union Jack had been excluded from a display of flags of the world. He and Innes promptly fashioned one of their own and proudly hung it aloft, "where its isolation drew attention to our grievance." Not all of the tour's discords would be handled so easily.

On October 2, the *Elbe* steamed into the New York harbor, where Conan Doyle would have paused at the rail to admire the Statue of

Liberty, erected only eight years earlier. While hundreds of hopeful immigrants were taken by barge to Ellis Island, Conan Doyle disembarked to face a circle of reporters eager to interview the creator of Sherlock Holmes. His open, agreeable manner made a highly favorable impression, as did his sturdy appearance. "He is tall, straight, athletic," observed the *New York Times*, "and his head that his blue eyes make radiant with affability must have been modeled by Energy herself, so profoundly impressed is it with her mark. His forehead is not colossal, yet it is as if it were built of the same marble as the Titans. His look is merry, quick, curious, inventive, and resolutely fixed on the things that happen, and not on an invisible star." With such descriptive powers at its command, it hardly mattered that the *New York Times* did not yet carry photographs.

Major James Pond, who organized the tour, was also present when the *Elbe* docked. A veteran of the Civil War, Pond had been a lecture agent for more than twenty years, and a central figure in promoting the "improving talk" as a form of entertainment in America. His clients had included the late Henry Ward Beecher, who generally read from his renowned *Seven Lectures to Young Men*; James Whitcomb Riley, author of the dialect poem "Little Orphant Annie"; and Mark Twain, whose *Pudd'nhead Wilson* appeared while Conan Doyle was in New York. With "a goat's beard and a nasal voice," the large, gangly Pond seemed to Conan Doyle to be the very embodiment of an American. What Conan Doyle did not know was that Pond had a reputation for being something of a slave driver. Pond would run his star attraction through more than thirty cities, many of them more than once. One typical stretch found Conan Doyle giving lectures in three different cities—New York, Princeton, and Philadelphia—in only twenty-four hours. Worse yet, Conan Doyle's agreement with Pond had him paying his own expenses, which mounted quickly as he caromed from one city to the next. The ambitious itinerary included Boston, Washington, D.C., Amherst, Buffalo, Toronto, Niagara Falls, Toledo, Indianapolis, Cincinnati, Chicago, and Milwaukee. Conan Doyle often had to sleep aboard trains to stay on schedule. What little free time he had was given over to literary soirees and society events, where "the exuberant hospitality of those pre-prohibition days" once again tested his resolve concerning alcohol. "It was all done in kindness," he wrote, "but it was dangerous for a man who had his work to do."

Unlike other authors who fell into Major Pond's orbit, Conan Doyle never said an unkind word about the "considerable programme" that had been imposed on him, though he admitted he was "forced to do rather more than to pay my expenses, and rather less in the way of seeing the country."

Originally, Conan Doyle intended to offer a selection of three different lectures to his American audiences. The first concerned the "Tendency of Fiction in England," and drew on the works of Thomas Hardy, Robert Louis Stevenson, Rudyard Kipling, and others. The second would address the work of George Meredith, whom Conan Doyle regarded as "the Novelist's Novelist." And finally there would be a lecture entitled "Readings and Reminiscences," in which he would draw on his own life and works. In the end, Conan Doyle dropped the first two speeches and limited himself almost exclusively to the third. At the tender age of thirty-five, he had misgivings about holding forth on his own achievements, which struck him as unseemly. "It is naturally repugnant for a man to stand up on a public platform and to talk about himself and his own work," Conan Doyle told his audiences, "for never until a man attempts to do so before an audience does he realize how very insignificant both himself and his own works are, and how very difficult it is to make either the one or the other interesting to any third person. It would be more pleasant for me to speak of the work of my friends and contemporaries. Before I came to this country, however, it was pointed out to me that if anybody should come to hear me lecture, it would not be because they want my criticism on this or that, but because something I have written has come in their way and they want to make a bond of sympathy between us."

For many of the Americans who came to hear him, that bond of sympathy rested with Sherlock Holmes. More than a few were surprised to see the man before them looking so hale and hearty, as opposed to the pale, cadaverous, violin-playing figure they had imagined. Almost from the moment Conan Doyle alighted in New York, he was deluged with questions about the detective. At a group interview, one reporter asked whether he had been influenced by

Edgar Allan Poe when he created Sherlock Holmes. Many of the other journalists present, it seems, believed that Conan Doyle would take umbrage at the question. "A hush fell in the room," wrote the reporter from the *New York Times*. "It could be heard as distinctly as if the string of a violin had snapped." As it happened, Conan Doyle wasn't at all affronted. "Oh, immensely!" he responded, apparently warming to the question. "His detective is the best in fiction."

"Except Sherlock Holmes," another reporter ventured.

Conan Doyle would not be swayed. "I make no exception," he answered. In some retellings of this incident, Conan Doyle is reported to have thundered his reply with angry bluster, as though consigning Sherlock Holmes to literary hell. According to the *Times*, however, he answered the question "very earnestly," and went on to elaborate. "Dupin is unrivaled," he stated. "It was Poe who taught the possibility of making a detective story a work of literature."

As far as Conan Doyle was concerned, Sherlock Holmes was to remain at the bottom of the Reichenbach Falls forever—"I was tired of that sort of thing anyway," he told one newspaper. Nonetheless, he gave considerable attention to the detective in his lectures. Speaking of his early years in Southsea, he remarked, "At this period a gentleman appeared in my life who certainly has been a very good friend to me, and to whom I think I afterward behaved in a very ungrateful manner—I mean the late Sherlock Holmes, of Baker Street." Conan Doyle went on to speak of Poe and Joseph Bell before reading two long passages that demonstrated how he had transferred their influence to his own detective. In the first reading, from *The Sign of the Four*, Sherlock Holmes conjured a vivid portrait of Dr. Watson's late brother from a battered pocket watch. In the second, Holmes and his brother Mycroft gazed out a window and constructed the entire life history of a passerby. For Conan Doyle's audiences, hearing these passages read aloud by the author himself was surely worth the price of admission.

Many authors took advantage of lecture tours to indulge their theatrical leanings. Dickens, for example, had often appeared in various costumes to impersonate characters from his novels. Conan Doyle, a nervous public speaker, preferred a more straightforward approach. "Indeed," he wrote, "I read to them exactly as in my boyhood I used to read to my mother." He had no costumes or props, not counting the large red handkerchief he used repeatedly to mop his brow.

Conan Doyle's audiences could not have failed to notice his jitters. On one occasion, his collar popped open as he approached the lectern, in the manner of a stage comedian's pop-up shirtfront, and Major Pond was obliged to hand over his own collar stud. At another lecture, Conan Doyle tripped on his way to the stage and stumbled toward the audience, throwing books and papers before him. "There was much laughter," he noted, "and a general desire for an encore." Without Louisa to look after him, Conan Doyle seems to have cut a somewhat bedraggled figure. One reporter observed that he had tied his tie so carelessly that a laundry mark reading "A. Conan Doyle" protruded below his vest.

If he lacked polish, however, Conan Doyle compensated with his natural warmth, his self-effacing charm, and his obvious passion for America. "Few foreign writers who have visited this country have made more friends than A. Conan Doyle," reported the *Ladies' Home Journal*. "His personality is a peculiarly attractive one to Americans because it is so thoroughly wholesome . . . he spoke with undisguised enthusiasm of his early acquaintance with American books and of his delight in them. No American boy could have come more intimately into association with the early American writers than did the boy whose early youth was spent in Edinburgh."

It was a time when a favorable impression counted for a great deal. Conan Doyle later declared that he could scarcely pick up a newspaper in America without reading some negative comment about Britain, much of it centered on the question of Irish home rule. One night in Detroit, at a dinner held in his honor, Conan Doyle listened with growing distress as one of the speakers, who was well in his cups, launched an outspoken attack on Britain. Affronted, Conan Doyle rose from his seat and asked if he might be allowed a response. His remarks, as he later recounted them for Bram Stoker, expressed his hopes for the future of the Anglo-American alliance: "You Americans have lived, up to now, within a ring fence of your own. Your country has become so vast, and you have had so much to do in peopling it and opening it out, that you have never had to think seriously of outside international politics, and you have lived to some extent in a world of prejudice and of dreams. This period is now drawing swiftly to an end. Your country is filling up, and soon you will have surplus energies which will lead you on into world politics and bring you into closer actual relations with other powers. Then your friendships and your enmities will be guided not by prejudice nor by hereditary dislikes, but by actual practical issues. When that day comes, and it is coming soon, you will find that the only people who will understand you—who will see what your aims are and who will heartily sympathize with you in them—are your own people, the men from whom you are sprung. In a great world crisis you will find that you have no natural friend among the nations save your own kin; and to the last they will always be at your side."

Whether Conan Doyle spoke these words precisely is a matter for speculation; there would be many revisions of the tale in years to come. The underlying sentiment remained unchanged, however, and clearly it meant a great deal to him. With the benefit of hindsight, Conan Doyle's concerns over a "great world crisis" were remarkably prescient.

Conan Doyle hoped to have occasion to meet American writers on his travels. "Met Bret Harte once at dinner," he told a reporter, "but have never had the good fortune to run across Mark Twain." To his lasting sorrow, he had arrived in New York just five days before the death of Oliver Wendell Holmes in New England. At the end of October, he traveled to Cambridge and made a pilgrimage to the Mount Auburn Cemetery, where Holmes was buried. "It was one of the ambitions of my lifetime to look upon his face," he wrote, "but by the irony of Fate I arrived in his native city just in time to lay a wreath upon his newly turned grave." Not surprisingly, while visiting Baltimore the following month, Conan Doyle also found time to visit the grave of Edgar Allan Poe.

Toward the end of November, an invitation came from Rudyard Kipling and his American wife, Caroline, who were then living near Brattleboro, Vermont. Not yet thirty years old, Kipling had published *The Jungle Book* that year, and Conan Doyle ranked him as "England's best novelist since Dickens." Under normal circumstances, Conan Doyle would have leapt at the invitation. At the time, however, he felt uncomfortable about Kipling's vocal responses to America's anti-British posturing. "Kipling pulled a few feathers out of the Eagle's tail in retaliation," Conan Doyle wrote. "The result at the time was to add oil to flames, and I, as a passionate believer in Anglo-American union, wrote to Kipling to remonstrate."

Apparently Kipling took these remonstrances in good humor; he responded by inviting Conan Doyle up to Vermont for Thanksgiving. Conan Doyle and Innes traveled by train from Buffalo, and enjoyed "two great days in Vermont." Ever resourceful, Conan Doyle managed to scare up a set of golf clubs to offer Kipling a few pointers, "while the New England rustics watched us from afar, wondering what on earth we were at." Later, Conan Doyle would arrange to share another of his sporting enthusiasms when he had a pair of skis sent to Kipling from Norway.

The two authors parted on good terms, having agreed to disagree on some of the baser aspects of American culture. As a final word on the subject, Conan Doyle is supposed to have urged Kipling to "stop talking about spittoons." These differences aside, they would correspond for years to come. "He is a wonderful chap," Conan Doyle told the Ma'am.

Having promised to spend Christmas with his family, Conan Doyle and his brother sailed from New York aboard the Cunard liner *Etruria* on December 8. The tour had been an enormous success; Major Pond had tried to persuade Conan Doyle to extend his stay, and offered a record-breaking sum if he would agree to an even more rigorous return engagement. Conan Doyle sidestepped Pond's offer but told a newspaper he would be back the following year. In fact, it would be twenty years before he saw America again.

Privately, Conan Doyle regretted that his profits from the tour—roughly £1,000—had not been higher. "Thackeray and Dickens made money," he wrote in a professional journal the following year, "and when we have another Thackeray and Dickens they may do the same; but the British lecturer whose credentials are more modest will find that the margin left over, after his expenses are paid, is probably less than the sum he could have easily earned in his own study." Be that as it may, Conan Doyle felt comfortable enough at the end of his tour to invest $8,500 in the faltering *McClure's Magazine,* rescuing it from near extinction.

The *Etruria* docked in Liverpool on December 15. Conan Doyle had spent most of the voyage lying low in his cabin, recovering from the exhausting schedule, while Innes enjoyed the amenities of the ship. The travelers made their way to London, where Conan Doyle promptly set off for Davos to join the family for Christmas. If his spirits lifted at the prospect, they quickly sank again at the grim news that greeted him in London. Driving along the Strand in a hansom cab, Conan Doyle caught sight of a yellow newspaper poster. It read: "Death of Stevenson." Robert Louis Stevenson, with whom Conan Doyle had been corresponding for many months, had succumbed to a fit of apoplexy at the age of forty-four. In time, Conan Doyle would write at length of Stevenson's legacy, and of the "strange Stevenson glamour" that gave life to *Dr. Jekyll and Mr. Hyde, Kidnapped,* and *Treasure Island*. Stevenson's executors, in the meantime, asked if Conan Doyle would consider finishing Stevenson's last novel, *St. Ives,* but Conan Doyle did not feel he could do it justice. Arthur Quiller-Couch took over instead.

At that moment, however, the loss struck Conan Doyle at a far more personal level. "Something seemed to have passed out of my world," he remarked.

In time, as the fatigue and irritations of Major Pond's itinerary faded, Conan Doyle looked back on his first experience of America with fondness. "My memories are the confused ones of a weary man," he admitted, but there was one anecdote he would repeat for the rest of his life. It involved a cab driver who, upon dropping Conan Doyle at his destination, requested a ticket to that evening's lecture instead of his fare.

"How on earth did you recognize me?" Conan Doyle asked.

The cabman replied: "If you will excuse me, your coat lapels are badly twisted downward, where they have been grasped by the pertinacious New York reporters. Your hair has the Quakerish cut of a Philadelphia barber, and your hat, battered at the brim in front, shows where you have tightly grasped it, in the struggle to stand your ground at a Chicago literary luncheon. Your right shoe has a large block of Buffalo mud just under the instep; the odor of a Utica cigar hangs about your clothing and the overcoat itself shows the slovenly brushing of the porters of the through sleepers from Albany. The crumbs of the doughnut on the top of your waistcoat could only have come there in Springfield. And, of course, the labels on your case give a full account of your recent travels—just below the brass plaque reading 'Conan Doyle.' "

14

Duet with an Occasional Chorus

It is my habit, you see, to talk of that which interests myself, and so I hope that I may interest you.

—BRIGADIER GERARD IN "HOW THE BRIGADIER CAME TO THE CASTLE OF GLOOM"

In America, Conan Doyle spoke often of the English novelist George Meredith, who had been one of his "youthful cults." Originally, Conan Doyle hoped that his thoughts on Meredith might constitute an entire evening's entertainment, much as they had years earlier when he addressed a meeting of the Portsmouth Literary and Scientific Society. On that occasion, Conan Doyle lamented that Meredith's dense prose rendered him unpalatable to the general public, and perhaps lesser known than the author of the latest "shilling shocker" might be—a self-deprecating reference to his own recently published *A Study in Scarlet*.

Shilling shockers aside, Conan Doyle was aware that his own popularity had now surpassed that of the much-admired Meredith, a fact that caused him some distress. He never missed an opportunity to praise Meredith's masterwork, *The Ordeal of Richard Feverel*, but regretted the "handicap" of the author's overly ornate style. "If his own generation finds him hard to understand," Conan Doyle asked, "what will our descendants make of him?"

For some time, Conan Doyle had been making regular pilgrimages to Meredith's home in Surrey. Even at close quarters, he discovered, Meredith could be fairly cryptic. On one occasion, when Conan Doyle had traveled down in the company of fellow authors James Barrie and Arthur Quiller-Couch, the three men listened in dutiful confusion as Meredith read aloud his poem "To the British Working Man."

"I don't know what the British working man made of it," Conan Doyle remarked, "but I am sure that we three were greatly puzzled as to what it was all about."

Nonetheless, Conan Doyle returned to Surrey many times. Once, as the two writers sat down to lunch, Meredith asked "with a very earnest air" if Conan Doyle could undertake to drink an entire bottle of Burgundy. Age and failing health had denied Meredith the wines he collected in his youth, but he enjoyed watching his guests make use of his cellar. "I answered that I saw no insuperable difficulty," Conan Doyle recalled. "A dusty old bottle was tenderly carried up, which I disposed of, Meredith taking a friendly interest in its dispatch."

Perhaps the wine made Conan Doyle particularly attentive when Meredith held forth on the subject of Napoleon's marshals, a topic of great interest to both men. If so, it led to one of Conan Doyle's finest inspirations. A new translation of *The Memoirs of Baron de Marbot*, originally published in Paris in 1844, had touched off a fresh wave of interest in the Napoleonic era. De Marbot, a French baron and officer under Napoleon's command, had recorded his "hairbreadth escapes and dare-devil exploits" with great verve and a pompous but engaging style. Meredith recommended the memoir highly to Conan Doyle, who came to regard it as "the first of all soldier books in the world."

It required a certain "robust faith," Conan Doyle allowed, to credit all of the Frenchman's outlandish claims of bravery, but therein lay the book's charm. De Marbot made such an impression that Conan Doyle transferred the French officer's verve and vainglorious manner into a new fictional hero, Brigadier Etienne Gerard of the Hussars of Conflans—"gay-riding, plume-tossing, debonair, the darling of the ladies and of the six brigades of light cavalry."

It proved to be one of his happier brainstorms. With Brigadier Gerard, Conan Doyle not only indulged his love of historical fiction but also created a new character who could sustain his readers' interest through a series of episodic tales, in the manner of the late Sherlock Holmes. Where his long historical novels tended to wander or bog down in detail, the new stories hurtled along with the speed of the Brigadier's own "heroic and admired" saber thrusts.

Each adventure found the flamboyant soldier thrown into an unlikely situation—and facing impossible odds—only to emerge triumphant through reckless nerve and dumb luck. In "How the Brigadier Slew the Fox," Gerard becomes lost behind enemy lines and blunders into a foxhunt. Forgetting himself in the excitement, he not only chases down the fox but kills it with a lusty swipe of his saber, much to the dismay of the English huntsmen, whose frantic cries and wild gestures he interprets as cheers of encouragement. "They are not really such a phlegmatic race, the English," observes Gerard. "A gallant deed in war or in sport will always warm their hearts."

"How the Brigadier Won His Medal," the new character's debut, appeared in the December 1894 issue of *The Strand*. Conan Doyle had read it aloud to audiences in America, whose generous responses encouraged him to think he had a success on his hands. As he settled back into the routine of Davos, he quickly turned out another seven adventures. These appeared in *The Strand* throughout 1895, and were collected in book form as *The Exploits of Brigadier Gerard*.

Though Conan Doyle often dismissed this collection as his "little book of soldier stories," Brigadier Gerard soon emerged as one of his most popular creations. Greenhough Smith was delighted to have another continuing series of stories, and the readership warmed to Conan Doyle's affable humor. "It is pleasant to see so many people fond of the Brigadier," Conan Doyle commented, "for I was a bit fond of him myself."

In Davos that winter Conan Doyle brushed up on his skiing, often in the company of his sister Lottie, and mapped out trails with the Branger brothers. As the family removed to Maloja for the summer, Conan Doyle began work on *Rodney Stone*, another historical novel. This time he chose a Regency setting, and focused on the sport of bare-knuckle boxing in the days before the Marquis of Queensberry imposed rules on the sport. "Why that subject," asked publisher George Newnes, "of all subjects on earth?" For Conan Doyle, whose boxing prowess had won him respect aboard the *Hope*, the topic seemed natural enough. He loved the sport and had participated in matches for most of his life. "An exhibition of hardihood without brutality, of good-humoured courage without savagery, of skill without trickery, is, I think, the very highest which sport can give," he wrote. "Better that our sports should be a little too rough than that we should run a risk of effeminacy." Modern readers may shake their heads at this, but for Conan Doyle the boxing ring offered a present-day equivalent of the knightly tournament, a chance to test one's mettle in ritual combat.

As always with his historical works, Conan Doyle surrounded himself with research material. He drew on the life of Beau Brummell and several other period chronicles to capture the flavor of the times, and immersed himself in "pugilistica"—the science and history of boxing.

Rodney Stone began serialization in *The Strand* in January 1896, with the book edition appearing later in the year. It not only sold well but did much to revive interest in boxing. The book would be reprinted and serialized many times over the next thirty years, and Conan Doyle came to regard it as one of his notable successes.

Not all of the critics admired the novel. When the first book edition appeared, no less a figure than Max Beerbohm panned the novel in *The Saturday Review*. Referring to Conan Doyle's medical background, Beerbohm commended the author as "the first to have carried the bedside-manner into literature." The very sight of Conan Doyle's kindly face and gold-rimmed eyeglasses, Beerbohm continued, filled the reader with confidence. However, in this instance, the critic believed, Conan Doyle had lost the patient. "[S]uch slight plot as there is bobs up only at the beginning and end of the book," he wrote. "And yet he is quite pleased with himself, this obstinate medico. He hints that he means to perform, shortly, a second operation. No, no, Doctor Doyle! You're a very good general practitioner, I've no doubt. But you've bungled the post-mortem. Operations of this kind require great special knowledge and most delicate handling. . . . You had far better have stuck to your ordinary practice."

In the spirit of his novel, Conan Doyle might have preferred to settle the matter with his fists. Instead, he contented himself with a letter of rebuttal to *The Saturday Review*, pointing out the "historical and social errors" in Beerbohm's review. "He may be upon safe ground when he refers to my bedside manner and gold-rimmed glasses, but he is very ignorant of the period about which he writes."

Conan Doyle felt more charitable toward the writer Grant Allen, a fellow *Strand* contributor he had met on a business trip to London in October 1895. Allen, whose candidly sexual novel *The Woman Who Did* had created a sensation that year, was shortly to become an important figure in detective fiction. His novel *An African Millionaire*, published in 1897, featured a roguish master of disguise named Colonel Clay. Like E. W. Hornung's Raffles, who made his debut two years later, Colonel Clay helped to establish the now familiar convention of casting a thief in the hero's role.

At their first meeting, Allen and Conan Doyle probably did not discuss detective fiction. As a younger man, Allen had suffered from tuberculosis. He cured himself, he insisted, without the expense and inconvenience of a long stay in a foreign sanatorium. Instead, he found the pure air of Hindhead, a village in Surrey, to be just as beneficial. In Allen's opinion, Conan Doyle could bring Louisa back to England without danger of a relapse, so long as they took up residence in Hindhead. "It was quite a new idea to me that we might actually live with impunity in England once more," Conan Doyle wrote, "and it was a pleasant thought after resigning oneself to a life which was unnatural to both of us at foreign health resorts."

Eager to investigate, Conan Doyle went down to Hindhead, roughly fifty miles southwest of London. Impressed by the dry conditions and sheltered landscape, he arranged to purchase a large plot of land near the center of the village. Having sold off the house in South Norwood, he commissioned the architect Henry Ball to build a new one in Surrey. Ball, Conan Doyle's mind-reading partner from

Southsea, drew up a set of plans that included a tennis court, horse stables, and modern electric lighting. Louisa, who had despaired of ever regaining any domestic stability, greeted the news warmly. "The thought of it," Conan Doyle wrote, "brought renewed hope to the sufferer."

While waiting for the house to be built, Conan Doyle decided to take Louisa to Egypt for the winter, hoping that the hot, dry climate would finish off her cure before their return to England. Once again they left the children with Mrs. Hawkins as they set off on their travels, though Louisa had reason to hope that these periods of separation were coming to an end. With his sister Lottie as companion and nurse, Conan Doyle and Louisa traveled by stages from Caux to Rome, then sailed from the seaport of Brindisi to Alexandria. Arriving in Egypt, the party established itself amid the potted palms and ceiling fans of the opulent Mena House Hotel, "in the very shadow of the Pyramids," seven miles out of Cairo on "the most monotonous road in the world." A bastion of empire, the hotel's lounges formed a hub of British society, with dashing officers in khaki making themselves charming to the ladies while turbaned waiters circulated trays of cooling drinks. Conan Doyle warmed to the social life of Cairo, as did his sister, who was "just at an age to enjoy it." This was a gallant thing to say of Lottie Doyle, who at the age of twenty-nine would have seemed a bit long of tooth to many of the young officers stationed in Egypt.

As always, Conan Doyle kept to a steady work schedule, though he found the desert heat enervating. He brought research materials along to finish up the first set of Brigadier Gerard stories, and also found time to adapt a play from a novel by his friend James Payn, the editor of *Cornhill Magazine*. His researches into the Napoleonic era set him off on another historical novel, *Uncle Bernac,* which had been commissioned by the editor of *Queen* magazine. When his creative energy flagged, he took local forms of exercise. He climbed the Great Pyramid of Giza, which he considered an "uncomfortable and useless feat," and made use of a golf course near the hotel. Here, he later remarked, "if you sliced your ball, you might find it bunkered in the grave of some Rameses or Thothmes of old." This marked an improvement over his golf outings in Davos. There his efforts to set up a course were foiled by inquisitive cows, which had a "curious trick" of knocking down the flags and eating them.

Conan Doyle also hoped to practice his horsemanship in Egypt, availing himself of an assortment of "weird steeds" available at a nearby livery. "As a rule they erred on the side of dullness," he wrote, "but I have a very vivid recollection of one which restored the average. If my right eyelid drops somewhat over my eye it is not the result of philosophic brooding, but it is the doing of a black devil of a horse with a varminty head, slab-sided ribs, and restless ears." Apparently there was ill feeling on both sides; the horse not only dragged Conan Doyle on a mad dash across the desert, but also pitched him to the ground and kicked him in the forehead. The wound required five stitches, and the sagging eyelid can be seen in every subsequent photograph.

Conan Doyle celebrated the New Year of 1896 with his wife and sister in Cairo. Two days later, the three of them set off on a Nile cruise organized by the Thomas Cook travel agency. They sailed aboard a paddle-wheel steamer called *Nitocris*, which carried a crew of sixteen and had berths for eight passengers. The journey covered some eight hundred miles, reaching as far south as the Sudanese border, with frequent stops to explore ancient tombs and temples. Conan Doyle marveled at the "majestic continuity" of Egyptian history: "There is nothing like this in the world. The Roman and the British Empires are mushrooms in comparison." Even so, with his growing interest in spiritualism, Conan Doyle could not reconcile himself to the Egyptian preoccupation with the preservation of the earthly body. "What a degraded intelligence does it not show!" he exclaimed. "The idea that the body, the old outworn greatcoat which was once wrapped round the soul, should at any cost be preserved is the last word in materialism."

As the tour moved south, it entered potentially dangerous territory. With the new Conservative government in Britain making noise about a reconquest of the Sudan, bands of restless Sudanese natives were making their feelings known by lobbing warning shots at passing English vessels. As reports of further hostilities circulated aboard the *Nitocris*, Conan Doyle concluded that the tour managers were taking unnecessary risks. "If I were a Dervish General," he noted, "I would undertake to carry off a Cook's excursion party with the greatest ease." Happily, the *Nitocris* returned its passengers to Cairo unharmed, but Conan Doyle continued to meditate on the idea of a tour party "plunged into frightful disaster." In time, he produced a new novel called *The Tragedy of the Korosko*, which appeared in America as *A Desert Drama*, in which a party of tourists falls prey to desert bandits. The book would appear in February 1898, after a well-received serialization in *The Strand*.

Returning from the Nile cruise safely, Conan Doyle left Louisa and Lottie in the comfort of the hotel while he rode fifty miles into the desert to visit the famous Coptic monastery at the Natron Lakes. When he got back to Cairo several days later, he learned that "great historical events" had transpired in his absence. The tensions in the region, escalated by disagreements over the deployment of British forces along the Nile, had now erupted into open warfare. The British-controlled Egyptian army, under the command of Lord Kitchener, was marching on the Sudanese dervishes loyal to the Khalifa Abdullah el Taashi. "Egypt had suddenly become the storm centre of the world," he wrote, "and chance had placed me there at that moment."

Conan Doyle, who had chronicled so many great military campaigns of the past in his novels, longed to see the modern British fighting man in action. As a civilian, he knew, he could not hope to get up to the front lines. Not to be denied, he wired to the *Westminster Gazette* in London and wrangled an appointment as an honorary war correspondent. With these credentials in hand, he kitted himself out with a khaki coat and riding breeches, and purchased an Italian revolver and cartridges. Leaving Louisa and Lottie in the safety of the hotel, he set off for the Sudanese border.

Traveling by train, boat, and camel, Conan Doyle headed south to Aswan, well short of the actual combat zone, where the men of the press had gathered. Impatient as he was to see action, he could not fail to be impressed by the unruffled demeanor of the British officers. He came to know four young men, all suffering from fever, who insisted on remaining at their posts. Every morning each of the four would toss a half crown into a hat, then take their temperatures. The man with the highest fever took the pot. Only once, when a telegram had been posted at headquarters, did Conan Doyle see signs of agitation among the troops. The notice, he assumed, brought news of advancing forces. "I pushed my way in, and thrust my head among all the bobbing sun helmets," he reported. "It was the account of the Oxford and Cambridge boat race."

A group of cavalry officers was preparing to join the main body of troops at Wadi Halfa, and the press contingent was ordered to join them. Instead, Conan Doyle decided to try his luck with the "big pressmen" from London, who determined that they would be happier making the trip on their own. "There was some risk in our lonely journey along the right bank of the river with our left flank quite unprotected," he wrote, "but on the other hand the dust of a great body of horsemen would be insufferable." On reflection, breathing a little dust would certainly have been preferable to the very real danger of falling into the hands of marauding dervishes, but Conan Doyle's taste for adventure overcame his more sober impulses. He and his fellow travelers set off in the darkness mounted on camels, attended by a retinue of servants.

Camels, Conan Doyle found, were no more congenial than his "varminty" Egyptian horse had been. "It is the strangest and most deceptive animal in the world," he wrote. "Its appearance is so staid and respectable that you cannot give it credit for the black villainy that lurks within. It approaches you with a mildly interested and superior expression, like a patrician lady in a Sunday school. You feel that a pair of glasses at the end of a fan is the one thing lacking. Then it puts its lips gently forward, with a far-away look in its eyes, and you have just time to say, 'The pretty dear is going to kiss me,' when two rows of frightful green teeth clash in front of you, and you give such a backward jump as you could never have hoped at your age to accomplish."

Fortunately, Conan Doyle's camel was the only serious threat he had to face; the party completed its journey to Wadi Halfa without encountering any Sudanese forces. "I am still haunted by that purple velvet sky," he was to write in his autobiography, "by those enormous and innumerable stars, by the half-moon which moved slowly above us, while our camels with their noiseless tread seemed to bear us without effort through a wonderful dream world."

Disappointment awaited the travelers at their destination, as the start of the campaign appeared to be on hold. "There was a whiff of real war in the little fortress," Conan Doyle found, "but no sign of any actual advance." Over dinner, Kitchener himself assured a crest-fallen Conan Doyle that no fighting could take place until his men and equipment were in position. The other correspondents elected to stay in place. Conan Doyle, as much as he might have wished it otherwise, knew that Louisa could not tolerate the heat of the coming summer. Donating his camel to the cause, he hitched a ride back to Cairo on a passing cargo boat, surviving for the entire journey on a diet of apricots in syrup. "I never wish to see a tinned apricot so long as I live," he said.

The Conan Doyle party sailed for England in late April. He brought back many souvenirs, the most prominent being an infestation of chiggers, which had burrowed into his wrists while he slept along the banks of the Nile.

The new home in Hindhead was not yet completed when the Conan Doyles returned. With their children in tow, they moved into a rented property in the nearby town of Haslemere, and later to a hotel in Hindhead where they could supervise the construction of the house. It must be said that Conan Doyle did not seem in any great hurry to renew his acquaintance with his children. He had spent six months in Egypt, but within three weeks of his return to England he set off on a sentimental visit to Southsea, where for several weeks he tailored his work schedule around cricket matches and visits with old friends. While there, it seems that he extended a generous hand to his old colleague Arthur Ford, the ophthalmic surgeon who trained him to perform eye tests. Ford, who had six children, had fallen on hard times. Acting on an apparent impulse, Conan Doyle bought the house Ford had been renting, and presumably offered security and generous terms to his old friend.

In October 1897, Conan Doyle and his family moved into their new home. The gabled, redbrick mansion made an impressive reflection of the author's fame and wealth, and also his far-flung interests as a traveler and sportsman. A long, winding drive brought visitors to the western entrance, which opened into a two-story entry hall, warmed by a brick fireplace, where the Doyle family's coats of arms were set into stained-glass windows. Guest bedrooms and an enormous billiards room held out the promise of entertaining on a lavish scale, as did the stately dining room, which could seat up to thirty people. In the wood-paneled drawing room, a special display shelf ran along the walls near the ceiling, holding an eccentric collection of walrus tusks, antique weapons, stuffed birds, and sporting trophies. The sheltered conditions that made Hindhead so favorable to Louisa's health also allowed for large, bright windows without the risk of unwelcome drafts. Electric lights, not yet common outside the larger cities, ran off a special generator. Conan Doyle calculated the total value of his new home at £10,000, perhaps half a million dollars in modern terms. He named the house Undershaw—"shaw" being an Anglo-Saxon word to describe a nearby grove of hanging trees. Bram Stoker, who visited in 1907, found the house "cozy and snug to a remarkable degree," and added that the many curios and artworks created an effect like a "fairy pleasure house." Stoker's reaction is not surprising; by that time Conan Doyle had built an electric monorail train on the grounds at the back of the property, which featured a special gyroscopic balancing mechanism. The train was large enough to carry passengers, much to the delight of his daughter and son, who were now eight and five years old.

For Conan Doyle, who had spent his childhood bouncing from one flat to another in Edinburgh, Undershaw brought a welcome stability. His own children, after the upheavals of the previous four years, now had a beautiful home and four acres of wooded land to explore. A visitor from the *Windsor Magazine* noted that the "youthful branches of the family are here, there, and everywhere," and Conan Doyle encouraged their budding interest in croquet, horses, and other outdoor sports. He shared his love of boxing and cricket with Kingsley, and went hiking and riding with Mary. For Louisa, the new house offered the same domestic pleasures she had enjoyed in South Norwood, though she now had a large staff to manage, including a butler, Cleeve, and various cooks and parlor maids. As a further concession to her health, the interior doors of the new home were designed to open at a light touch. Louisa now suffered from arthritis, which made turning knobs difficult. She continued to receive a great deal of help from her mother, who came to live in a neighboring cottage. Conan Doyle's mother, now fifty-nine, remained in Masongill.

From his new study, Conan Doyle began producing a number of short stories, many of which were "concerned with the grotesque and with the terrible—such tales as might well be read 'round the fire' upon a winter's night." These were eventually collected as *Round the Fire Stories*, and the accumulation of sealed rooms, rotting corpses, and severed hands showed that Conan Doyle's interest in Edgar Allan Poe had not faded.

Although *The Tragedy of the Korosko* appeared soon after the move to Hindhead, Conan Doyle's novels were no longer appearing at quite so furious a clip. *Uncle Bernac,* slightly revised from its magazine serialization, had appeared earlier in 1897, and Conan Doyle had complained during the writing that "I never seem to be quite in the key." Many of the critics agreed with him, especially Max Beerbohm, who gave him another drubbing in *The Saturday Review*. "In his reconstruction of Napoleon," Beerbohm wrote, "he has omitted nothing, except Napoleon." This was not entirely justified; much of the novel's weakness could be traced to the fact that Napoleon, in an incidental role, seemed so much more vivid than Conan Doyle's own characters—as even Beerbohm acknowledged. The criticism irritated Conan Doyle, but this time he allowed it to pass unchallenged.

He was less restrained when his next book, *A Duet with an Occasional Chorus,* came under attack after its publication in March 1899. Conan Doyle discovered that many of the negative reviews were the work of a single critic, William Robertson Nicoll, who wrote under various pseudonyms for several publications. Conan Doyle was outraged, and wrote a hotly worded letter to the *Daily Chronicle* to address this "growing scandal." To the uninitiated, he argued, it would seem that a particular book had drawn a chorus of praise or blame, when in fact the entire battery of reviews might be traced to one person. "If all these strings are pulled simultaneously a prodigious consensus of opinion seems to exist," he wrote. "And yet there is only one pair of hands to pull them." Conan Doyle expressed himself with such vehemence, he later admitted, that Nicoll did not know whether to answer "in print or in the law courts." The matter blew over in time, and Conan Doyle came to consider Nicoll a friend.

It is understandable that Conan Doyle should have felt protective of *A Duet*, as the novel came to be known. This "domestic study," as he called it, traced the fortunes of Frank Crosse and his courtship of Maude Selby, who "had come like an angel of light across the shadowed path of his life." Conan Doyle gave a warm and affectionate account of their romance and early marriage—"never more to part," he declared, rather artlessly in the circumstances, "until the coffin-lid closed over one or the other."

A Duet, the author contended, was "an attempt at quite a different form of literature—a picture in still life, as it were. It was partly imaginative and partly founded upon early experiences of my own and of friends." One wishes he had been more specific as to where experience left off and imagination began. In every way, *A Duet* is both the most revealing and confounding book of his career. Many of its incidents, such as the visits of the young lovers to Samuel Pepys' grave and the home of Thomas Carlyle, are clearly drawn from his own experiences. Others may well have been. On a tour of Westminster Abbey, "the most august and tremendous monument that ever a nation owned," Frank gives a passionate tribute to "our kings and our warriors and our thinkers and our poets" that might easily have been spoken by Conan Doyle himself.

Not all of the book's episodes are so innocuous. In the preface to a later edition, Conan Doyle wrote that his aim had been "in an age of pessimism, to draw marriage as it may be, and as it often is, beautiful and yet simple, the commonplaces of life being all tinged, and softened, and glorified by the light of love. No startling adventures are here, for they do not come to such people as I have portrayed, nor would I have them sparkling and talking aphorisms, for this also is unusual in suburban villas."

Yet, taken on those terms, *A Duet* does present one very startling adventure, and it was this that drew fire from the multifaceted William Robertson Nicoll. Soon after his marriage, Frank Crosse receives a letter from a woman named Violet Wright, with whom he has enjoyed a "prematrimonial experience." Threatening a confrontation with his new wife, Miss Wright summons him to "our old private room" at an establishment called Mariani's.

"Mariani's is a quiet restaurant," Conan Doyle explained, "famous for its *lachryma christi spumante*, and situated in the network of sombre streets between Drury Lane and Covent Garden. The fact of its being in a by-street was not unfavourable to its particular class of business. Its customers were very free from the modern vice of self-advertisement, and would even take some trouble to avoid publicity. Nor were they gregarious or luxurious in their tastes. A small, simple apartment was usually more to their taste than a crowded salon, and they were even prepared to pay a higher sum for it."

This was heady material for 1899, even though the encounter between Frank and Violet is entirely chaste. Conan Doyle is careful to say that the very thought of infidelity nauseated Frank, and shows him to be steadfast in his resistance to Violet's charms:

> "Frankie, you have not kissed me yet."
>
> She turned her smiling face upwards and sideways, and for an instant he leaned forward towards it. But he had himself in hand again in a moment. It gave him confidence to find how quickly and completely he could do it. With a laugh, still holding her two hands, he pushed her back into the chair by the table.
>
> "There's a good girl!" said he. "Now we'll have some tea, and I'll give you a small lecture while we do so."
>
> "You are a nice one to give lectures."
>
> "Oh, there's no such preacher as a converted sinner."
>
> "You really are converted then?"
>
> "Rather. Two lumps, if I remember right."

Few of today's readers will require smelling salts to get through this passage, but with this setting and situation, Conan Doyle was testing the limits of Victorian propriety. Only one year later, publication of Theodore Dreiser's *Sister Carrie* would be halted and delayed by twelve years because of the novel's frank portrait of a "fallen" woman. Conan Doyle's treatment of the subject seems naive in comparison, but it was enough to excite charges of needless and offensive prurience. In subsequent editions, Conan Doyle revisited the episode and "softened down some crudities." Again, these crudities emerge today as winningly quaint; there is some minor business about a cigarette to help Frank control his passions, and some ungentlemanly outbursts—"Oh, bother the tea!" he shouts at one stage, and then urges Violet to "go to the devil!"

Though he did some minor tinkering, Conan Doyle insisted that the scene be allowed to stand. "I did not set out to write a fairy tale," he declared, "but to draw a living couple with all the weaknesses, temptations, and sorrows which might come to test their characters and to overshadow their lives. Frank is no ideal hero, but an everyday youth no better than his fellows." Conan Doyle's insistence on this point bears examination, and naturally raises the question of whether he had drawn on experiences of his own in establishments such as Mariani's. Subsequent events render this unlikely, and though his familiarity with the setting is provocative, throughout his career he also demonstrated a familiarity with opium dens, the court of Louis XIV, and the lost city of Atlantis. There is no reason to assume that he drew on firsthand experience in any of these instances.

Even so, *A Duet* would always stand apart from his other books. Conan Doyle turned down large sums for the serial rights, in the belief that it would be diminished in that form, and bitterly regretted that the publisher, Grant Richards, took a heavy loss on the novel. He found some consolation in letters of praise from Swinburne and H. G. Wells, but the critical consensus—even apart from William Robertson Nicoll—was overwhelming. One reviewer found the novel "quite unworthy of Mr. Conan Doyle's reputation" and "a rather daring experiment on the docility of his public." Even Andrew Lang, who had been instrumental in the publication of *Micah Clarke*, could not find a kind word for *A Duet*. "We cannot pretend to be interested in Frank and Maude," he wrote a few years later. "It may be a vulgar taste, but we decidedly prefer the adventures of Dr. Watson with Sherlock Holmes."

Conan Doyle took these criticisms very much to heart. He could acknowledge, he told his mother, that he had failed with *The Mystery of Cloomber, The Firm of Girdlestone,* and even the more recent *Uncle Bernac,* but in his "innermost soul" he could not dismiss *A Duet* so easily. He believed that the effect of the book had less to do with a collection of incidents than with a general sensibility. In the preface to a later edition he wrote, "It is atmosphere—the subtle, indefinable, golden-tinted atmosphere of love—which I have wished to reproduce. . . . It is on these points that I have succeeded or failed, for I have attempted no other."

In light of this remark, *A Duet* may be seen as a mood piece, a love letter of sorts. In that spirit, one begins to understand the depth of his feeling for it, especially when he had the manuscript specially bound as a present for the woman who, as he told his mother, "kept my soul and my emotions alive."

Unfortunately, that woman was not his wife.

15

Thoughts He Dare Not Say

I had an intuition that I should marry you from the first day that I saw you, and yet it did not seem probable. But deep down in my soul I knew that I should marry you.

—FRANK CROSSE IN *A DUET WITH AN OCCASIONAL CHORUS*

Conan Doyle met Jean Leckie on March 15, 1897. For the rest of his life, he would always mark the anniversary by presenting her with a single white flower—a snowdrop.

The circumstances of their meeting are not known, and Conan Doyle kept the details deliberately vague. In his autobiography, Jean Leckie would not be mentioned until the chronicle had moved ahead another ten years, and she was then presented as "the younger daughter of a Blackheath family whom I had known for years, and who was a dear friend of my mother and sister." By that time it was certainly true that the Leckies and the Doyles had become intimates, but this was the result, rather than the cause, of the relationship between Conan Doyle and Jean.

"There are some things which one feels too intimately to be able to express," he declared, gracefully sidestepping any closer examination of the issue. The reason for his ambiguity is clear enough. The early years of his romance with Jean Leckie had been the most wrenching period of his life. He claimed to have fallen in love with Jean at the moment he saw her, but at the time, he was still very much a married man. His rigid sense of honor, the code of chivalry that guided his life and shaped his fiction, now faced its sternest test. "I have asked myself," said the beautiful young heroine of *The White Company*, "if the best which can be done with virtue is to shut it within high walls as though it were some savage creature." No doubt there were times in those years when Conan Doyle asked himself the same thing.

By all accounts, Jean Leckie was a remarkable woman. The daughter of well-to-do Scottish parents, she had a striking appearance, with curly dark-blond hair and bright green eyes. Quick-witted and widely read, she was also a skilled horsewoman and a trained mezzo-soprano. Even her lineage seemed calculated to appeal to Conan Doyle; her family claimed descent from the Scottish hero Rob Roy. At the time of their meeting, she was twenty-four years old. Conan Doyle was thirty-seven.

Three and a half years had passed since the diagnosis of Louisa's tuberculosis, and her condition precluded any sexual relations with her husband. For all its surface of rectitude, Victorian society offered any number of ways in which Conan Doyle might have gratified his impulses, had he chosen to do so. The Violet Wright episode in *A Duet* demonstrates that he was familiar with at least one of his options, but Conan Doyle held himself to a different standard. He had pledged himself to Louisa, as he wrote in *A Duet*, "until the coffin-lid closed over one or the other." In his view, her illness changed nothing, and he remained determined to honor his marriage vows. There is every reason to suppose that Conan Doyle remained celibate for the rest of Louisa's life.

The circumstances had been difficult enough up to this point. Now, having met and fallen in love with Jean, the conflict between duty and desire became a torment. From the first, he told Jean that he would not divorce Louisa and would not be unfaithful to her. Jean accepted this, and in the early stages they were careful not to spend too much time together, possibly for fear of yielding to temptation. "I fight hard against all the powers of darkness" he declared, "and I win."

Conan Doyle felt no hesitation in discussing his dilemma with the Ma'am. It may seem odd that a man in his situation should take the problem to his mother, but Conan Doyle took all of his problems to his mother. There were few decisions in his life—his marriage to Louisa, his career changes, the death of Sherlock Holmes—that did not first get an airing in Masongill. He felt no shame in having fallen in love with Jean and was confident that his mother would approve of the virtuous path he had chosen. Moreover, Mary Doyle's own marriage had presented a set of challenges that were not entirely dissimilar. Whatever her relationship with Bryan Waller may have been, her marriage to Charles Doyle had been sorely tested through the long years he spent in custodial care.

Very early, Conan Doyle arranged to introduce Jean to his mother. Mary Doyle not only gave her approval but even went so far as to chaperone the couple on visits to the country. As a sign of the Ma'am's favor, Jean was given a family heirloom, a bracelet that had belonged to Conan Doyle's Aunt Annette. Gradually, other members of the family were informed of the relationship. By the end of 1899, Conan Doyle's sister Lottie had become friendly with Jean. In a letter to his brother Innes, Conan Doyle gave assurances that Touie—as Louisa was still known—would be shielded from any pain or dishonor. "She is as dear to me as ever," he wrote, "but, as I said, there is a large side of my life which was unoccupied but is no longer so."

Also by the end of 1899, Jean's parents and her brother Patrick had also been apprised of the situation. One gathers that they gave their approval; Conan Doyle received a pearl and diamond stud-pin from the Leckies as a Christmas present. Incredibly, even Mrs. Hawkins, Louisa's mother, seems to have been aware of the arrangement and condoned her son-in-law's behavior.

Amid all these secret meetings and expressions of goodwill, Louisa, whose failing health kept her at home much of the time, appears to have remained oblivious. Conan Doyle intended that she should never know of his divided affections. He may not have loved her with the same intensity of his feelings for Jean, but their marriage had been happy. "I have nothing but affection and respect for Touie," he wrote to his mother. "I have never in my whole married life had one cross word with her, nor will I ever cause her any pain." One might well debate whether this course of action was truly in his wife's best interests, but there is no doubt that Conan Doyle felt he was doing his best for all concerned.

As for cross words, his children might have remembered matters differently. Conan Doyle loved his children and had been an attentive, affectionate father when he happened to be at home. In this period, however, as the strain of his suppressed desires took its toll, he became distracted and quick-tempered. For much of their lives, Kingsley and Mary had been cared for by relatives. Now, even in the secure atmosphere of Undershaw, their father remained aloof. His work and busy social calendar took him away often. When he returned, he behaved in a gruff and distracted manner. His moodiness became evident in his work habits. In Southsea and South Norwood, he could write in a crowded room. Now, when he entered his study at Undershaw, the children were instructed to tiptoe past the door. If he became a brusque, occasionally frightening figure to his children in these days, Conan Doyle was no different from many men of his time. For Kingsley and Mary, however, who had known great warmth and affection in happier times, the change would have been unsettling.

One of the books he wrote in the study at Undershaw, while his children crept past the door, was *A Duet with an Occasional Chorus*. In light of his inner turmoil, this novel of an idyllic courtship and marriage—which drew so heavily on his early years with Louisa—seems a curious choice of subject. Their duet, as he was painfully aware, had now become a trio. Even so, the novel may have presented an opportunity to express himself to both partners. On the one hand, *A Duet* can be seen as a tender and fitting tribute to his dying wife, who had stood by him through the early years of struggle. At the same time, his decision to present the manuscript to Jean suggests that its pages contained a message for her as well. Possibly Conan Doyle wished to give Jean a taste of a more conventional courtship, one he might have offered if matters had stood differently. Perhaps the novel allowed him to set out, in an acceptable way, his hopes for the future happiness they might enjoy. By doing so in fiction, he did not appear to be longing for Louisa's death.

There remains, however, the problem of the scandalous scene at Mariani's establishment for discreet couples. Conan Doyle had made his feelings on extramarital sex very plain to Jean, and his description of the "dingy little room" at Mariani's suggests that he had not revised his view. If Frank's confrontation with Violet did not reflect actual experience, however, it conveyed something to Jean that Conan Doyle wished her to know—that he was a man of honor, a man in control of his urges, but also a man who had lived a full life. He put a great deal of himself into the description of Frank, who had inherited an artistic temperament and literary ambition from his mother. "Strength, virility, emotional force, power of deep feeling—these are traits which have to be paid for," Conan Doyle wrote. "There was sometimes just a touch of the savage, or at least there were indications of the possibility of a touch of the savage, in Frank Crosse. His intense love of the open air and of physical exercise was a sign of it. He left upon women the impression, not altogether unwelcome, that there were unexplored recesses of his nature to which the most intimate of them had never penetrated. In those dark corners of the spirit either a saint or a sinner might be lurking, and there was a pleasurable excitement in peering into them, and wondering which it was. No woman ever found him dull."

If to some extent *A Duet* had been an exercise in make-believe for Jean, it also carried a warning: Conan Doyle had his demons. He expressed further concern over these "dark corners of the spirit" in a poem he composed during this period. Conan Doyle had been experimenting with poetry for many years, and his first collection of verse, *Songs of Action,* appeared in 1898. Most of his poems were narrative ballads of fighting men and sporting events, and many revealed the author's careful study of Rudyard Kipling, his former golfing companion. One of Conan Doyle's better efforts, a comic poem entitled "Bendy's Sermon," told the story of a prizefighter-turned-preacher named Bendigo, whose fighting instincts return when hecklers disrupt a sermon: "He vaulted from the pulpit like a tiger from a den / They say it was a lovely sight to see him floor his men . . . Platt was standin' on his back and lookin' at his toes, / Solly Jones of Perry Bar was feelin' for his nose, / Connor of the Bull

Ring had all that he could do / Rakin' for his ivories that lay about the pew."

Poems of this sort suggest that Conan Doyle's tastes ran toward the likes of Ernest Lawrence Thayer, whose "Casey at the Bat" appeared a few years earlier. Nevertheless, while gathering up a collection of poems with titles such as "Corporal Dick's Promotion" and "The Farnshire Cup," Conan Doyle slipped in a deeply personal, highly introspective effort called "The Inner Room." In it, he conceived of his own personality as a "motley company" of conflicting impulses, each represented by a different character—a soldier, a priest, an agnostic—and all of them struggling for control of his soul. The soldier is "Bluff and keen; / Single-minded, heavy-fisted, / Rude of mien." The priest is "schism-whole" and "loves the censer-reek / And organ-roll." Trailing behind the priest is a skeptical "younger brother" who is "Peering forwards anxious-eyed, / Since he learned to doubt his guide."

Sitting quietly among these figures is "a stark-faced fellow, / Beetle-browed, / Whose black soul shrinks away / From a lawyer-ridden day, / And has thoughts he dare not say / Half avowed." This is quite possibly the most personal and revealing line Conan Doyle ever wrote. If the stark-faced fellow represents Conan Doyle's own guilty conscience, we are left to wonder what the "lawyer-ridden" event might be, and why it has caused him such anxiety. Can it be that in his darkest moments he considered divorcing Louisa, and perhaps removing her to some distant health resort, leaving him free to pursue a new life with Jean? Within ten years he would join England's Divorce Law Reform Union. His concern over the issue, it must be said, rested with obtaining equal divorce rights for women, since the current system gave an unfair bias toward the husband. Conan Doyle's convictions on this issue probably owed more to his mother's unhappy circumstances than his own. Even so, his active role in the Union—he would serve ten years as its president—demonstrates that the notion of divorce was not repellent to him. It is possible, then, that in fleeting moments he contemplated a divorce from Louisa, even if such thoughts were only "half avowed."

If so, the "stark-faced" figure was only one of the many warring figures in Conan Doyle's "Inner Room." The poem concludes:

If the stark-faced fellow win,
  All is o'er!
If the priest should gain his will,
  I doubt no more!
But if each shall have his day,
I shall swing and I shall sway
In the same old weary way
  As before.

Soon enough, this "motley company" would merge into a single figure, one that combined the unconventional thoughts of the agnostic, the crusading zeal of the soldier, and the unshakable faith of the priest. Conan Doyle had long since started down the path toward psychic belief, but he had not yet made the transition from "anxious-eyed" skeptic to "schism-whole" believer. Once he had accepted this "new revelation," as he would call it, his doubts and longings would merge into a spiritualist system of belief, and the voices of the inner room would fall silent. "There are strange red depths in the soul of the most commonplace man," he was to write in *The Lost World*. Only his absolute conviction in the "serenity of psychic knowledge" would quiet those rumblings once and for all. In the words of his poem, he would "doubt no more."

For the time being, however, Conan Doyle continued in the "same old weary way" to struggle with his internal conflicts. He did not bear his burdens cheerfully. His temper flared often. He took offense easily, and could be curt with associates. Friends noticed that he appeared stiff in manner and bearing. "I have lived for six years in a sick room," he told his mother, "and, oh, how weary of it I am: Dear Touie: It has tried me more than her—she never dreams of it and I am very glad."

Desperate for distraction, Conan Doyle seized on any activity that might take him away from home for a day or two. He spent time at the Reform Club in London, accepted lecturing invitations, and set off on numerous sporting junkets. Sometimes he stayed away for longer periods. He traveled through Italy with his brother-in-law, Willie Hornung, in the spring of 1898, meeting up with H. G. Wells and his wife. Wells, whose most recent novels included *The Time*

Machine, *The Invisible Man*, and *The Island of Dr. Moreau*, had come to Siena to visit George Gissing, the author of *New Grub Street*. The four writers spent several weeks together.

In the fall of 1899, the novelist Grant Allen, who had become a good friend in Hindhead, fell fatally ill. He called Conan Doyle to his bedside to ask if he would complete his latest detective novel, *Hilda Wade,* which had already begun serialization in *The Strand*. Conan Doyle was glad to be able to relieve his friend's anxiety, though he felt his contributions were "pretty bad."

Some of his activities were probably suggested by thoughts of Jean. She loved horses, but Conan Doyle had never been too adept a rider. At Undershaw, where he kept a stable of six horses, he sharpened his skills and joined a local foxhunt. Soon enough, he lost his taste for blood sports, fearing that they "blunt our better feelings." His foray into the world of music, another of Jean's passions, was also mercifully short-lived. As a student in Feldkirch, he had played the tuba. Now, having fallen in love with a trained opera singer, he took up the banjo.

Stranger still, within months of meeting Jean, Conan Doyle's thoughts drifted back toward Sherlock Holmes. It had been four years since the unfortunate incident at Reichenbach, and in that time Conan Doyle had shown no inclination to revive his famous detective. Only one year earlier, at a dinner in his honor, Conan Doyle repeated his assertion that the death of Holmes had been "justifiable homicide."

"For a man who has no particular natural astuteness to spend his days in inventing problems and building up chains of inductive reasoning is a trying occupation," he told his audience. "Besides, it is better not to rely too much upon the patience of the public, and when one has written twenty-six stories about one man, one feels that it is time to put it out of one's power to transgress any further." In America, he had made the point even more forcefully. "The strain was something I could not endure any longer," he told a reporter in Rochester. "Of course had I continued I could have coined money, for the stories were the most remunerative I have written; but as regards literature, they would have been mere trash."

Now, in his study at Undershaw, Conan Doyle edged toward a

compromise. Writing a play about Sherlock Holmes, rather than a new series of stories, might bring him the rewards without the compromise to his literary principles. There are many reasons why Conan Doyle might have allowed himself this concession. The construction of Undershaw had been costlier than expected and a quick success with Sherlock Holmes would repair the damage to his bank balance. His recent books had sold respectably, but not in the huge numbers of his Holmes collections. He may also have wished, in some sense, to puff himself up a bit for Jean, who had not known him during the heady first days of *The Strand*.

In any event, Conan Doyle made it clear that the play would simply be a curtain call of sorts for Sherlock Holmes, and not a return from the grave. The idea of playing Holmes soon caught the attention of Herbert Beerbohm Tree, whose fame as an actor and manager was second only to that of Henry Irving. Tree, who had recently scored a major hit as Svengali in a stage version of *Trilby*, came down to Undershaw to hear an early version of the play. The actor evidently liked what he heard. He not only wanted to play Holmes, but also Professor Moriarty, who had a large role in the production. With all appropriate deference, Conan Doyle pointed out that this idea, while interesting, might prove impractical, as Holmes and Moriarty shared the stage for much of the play. Undaunted, Tree declared that he had a solution—he would play Holmes in a beard. Puzzled, Conan Doyle withdrew to reconsider the matter.

For a time, Conan Doyle decided to bury the play in a desk drawer, where it might have languished forever but for the interest of William Gillette, the distinguished American actor. Born in 1853, Gillette had achieved early fame starring in plays of his own composition, including *Held by the Enemy* and the wildly successful *Secret Service*. Accustomed to working from his own scripts, Gillette saw difficulties in staging Conan Doyle's play as written and asked for permission to revise it. Conan Doyle assented. Eager to do justice to the character, Gillette made a study of the original stories. Holmes, the actor soon realized, was not a conventional matinee idol, and Gillette began to doubt whether the detective would work onstage. Accordingly, Gillette began to imagine the production as a more traditional melodrama, complete with a romantic interest for Holmes.

He made a cautious approach to Conan Doyle, asking if he might allow his detective to get married for the sake of the play. By now Conan Doyle had grown weary of the enterprise. His reply, relayed by telegram, has become a famous piece of Sherlockian lore: "You may marry him, murder him, or do anything you like to him."

In May of 1899, Gillette came to England and traveled to Undershaw to read the play for Conan Doyle. No doubt this was an anxious prospect for Gillette, as his script had almost completely erased Conan Doyle's original effort. By one account, Conan Doyle listened intently to the reading, pondered it for a moment, and then gave a genial benediction: "It's good to see the old chap again."

In truth, Gillette's Sherlock Holmes had little more than a nodding acquaintance with Conan Doyle's creation. Though the play drew on elements of "A Scandal in Bohemia" and "The Final Problem," Gillette shrewdly tailored the character to suit his own talents. His Sherlock Holmes, in keeping with the demands of melodrama, emerged as a man who would keep his head when trapped in a gas chamber but could also play romantic scenes with the imperiled heroine, Miss Alice Faulkner. To this day, Holmes purists writhe in agony at Gillette's proclamation of love for his client: "Your powers of observation are somewhat remarkable, Miss Faulkner—and your deduction is quite correct! I suppose—indeed I know—that I love you."

Gillette may have taken liberties, but he created a lasting entertainment. In all, the actor would play the detective more than thirteen hundred times onstage, along with various radio adaptations and a 1916 movie. Gillette became the embodiment of Sherlock Holmes for a generation of theatergoers. This was especially true in America, where the artist Frederick Dorr Steele, who illustrated many of the later tales, drew on a likeness of the actor. Many of Gillette's inventions and mannerisms were absorbed into the Holmes mythology. He may have been the first to utter the words "Elementary, my dear Watson," though the line does not appear in any published version of the script—nor in any story by Conan Doyle. It was Gillette who gave a name, "Billy," to the Baker Street page boy, a convenience later adopted by Conan Doyle himself.

Legend holds that Gillette also introduced the familiar curved-stem calabash pipe, which was to become such a familiar totem. The actor was himself a dedicated pipe smoker and relished the opportunity to smoke onstage. According to received wisdom, Gillette settled on the calabash because its shape and balance allowed him to "talk around" the pipe. Actually, there is no evidence that Gillette ever used a calabash, and the pipe's weight would have made it an unwieldy stage prop. Gillette seems to have favored a lighter, bent-stem briar. It has recently been suggested, in the pages of *The Baker Street Journal*, that the famed calabash may originally have come to light as an oversized comedy prop. In a handful of comedy shorts from the 1930s and 1940s, calabashes are found in the hands of Holmes impersonators who did not share Gillette's reverence for the character—such as Abbott and Costello, Robert Woolsey, and the Three Stooges.

With or without a calabash, the role of Sherlock Holmes would be a fixture of Gillette's repertoire for thirty years. In that time, he and Conan Doyle would become firm friends, which occasionally proved useful for the American actor. During World War I, one of Gillette's stage props for *Secret Service*—a map of the British embassy in Paris—led to his arrest in London as a spy. He put the police in touch with Conan Doyle to vouch for his story. Later still, when Gillette came out of semiretirement for a farewell tour of *Sherlock Holmes*, Conan Doyle wrote an open letter to celebrate the occasion. "That this return should be in *Sherlock Holmes* is of course a source of personal gratification," Conan Doyle wrote, "my only complaint being that you make the poor hero of the anaemic printed page a very limp object as compared with the glamour of your own personality which you infuse into his stage presentment."

Gillette's glamour was apparently lost on the early critics of the play. *Sherlock Holmes* did not reach Britain until September 1901, having spent more than a year touring the United States. The opening night at the Lyceum, where *A Story of Waterloo* had premiered six years earlier, was marred by Gillette's failure to make himself heard in the far reaches of the house. At the conclusion, loud expressions of discontent issued from the balcony, drawing a reproachful curtain speech from the actor. The incident probably contributed to the play's lukewarm reviews. One critic described Gillette's performance as "a mere burlesque" of Holmes, while another dismissed the play as "nothing more than a crude and commonplace, though exciting, melodrama." Others found the plot predictable. Professor Moriarty, wrote the critic from the *Times*, should have known better than to snatch up a revolver that Holmes had casually abandoned: "If he had ever seen a melodrama, he would have known that the cartridges had been withdrawn." The boisterous element in the balcony, the writer went on to suggest, may well have been in the professor's employ.

Despite the critical indifference, Gillette's first season was a galloping success. He played eight months at the Lyceum, and by the time he came off, four touring companies were playing around the country.

Conan Doyle was gratified by the play's popularity, but he had little to do with the production. As the nineteenth century drew to a close, his thoughts turned to the mounting tensions in South Africa, where Britain would soon be fighting a costly war against the Boers, the Dutch settlers whom Conan Doyle regarded as "the most formidable antagonist who ever crossed the path of Imperial Britain."

"Our military history has largely consisted in our conflicts with France," he wrote, "but Napoleon and all his veterans have never treated us so roughly as these hard-bitten farmers with their ancient theology and their inconveniently modern rifles."

This time, Conan Doyle would manage to get himself into the thick of it.

16

The Helpful Mud Bath

If you want to write good copy you must be where the things are.

—EDWARD MALONE IN *THE LOST WORLD*

In December of 1899, Conan Doyle announced to his startled family that he wished to join the army and fight the Boers. This proved more difficult than he imagined. When three sets of enlistment forms drew no response, he went to a recruitment center in Hounslow and waited patiently to enlist in the Middlesex Yeomanry. As fate would have it, the colonel who interviewed him was perhaps the only man in Britain who had never heard of him. Running a critical eye over the beefy, forty-year-old candidate, the colonel inquired as to whether Conan Doyle had any military experience. On his forms, Conan Doyle had exaggerated slightly when describing his experiences with the army in Egypt. "Two white lies are permitted to a gentleman," he remarked later, "to screen a woman, or to get into a fight when the fight is a rightful one. So I trust I may be forgiven."

The question of whether this fight was a rightful one has troubled historians for a century. The Boer War, also known as the South African War, pitted Great Britain against the allied governments of the South African Republic (also known as the Transvaal) and the Orange Free State. The Boers, European settlers of mainly Dutch extraction, occupied both republics, and though both were nominally independent, they remained under British political control.

The growing trade in gold and diamonds had brought an influx of British colonists, prompting Boer president Paul Kruger to levy punitive taxes. Protests from Britain aggravated the situation, and soon Kruger demanded that the British leave South Africa altogether. Joseph Chamberlain, then the British secretary of state for the colonies, was equally determined that they should remain. Kruger issued an ultimatum in October 1899, and war was declared soon afterward.

With their vastly superior numbers, the British forces did not expect much opposition, but the Boers proved to be, in Conan Doyle's phrase, "one of the most rugged, virile, unconquerable races ever seen upon earth." Virility aside, the Boers had the advantage of modern weaponry and highly mobile troops. The British soldiers, by contrast, were poorly equipped and had no experience of the harsh African conditions. While the Boers made use of such modern innovations as concealed trenches and barbed wire, British tactics had not changed appreciably since Waterloo.

The disparity took an immediate toll. In mid-December, the British forces lost three major battles. As Lord Roberts and Lord Kitchener were dispatched to relieve the British commander-in-chief, the call went out for volunteers. Conan Doyle had been among those urging able-bodied men to step forward. "The suggestion comes from many quarters that more colonials should be sent to the seat of war," he wrote in a letter to the *Times* of London. "But how can we in honour permit our colonial fellow-citizens to fill the gap when none of our own civilians have gone to the front?"

Having stated this position publicly, Conan Doyle felt a duty to set an example. He presented himself at Hounslow, expecting to be accepted as a private in "the greatest army which ever at any time of the world's history has crossed an ocean."

His mother was not quite so swept up in the spirit of adventure. "How dare you!" she wrote upon learning of his plans. "What do you mean by it? Why, your very height and breadth would make you a simple and sure target!" She went on to remind him of his obligations at home, and spoke of the "pleasure and solace" his writings brought to his readers. "There are hundreds of thousands who can fight for *one* who can make a Sherlock Holmes or a Waterloo," she continued. "For God's sake listen to me; even at your age . . . I am coming down if you leave me in uncertainty. This is altogether too dreadful."

Mary Doyle's reaction is not surprising. Her younger son Innes was already in the army, and would go to South Africa if called. Moreover, she did not share her older son's confidence in the justice of the cause. In her view, the war was nothing more than a scramble for gold.

The Ma'am had all but threatened to box Conan Doyle's ears, but he would not be swayed. He informed his mother that he "rather felt it was his duty" to volunteer. "I learned patriotism from my mother," he told her, "so you must not blame me." Whatever his value as a soldier, he went on to say, he felt sure he could serve his country as a role model. "What I feel is that I have perhaps the strongest influence over young men, especially young athletic sporting men, of any one in England, (bar Kipling). That being so, it is really important that I should give them a lead."

Certainly Conan Doyle believed every word of what he told his mother, but his motives were not entirely geared toward Britain's young men. At forty, he knew that this would be his last chance to see action on a battlefield. Much of his career had been spent praising the spirit of fighting men, and he drew his own sense of honor from Britain's knights of old. The Boer War would give him a chance to test his steel in combat.

None of this made any impression at the Hounslow recruitment center. Conan Doyle was promptly dismissed amid unkind remarks about his age and weight. Crestfallen, he returned to Undershaw. Soon, however, a fresh opportunity presented itself. A friend named John Langman had arranged to send a fifty-bed hospital unit to South Africa at his own expense. Langman's son Archie, whom Conan Doyle had known in Davos, would go along to manage the outfit. Conan Doyle was offered a spot on the medical staff. He would help to select the personnel and then ship out to South Africa as an army doctor.

Conan Doyle gratefully accepted the post, and offered to pay all expenses for himself and his butler, Cleeve, whom he soon drafted into the expedition. In all, the unit would require a staff of some fifty men, and Conan Doyle spent a week helping to sort through the list of candidates. Langman had chosen his friend Dr. Robert O'Callaghan as chief surgeon for the team. The appointment made Conan Doyle uneasy: O'Callaghan, he remarked, was "in truth an excellent gynaecologist, which is a branch of the profession for which there seemed to be no immediate demand." A pair of "really splendid younger surgeons" named Scharlieb and Gibbs helped to compensate. Army regulations mandated that a military officer also be assigned to the unit. "[T]his proved to be one Major Drury, a most amusing Irishman," Conan Doyle reported. "To leave the service and to 'marry a rich widow with a cough' was, he said, the height of his ambition."

Conan Doyle sailed for Africa on February 28, 1900, aboard the P & O liner *Oriental*. Louisa and the children, meanwhile, had set off for Naples in the interests of her health. The Ma'am, though still angry with her "very naughty son," traveled down to Tilbury to see him off. Jean was also there, having sent flowers to Conan Doyle's cabin, but she remained hidden in the crowds on the dock. It has been suggested that she couldn't bear to say good-bye, but her low profile implies that matters between them may not have been entirely open at this stage.

The transport reached Cape Town three weeks later, on March 21. The new arrivals soon learned that the tide of the fighting had turned: British forces under the command of Roberts had advanced and captured Bloemfontein, the Boer capital of the Orange Free State. Within two weeks, Conan Doyle and the Langman hospital unit were on the scene.

Bloemfontein was a dusty hodgepodge of military tents, tin-roofed houses, and imposing government buildings when Conan Doyle reached it on April 2. Many black Africans, who had for the most part held themselves separate from the fighting, remained in the town, as did a number of Boer civilians who continued in various municipal posts under the British administration. Food and supplies grew scarce as the population swelled; the single-track railway line that served the town strained to cope with the sudden influx of soldiers and the forty tons of hospital supplies that accompanied the Langham unit.

When the equipment arrived, Conan Doyle joined in the backbreaking labor of setting up the hospital in the pavilion of the Bloemfontein Ramblers' Cricket Club. It made an unlikely setting; enormous marquee tents went up on the playing field, with smaller tents on the periphery for the staff. Incongruously, the far end of the pavilion held a stage set for an amateur production of *HMS Pinafore*. Soon enough, its decks would do service as a latrine.

Conan Doyle worked himself to the point of exhaustion unloading the medical packing cases. In a letter to Louisa, he gave a proud description of himself, sunburned and caked with dirt, wearing a pith helmet, breeches, and puttees—leather leggings—and a military-issue undershirt, which was dyed pink to mask any splatters of blood. "You would have smiled if you could have seen me," he wrote.

With the tents and equipment readied, Conan Doyle believed the Langman Hospital was ready to meet any crisis. "Two days later," he wrote, "wagons of sick and wounded began to disgorge at our doors and the real work had begun."

The Langman unit was only one of several hospitals at Bloemfontein, but it soon had more patients than it could handle. The vast majority were victims of disease, rather than combat injury. Roberts had captured the town itself, but the water supply—some twenty miles away—remained in enemy hands. When the Boer commander shut off the pumps, British troops were put on strict rations. Soon enough, the men began looking elsewhere for potable water. Unfortunately, many of them dipped into the nearby Modder River, a cesspool of animal carcasses and debris from a Boer camp upstream. Within days, a full-blown epidemic of enteric, or typhoid fever, ripped through the British forces.

"The outbreak was a terrible one," Conan Doyle wrote. "[W]e lived in the midst of death—and death in its vilest, filthiest form."

The conditions were so horrific that Conan Doyle hesitated to supply much in the way of detail. The debilitating fever of the disease, and its lacerating effect on the bowels, left its victims so weak that only a few had the strength to stagger as far as the latrines. "The rest did the best they could," Conan Doyle said, "and we did the best we could in turn." With every bed filled, dozens of patients had to be laid out on the floor of the ward. Soon the epidemic overwhelmed the hospital's resources, and the "constant pollution" of the disease made it impossible to maintain sanitary conditions. As he moved through the ward, Conan Doyle's boots squelched on the sodden floor. "The worst surgical ward after a battle would be a clean place compared to that pavilion," he wrote.

The epidemic dragged on for a month. "Four weeks may seem a short time in comfort," Conan Doyle remarked, "but it is a very long one under conditions such as those, amid horrible sights and sounds and smells, while a haze of flies spreads over everything, covering your food and trying to force themselves into your mouth—every one of them a focus of disease."

At the height of the contagion, patients died at an appalling rate. "Coffins were out of the question," said Conan Doyle, "and the men were lowered in their brown blankets into shallow graves at the average rate of sixty a day."

Soon, the disease began to take its toll on the hospital staff. Dr. O'Callaghan, the gynecologist, saw that he was overmatched and decamped for London. Major Drury, whom Conan Doyle found to be "rather too Celtic in his methods," sought consolation from alcohol. Scharlieb and Gibbs worked frantically against worsening odds, aided by the timely appearance of a pair of Red Cross nurses. Although Conan Doyle and the rest of the staff had been inoculated against typhoid aboard the *Oriental*, more than a dozen hospital workers fell victim to the disease. Three of them died.

All the while, Conan Doyle stayed at his post, bending to his task with a grim determination. He had come to South Africa for a taste of adventure, hoping to see a bit of action on the battlefield. Instead, he found a disaster beyond all imagining, one that might have tested the nerve of his own epic heroes. His training and his life of comfort had not prepared him for a crisis of this scale. No one would have looked askance if he had followed O'Callaghan back to London. Instead, he set his jaw and did his work. At last, he was doing his bit.

"It was difficult to associate him with the author of Sherlock Holmes," wrote a newspaper artist who visited Bloemfontein at the worst of the epidemic. "He was a doctor pure and simple, an enthusiastic doctor too. I never saw a man throw himself into duty so thoroughly heart-and-soul."

At last, a British force moved to recapture the water pumps from the Boers. Conan Doyle rode along to observe, and spent the night before the battle huddled beneath a wagon, shivering in his thin coat. Although he had once nearly frozen to death in the Arctic, he claimed that this experience left him "colder than I can ever remember being in my life." When morning came, the enemy had retreated and the pumps were easily taken. By now, conditions at Bloemfontein had improved to such an extent that Conan Doyle was able to spend a few days with the troops as they advanced toward Pretoria, the capital of the South Africa Republic.

The experience of traveling with these "gallant lads" meant a great deal to Conan Doyle. For all the horrors of Bloemfontein, he had still not seen any close fighting, and he longed for it. He finally got his wish when the unit came under heavy artillery fire at Vet River. He wrote an account at the time and included it as a chapter in his autobiography, published nearly a quarter of a century later. At times, his account reads like something out of *Biggles in Africa* rather than a sober military chronicle: "Boom! Boom! Boom! Cannon at last! . . . Right between the guns, by George! Two guns invisible for the dust. Good heavens, how many of our gunners are left? Dust settles, and they are all bending and straining and pulling the same as ever." Conan Doyle is often chastised for such writings; his critics charge that he masks the realities of war behind a veneer of rugged sportsmanship and the stiff upper lip. It would be more accurate to say that he wished to celebrate the bravery of the British soldier, just as he had always done in his historical fiction. After Bloemfontein, he had few illusions about war, but he retained his admiration for the "splendid stuff" of the fighting man.

Even here, Conan Doyle could not escape the long shadow of Sherlock Holmes. Moving past a line of soldiers, Conan Doyle paused to examine a New Zealander's bullet wound. "I've read your books," said the injured soldier. On another occasion, he was asked to name his favorite Sherlock Holmes tale. Distracted, the author allowed as how he had always liked the "one about the serpent," though he couldn't remember the title at the moment.

After a week, Conan Doyle headed back to Bloemfontein. "For them the bullets," he wrote, "for us the microbes, and both for the honour of the flag." Returning to camp, he fell ill with some form of fever. He continued with his duties, but complained of something "insidious" in his system. Possibly it was a form of typhoid, as it would be another ten years before his digestion "recovered its tone." Conan Doyle's ribs also took a beating in a staff football match, and he had to go around for some time encased in a plaster corset.

British forces swept Pretoria in early June, and it was thought the war would soon be over. When a relief doctor arrived in Bloemfontein, Conan Doyle decided to ship out. There were "potent influences" drawing him back to London, and foremost of these was his decision to write what he called an "interim" history of the war. He had been taking notes, interviewing commanders and soldiers, and sketching out chapters almost from the moment he arrived in the country. His interest in writing a book led to charges that he went to South Africa "on business principles," while others accused him of abandoning his unit before its work was done. Both charges were unjust; he made no profit from his military service and at the time of his departure the Langman unit was scheduled to be disbanded. "I believe," he wrote to his mother, "that between my history and my work there are few men in South Africa who have worked harder."

Conan Doyle was anxious that his book should be the first history of the war to appear, though he knew that others would soon follow. Before departing, he obtained leave to visit Pretoria, an essential stop if he hoped to have his book ready "before that of my rivals." It could be argued that perspective and accuracy count for more than speed in the writing of history, but Conan Doyle saw himself in the role of a war correspondent sending a dispatch from the front.

In Pretoria, Conan Doyle had an interview with Lord Roberts, the commander of the British forces. Press reports in London were drawing attention to the appalling state of the British field hospitals, and Roberts wanted firsthand information. Conan Doyle had strong feelings on the subject, and would later urge compulsory immunization against typhoid, but with Roberts he took care to emphasize the hard work done by the hospital workers. He later took the same line with a royal commission in London, where his words carried greater weight because of his status as independent volunteer.

Before leaving Pretoria, Conan Doyle visited a Boer prisoner-of-war camp where captured British soldiers had been held only two weeks earlier. At the time of their release, a group of soldiers had been busily using spoons to dig an escape tunnel. Conan Doyle posed for a photograph waist-deep in the tunnel, then mailed copies to his friends with the inscription: "Getting out of a hole, like the British Empire."

In July, Conan Doyle sailed for England aboard the S.S. *Briton*, spending much of the journey writing in his cabin. "I have my history done within four chapters of the end," he wrote to the Ma'am, "unless the war is unduly prolonged." He had no way of knowing that the war would, in fact, be unduly prolonged. The Boers had now turned to guerrilla warfare, which would draw the conflict out for another two years.

In August, Conan Doyle rejoined his family at Undershaw and resumed his normal routine. Part of that routine, at this stage of his life, involved clandestine meetings with Jean Leckie. Within days of his return to England, Conan Doyle invited Jean to come and watch him play in a cricket match at Lord's. Willie Hornung, his brother-in-law, also happened to be in the crowd, and registered surprise at the sight of Conan Doyle walking arm-in-arm with a woman who was not his wife. Apparently Conan Doyle had not fully acquainted his sister Connie with the circumstances of his arrangement with Jean. That evening, he presented himself at their house in Kensington to explain. For the moment, all appeared well. Connie agreed to come to Lord's the following day to lunch with her brother and Jean. Hornung declared himself ready to support Conan Doyle without question.

Their goodwill soon evaporated. The following morning, Conan Doyle received a telegram to the effect that Connie had a toothache and would not be able to meet Jean after all. Conan Doyle, unconvinced by this excuse, went back to Kensington. He found Willie Hornung in a confrontational mood. "I suppose their hearts spoke first and then they were foolish enough to allow their heads to intervene," Conan Doyle wrote to his mother. "Willie's tone was that of an attorney dissecting a case, instead of a brother standing by a brother in need."

In Hornung's view, Conan Doyle had attached too much importance to the fact that his relations with Jean remained platonic. To his way of thinking, it made little difference whether the couple had consummated their affair or not. The mere fact of the relationship—and their lack of discretion in flaunting it at Lord's—constituted an affront to Louisa and a betrayal of Conan Doyle's marriage vows. Struggling to control his temper, Conan Doyle repeated his conviction that so long as his relations with Jean remained chaste, he had brought no dishonor to Louisa. This distinction, for him, represented "the difference between guilt and innocence." Refusing to speak further on "so sacred a matter," Conan Doyle left the house.

Hornung's opinions were not entirely without merit, but Conan Doyle was impervious to all opposing views. He had an obstinate faith in his own judgment—whether it applied to Jean, the Boer War, or, later, the existence of fairies—and would not be second-guessed in any matter so close to his heart. It seemed ridiculous, he told his mother, that Connie and Willie should condemn him when she, his other siblings, and Louisa's mother had all given their blessing. Even if they did disapprove, they owed him their support as the de facto head of the family. "When have I failed in loyalty to any member of my family?" he asked the Ma'am. "And when before have I appealed to them?"

Here Conan Doyle was probably alluding to financial as well as moral support. For years, ever since Sherlock Holmes made him rich, Conan Doyle had handed out money to his family with a free hand. He sent blank checks to his brother Innes so that he could play polo with his fellow officers. When his sister Lottie married Captain Leslie Oldham of the Royal Engineers, Conan Doyle sent money to help them get started. His two youngest sisters, Ida and Dodo, also benefited from their famous brother's generosity.

The Hornungs, too, had received an allowance from Conan Doyle after their marriage, though they would not have needed it after the success of the first Raffles book in 1899. Still, Conan Doyle felt he was due a certain consideration. "I expected the attitude of a friend, and a brother, from William and I got neither," he told his mother. Mary Doyle tried to intervene, but the rift lasted for some time.

There would not have been much time to dwell on it, however, as Conan Doyle was now preparing himself for another of his abrupt changes of direction. Upon leaving South Africa, he had spoken of the "potent influences" that were drawing him back to England. The first of these was his history of the war. The second, it now emerged, was politics. Even before the start of the war there had been press speculation about Conan Doyle as a potential member of Parliament. Now, he recorded, "a political crisis and a general election were coming on, and it was on the cards that I might be a candidate." In fact, both the Conservatives and the Liberals courted him for the October elections. Conan Doyle's fame as an author, coupled with his well-known concern for public issues, made him an attractive prospect for both parties.

The general election of 1900 would come to be known as "The Khaki Election," after the uniforms worn by the British troops in South Africa. Other issues were on the docket, such as Home Rule for Ireland and free trade, but the Boer War dominated the platforms of both parties. The ruling Conservatives favored seeing the war through to its conclusion, while many factions within the Liberal Party opposed the conflict. Under the guidance of Joseph Chamberlain, Conan Doyle decided to stand with the Liberal Unionists, who had forged an alliance with the Conservatives based on their mutual desire to continue the campaign in South Africa.

Looking back on his decision in later years, Conan Doyle admitted that he could think of no good reason why he should have wished to enter Parliament at all. "It certainly was from no burning desire to join that august assembly," he wrote. The stresses of his personal life may have nudged him toward the public arena, but he would not have entered politics simply to get out of the house. He had been troubled for some time by a nagging sense that he had not yet found his mission in life. "Deep in my bones I felt that I was on earth for some big purpose," he wrote, "and it was only by trying that I could tell that the purpose was not political." Being a world-famous author, it appears, had not satisfied this longing. In a letter to his mother, he expressed an urge to test himself in a new forum. "What is to be gained?" he asked. "A full and varied and perhaps useful life. The assurance that come what may I have at least tested my fate, and done my duty as a Citizen."

Party elders offered him several "safe seats" where Conan Doyle would be assured of a victory, but he made up his mind that he wanted a fight. At length it was decided that he would stand in Central Edinburgh, considered the "premier Radical stronghold of Scotland." Although he had spent his boyhood there, Conan Doyle knew that carrying the district would be a difficult feat. "It was no light matter to change the vote of a Scotsman," he allowed, "and many of them would as soon think of changing their religion."

In late September, Conan Doyle went up to Edinburgh and launched into a ten-day marathon of nonstop electioneering. "I was fresh from the scene of war and overflowing with zeal to help the army," he wrote, "so I spared myself in no way. I spoke from barrels in the street or any other pedestal I could find, holding many wayside meetings besides my big meetings in the evening, which were always crowded and uproarious."

He gave as many as ten speeches a day, matching the rigorous pace set by his Liberal Party opponent, a wealthy local publisher named George Mackenzie Brown. A typical day began at dawn with a breakfast speech for brewery workers and ended after midnight with an address for two hundred employees of the local tram line. He shook hands with factory workers and coal miners until his hand turned black with grime. The locals were greatly impressed by the candidate's energy. "Mun," declared one, "the perspiration was just runnin' down the stair."

Conan Doyle adopted a simple strategy. Again and again he stressed that he and Mr. Brown agreed on most of the "social issues," or matters of local concern. They differed strongly, however, on the war in South Africa, so this was the issue on which the electors must cast their votes. "He spoke to them as an Edinburgh man to Edinburgh men," wrote *The Scotsman*, reporting on a speech before several hundred foundry workers. "He was born and bred in the city, and it was a great joy to him to be amongst them again, and it was his proudest ambition to serve his fellow-townsmen in Parliament."

For a man with no political experience whatever, Conan Doyle had fastened upon a solid game plan. He may have presumed too much on his hometown roots, as he had not actually lived in Edinburgh for twenty years, but potential voters turned out in droves to see the local boy who made good. His speeches were direct and easily understood, and he never failed to underline the danger of failing to return the present government to power. It would be a disaster, he told one gathering, to "swop horses in the middle of a stream." He told another group that it would be pointless to focus on trivial local matters at such a time, as that would be "like a man wanting to tidy his sitting-room while his house was on fire."

Not everyone in his audiences agreed with him, and they were not shy about shouting out their views. In Edinburgh, Conan Doyle reported, the "art of heckling has been carried to extremes." The noise level in some of the meeting halls, he said, came to resemble "feeding-time at the Zoo." Conan Doyle quickly learned how to handle himself without getting ruffled. "The heckling of the candidate was carried on with great liveliness," *The Scotsman* reported of one session, "his ready and straight replies being received with loud cheers."

Some of the hecklers took to addressing him as Sherlock Holmes, as in: "Sherlock Holmes! Are ye no' a believer in home rule?" Here, too, Conan Doyle learned to curb his natural irritation. "This title," reported a Glasgow paper, "the doctor acknowledges genially."

As the polling date drew near, Conan Doyle stated that his hecklers had convinced him of one thing—that there was no single local issue of pressing importance to the voters. "The proof of that," *The Scotsman* noted, "lay in the great variety of subjects on which he had been questioned, these subjects ranging from trout fishing to the exact position of the Episcopalians in India." The remark drew laughter from Conan Doyle's supporters, but his indifference to local concerns undoubtedly cost him votes.

As his campaign came to a close, Conan Doyle pulled out all the stops for an appearance before the Edinburgh Literary Institute. Crowds had waited for an hour to hear his address, and police were needed to contain a party of "unenfranchised youths" who threatened to disrupt the proceedings. When the doors finally opened there was such a rush for seats that dozens of people had to stand in the aisles and passageways. Conan Doyle took the stage amid great cheering, quickly turning his remarks toward the war. He painted a vivid portrait of a hopeful South Africa turning toward Edinburgh for deliverance. *The Scotsman* paraphrased his remarks: "This general election meant everything to our Colonists in South Africa, who looked to Edinburgh as the centre of their thoughts, and the heart of the Scottish people. In all the little towns in South Africa the excitement was intense, and crowds gathered in front of the screens on which the election results were displayed. [Conan Doyle] asked them to enable their brethren in South Africa to say on Friday morning, as they looked upon those screens—'Thank God, Edinburgh has gone straight!' " This stirring rhetoric, *The Scotsman* noted, brought "loud and continued cheering" from the assembly.

As the cheers subsided, Conan Doyle played his trump. His hecklers had repeatedly called for Sherlock Holmes; Conan Doyle gave them the next best thing. Dr. Joseph Bell, now sixty-three years old, emerged from the crowd and stood beside his former pupil. Stepping forward, Bell remarked that he had probably known the candidate—"my former dresser"—longer than anyone in the hall. "If Conan Doyle does half as well in Parliament as he did in the Royal Edinburgh Infirmary," Bell declared, "he will make an unforgettable impression on English politics." The crowd gave another thunderous ovation.

On the eve of the election, Conan Doyle had every reason to think he might score an upset victory. He told his mother that he hoped he would carry Central Edinburgh and give a boost to all the other Liberal Unionist candidates. "May there be no contretemps," he added.

Just as the polls opened, there was a contretemps. Overnight, three hundred placards went up across the city that branded Conan Doyle as a "Papist conspirator, a Jesuit emissary, and a Subverter of the

Protestant Faith," whose candidacy constituted an assault on "everything dear to the Scottish heart." Conan Doyle denounced the smear campaign as the work of an "Evangelical fanatic" named Jacob Plimmer, who operated an outfit called the Dumfermline Protestant Defense Organisation. Plimmer, Conan Doyle said, had declared it his "special mission to keep Roman Catholic candidates out of Parliament."

As the voters went to the polls, Conan Doyle tried frantically to repair the damage. He sent a telegram to Plimmer threatening legal action and communicated with his opponent, George Mackenzie Brown, who issued a statement denouncing the "slanderous attack."

The exact nature of this slander only added to the confusion. Plimmer's attack implied a sinister agenda in Conan Doyle's religious background. Conan Doyle told his supporters that he "doubted that anyone in the world held broader views" on the question of religion, and this was quite possibly the literal truth. But the fact remained that he had been raised a Catholic, and educated by Jesuits, which meant that Plimmer's charges could not be denied unequivocally.

Conan Doyle lost the election by 569 votes. It is not certain that Plimmer's attack cost him the victory, though Conan Doyle would always believe it had. In his autobiography, he stated that he "narrowly missed the seat, being beaten by a few hundred votes." Those few hundred votes were not quite as trifling as they might seem, given that the total number of votes cast numbered fewer than 5,500. The final tally gave Mr. Brown a total of 3,028 votes as opposed to Conan Doyle's 2,459. Even so, Conan Doyle had surpassed all expectations, and reduced the previous Liberal majority by 1,500 votes.

By that standard, Conan Doyle's campaign was hailed as a victory for the party, but he felt a great deal of disgust over the devious tactics. He himself had refused to stoop to such a level. "We have a letter which would damn our opponent utterly but I won't let them use it," he had confided some days earlier. "It is below the belt." He wrote an eloquent letter to *The Scotsman* to protest this "very grave public scandal," but in the end he decided against lodging an official appeal.

At his final appearance before his supporters, Conan Doyle

showed himself to be a magnanimous loser. He assured his committee and the members of various Unionist associations that he did not care "a snap of the finger" about being beaten, because the greater cause—the policy in South Africa—had been carried across Britain. When a voice in the crowd shouted that he would have won if not for the "dirty placards," Conan Doyle would not be drawn into recrimination. His opponent was a man of honor, he stated, and that was what mattered. The meeting concluded with a rousing chorus of "For He's a Jolly Good Fellow."

Less than three weeks later, Conan Doyle shared a platform at London's Pall Mall Club with a young man who had just won his first seat in Parliament. Both men, in the words of the club's president, had distinguished themselves in the field of literature before turning their attentions to politics. The two figures made an interesting contrast. Conan Doyle shared some of his experiences in Bloemfontein. The other speaker, twenty-five-year-old Winston Churchill, spoke of the dangers of press censorship. Churchill had gone to South Africa as a war correspondent, only to be captured by the Boers. His daring escape made him a celebrity, and helped sweep him to victory in the October election.

Listening to the young Churchill that evening, Conan Doyle must have reflected on his own recent defeat. "I am 41," he had noted in his journal while deciding whether to enter politics. "So it is now or never." Seeing the promising new M.P. address his audience, Conan Doyle may well have felt twinges of regret over the lost opportunity.

If so, his regrets would have been short-lived. He cared deeply for the issues at stake, but disliked the machinations of party politics, a process he likened to "a mud bath—helpful but messy." He could not see himself tied to one party at the cost of his own independence of thought. As the years passed, he came to regard Jacob Plimmer and his "Dumfermline Protestant Defense Organisation" in an entirely new light:

"Looking back," he declared, "I am inclined to look upon Mr. Plimmer as one of the great benefactors of my life."

17

The Footprints of a Gigantic Hound

"Holmes!" I cried. "Is it really you? Can it indeed be that you are alive?"

—DR. WATSON IN "THE ADVENTURE OF THE EMPTY HOUSE"

In March 1901, while the nation was still in mourning over the death of Queen Victoria in January, Conan Doyle opened a fresh round of negotiations with the editor Greenhough Smith. "I have the idea of a real creeper for *The Strand*," he wrote. "It is full of surprises, breaking naturally into good lengths for serial purposes. There is one stipulation. I must do it with my friend Fletcher Robinson, and his name must appear with mine. I can answer for the yarn being all my own, in my own style without dilution, since your readers like that. But he gave me the central idea and the local colour, and so I feel his name must appear. I shall want my usual £50 per thousand words for all rights if you do business."

Bertram Fletcher Robinson, known as "Bobbles" to his friends, was only twenty-eight years old when Conan Doyle took him on as a collaborator. A promising journalist, Robinson had been a correspondent for the *Daily Express* in South Africa. His friendship with Conan Doyle took hold when they shared a "very joyous voyage" back from South Africa aboard the *Briton*, whose passenger list included many aristocrats and prominent military figures. "Only one cloud marred the serenity of that golden voyage," Conan Doyle would recall. "There was a foreign officer on board, whose name I will not mention, who had been with the Boers and who talked with great indiscretion as to his experiences and opinions."

Chief among these indiscretions was the accusation that the British army, in violation of international law, was using soft-tipped dumdum bullets, which expanded on impact for maximum damage, in the campaign against the Boers. The mere suggestion sent Conan Doyle into a rage, and only Robinson's intervention averted what might have become a "serious incident."

The following March, the two men took a short golfing break in Cromer, on the north coast of Norfolk. Robinson, who had a strong interest in the folklore of his native Devon, kept his friend entertained with an account of a local legend involving a large, ghostly hound. This story, it seemed to Conan Doyle, had strong possibilities. He wrote a note to his mother of his plan to do "a small book" with Robinson, and he mentioned the title: *The Hound of the Baskervilles*.

British folklore has many phantom dogs and hellhounds. The exact origin of the legend that so entranced Conan Doyle has excited much speculation over the years. Because Robinson was a Devonshire man, and *The Hound of the Baskervilles* came to be set in that region, it is widely assumed that Robinson drew on a tale from his own boyhood. Much later, Greenhough Smith would recall that Robinson had taken his inspiration from a Welsh guidebook. Conan Doyle's own boyhood would have had its Scottish "bokey hounds." Whatever the source, the notion of a fiery hound sent Conan Doyle scrambling for his writing materials. Within hours, according to one account, he and Robinson had sketched out a rough plot line.

It is difficult to know what Conan Doyle had in mind when he suggested a collaboration with Robinson. In the past, such partnerships had not been especially fruitful. He would not have been eager to repeat the experience of *Jane Annie*, and a similar exercise with his brother-in-law Willie Hornung had been abandoned after a few days. Clearly Conan Doyle felt obliged to give due credit to his new friend. Though he wanted Robinson to share the billing, Conan Doyle expected to do all of the writing himself. Robinson may have had other ideas.

As work progressed, Robinson invited Conan Doyle to Dartmoor, a bleak expanse of moor in southwest Devon, to soak up atmosphere. They divided their time between Robinson's home and a hotel near the famous Dartmoor prison. "One of the most interesting weeks that I ever spent was with Doyle on Dartmoor," Robinson wrote a few years later. "Dartmoor, the great wilderness of bog and rock that cuts Devonshire at this point, appealed to his imagination. He listened eagerly to my stories of the ghost hounds, of the headless riders and of the devils that lurk in the hollows—legends upon which I had been reared, for my home lay on the borders of the moor."

All the while, the novel continued to take shape. "Mr. Doyle stayed for eight days and nights," recalled Robinson's coachman. "I had to drive him and Bertie about the moors. And I used to watch them in the billiards room in the old house, sometimes they stayed long into the night, writing and talking together." This gentleman, it is worth noting, was named Harry Baskerville. It was his impression that his name inspired the famous title, though this is certainly debatable, since Conan Doyle mentioned the title to his mother before the Dartmoor trip.

With Robinson as guide, Conan Doyle visited such sites as Grimspound, a Bronze Age ruin, and Fox Tor Mire, a treacherous bog. One need not be a "perfect reasoning machine" to trace the parallel to *The Hound*'s Grimpen Mire, where a misstep means "death to man or beast." Conan Doyle may also have passed through a hamlet called Merripit, and heard tales of convicts who escaped from the nearby prison. *The Hound of the Baskervilles* features a Merripit House, home of the Stapletons, and an escaped convict named Selden—the infamous Notting Hill murderer—whose presence on the moor causes much consternation.

Over the years, the extent of Robinson's participation has been a subject of furious debate. Did he merely suggest the idea, as Conan Doyle told Greenhough Smith, or did Robinson actually have an uncredited role in the writing of the book? Harry

Baskerville, Robinson's driver, claimed to have seen the two men "writing and talking together" on more than one occasion. One wonders, however, whether Conan Doyle would have been so quick to share writing duties with a young, relatively unknown journalist. "Bobbles" may have been a charming companion, but Conan Doyle was well aware of his own status and reputation as a novelist. If any doubt existed as to the pecking order of this collaboration, Conan Doyle soon made a decision that effectively decided the matter. As originally conceived, *The Hound of the Baskervilles* did not feature Sherlock Holmes. Soon, however, Conan Doyle realized he would need a strong central figure to hold the plot together. "Why should I invent such a character," he is supposed to have said, "when I have him already in the form of Holmes?"

By every measure, this was a remarkable decision. Holmes had been dead for nearly eight years, and Conan Doyle had often protested that he would remain so. Moreover, the decision to cast *The Hound of the Baskervilles* as a Sherlock Holmes story made Robinson's collaboration a liability, though Conan Doyle may not have realized this at the time. A letter to his mother, written from the hotel in Devonshire, suggests that the partnership had survived the introduction of Holmes. "Robinson and I are exploring the moor over our Sherlock Holmes book," Conan Doyle wrote. "I think it will work out splendidly—indeed I have already done nearly half of it. Holmes is at his very best, and it is a highly dramatic idea—which I owe to Robinson." In Conan Doyle's mind, then, Robinson was mainly an idea man, though *The Hound* was still considered "our" book.

With Sherlock Holmes recalled to duty, *The Hound of the Baskervilles* was soon complete. Conan Doyle's stated reason for reviving the detective—that he needed a strong central character—certainly made sense, but there were other factors at work, just as there had been with his Sherlock Holmes play. Money would have been high on the list of motivations. *A Duet* had been a commercial failure, and Conan Doyle would draw no income from his writings about the Boer War. His other fiction continued to sell respectably, but with Sherlock Holmes, Conan Doyle felt no qualms about doubling his price. "Now it is evident," he told Greenhough Smith, "that this is a very special occasion since as far as I can judge the revival of Holmes would attract a great deal of attention." As for the money, he continued, he felt sure of where he stood with the magazine's editorial board. "Suppose," he asked, "I gave the directors the alternative that it should be without Holmes at my old figure or with Holmes at £100 per thou., which would they choose?" Once again, *The Strand* offered no resistance. They cheerfully accepted Conan Doyle's new terms.

Conan Doyle often sacrificed his profits if a particular subject or cause appealed to him, but he remained a canny businessman. He understood that a new Holmes book would be a major event, and spark a fresh round of sales for *The Adventures* and *The Memoirs of Sherlock Holmes*. Moreover, William Gillette's play had become a sensation in the United States, creating even more interest in the detective. The circumstances had never been better for a new Holmes adventure.

Nevertheless, Conan Doyle did not want to be saddled with the responsibilities of a fully resurrected Sherlock Holmes. As with his play, he made it clear that the detective was still dead. *The Hound of the Baskervilles* was to be presented as a previously untold tale from Dr. Watson's battered tin dispatch box, one that predated the detective's fatal encounter with Professor Moriarty.

The first installment appeared in the August 1901 edition of *The Strand*. On the morning of publication, a long line of expectant readers waited outside the magazine's offices, and bribes were offered for advance copies. To the delight of Greenhough Smith, the magazine's circulation rose by thirty thousand copies.

Almost unnoticed in the excitement was a modest footnote under the first column of text. In negotiating his fee, Conan Doyle had to give way on his demand that Fletcher Robinson share equal billing with him. Instead, alert readers were notified that: "This story owes its inception to my friend, Mr. Fletcher Robinson, who has helped me both in the general plot and in the local details." In the book edition, which he dedicated to Robinson, Conan Doyle expressed much the same sentiment. In subsequent editions, however, the wording changed. By the time the novel appeared in America, it no longer owed its inception to Robinson; instead, Conan Doyle expressed gratitude to his friend for having "suggested the idea." Still later, in an omnibus edition of the longer Holmes stories, Conan Doyle acknowledged that the book "arose from a remark" by Robinson but felt compelled to assure his readers that "the plot and every word of the actual narrative was my own."

These shifting statements, like Dr. Watson's war wound, have provoked much comment over the years. It is difficult to tell whether the confusion arises from Conan Doyle's generosity, or Robinson's actual contributions, or some combination of the two. It appears that Robinson received some payment for his role in the novel's evolution. The writer Archibald Marshall claimed that Conan Doyle signed over one-quarter of the initial profits to Robinson. Marshall wrote: "As I put it to Bobbles at the time, 'Then if you write "How do you do?" Doyle gets six shillings and you get two.' He said he had never been good at vulgar fractions, but it sounded right, and anyhow what he wrote was worth it."

Marshall's statement certainly implies that Robinson shared in the composition. If so, it seems he placed no great value on his efforts. In describing the week he spent with Conan Doyle in Devon, Robinson made no claims to authorship. "He made the journey in my company shortly after I had told him, and he had accepted from me, a plot which eventuated in the *Hound of the Baskervilles,*" Robinson wrote. "How well he turned to account his impressions will be remembered by all readers of the *Hound*."

Indirectly, Robinson gave the impression that he played a more substantial role. He presented Harry Baskerville with an inscribed copy of the cook—"with apologies for using the name." Very occasionally his byline identified him as the "Joint Author" of *The Hound*. After his death, he was quoted as having claimed to have written "most" of the first installment of the book, which included chapters one and two.

If Robinson made such a statement, one can understand Conan Doyle's need to reassert his own claim over the manuscript, even if it meant diminishing his acknowledgment to Robinson. Possibly Robinson sketched out preliminary drafts or source material, and

Arthur Conan Doyle as a young doctor in Southsea, around the time he wrote *A Study in Scarlet*, the first adventure of Sherlock Holmes. “There was a time in my life which I divided among my patients and literature,” he later remarked. “It is hard to say which suffered most.”

Sir Arthur relaxing in the vast billiards room at Windlesham, the home he purchased in 1907. "He was a great, burly, clumsy man," a friend once wrote of him, "with an unwieldy-looking body that was meant for a farm bailiff, with hands like Westphalian hams, and a nervous halting voice whose burrs recalled the banks and braes of Scotland."

"Now, Watson, the fair sex is your department." Conan Doyle's mother, the former Mary Foley (right), would always be known as "the Ma'am" His first wife, Louisa Hawkins (left), succumbed to tuberculosis in 1906. The following year he married Jean Leckie, shown here as she appeared in 1897.

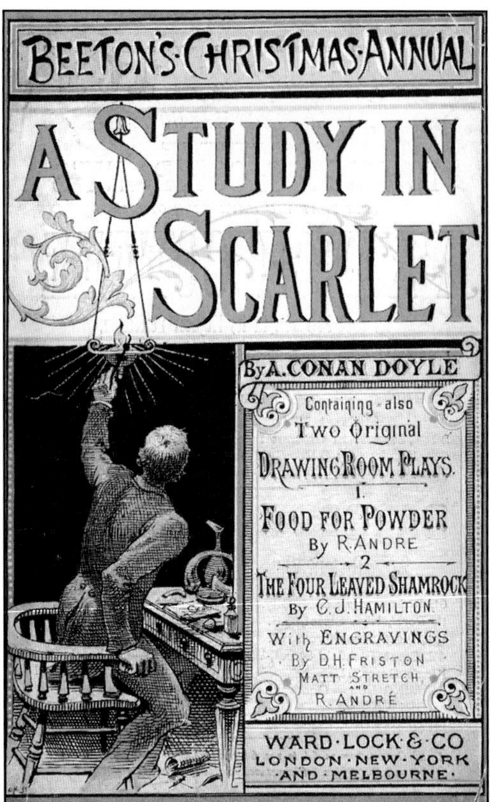

"I came of age in 80 degrees north latitude," said Conan Doyle (third from left) of his seven months aboard a whaling ship. The voyage interrupted his medical studies under Dr. Joseph Bell (above), whose uncanny powers of observation helped to inspire the debut of Sherlock Holmes in *Beeton's Christmas Annual* of 1897.

Conan Doyle mounted an energetic defense of both George Edalji (above), accused in a series of bizarre cattle mutilations, and Oscar Slater (left), wrongfully imprisoned for the murder of a Glasgow spinster. He was equally vigorous in his campaign to promote his novel *The Lost World*, even donning a false beard to impersonate its hero, Professor Challenger.

In later years, Conan Doyle gave himself over to Spiritualism, a subject he considered to be "infinitely the most important thing in the history of the world."

Left, a spirit photograph taken in 1919 reveals a ghostly presence said to be the author's late son, Kingsley.

Below, Francis Griffiths admires a group of fairies in one of the infamous Cottingley photographs, which Conan Doyle championed in *The Coming of the Fairies*.

Enormous crowds gathered to hear the "St. Paul of Spiritualism" on his lecture tours of Australia, New Zealand, and the United States.

In Atlantic City in 1922, the Conan Doyle family was joined by the magician Harry Houdini for a bit of "skylarking" on the beach, moments before an ill-fated séance conducted by Lady Conan Doyle.

"I am amazed, fairly paralyzed at the sight of New York," Conan Doyle said of his second visit to the city in 1914. "It seems as though someone had gone over the city with a watering pot and these stupendous buildings had grown overnight as a result." Seen here on a return trip in 1922, he relished the opportunity of showing his family the sights, in spite of "that peculiar brew of damp heat for which the island city is notorious."

later exaggerated his role as his ego and professional circumstances demanded. If so, no evidence is currently available. The surviving portions of the manuscript are all in Conan Doyle's hand.

If Robinson did, in fact, let it be known that he wrote a portion of the novel, it is curious that he should have laid claim to the first two chapters. Together they form the very model of the classic Baker Street curtain-raiser. When a visitor leaves his walking stick, but not his calling card, Holmes invites Watson to gather whatever clues he can from the stick. Watson, attempting to apply his friend's methods, offers a series of plausible conjectures, building a portrait of a middle-aged country practitioner. Holmes appears greatly impressed. "Some people without possessing genius have a remarkable power of stimulating it," he announces. "I confess, my dear fellow, that I am very much in your debt."

"Has anything escaped me?" Watson asks proudly. "I trust that there is nothing of consequence which I have overlooked?"

The answer leaves him crestfallen: "I am afraid, my dear Watson, that most of your conclusions were erroneous. When I said that you stimulated me I meant, to be frank, that in noting your fallacies I was occasionally guided toward the truth."

Holmes goes on to correct Watson's misapprehensions in glorious detail, concluding that the owner of the stick is actually "a young fellow under thirty, amiable, unambitious, absent-minded, and the possessor of a favourite dog, which I should describe roughly as being larger than a terrier and smaller than a mastiff." Presently, the young and amiable Dr. James Mortimer appears—with his dog in tow—to consult on the recent death of Sir Charles Baskerville, and its possible connection to an ancient Baskerville family curse.

The consultation ends with perhaps the most classic passage in the entire Holmes saga. Dr. Mortimer, having related how the body of Sir Charles came to be discovered, tells Holmes that no one observed any traces on the ground around the body. But Mortimer himself did observe a strange cluster of markings, and it is for this reason that he has come to Baker Street:

> "Footprints?"
> "Footprints."

"A man's or a woman's?"

Dr. Mortimer looked strangely at us for an instant, and his voice sank almost to a whisper as he answered:

"Mr. Holmes, they were the footprints of a gigantic hound!"

If these words were not written by Conan Doyle, at least one biographer will eat his deerstalker hat.

After its serialization in *The Strand*, *The Hound of the Baskervilles* appeared in book form and became a massive best-seller. This success brought new pressure to bear for further Holmes adventures. Within months, Conan Doyle received an offer he could scarcely afford to refuse. Years earlier, the King of Bohemia had offered Sherlock Holmes carte blanche in the matter of the Irene Adler photograph. Now the American magazine *Collier's Weekly* extended virtually the same terms to Conan Doyle. The magazine bid $25,000 for six new Sherlock Holmes stories, or $30,000 for eight, or $45,000 for a series of thirteen. Greenhough Smith sweetened the deal with a promise of a further £100 per thousand words. Even in today's market, this would be a respectable sum. At the time, it was staggering. Bowing to the inevitable, Conan Doyle signaled his acceptance with a laconic postcard: "Very well. A.C.D."

The Ma'am, after pleading so strenuously for the detective's life, now expressed reservations about his return, fearing that Sherlock Holmes could not possibly live up to his own reputation. "I don't think you need have any fears about Sherlock," Conan Doyle assured her. "I am not conscious of any failing powers, and my work is not less conscientious than of old. . . . I have done no short Sherlock Holmes stories for seven or eight years and I don't see why I should not have another go at them."

Initially, at least, Holmes showed no ill effects from his mishap in Switzerland. Conan Doyle still complained of the difficulty in manufacturing suitable plots, but the long layoff had refreshed his ingenuity. His own life, it seems, provided some inspiration, as many of the new stories were to feature secret love affairs. Conan Doyle also had the advantage of discussing—and occasionally borrowing—the plots his brother-in-law Willie Hornung was devising for his popular Raffles series.

In later years, Conan Doyle would be sensitive to charges that the new Holmes stories had not measured up. "The most trenchant criticism of the stories as a series came from a Cornish boatman," he later wrote in an article for *The Strand*, "who remarked to me: 'When Mr. Holmes had that fall he may not have been killed, but he was certainly injured, for he was never the same afterwards.' " Whenever possible, he answered his critics directly. In "The Adventure of the Priory School," Holmes examines the track left by a bicycle's tires and announces which direction the rider had gone. "I had so many remonstrances upon this point," he noted, "varying from pity to anger, that I took out my bicycle and tried." He found that his readers were right and he was wrong. Nevertheless, he remained fond of the later efforts. Whenever he was asked to list his favorite Holmes adventures, he took care to include examples from the post-Reichenbach period.

For the moment, as he sat down to begin the new series, there remained the difficulty of retrieving Sherlock Holmes from his watery grave. Conan Doyle handled this with exceptional panache in "The Adventure of the Empty House." The story opens with the news of the murder of the Honorable Ronald Adair, an event in which "all London was interested, and the fashionable world dismayed." As Dr. Watson contemplates this mystery, he is confronted by an elderly bookseller, armed with a copy of *The Origin of Tree Worship*, who proves to be none other than a disguised Sherlock Holmes. Watson, after a brief fainting spell, demands to know how his friend "succeeded in climbing out of that awful abyss." The answer, though implausible, is no less delightful in its utility. Holmes, we learn, has a useful knowledge of *baritsu*, the Japanese system of wrestling, which enabled him to slip out of Professor Moriarty's grasp and thus avoid falling into the chasm. He then scrambled up a sheer cliff to avoid leaving footprints, and allowed the world to think him dead so that he might avoid the vengeance of Moriarty's henchmen.

The manner in which Holmes occupied himself during this

interval—known to Sherlockians as "The Great Hiatus"—is a source of enduring delight to his admirers: "I travelled for two years in Tibet, therefore, and amused myself by visiting Lhassa, and spending some days with the head lama. You may have read of the remarkable explorations of a Norwegian named Sigerson, but I am sure that it never occurred to you that you were receiving news of your friend. I then passed through Persia, looked in at Mecca, and paid a short but interesting visit to the Khalifa at Khartoum, the results of which I have communicated to the Foreign Office. Returning to France, I spent some months in a research into the coal-tar derivatives, which I conducted in a laboratory at Montpellier, in the south of France."

At least, as he himself might have said, the two years had not been without features of interest. Conan Doyle credited Jean Leckie with providing the basic plot for the story, but the breezy style and wit suggests that the author had learned to enjoy his famous creation once again. Both *Collier's* and *The Strand* promoted "The Adventure of the Empty House" with undisguised glee. "Sherlock Holmes Returns!" announced a handbill in America. "The Tale of his Marvellous Escape will appear in Collier's Household Number for October." *The Strand* took a similar tone: "The news of his death was received with regret as at the loss of a personal friend. Fortunately, that news, though based on circumstantial evidence which at the time seemed conclusive, turns out to be erroneous."

Even as Holmes and Watson settled back into the rooms at Baker Street, an important transition had taken place. For the author, and for the rest of the world, a new century had begun. For Sherlock Holmes, only two years had elapsed. He was now a figure of the past, rooted in the era of gaslight, swirling fog, and hansom cabs, rather than the modern, forward-looking detective who first captured the public's imagination. With this decision, the longevity of Sherlock Holmes was assured. As Vincent Starrett, perhaps the greatest of all Sherlockians, was to write in a poem called "221B":

> Here, though the world explode, these two survive,
> And it is always eighteen ninety-five.

The new Sherlock Holmes adventures made a welcome change from Conan Doyle's other best-seller of this period: the five-hundred-page volume on *The Great Boer War*. As the war had not yet ended when Conan Doyle's chronicle appeared in October 1900, the book carried the subtitle of "An Interim History of the Boer War." Interim or not, the book stands as a rigorous work of military scholarship, drawing together field reports, battle maps, troop statistics, and casualty data. It appeared too prematurely to be regarded as the definitive history of the conflict, as Conan Doyle had hoped, but it was enormously influential in helping to usher in an era of military reforms. Conan Doyle's history, and an article he published in *Cornhill Magazine*, called attention to many of the outmoded tactics that had proven ineffective in South Africa. His list of suggested reforms ranged from camouflage and artillery placement to the abandonment of anachronistic cavalry swords and lances. He also counseled the formation of civilian rifle clubs, so that future generations of British soldiers might learn to shoot as well as their Boer counterparts had. In the latter instance Conan Doyle led the way by establishing an Undershaw Rifle Club on his own property, supplying all the weapons and ammunition himself, and holding practice sessions twice a week. Lord Roberts himself supported the proposal, and visited Hindhead to inspect Conan Doyle's target range.

In his article for *Cornhill Magazine*, Conan Doyle emphasized the need to move toward a more democratic, less class-conscious military. "Above all," he wrote, "let us have done with the fuss and feathers, the gold lace, and the frippery! Let us have done also with the tailoring, the too-luxurious habits of the mess, the unnecessary extravagance which makes it so hard for a poor man to accept a commission!" Here, Conan Doyle spoke with some heat. His own wealth made it possible to provide his brother Innes, a career officer, with the luxuries needed to keep pace with his fellow officers. Conan Doyle felt strongly that his brother would have been no less deserving if he himself had remained a humble Southsea physician.

With the benefit of historical hindsight, Conan Doyle's proposals appear modest and sensible, but they provoked a great deal of heated discussion at the time. Conan Doyle primed the debate in the letters column of the *Times* of London. He pressed his agenda with "some freedom and possibly even some bitterness," but though his views mirrored those of many officials, the military establishment as a whole dismissed him as a presumptuous civilian. In 1902 a royal commission was appointed, but reforms were slow in coming.

To some extent, Conan Doyle courted controversy where the military was concerned. When Boer guerrilla parties began derailing British supply trains, killing and injuring many soldiers, Conan Doyle wrote to the *Times* to suggest a solution. "Would it not be perfectly feasible to put a truck full of Boer irreconcilables behind every engine which passes through a dangerous part of the country?" he asked. "Such a practice as I suggest would infallibly put an end to it, and is so obvious that it is difficult to imagine why it has not been done. The Germans in 1870 continually carried French hostages in the trains." The suggestion was not popular, but this did not greatly concern him. "Let both sides wear the gloves," he told his critics, "or let both sides take them off."

If Conan Doyle's suggestion was ugly, the war in South Africa had turned uglier still. As the conflict wore on, and the outmanned Boers fell back entirely on guerrilla raids, the British responded in kind. Boer farms were burned, and crops and livestock were destroyed. Reports of rape and looting were rampant. Boer women and children, as they were burned out of their homes, were herded into concentration camps, ostensibly for their own protection. When typhoid and measles swept the camps, an appalling death toll was recorded.

In Britain and abroad, loud protests were heard. W. T. Stead, editor of the *Review of Reviews*, published a pair of pamphlets—"Shall I Slay My Brother Boer?" and "Methods of Barbarism"—in which he attacked the British actions in South Africa. These diatribes created a climate of suspicion and uncertainty at home, while a wave of impassioned reports in the foreign press sparked anti-British sentiment abroad. Conan Doyle had known Stead ever since his fact-finding trip to Berlin years earlier, but he felt it his duty to stem what he called an "extraordinary outbreak of defamation." In January 1902 he began writing a pamphlet entitled "The War in South Africa: Its Causes and Conduct." Drawing heavily on eyewitness statements and army documents, Conan Doyle completed the task in only eight days. The finished "pamphlet" ran to sixty thousand words, which made it longer than *The Hound of the Baskervilles*.

He would have preferred, Conan Doyle said, to see a government official take up the defense of British policies, but this had not happened. "For some reason, which may be either arrogance or apathy, the British are very slow to state their case to the world," he wrote. "In view of the persistent slanders to which our politicians and our soldiers have been equally exposed, it becomes a duty which we owe to our national honour to lay the facts before the world."

In the booklet, Conan Doyle tried to address the criticisms point by point. A chapter called "The Farm-Burning" answered charges that troops were causing wanton destruction to Boer property, and quoted official dispatches to show that such activity had been prohibited at the early stages of the campaign. Only when private homes had become staging areas for guerrilla assaults, Conan Doyle argued, did the burnings begin. "Guerrilla warfare cannot enjoy all its own advantages and feel none of its own defects," he wrote. "It is a two-edged weapon, and the responsibility for the consequences rests upon the combatant who first employs it."

A chapter on "The Concentration Camps" casts the matter of Boer internment as a moral obligation: "[W]hen large numbers of farmhouses were destroyed under the circumstances already mentioned, it became evident that it was the duty of the British, as a civilised people, to form camps of refuge for the women and children where, out of reach, as we hoped, of all harm, they could await the return of peace." He went on to detail the exact quantities of meat, flour, coffee, sugar, and milk allotted to every inhabitant, in an attempt to illustrate their humane treatment. He made no effort to deny the high mortality rate of the camps, but went on to state, with some authority, that this tragedy was the result of disease, and that the British army had done no better where their own troops were concerned. "I cannot believe," he concluded, "that any impartial mind can read the evidence without seeing that the British Government was doing its best under difficult circumstances to carry out the most humane plan possible, and that any other must involve consequences from which a civilised nation must shrink." This is a point that has troubled the British conscience ever since; if Conan Doyle's words read as an apologia, he intended to show—as he truly believed—that the intention had been honorable. It must be added that the phrase "concentration camp" had not yet acquired the horrific resonance of the present day.

Conan Doyle's thoughts on the "Further Charges Against British Troops," which included accusations of rape, were not as admirably balanced. W. T. Stead and others had written that incidents of rape were widespread and had not met with appropriate condemnation from officials. "It is an unpleasant fact," Stead had written, "but it has got to be faced like other facts. No war can be conducted—and this war has not been conducted—without exposing multitudes of women, married and single, to the worst extremities of outrage. It is an inevitable incident of war." Conan Doyle examined a handful of reports, and quoted at length from Boer prisoners and impartial witnesses in an effort to discredit the charges. He attempted to show a disparity between the published reports and the actual facts; in one instance, he claimed the accused soldier had done no more than use "coarse terms in his conversation." In cases where the charges were found to be true, he reported, severe punishments had been given. Conan Doyle's findings were true so far as he could verify them, but subsequent investigations showed that the army's record was not quite as unblemished as he might have hoped.

Whatever the pamphlet's strengths and weaknesses, Conan Doyle had stated the British position with passion and great eloquence. In the *Times*, he appealed for contributions to assist in translating the work and distributing it abroad. Money poured in from all quarters—including, it was said, a sub-rosa contribution of £500 from Edward VII. "It was not long before we had the most gratifying evidence of the success of these efforts," he noted in his autobiography. "There was a rapid and marked change in the tone of the whole Continental press, which may have been a coincidence, but was certainly a pleasing one."

A considerable sum remained when production and distribution ceased later that year, so Conan Doyle proposed that a fund be established to bring worthy South African students to Edinburgh

University. This was perhaps his finest moment of the entire episode. Regrettably, nothing seems to have come of the idea.

Conan Doyle's talents as a public crusader had now come into full flower. As with his earlier warnings about Koch's tuberculosis cure and his subsequent efforts with the spiritualist movement, he showed himself to be a formidable propagandist. The public showed a natural interest in anything he might say, and Conan Doyle's lucid style and narrative power gave authority to whatever cause he might espouse. He had gone into the elections in Edinburgh in search of "some big purpose" in life. For the moment, he had found that purpose in what he called "an appeal to the world's opinion." He would always consider the episode one of the "most pleasing and complete" of his life.

On October 24, 1902, in recognition of his services to the Crown during the war, Conan Doyle presented himself at Buckingham Palace to receive a knighthood. At first, he felt strongly inclined to refuse the honor. He disparaged the title as "the badge of the provincial mayor," and believed that the "big men"—such as Kipling and Chamberlain—would not stoop to accept such honorifics. "All my work for the State would seem tainted if I took a so-called reward," he wrote to his mother. "I tell you it is unthinkable. Let us drop the subject."

The Ma'am would not drop the subject. She pelted her son with reproachful letters, and traveled to Hindhead to press her case in person. In the end, she wore him down. To refuse the honor, she said, would constitute an insult to the king.

Certainly His Majesty would have been disappointed. He was extremely fond of Sherlock Holmes, whose adventures were said to be among the few stories he ever finished reading. Earlier in the year, at a royal command performance of Gillette's play, the king summoned the actor to the royal box at the intermission and kept him talking so long that the audience grew restless. Of all the names on the Honours List, then, one assumes that Conan Doyle's brought a particular satisfaction to the monarch.

If Conan Doyle accepted his knighthood under duress, there was some consolation at the ceremony itself. Oliver Lodge, the distinguished physicist who shared an interest in spiritualism, was also being honored that day. "[W]e plunged at once into psychic talk," Conan Doyle recalled, "which made me forget where I was, or what I was there for."

He returned to the earthly plane in time for the investiture, but found he had difficulty adjusting to his new status as Sir Arthur Conan Doyle. "I feel," he told Innes, "like a new-married girl who isn't sure of her own name. They have also made me Deputy-Lieutenant of Surrey, whatever that means." In his autobiography he said nothing of his discomfiture, dwelling instead on the many letters and telegrams of congratulation he received. One in particular, from the editor H. A. Gwynne, compared his efforts in the war to those of a successful general. "This may well be the exaggeration of friendship," Conan Doyle wrote, "but it is at least pleasing to know that those who were in a position to judge did not look upon me as a mere busybody who butts in without due cause."

Many years later, when the Ma'am was long dead, Conan Doyle allowed himself a discreet final word on the subject. In "The Adventure of the Three Garridebs," Dr. Watson mentions in passing that Sherlock Holmes had been offered a knighthood—and that he had refused the honor. Though Watson was notoriously vague about dates, in this instance he fixed it precisely. It was 1902, "shortly after the conclusion of the South African War."

18

The Bondage of Honor

That paladin of lost causes found in the dubious circumstances of the case a matter after his own heart.

—WILLIAM ROUGHEAD, AUTHOR OF "TRIAL OF OSCAR SLATER," ON CONAN DOYLE

One winter day in 1904, as Conan Doyle drove through the gates of Undershaw in his twelve-horsepower Wolseley "motoring machine," the car clipped a gatepost, bounced onto a steep slope, and rolled over on top of him. His brother Innes, who had been riding with him, was thrown clear of the open passenger compartment. Conan Doyle, who had learned to drive only a short time earlier, was trapped underneath. For a moment, the car's steering column caught the brunt of the impact, which undoubtedly saved his life. Before he could scramble free, however, the steering column sheared off, pinning him facedown in the gravel drive with much of the car's weight settling across his back and shoulders. "I felt the weight getting heavier moment by moment," he recalled, "and wondered how long my vertebrae could stand it." Before the question could be answered, a crowd of men gathered to raise the car and pull him free.

Conan Doyle's lucky escape, according to some of his admirers, owed much to his superb physical conditioning. He had taken a course of "muscular development" with a famous bodybuilder named Eugene Sandow, and it was thought that his enhanced physique enabled him to withstand the weight of the overturned car. As the Wolseley weighed more than a ton, one must allow that luck probably played a greater role.

Conan Doyle required a great deal of luck where his car was concerned. "[T]he secret of safe brakes had not yet been discovered," he wrote, "and my pair used to break as if they were glass. More than once I have known what it is to steer a car when it is flying backwards under no control down a winding hill." This does not seem to have discouraged him. Motoring was a new sport, and he wanted to participate. He had traveled all the way up to Birmingham to take delivery of the Wolseley, and drove the 170 miles back to Hindhead as a form of self-tutorial. "I had invested in the sort of peaked yachting cap which was considered the correct badge of the motorist in those days," he recalled, "but as I paced the platform of New Street Station a woman removed any conceit I might have over my headgear by asking me peremptorily how the trains ran to Walsall. She took me for one of the officials."

He may have looked like a railway conductor, but he did not display the same competence with heavy machinery. While demonstrating the new car for his mother, Conan Doyle managed to slam into a cartload of turnips. The Ma'am, unperturbed by the sudden shower of vegetables, continued with her knitting. Not surprisingly, perhaps, Conan Doyle also became one of the first men in Britain ever to receive a speeding ticket, prompting an angry letter to the *Daily Mail*. Undeterred, he expanded his motor fleet to include a second, more powerful car and a motorcycle.

Motoring was only one of Conan Doyle's enthusiasms in those days. In 1902 he had taken off from London's Crystal Palace as a passenger in a hot air balloon, reaching an altitude of 6,000 feet before touching down in a field some twenty-five miles away. "A man has a natural trepidation the first time he leaves the ground," he admitted. "[F]or the first minute or so one feels very strange, and keeps an uncommonly tight grip of the side-ropes." Later, he would also make a noisy ascent in an early biplane, an experience he did not enjoy quite as much. Having seen the ground from this new vantage, however, he expressed the hope of making a parachute jump one day. "I think the man who first tried coming down in a parachute was the pluckiest man on earth," he told a twenty-two-year-old interviewer named P. G. Wodehouse. "I should like to try it, just for the sake of one great experience!"

Airplanes featured prominently in his short story "The Horror of the Heights," which appeared some years later, but most of his fiction of this period dealt with heroes of the past. A new series of Brigadier Gerard stories began running in *The Strand* in 1902, which were collected the following year as *The Adventures of Gerard*. *The Return of Sherlock Holmes* appeared in 1905, gathering together thirteen of the revived detective's new adventures.

At the end of 1905, *The Strand* began the serialization of *Sir Nigel*, Conan Doyle's latest historical effort. The novel emerged as a sort of prelude to *The White Company*, reintroducing many of the same characters as it traced the early career of Nigel Loring. Once again Conan Doyle paid an affectionate tribute to his mother in the form of Dame Ermyntrude, who counsels the young Nigel on "the emptiness of sordid life, the beauty of heroic death, the high sacredness of love and the bondage of honour."

Conan Doyle had great hopes for the book, which appeared at the end of the following year. Initially he had considered forgoing the lucrative serialization rights, although this strategy had done no favors for *A Duet*. Any lingering doubts about serial publication vanished when the American rights sold for $25,000. As he told a newspaper interviewer, "One must live, after all."

The book sold extremely well, and Kipling himself wrote to say that he had read it "at one gulp." Once again, however, Conan Doyle felt disappointed by the critical reception. He filled a scrapbook with glowing reviews, but most of them treated the novel as a routine adventure tale. Conan Doyle had aimed higher, and considered the book his "high-water mark in literature." His heart must have quailed when he reached the end of a cordial notice in *The Bookman*: "In short," the reviewer proclaimed, "*Sir Nigel* is the boy's book of the year."

Soon after *Sir Nigel* made its debut in *The Strand*, Conan Doyle was compelled to return to politics for the general election of 1906.

In spite of his loss in Central Edinburgh, he had shown himself to be a great asset to the Liberal Unionist party. A personal appeal from Joseph Chamberlain induced him to accept the candidacy for the Scottish "Border Burghs," consisting of the small towns of Galashiels, Hawick, and Selkirk.

Once again, Conan Doyle contested a Liberal stronghold, and once again the Liberal Unionists had allied with the Conservatives on a central issue. This time, the devisive issue of free trade versus tariff reform dominated the campaign. It was a subject of some concern to the constituency, many of whom were employed by the local wool industry.

The party elders had approached Conan Doyle well in advance, and in the months leading up to the campaign he made several trips north to lay the groundwork for his campaign. Politicking in the Border Burghs proved especially grueling, since every speech and appearance had to be repeated in each of the three towns. Conan Doyle gamely took part in the annual tradition of "common riding," a horse race of sorts to mark the boundaries of the community grounds in Hawick. Still an unseasoned rider, he "nearly made the acquaintance of the Hawick turnpike." Afterward, he was surprised to read a press account that had him dancing a lively hornpipe before the voters. Actually, he had been tapping his foot to keep time with an "interminable ballad."

Conan Doyle's opponent, "Tommy" Shaw, was so certain of his victory that he scarcely troubled himself to appear, consigning most of his campaigning to a deputy. As it turned out, Shaw's confidence was entirely justified—Conan Doyle lost the election by a margin similar to his Edinburgh defeat. The result could hardly be counted as surprising; the election also saw a resounding defeat of the Conservative government.

This marked the end of Conan Doyle's political career, and he felt no regret in giving up the "vile business" of electioneering. "And yet," he wrote, "I was deeply convinced that public service was waiting for me somewhere." For the moment, the nature of that public service remained obscure.

In *Sir Nigel*, the young hero speaks of proving his love through honorable feats. "I take my oath," he declares, "that I will do three deeds in your honour as a proof of my high love before I set eyes upon your face again, and these three deeds shall stand as a proof to you that if I love you dearly, still I will not let the thought of you stand betwixt me and honourable achievement!" Conan Doyle might just as easily have spoken these words to Jean Leckie. He still loved her, but the bondage of honor he owed to Louisa still kept them apart. In the meantime, he would show himself worthy of her sacrifice through a series of manly, virtuous trials such as politics, sports, and even, if need be, jumping out of an airplane.

By the time of Conan Doyle's second parliamentary candidacy, he and Jean had known each other for nearly nine years. Whatever pleasure they found in each other's company was shadowed by an unspoken truth: their hopes for future happiness constituted a deathwatch for Louisa. The strain took its toll on both of them. At times, Conan Doyle wondered if it might be better for all concerned if Jean left him for a younger, available man. She assured him that she would not. As Conan Doyle told his mother, "The dear soul gets these fits of depression (it is her artistic nature), and then her remorse is terrible and she writes, poor soul, as if she has done some awful thing. I never love her more than at such moments."

At the same time, Conan Doyle remained committed to Louisa's care and happiness, so that his soul, as he confided to the Ma'am, "is inevitably rather wrenched in two all the time. I am most careful at home and I am sure that at no time have I been anything but most considerate and attentive. But the position is difficult, is it not?" Meanwhile, all of his own anxieties and desires were subsumed in furious activity. At one stage he spoke of the need to "steady myself down" with rigorous study of the French writer Ernest Renan. "That, with plenty of golf and cricket, ought to keep me right—body and mind."

In the end, golf and French literature were not enough. His black moods became more frequent, and longer in duration. "Nothing could exceed his energy when the working fit was upon him," he had written of Holmes in *A Study in Scarlet*, "but now and again a reaction would seize him, and for days on end he would lie upon the sofa in the sitting-room, hardly uttering a word or moving a muscle from morning to night."

In the spring of 1906, Louisa's health took a turn for the worse. Sensing that the end was near, she called her daughter, Mary, to her bedside. Mary must not be shocked or surprised, Louisa said, if her father should marry again. If he did, the dying woman insisted, he would have her blessing. There is no reason to suppose that Louisa knew of her husband's attachment to Jean. For thirteen years, however, she had realized he would almost certainly outlive her. Throughout their marriage, her family's happiness had been her greatest concern, and this had not changed as she prepared for death. '[N]o man could have had a more gentle and amiable life's companion," Conan Doyle once wrote of her. He may not have felt the same "union of souls" that he did with Jean, but he loved Louisa and treasured the early years of happiness they had shared.

In June, Louisa began slipping in and out of delirium. Conan Doyle issued hopeful bulletins to the family—"Better; sat up to tea; I hope for the best"—but at the end of the month it was clear she was fading. She died on July 4, at the age of forty-nine, with her husband and mother at her bedside. "She told me that she had no pain and was easy in her mind," Conan Doyle noted in his journal. "I was much in her room after her death and standing by her body I felt that I had done my best."

He may have wished to believe so, but as his wife was laid to rest in Hindhead, the cumulative stresses of the thirteen-year illness sent Conan Doyle to his lowest ebb. Tortured by insomnia, he grew weak and listless. His work ceased. The intestinal complaint of his South Africa days returned to plague him. He carried flowers to his wife's grave and spent dark hours alone with his thoughts. It would be months before he roused himself.

Toward the end of 1906, as Conan Doyle glanced through the logjam of papers and correspondence on his desk, a magazine article caught his attention. It concerned a young man named George Edalji, who had been accused in a strange series of cattle mutilations. Having been imprisoned for the crime and then released without explanation, Edalji was seeking to prove his innocence in the matter. His appeals to police and government officials had gone unanswered, so Edalji now appealed to the public for help in clearing his name. Suddenly, Conan Doyle found, after the long "days of darkness," he felt able to turn his energies toward "an entirely unexpected channel."

Conan Doyle often protested that he possessed none of the deductive talent of Sherlock Holmes. Nevertheless, over the course of his career a number of true-life crimes were referred to him. If a problem especially intrigued him, or if he detected any miscarriage of justice, he would readily use his abilities and influence in service of the victim. Like Holmes, he possessed a powerful memory and an encyclopedic knowledge of crime. Once, when he read a report of a young bride found dead in her bathtub, he noted a disturbing parallel to an earlier drowning. He communicated with Scotland Yard, helping to draw attention to a serial killer who came to be known as "The Bluebeard of the Bath." Closer to home, Conan Doyle once put his talents to use in defending a luckless collie named Roy, who had been accused of killing a sheep. He was able to demonstrate that the canine defendant, who suffered from a debilitating illness, could not have committed the crime. The magistrate dismissed the case, and Roy went free.

George Edalji's troubles were more serious. At the time, Edalji was a thirty-year-old solicitor living with his parents in Great Wyrley, near Birmingham. His father, the Reverend Shapurji Edalji, was a Parsee Indian who had embraced the Church of England. He and his English wife had three children, of whom George was the eldest. An Indian vicar was something of an oddity in Birmingham at that time, and the family came in for a great deal of racial abuse, usually in the form of shouted insults, cruel practical jokes, or trash strewn in their yard.

By most accounts, George Edalji was a frail, anxious young man whose large, bulging eyes gave him the look of a sideshow hypnotist. He had distinguished himself in law school and published a well-regarded book on railway law by the age of twenty-five. He had few friends, however, and was considered a curiosity in the rural mining district of Great Wyrley.

Some years earlier, the Edalji family had received a series of threatening letters. The chief constable of the local police, Captain George Anson, came to believe that these letters were the work of George himself, who was then a sixteen-year-old grammar school student. Reverend Edalji argued the point strenuously, pointing out that his son had been sitting in plain sight when many of the letters were pushed under the door. Nonetheless, Captain Anson remained convinced that George was the culprit and would benefit from a stretch in custody. After a time, the offending letters ceased.

In 1903, the village suffered an outbreak of horse and cattle mutilations. Over a span of six months, as many as sixteen animals were found with long, shallow slits along the stomach—deep enough to cause profuse bleeding without puncturing the organs, leaving the animals to bleed to death. Anonymous letters came to light, taunting the police with talk of a bloodthirsty gang whose members included "Edalji the lawyer." Although other supposed gang members had also been mentioned by name, Captain Anson focused his attentions on George, who now worked in Birmingham but still lived at his parents' home. The police formed a theory: George was not only a mad slasher but had also written the letters denouncing himself. His possible motives for doing so were not discussed.

When an injured pony was discovered in a field not far from the Edaljis' home, George was taken into custody. A search of the house produced four bloody razors, a pair of mud-caked boots, and clothing that bore suspicious-looking stains and horsehairs. Reverend Edalji swore that his son had been asleep in the same room with him when the attack occurred, but the police discounted this as a possible alibi. The prosecution went ahead, in spite of the fact that the incriminating razors proved to be stained with rust rather than blood, and the mud on George's boots had not come from the crime scene. The police case rested on the testimony of a handwriting expert, Thomas Gurrin, who confirmed that George Edalji was, in fact, the author of the incriminating letters. As it happened, Gurrin had already helped to convict at least one innocent man, but this would not be made public until the following year. In the meantime, Edalji drew a stiff prison term: seven years of hard labor.

While Edalji broke rocks in a prison quarry, another animal was found slashed in Wyrley and the police received further anonymous communications. Here, too, the officials had a ready explanation—the original attacks had been part of a bizarre religious cult, so the further incidents could be put down to members of Edalji's gang. Edalji, the presumed ringleader, remained behind bars.

By this time, the case had provoked a great deal of protest, culminating in a petition to the Home Office signed by ten thousand people. After three years, the public pressure appeared to pay off: Edalji was released in October 1906, though no reason was given and his name was not cleared. Since his conviction had not been overturned, he could no longer practice law or claim any compensation. He found work as a law clerk and published an account of his ordeal in the newspapers.

It was then that the story came to Conan Doyle's attention. "I realized that I was in the presence of an appalling tragedy," he wrote, "and that I was called upon to do what I could to set it right."

After reviewing the trial records and visiting the crime scene, Conan Doyle arranged an interview with Edalji. "I had been delayed, and he was passing the time by reading the paper," Conan Doyle wrote. "He held the paper close to his eyes and rather sideways, proving not only a high degree of myopia but marked astigmatism. The idea of such a man scouring fields at night and assaulting cattle while avoiding the watching police was ludicrous to anyone who can imagine what the world looks like to eyes with myopia of eight diopters."

Conan Doyle knew that Edalji's vision could not be fully corrected with eyeglasses. It seemed unlikely, therefore, that Edalji could even locate a farm animal in a darkened field, much less perform delicate knifework upon it. Ironically, Conan Doyle's aborted career as an eye specialist lent a great deal of credence to this diagnosis.

Convinced of Edalji's innocence, Conan Doyle marshaled the evidence in his favor. Additional handwriting experts were consulted, who contradicted the earlier verification and stated that Edalji had not written the incriminating letters. The stains on Edalji's clothing—never conclusively shown to be fresh blood—were dismissed by Conan Doyle: "The most adept operator who ever lived would not rip up a horse with a razor upon a dark night and have only two threepenny-bit spots of blood to show for it. The idea is beyond argument." Horsehairs had also been found on the clothing, but this was not entirely persuasive—Edalji's jacket had been carried to the police lab in a sack containing a strip of horsehide.

Many others had taken up Edalji's case by this time, but Conan Doyle's name drew more publicity than ever. As more than one newspaper commented, it seemed as if Sherlock Holmes himself had rallied to Edalji's defense. Conan Doyle brushed aside the suggestion: "There is a good deal of difference between fact and fiction," he told the *Daily Telegraph*, "but I have endeavoured to get at facts first before coming to any conclusion." Indeed, Conan Doyle's efforts more closely resembled those of Mycroft Holmes, the detective's older, less ambulatory brother. Most of the facts had been assembled by others, but Conan Doyle used his narrative gifts to cast the evidence into a compelling and seemingly unanswerable argument. He began with a letter-writing campaign in the newspapers and then, in late January 1907, published an eighteen-thousand-word pamphlet called "The Story of Mr. George Edalji."

"I have examined a very large number of documents," he wrote, "and tested a long series of real and alleged facts. During all that time I have kept my mind open, but I can unreservedly say that in the whole research I have never come across any considerations which would make it, I will not say probable, but in any way credible, that George Edalji had anything to do, either directly or indirectly, with the outrages or with the anonymous letters."

In the course of his research, Conan Doyle's suspicions came to rest with a pair of brothers, Royden and Wallace Sharpe, who had a long history of antagonism toward the Edalji family. The indications were never more than circumstantial, but Royden, in particular, had an impressive list of qualifications. He was known to have forged letters in the past, he had worked for a butcher, and he was thought to have slashed railway property with a knife. He had known George Edalji, and possibly nursed a grudge against him, since grammar school—though he himself had been expelled—and his ten months of service aboard a cattle boat happened to correspond with a lull in the abuse against the Edaljis. Conan Doyle pursued this line of inquiry with such energy that he, too, began to receive threatening letters. The evidence against the Sharpes wasn't strong enough to prosecute a case, but, as Conan Doyle had forcefully stated, it easily outweighed the evidence against George Edalji.

With Conan Doyle's pamphlet fanning the flames, the Edalji case became a subject of national outrage. "I am firmly convinced," he told one journalist after another, "that if ever a man was innocent, Edalji is." Before long the foreign press took up the story. In America, the *New York Times* carried the details on its front page. "Conan Doyle Solves a New Dreyfus Case," read one headline. "Creator of 'Sherlock Holmes' Turns Detective Himself."

With international attention focusing on the case, the British government was soon forced to take action. An Edalji Committee was formed in the spring of 1907, leading to an official investigation under the auspices of the home secretary. In time the government commission found Edalji innocent of the animal attacks, but guilty of writing the defamatory letters. As a result, Edalji received a pardon, but no compensation of any kind. Here, too, critics charged that the findings could not have been impartial: Sir Albert de Rutzen, a member of the three-man commission, was the cousin of Captain George Anson, the chief constable of the Great Wyrley police.

Conan Doyle believed the entire episode constituted an ugly blot on British justice. "After many years," he noted in his autobiography, "I can hardly think with patience on the handling of this case."

Recent investigations suggest that the final chapter of the Edalji case has yet to be written. "He was of irreproachable character," Conan Doyle insisted. "Nothing in his life had ever been urged against him." Subsequent research indicates that Edalji may not have been entirely pure of heart. Rumors of gambling debts and misappropriation of client funds have surfaced, indicating that the story may yet take another twist. As a 1907 editorial in the *New York Times* noted, "[Conan Doyle] may have been misled by the literary artist's natural desire to round out his story perfectly. Truth may be stranger than fiction, but it usually lacks what is known in literature as 'construction.' " Whatever fresh allegations may emerge, however, the basic tenets of Conan Doyle's argument are likely to stand. He threw himself into the episode because the police case against

Edalji was deeply flawed. Conan Doyle exposed those flaws, and alerted the world to a serious miscarriage of justice. His pride in having done so was entirely warranted.

Conan Doyle always regretted that his efforts had not brought about a more definitive result. Personally, however, the investigation had done him a world of good. His indignation over the Edalji affair burned away the lassitude that gripped him after Louisa's death, and channeled his grief and depression into a productive form. Several months had passed in the single-minded pursuit of Edalji's vindication; when he paused in his labors, he felt ready to resume a more normal life.

On September 18, 1907, Conan Doyle married Jean Leckie in a small private ceremony at St. Margaret's Church in Westminster. The wedding was very much a family affair; his brother-in-law the Reverend Cyril Angell, Dodo's husband, conducted the ceremony, and Innes served as best man. Conan Doyle wore a traditional frock coat and striped trousers, while the bride appeared "surpassingly decorative," according to one newspaper, in a dress of ivory silk and Spanish lace. Connie and Willie Hornung, having withdrawn their earlier objections to the relationship, joined in the celebrations.

Afterward, Conan Doyle carried his bride up the stairs of the Hotel Metropole for a lavish reception. Among the 250 guests were Jerome K. Jerome, Bram Stoker, J. M. Barrie, George Newnes, and Greenhough Smith. Even Dr. Reginald Hoare, who had given Conan Doyle room and board some thirty years earlier, came down from Birmingham to raise a glass to his former pill-roller. George Edalji also attended, and Conan Doyle claimed that there was no guest he felt prouder to see.

Although Conan Doyle had been secretive about the plans, the wedding received extensive coverage in the press. The *Daily Telegraph* devoted a lengthy column of text to the bride's "particularly beautiful dress," while the *Morning Post* remarked on the "beaming countenance" of the groom. The foreign papers also took note: "Lady Doyle a Very Handsome Woman," opined the *New York Times*; "Sherlock Holmes Quietly Married," reported the *Buenos Aires Standard*. Mysteriously, one New York paper informed its readers that the groom had "long been regarded as a confirmed bachelor."

After a honeymoon that featured a Mediterranean cruise, the newlyweds settled into their new life together. Happily, Kingsley and Mary, who were now both in their teens, were greatly attached to Jean, and their father's new happiness marked a warming of their relationship with him. As Jean felt eager to make a fresh start, it was decided that the family would leave Hindhead. Undershaw was leased and Conan Doyle bought a new home, called Windlesham, in the Sussex town of Crowborough, on the edge of the Ashdown Forest. Jean's parents lived nearby, having left Blackheath following Mr. Leckie's retirement.

The new home offered many of the same features as Undershaw, including a gabled roof and an even more impressive billiards room, which ran the width of the house and did double duty as a ballroom. Jean's harp and piano stood at one end, the billiards table at the other. A large oil portrait of Conan Doyle, painted by *The Strand* illustrator Sidney Paget, looked down on a quirky collection of personal relics, including a stag's head, several animal-skin rugs, and a vast array of Napoleonic weapons. Upstairs, Conan Doyle's new study stretched to include two of the home's five gables, and commanded a dramatic view of the Sussex Downs. In one corner stood a bust of Sherlock Holmes, not unlike the one smashed by Colonel Moran's air gun in "The Adventure of the Empty House."

Conan Doyle would spend the rest of his life at Windlesham, extending it with additions and improvements over the years. With London no longer as accessible, he also kept a flat near Victoria Station for his frequent business and social engagements. Once again, Conan Doyle found himself reveling in what Dr. Watson had called the "home-centered interests" of a newly married man. His literary output slowed in the first years at Windlesham, and he resolved to write only when inspiration seized him. He often found himself diverted by the gardening duties he shared with Jean, along with his golf and other sports. Not all of his diversions were pleasant; in January 1909, a sudden intestinal blockage—the result of his Bloemfontein ailment—brought a team of specialists to his bedside. Surgery was performed, and the *Times* posted daily bulletins of his rapid recovery.

The Edalji case had brought Conan Doyle a considerable reputation as a champion of the oppressed. Now, as he settled down to work in his new study, a second, even more notorious criminal case claimed his attention. The story had begun on a gray December evening in Glasgow in 1908, when an elderly spinster named Marion Gilchrist sent her paid companion, Helen Lambie, around the corner to buy a newspaper. When Miss Lambie returned ten minutes later, an unknown man rushed past her into the street. Entering the parlor, she found Miss Gilchrist dead on the floor. She had been bludgeoned to death. Her personal papers were scattered, and her jewels rifled, but only one item appeared to be missing—a diamond brooch.

Police were quick to implicate a German immigrant named Oscar Slater, who had recently pawned a diamond brooch. Slater appeared to confirm his own guilt by fleeing the country under an assumed name, aboard the *Lusitania*. When the liner reached New York, Slater was found in possession of a small upholsterer's hammer, thought to be the murder weapon. Extradition was threatened, but Slater returned to Britain voluntarily, convinced that he could easily prove his innocence.

Slater was guilty of many things—gambling, petty theft, and possibly even prostitution—but he was not the murderer of Marion Gilchrist. As in the Edalji case, however, the police tailored the facts to fit their suspect, suppressing contrary evidence where necessary. Witnesses who had seen a mysterious man flee the victim's apartment were coached with Slater's photograph, and the suspect's alibi—he had been at home with his mistress and a servant—was overlooked. Worse yet, the only real piece of evidence linking Slater to the crime scene—the diamond brooch—did not match the description of the victim's jewelry and was indisputably shown to have been hocked before the murder took place.

Astonishingly, Slater was soon found guilty and sentenced to death. No court of criminal appeal existed in Scotland at the time. Slater's only option, then, was to ask the government for mercy. Public opinion now turned in his favor, and a petition asking for clemency gathered a staggering twenty thousand signatures. Two days before the execution was scheduled to take place, Slater's sentence was commuted to life in prison.

In April 1910, a prominent Edinburgh lawyer named William

Roughead published a booklet entitled "Trial of Oscar Slater," which set out the inconsistencies of the evidence and presented a transcript of the trial. Conan Doyle, who had already been approached by Slater's lawyers, was among those stirred by Roughead's accusations. Though he had little stomach for another investigation, he recognized that "this unhappy man had in all probability no more to do with the murder for which he had been condemned than I had." The Edalji case had discouraged him, however, and he knew that the officials involved in Slater's prosecution would close ranks in a similar manner. "What confronts you is a determination to admit nothing which inculpates another official," he wrote, "and as to the idea of punishing another official for offences which have caused misery to helpless victims, it never comes within their horizons."

For all of that, Conan Doyle felt obliged to do something. Once again he decided to publish a booklet, using his name and influence to attract a wider audience for Slater's grievance. With William Roughead's assistance, he assembled "The Case of Oscar Slater," published in the summer of 1912. It was an eighteen-thousand-word summary of the case that examined Roughead's information in greater detail. The booklet presented an effective rebuttal of many of the initially damning indictments of Slater's actions and motives. Slater had, for example, been traveling under a false name when he made his flight to America. Conan Doyle pointed out that Slater had made the trip in the company of his young mistress and wished to avoid being found out by his wife. This explanation, while not exactly laudable, did not make Slater guilty of murder. Slater had used his real name in a hotel in Liverpool before departure, Conan Doyle pointed out, something he would not have done had he been hiding from the police.

As for the hammer found among Slater's effects, Conan Doyle did not express much confidence in its value as a murder weapon. It was "an extremely light and fragile instrument," he insisted, and "any task beyond fixing a tin-tack, or cracking a small bit of coal, would be above its strength." A doctor who examined Miss Gilchrist's body at the crime scene offered some corroboration on this point; he concluded that the victim had been dispatched with a heavy mahogany chair, found to be "dripping" with blood.

"The Case of Oscar Slater," published cheaply to encourage a wide readership, revived the calls for a new trial. In the House of Commons, questions about the case were addressed to McKinnon Wood, the secretary of state for Scotland. The reply offered little cause for optimism: "No new considerations have, in my opinion, emerged such as would justify me in reopening the case."

Meanwhile, new disclosures came to light, along with further evidence of police negligence. Slater's alibi, it emerged, had been confirmed by a grocer named MacBrayne, who saw him standing on his own doorstep at the time of the murder. MacBrayne had not been called to testify at the trial. An even more disturbing revelation came from Lieutenant John Trench, a Glasgow police detective. After a long struggle with his conscience, Lieutenant Trench came forward with an electrifying piece of information: on the night of the murder, Helen Lambie, the victim's companion, had named the man she saw fleeing from Miss Gilchrist's flat. That man was not Oscar Slater.

Incredibly, this allegation was not thought significant enough to warrant a new inquiry. For his troubles, Lieutenant Trench found himself dismissed from the force and denied a pension. Conan Doyle was mortified. "How the verdict could be that there was no fresh cause for reversing the conviction is incomprehensible," he wrote in *The Spectator*. "The whole case will, in my opinion, remain immortal in the classics of crime as the supreme example of official incompetence and obstinacy."

For the moment, all appeared lost. The next move—though Conan Doyle could not have known it at the time—would be Oscar Slater's.

19

A Perfectly Impossible Person

Most vividly of all, however, there stands out in my memory the squat figure of Professor Rutherford with his Assyrian beard, his prodigious voice, his enormous chest and his singular manner.

—ARTHUR CONAN DOYLE, *MEMORIES AND ADVENTURES*

My methods of work are not made out to any particular plan," Conan Doyle had told a reporter in 1905. "I write when the mood is on me. I never dictate a single word, but write the entire story with my pen. I write slowly and very seldom make any corrections afterward. Often when I have done so I have found the result so unsatisfactory that I have restored what I had originally written. If I do make an alteration it usually entails reconstruction of part of the story. First impressions always seem to me the best."

That interview appeared under the headline "Conan Doyle's Hard Luck as a Playwright," which gave an indication of the path his career would take in the first years of his new marriage. Much of his time would be spent writing and producing plays based on his own works, an enterprise that "if it was not lucrative it at least provided us with a good deal of amusement and excitement."

As for his "hard luck," this referred to a drama he had written featuring Brigadier Gerard, his popular hero of the Regency period. "I have offered it to nearly every London manager," Conan Doyle said, "but without success. They all seem to fight shy of it. Why, I cannot say. I am still confident, however, that it is a good play—and they are equally certain that it is not." Meanwhile, William Gillette's *Sherlock Holmes* continued to play to packed houses.

After several months, *Brigadier Gerard* found an unlikely champion in Lewis Waller, an actor who became known as "the flapper's idol" for his dashing portrayals of D'Artagnan, Hotspur, and Henry V. An experienced theatrical manager, Waller agreed to produce the play and star in the title role. As rehearsals began, Conan Doyle found it difficult to relinquish control of his character. In his novels, he could fill page after page with fond descriptions of gold-slashed lancers, jeweled swords, and finely wrought dueling pistols. In the theater, this passion for historical detail became troublesome. Arriving at a dress rehearsal, Conan Doyle was aghast to see a group of Hussar officers, lately returned from Napoleon's last campaign, marching onto the stage in sparkling chestnut and silver uniforms. "These men are warriors," he cried, "not ballet dancers!" At the playwright's insistence, the costly uniforms were taken outside and dragged through the dirt and mud. Such authenticity did not appeal to Waller. As the star of the show, he insisted that his own uniform remain unblemished.

Waller and his pristine costume debuted in the spring of 1906. He gave, in Conan Doyle's estimation, a "glorious performance," but the actor's heartthrob image seemed at odds with the material. Audiences were accustomed to seeing Waller as a steely-eyed hero; many of his fans failed to see the intended humor in his portrayal of the trouble-prone Brigadier. "Do you know," one first-nighter commented, "there are times when I can hardly keep from laughing?" Apparently the confusion was shared by many. The crowds neither laughed nor cheered, with the result that *Brigadier Gerard* was not a great success. Conan Doyle regretted the short run, but came away with a deep respect for the Spanish-born Waller. "I am not clear what blood ran in Waller's veins, Hebrew or Basque or both," he wrote. "I only know that it went to make a very wonderful man."

Three years later, the two men collaborated again on *The Fires of Fate*, an unabashed melodrama better suited to Waller's talents. Based on Conan Doyle's *The Tragedy of the Korosko*, Waller again played a dashing military man, Colonel Egerton, who is informed during the first act that a rare form of sclerosis of the spine will kill him in a year. After a brief flirtation with suicide, Egerton decides instead to lead a party of tourists on an adventurous expedition up the Nile River. In true Conan Doyle style, Egerton meets and falls in love with a pretty American, Sadie Adams of Massachusetts. Because of his illness, however, he must refrain from declaring his affections.

Destiny takes a hand when the party is captured by Dervishes. Realizing that a fate worse than death awaits the comely Miss Adams, Colonel Egerton, though gravely wounded by a blow to the head, manages to crawl off and signal for help. Reinforcements arrive and effect a rescue. A happy ending appears within reach, but for the problem of Colonel Egerton's terminal disease. Conan Doyle's solution, albeit inventive, appears rather dubious in the light of his medical training. Earlier, Egerton had learned that a fellow sufferer was cured by the impact of a railway accident. It emerges that a blow on the head from a Dervish has much the same effect, allowing Conan Doyle to bring the drama to a crowd-pleasing conclusion.

Conan Doyle considered the play to be his finest dramatic work, and on opening night—June 16, 1909—the audience seemed to agree with him. A scene in which the sinister Dervishes attack the helpless travelers—made more realistic by Conan Doyle's insistence on whips and cudgels—caused widespread alarm in the audience. In the front stalls, a friend of Innes Doyle had to be restrained from charging the stage to assist the besieged tourists. Later, Colonel Egerton's brave ordeal in signaling for help brought the audience to its feet. "Such moments to a dramatist," Conan Doyle wrote, "give a thrill of personal satisfaction such as the most successful novelist never can feel."

The thrill was short-lived. *The Fires of Fate* closed after a few months, and only lasted that long because both Waller and Conan Doyle put up money for the production expenses. Conan Doyle remained optimistic, blaming the unsteady box office receipts on an unseasonably hot summer, but Waller soon turned his attention to another project. Conan Doyle would always regret what he considered to be the play's premature burial.

As he cast about for his next theatrical venture, Conan Doyle turned his attention to a dusty, half-finished manuscript from his younger days. In 1894, as *A Story of Waterloo* went into rehearsal, the ever-ambitious Conan Doyle had made a start on a second play, called *The House of Temperley*, also intended as a vehicle for Henry Irving. The young playwright's interest in boxing suggested a colorful backdrop for the piece, though it seemed an unlikely milieu for the aging Sir Henry. After a brief attempt at collaboration with his brother-in-law Willie Hornung, Conan Doyle abandoned the project. Never one to waste an idea, he used the research and situations to produce the novel *Rodney Stone*.

The House of Temperley, subtitled *A Melodrama of the Ring*, followed the misfortunes of Sir Charles Temperley, an inveterate gambler who must risk his fortune and family honor on a bare-knuckle boxing match. Just before the fateful match is to take place, the boxer upon whom Temperley has staked ten thousand pounds is kidnapped. Temperley's own brother Jack, a soldier, must fight in his stead against the brutal Gloucester Dick.

A Story of Waterloo had been a sleek, modest production, with a simple set and a small handful of supporting actors. *The House of Temperley,* by contrast, was a great lumbering ox of a play, with forty-three actors, seven set changes, and a lengthy boxing match as its climax. As he revised and finished the long-dormant manuscript, Conan Doyle must have realized that its lavish scale would alarm all but the most iron-willed theatrical producers. Undiscouraged by the limited successes of *Brigadier Gerard* and *The Fires of Fate,* he decided to finance the bare-knuckle epic out of his own pocket.

The decision appears rash, but the role of impresario suited Conan Doyle's take-charge personality and allowed him to regain the creative control he enjoyed in fiction. With his usual optimism, he took out a costly six-month lease on the Adelphi Theater and engaged a director and a platoon of actors. He oversaw nearly every aspect of the production and insisted on an authenticity of period detail that extended to antique props and furniture—at even greater expense to himself.

Though Conan Doyle had tried to weave a love story into the first act, the play's real interest lay in the climactic bare-knuckle bout between Jack Temperley and Gloucester Dick. Conan Doyle brought in a military boxing instructor to coach the actors, and the resulting spectacle skirted a fine line between entertainment and blood sport. The actor who played Gloucester Dick would suffer a broken finger, a lost tooth, and a cracked rib.

As production expenses mounted into the thousands of pounds, on top of a £600 weekly outlay in payroll and rent, even Conan Doyle had to admit that he was "plunging rather deep." The opening night, on February 11, 1910, would have been a tense affair for the impresario. To his horror, the audience sat through the first act in what could only be called a respectful silence. Anxiously, Conan Doyle began scribbling notes—"too anaemic"—on his program. The crowd came to life, however, as the action shifted to the boxing ring. "Only those who attend a performance of the piece can have any idea how life-like these passages are made on the stage," wrote the reviewer for the *Athenaeum*. "Such zest cannot but affect an audience, and the play obtained the heartiest first-night reception of any of the year." A relieved Conan Doyle emerged to cheers at the final curtain.

The playwright's first-night elation soon gave way to a producer's nightmare. Despite enthusiastic reviews, *The House of Temperley* played to half-empty houses. "Ladies were afraid to come," Conan Doyle wrote, "and imagined it would be a brutal spectacle." As the play's main interest lay in watching the actors pummel each other with their fists, such reservations were not entirely unfounded. Conan Doyle added an appealing curtain-raiser called *A Pot of Caviare*, but ticket sales continued to dwindle. The death of King Edward VII on May 6 brought down the final curtain. The Adelphi, along with all of the other London theaters, went dark for the mourning period. *The House of Temperley* made a few scattered appearances toward the end of the month, but these ceased in early June.

One bright spot in this gloomy period was a meeting with Theodore Roosevelt—whose term as U.S. president had ended the previous year—at a small luncheon hosted by a mutual friend. Roosevelt, who was passing through London on the return leg of an African safari, dominated the gathering with what Conan Doyle called the "raciest" talk he had ever heard. The former president was "a very loud hearty man," Conan Doyle recalled, "with a peculiar wild-beast toothy grin, and an explosive habit of slapping his hand down for emphasis." Conan Doyle found much to admire in Roosevelt's exploits as a military man, sportsman, and adventurer. "Colonel Roosevelt is a superman if there ever was one," he told an American journalist. Roosevelt, for his part, respected Conan Doyle's political views and public crusades. A longtime fan of Sherlock Holmes, Roosevelt also inquired after the health of the great detective, whose latest adventure, "The Red Circle," had just appeared in *The Strand*.

As it happened, Sherlock Holmes was very much on Conan Doyle's mind. Even before *The House of Temperley* had officially closed, it was clear that the play's failure would leave him with heavy debts and an expensive lease on an empty theater. It was, he admitted, a "difficult—almost a desperate—situation." Desperate times called for desperate measures, so the beleaguered author returned once again to Baker Street and his ever-reliable cash cow.

Years later, Lady Conan Doyle would express wonder at the speed with which her husband wrote and produced his new play, which went from blank page to full production in little more than three weeks. Such efficiency, she declared, "must surely be a record." If so, it was born of necessity. The excitement and jolly times of Conan Doyle's theatrical ventures had now become, in his phrase, "a little too poignant." His losses must be recovered.

The new play took its inspiration from "The Speckled Band," one of the earliest and best of the Sherlock Holmes adventures, though Conan Doyle made substantial changes to the story. Much of the cast and crew of *The House of Temperley* transferred over to the new production, with better-known actors brought in for the leading roles. H. A. Saintsbury, who had given hundreds of performances as Holmes in a touring company of the Gillette play, stepped in to play the detective. A Shakespearean actor named Lyn Harding portrayed the villainous Dr. Grimesby Rylott—"Roylott" in the original story—

and argued so vehemently with Conan Doyle over the interpretation of the role that their mutual friend J. M. Barrie had to be called in to mediate. Conan Doyle eventually conceded to the actor's point of view, with the result that the character of Rylott nearly overwhelmed Sherlock Holmes.

A number of other changes were made as opening night approached. Conan Doyle had originally called the play *The Stonor Case*, but his colleagues, anxious to capitalize on a proven winner, persuaded him to revert to the more familiar *The Speckled Band*. A scene in which Holmes indulged his cocaine habit was revised to allow an intervention from Billy the page boy. A familiar episode from the original story—in which Dr. Roylott bends a fireplace poker and Holmes straightens it out again—had to be abandoned when no sufficiently pliable prop could be found.

One of the greatest difficulties concerned the title character, a poisonous snake who was to menace the heroine in the play's climactic scene. Yet again Conan Doyle insisted on using the most realistic props available. The production crew—and, one imagines, the actors—favored an artificial snake. Conan Doyle, seeking a more spine-tingling effect, imported a fearsome-looking rock python. Even he had to admit that the snake made a poor actor. The python, he wrote, "either hung down like a pudgy yellow bell rope, or else when his tail was pinched, endeavored to squirm back and get level with the stage carpenter, who pinched him, which was not in the plot."

One can only imagine the stage carpenter's trepidation as the curtain went up on June 4. Happily, all went according to the script and Conan Doyle emerged to a thunderous ovation at the final curtain. "It went wonderfully well," he reported to the Ma'am. "I don't think I have ever seen a play go so well."

The critics had high praise for the performances of H. A. Saintsbury and Lyn Harding, and many made special mention of Saintsbury's skill at disguises—a feature of the play Conan Doyle playfully concealed by assigning a program listing to "Mr. C. Later," who proved to be Holmes disguised as a butler.

The rock python fared less well, though Lyn Harding had coaxed it into taking an opening night curtain call. Critics had harsh words for its wan performance, which they variously described as "palpably artificial" and no more terrible than a "large and unwieldy sausage." Stung by the criticism, the crew rigged up an effective mechanical duplicate, but Conan Doyle would not allow the substitution. Later, however, the two snakes were furtively switched so that Conan Doyle expressed a strong preference for the fake, believing it to be real. Thereafter, the mechanical snake took over the part, leading to one of the most chilling scenes in the production. When Grimesby Rylott, in his death scene, crashed to the floor with the snake coiled firmly about his head, the audience watched with mounting alarm as the creature slowly uncoiled and slithered across the stage toward Dr. Watson, played by Claude King, who thrashed it thoroughly with his cane while the audience shrieked in terror. Presumably the artificial snake received a warmer reception at the final curtain.

The success of *The Speckled Band* allowed Conan Doyle to recoup his losses with interest. Two touring companies were already on the road by the time his irksome six-month lease on the Adelphi expired. The original production transferred to the Globe.

For all its success, even Conan Doyle had to admit that *The Speckled Band* was inferior to William Gillette's *Sherlock Holmes*. The detective was slow to appear in the Conan Doyle effort and gave little evidence of his customary brilliance. "The real fault of the play," the author wrote, "was that in trying to give Holmes a worthy antagonist I overdid it and produced a more interesting personality in the villain." Even so, Conan Doyle would always be grateful to the actors who had helped him out of his financial straits. More than a decade later, when a revival starring Saintsbury and Harding struggled to break even, Conan Doyle generously declined his royalties to help the production find its feet.

As *The Speckled Band* settled in for a long run, Conan Doyle decided to bring his career as a playwright to a discreet close. "I am not leaving stage work because it doesn't interest me," he told a journalist. "It interests me too much." Thereafter he advised his friends never to put money of their own into theatrical ventures.

Though Sherlock Holmes had allowed him to salvage a bad situation, Conan Doyle must have regretted the necessity of resorting to his old warhorse, the character who had so often overshadowed his other ambitions. Now, as his attention turned back toward fiction, and with Sherlock Holmes preying on his mind, Conan Doyle wandered down an oddly familiar path. Drawing inspiration from his own past, he set out to create an audacious new character, whom he modeled on a professor of medicine from the University of Edinburgh. This new character would be intensely brilliant and wildly eccentric, and his adventures would be chronicled by a less intelligent, but admirably stalwart companion.

If the scenario seemed familiar, the circumstances had changed. Nearly a quarter of a century had passed since *A Study in Scarlet*. With the creation of Professor George Edward Challenger—whose own wife describes him as "a perfectly impossible person"—Conan Doyle hoped to fashion a character who would challenge Holmes for the public's affections.

The idea evolved slowly. In a rock quarry near Windlesham, Conan Doyle had noticed the imprint of some "huge lizard's tracks" in the stone. The fossils so intrigued him that he alerted the British Museum, who dispatched an expert to take impressions.

Earlier, while cruising the Aegean with Jean on their honeymoon, he spotted a creature that looked exactly like a "young ichthyosaurus"—roughly four feet long, with a thin neck and tail, and four large side-flippers. "This old world has got some surprises for us yet," he remarked. These incidents, which added fuel to a growing interest in paleontology, may have provided the spark for Professor Challenger's first adventure.

At the time of his second marriage, Conan Doyle had spoken of waiting for inspiration before he attemped a new novel. That wait may have been longer than he intended. In his disappointment over the critical reception of *Sir Nigel*, he had allowed himself to be distracted by the call of the footlights. His crusades on behalf of George Edalji and Oscar Slater absorbed still more of his time, as did his work for the Divorce Law Reform Union, of which he had become president in 1909. The birth of his sons—Denis Percy Stewart in 1909 and Adrian Malcolm in 1910—also diverted his attention away from fiction.

Apart from his plays and pamphlets, Conan Doyle's name remained before the reading public through a series of other works. *Through the Magic Door,* an affectionate tribute to his literary influences, appeared in 1907, while *The Crime of the Congo,* a diatribe against Belgian oppression of Congolese natives, followed in 1909. A final Brigadier Gerard story entitled "Marriage of the Brigadier" was published in *The Strand* in 1910.

None of these approached the scope and ambition of his earlier works. By the time *The Last Galley,* a collection of stories, appeared in 1911, Conan Doyle had not published a new novel in five years. As he turned his energy back toward fiction, the critical indifference to his historical novels inspired him to attempt something new. "My ambition," he wrote to Greenhough Smith, "is to do for the boys' book what Sherlock Holmes did for the detective tale. I don't suppose I could bring off two such coups. And yet I hope it may."

The result was *The Lost World,* a vivid adventure tale that stands with *The Hound of the Baskervilles* and the Brigadier Gerard stories as the most thoroughly enjoyable of all Conan Doyle's works. Narrated by an agreeable Irish journalist named Edward Dunn Malone, *The Lost World* introduces the irascible Professor Challenger just as he is mounting an expedition to South America. Challenger and Malone are joined by Professor Summerlee, an academic rival of Challenger's, and Lord John Roxton, a globe-trotting sportsman. After many hardships and internal disputes, the four adventurers arrive at a remote Amazonian plateau, where a combination of isolation and unusual atmospheric conditions have created a kind of living time capsule. Here, the explorers discover, the world has been preserved just as it was in prehistoric times, and dinosaurs walk the earth.

The Lost World owed a great deal to Jules Verne, H. G. Wells, and Daniel Defoe—as many commentators have been eager to point out—but its greatest strengths were unique to Conan Doyle. His passion for research brought the prehistoric flora and fauna to life, while the engaging narration of Edward Malone made both Challenger and his adventures accessible to the reader, just as Dr. Watson had done for Sherlock Holmes.

Conan Doyle's reference to "boys' books" in his letter to Greenhough Smith gave a clear picture of his intent. He would not have used the term in a disparaging sense, but rather to identify the "ripping yarn" school of fiction that he hoped to nudge toward the mainstream. It would not have occurred to Conan Doyle that he was writing science fiction, as that phrase had not yet come into common use, but *The Lost World* can now be seen as an early masterpiece of the genre. In many ways, *The Lost World* is comparable to *A Study in Scarlet* as a milestone of its field, though Conan Doyle's influence as a writer of science fiction is seldom acknowledged.

Conan Doyle first experimented with science fiction in early stories such as "The Great Keinplatz Experiment," featuring a professor and a student who exchange bodies, and "The Los Amigos Fiasco," in which a botched electrocution transforms a condemned man into a superhuman being. Now, with *The Lost World*, he brought his mature powers to bear, creating a character who would not be overwhelmed by the hectic twists of the plot. "I was prepared for something strange," declares Malone at his first meeting with Challenger, "but not for so overpowering a personality as this. It was his size which took one's breath away—his size and his imposing presence. His head was enormous, the largest I have ever seen upon a human being. I am sure that his top-hat, had I ventured to don it, would have slipped over me entirely and rested upon my shoulders. He had the face and beard which I associate with an Assyrian bull; the former florid, the latter so black as almost to have a suspicion of blue, spade-shaped and rippling down over his chest. The hair was peculiar, plastered down in front in a long, curving wisp over his massive forehead. The eyes were blue-grey under great black tufts, very clear, very critical, and very masterful. A huge spread of shoulders and a chest like a barrel were the other parts of him which appeared above the table, save for two enormous hands covered with long black hair. This and a bellowing, roaring, rumbling voice made up my first impression of the notorious Professor Challenger."

After his trials as a playwright, *The Lost World* seemed to provide some relief for Conan Doyle. His high spirits and sense of humor are evident on every page, especially in a gleeful episode at London's Queen's Hall, where Professor Challenger produces a caged pterodactyl as proof of the success of his expedition: "Peering down into the box he snapped his fingers several times and was heard from the Press seat to say, 'Come, then, pretty, pretty!' in a coaxing voice. An instant later, with a scratching, rattling sound, a most horrible and loathsome creature appeared from below and perched itself upon the side of the case. Even the unexpected fall of the Duke of Durham into the orchestra, which occurred at this moment, could not distract the petrified attention of the vast audience."

As he fleshed out the character of Challenger, Conan Doyle drew on his memories of William Rutherford, a professor of physiology from his University of Edinburgh days. "He fascinated and awed us," Conan Doyle wrote of his old professor. "He would sometimes start his lecture before he reached the classroom, so that we would hear a booming voice saying: 'There are valves in the veins,' or some other information, when the desk was empty."

From Rutherford, Challenger received his arresting physical characteristics—the "Assyrian" beard, the rafter-shaking voice, the squat figure, the barrel chest. It cannot have displeased Conan Doyle that these characteristics made Challenger the physical opposite of Sherlock Holmes. Other members of the Edinburgh faculty also made their presence felt. The pioneering expedition of Sir Charles Wyville Thomson aboard the corvette *Challenger* gave Conan Doyle's hero his name, while the tall and somewhat imperious Sir Robert Christison, known to his students as "Dignity Bob," influenced the character of Professor Summerlee, Challenger's prickly rival-turned-colleague.

After running serially in *The Strand*, the book version of *The Lost World* appeared to enthusiastic reviews in October 1912. "It is decidedly the most imaginative of the author's works," declared *The Athenaeum*. "[H]e has produced a highly interesting tale of outlandish adventure of a sort to stir the pulses and arouse the wonder of even the 'jaded' novel reader," wrote the *Times*.

From the first, Conan Doyle showed a fondness and enthusiasm for Challenger that contrasted sharply with his feelings for Holmes. To publicize *The Lost World*, Conan Doyle even allowed himself to be photographed as Challenger in an explorer's outfit, wig, and long, dark beard. Shortly thereafter, Willie Hornung was surprised to find a black-bearded stranger on his doorstep, who introduced himself as a German friend of Hornung's famous relation, Sir Arthur Conan Doyle. Hornung, who was nearsighted, gave a cordial reception to the voluble German visitor, but turned angry when, after a few minutes, he recognized his brother-in-law behind the beard. Incensed by the prank, he showed Conan Doyle to the door.

When it became clear that *The Lost World* would be a success, Conan Doyle set to work on a sequel. *The Poison Belt,* which appeared the following year, begins as Edward Malone receives a strange message from Challenger: "Bring oxygen." Hurrying to the professor's home with a canister of oxygen, Malone joins up with Lord John Roxton and Professor Summerlee—his fellow adventurers from *The Lost World*—who are responding to the same cryptic summons. The professor, it emerges, has noticed a "blurring of Frauenhofer's lines in the spectra," which presages the end of humanity. The earth, he explains, will shortly pass through a band of poisonous ether that will extinguish all life on the planet.

Powerless to prevent the catastrophe, Challenger arranges to postpone the inevitable so as to witness "the last act of the drama of the world." Sealed in his wife's dressing chamber with five canisters of oxygen, Challenger and his companions watch in awe as the poison sweeps across the landscape. "No bird flew in the blue vault of heaven, no man or beast moved upon the vast countryside which lay before us," Malone records. "For a few short hours the knowledge and foresight of one man could preserve our little oasis of life in the vast desert of death, and save us from participation in the common catastrophe. Then the gas would run low, we too should lie gasping upon the cherry-coloured boudoir carpet, and the fate of the human race and of all earthly life would be complete."

Conan Doyle was by no means the first novelist to bring the world to an end, but he may well have been the first to play it for laughs. From beginning to end, the author's finely pitched humor saves the enterprise from gloom—especially in the early stages of the catastrophe, when the poison gas causes the adventurers to lose their inhibitions. "You know me as the austere man of science," says Professor Summerlee. "Can you believe that I once had a well-deserved reputation in several nurseries as a farmyard imitator? Would it amuse you to hear me crow like a cock?"

Later, when the poison belt has passed and the atmosphere has unexpectedly refreshed itself, the four men venture forth to view the devastation. Believing themselves to be the only survivors of the calamity, they are surprised to encounter an elderly woman who has been sustained by a store of oxygen used to treat her asthma. "Gentlemen," she says, "I beg that you will be frank with me. What effect will these events have upon London and Northwestern Railway shares?"

Conan Doyle has come in for criticism over the years for giving *The Poison Belt* a happy ending. As the story progresses we learn that humanity isn't dead at all, but merely sleeping under the effect of a potent narcotic. Challenger and his companions behold a wondrous scene of reawakening as the world stirs and resumes its business. Many commentators have chided Conan Doyle for taking the easy way out, but his business instincts would have admitted no alternative. Conan Doyle had further plans for Challenger. The world, therefore, would have to be spared.

In December 1912, even as Conan Doyle reveled in Challenger's success, a critic's barbs turned his attention back to Baker Street. In a rhymed address entitled "To Sir Arthur Conan Doyle," first published in America in *Life* magazine, a writer named Arthur Guiterman offered high praise for the "vigor and charm" of Conan Doyle's work but took exception to the famously outlandish opinions expressed by Sherlock Holmes in *A Study in Scarlet*:

> Faith! as a teller of tales you've the trick with you!
> Still there's a bone I've been longing to pick with you:
>
> Holmes is your hero of drama and serial;
> All of us know where you dug your material
> Whence he was moulded—'tis almost a platitude;
> Yet your detective, in shameless ingratitude—
>
> Sherlock your sleuthhound, with motives ulterior,
> Sneers at Poe's "Dupin" as "very inferior"!

Labels Gaboriau's clever "Lecoq," indeed,
Merely "a bungler," a creature to mock, indeed!

This, when your plots and your methods in story owe
Clearly a trifle to Poe and Gaboriau,
Sets all the Muses of Helicon sorrowing,
Borrow, Sir Knight, but be candid in borrowing!

The suggestion of ingratitude toward Poe, however jocular, must have rankled. "Poe is the master of all," Conan Doyle had written in *Through the Magic Door*. "If every man who receives a cheque for a story which owes its springs to Poe were to pay a tithe to a monument for the master, he would have a pyramid as big as that of Cheops."

Arthur Guiterman's poem, then, demanded a response. Conan Doyle's rebuttal, entitled "To An Undiscerning Critic," appeared in *London Opinion* on December 28. The spirit of the holiday season may have moderated his tone, but his poetry had seldom risen to such heights:

Sure, there are times when one cries with acidity,
"Where are the limits of human stupidity?"
Here is a critic who says as a platitude,
That I am guilty because "in gratitude,
Sherlock, the sleuthhound, with motives ulterior,
Sneers at Poe's Dupin as very 'inferior,' "

Have you not learned, my esteemed commentator,
That the created is not the creator?
As the creator I've praised to satiety
Poe's Monsieur Dupin, his skill and variety,
And have admitted that in my detective work,
I owe to my model a deal of selective work.

But is it not on the verge of inanity
To put down to me my creation's crude vanity?
He, the created, the puppet of fiction,

Would not brook rivals nor stand contradiction.
He, the created, would scoff and would sneer,
Where I, the Creator, would bow and revere.

So please grip this fact with your cerebral tentacle,
The doll and its maker are never identical.

20

The Ruthless Vegetarian

THE NOTETAKER: And how are all your people down at Selsey?
THE BYSTANDER: Who told you my people come from Selsey?
THE NOTETAKER: Never you mind.

—GEORGE BERNARD SHAW, *PYGMALION*

Not all critics, Conan Doyle learned to his sorrow, could be dispatched with such humor and grace. If Arthur Guiterman brought out the best in him, George Bernard Shaw would bring out the worst. "I have known no literary man who was more ruthless to other people's feelings," Conan Doyle once remarked of Shaw. "And yet to meet him was to like him."

Conan Doyle was by no means the first to remark upon Shaw's ill temper, but he may have been the first to attribute this ornery nature to a meat-free diet. "It was strange," Conan Doyle declared, "that all the mild vegetables which formed his diet made him more pugnacious and, I must add, more uncharitable than the carnivorous man."

Shaw had been a close neighbor of Conan Doyle's in Hindhead, and the two men had come to know each other well. Shaw's remarks on *Jane Annie* and *A Story of Waterloo* may have been forgotten, but one particular cruelty of Shaw's would always stand out in Conan

Doyle's memory. During a charity event at Undershaw, a group of amateur actors came together to stage a few scenes from *As You Like It*. Conan Doyle enjoyed the presentation thoroughly and congratulated the actors on a job well done. Shaw, on the other hand, went home and wrote a blistering review for the local paper—"spattering all the actors and their performance," Conan Doyle wrote, "and covering them with confusion, though indeed they had nothing to be ashamed of." For Conan Doyle, there could be no excuse for such an unwarranted display of spite. "One mentions these things as characteristic of one side of the man, and as a proof, I fear, that the adoption by the world of a vegetarian diet will not bring unkind thoughts or actions to an end."

Perhaps it was a bad carrot, then, that accounted for Shaw's bile in May 1912, one month after the sinking of the *Titanic*. At a time when the whole of Britain appeared united in its grief over the tragedy, Shaw felt compelled to offer a dissenting opinion. In Shaw's view, Britain's press had been guilty of "outrageous falsehoods" in the wake of the disaster. Writing in the *Daily News and Leader*, he put forward a series of deliberately inflammatory remarks intended to expose this hypocrisy. Under the heading of "Some Unmentioned Morals," Shaw lashed out at the gentlemen of the press for having lionized the *Titanic*'s captain and crew on the slender evidence of having gone down with the ship. "Why is it," Shaw asked, "that the effect of a sensational catastrophe on a modern nation is to cast it into transports, not of weeping, not of prayer, not of sympathy with the bereaved nor congratulation of the rescued, not of poetic expression of the soul purified by pity and terror, but of wild defiance of inexorable Fate and undeniable Fact by an explosion of outrageous romantic lying?"

A sampling of the newspapers of the time lends considerable weight to Shaw's view. In the immediate aftermath of the tragedy, when few details of the ship's final hours were known, many newspapers in both Britain and America printed rumor as fact, and filled their pages with highly charged accounts of heroism and melodrama. The confusion deepened as survivors arrived in New York aboard the *Carpathia*, which had responded to the *Titanic*'s distress calls. The survivors gave sketchy, often conflicting accounts of their ordeal. The press, starved for fresh material, often embroidered these slender facts beyond recognition.

A typical example was the tale of Ida Straus, who refused to leave her husband's side for a place in a lifeboat. The story was repeated over and over again on both sides of the Atlantic, complete with improbable commentary from the survivors. "And so she stayed," ran one passenger's unlikely quote, "clinging to her husband's arm, her face a study of quiet dignity, as the mighty ship went down to the depths."

Other accounts focused on episodes of cowardice and treachery. Breathless articles told of officers shooting third-class passengers to prevent them from storming the lifeboats. Others decried the "cowardly dastards"—especially J. Bruce Ismay, the managing director of the White Star line—who clambered to safety while women and children perished.

Nearly all of these early emotional accounts contained high praise for the "sublime and unselfish" Captain John Smith. One account had him shooting himself on the bridge of the ship. Another found him swimming through the icy waters, depositing a helpless infant in a lifeboat, and then swimming away with a cheery cry of "Be British, boys!" Still another placed him on the deck, calm and self-possessed as the icy waters rose to engulf him. "And then," wrote the *Daily Graphic*, "when all that human foresight could do and had been done unavailingly to save the *Titanic*, he still remembered his quiet little band of hard-working officers, and released them from duty. 'It's every man for himself at such a time as this,' he said. 'I release you. Look out for yourselves.' "

It was this sort of hyperbole that excited the wrath of Shaw. "It is commented upon as a heroic melodrama," he remarked in a private letter. "The whole attitude of the press is one of simple romantic insanity."

Shaw gave a forceful elaboration on this theme in his letter to the *Daily News and Leader*. "I ask, What is the use of all this ghastly, blasphemous, inhuman, braggartly lying? Here is a calamity which might well make the proudest man humble, and the wildest joker serious. It makes us vainglorious, insolent and mendacious. At all events, that is what our journalists assumed. Were they right or wrong? Did the press really represent the public? I am afraid it did. Churchmen and statesmen took much the same tone. The effect on me was one of profound disgust, almost of national dishonour. Am I mad? Possibly. At all events, that is how I felt and how I feel about it. . . . Our wretched consolation must be that any other nation would have behaved just as absurdly."

From a detached historical remove, one can only marvel at Shaw's perspective and clarity of thought. One must also wonder, however, at his motivation. It was not the first time he had expressed a deliberately provocative opinion in order to draw attention to himself, and he would do so again—to even greater effect—during the coming war. With the *Titanic*, however, he had struck a particularly raw nerve. It was one of those times, Conan Doyle remarked, when Shaw's "queer contrary impulses became perfectly brutal in their working."

Conan Doyle had personal grounds to recoil at Shaw's apparent callousness: he had lost a friend aboard the *Titanic*. The journalist W. T. Stead, who shared Conan Doyle's growing interest in spiritualism, had been among the casualties. Their friendship had survived Stead's attacks on British policy during the Boer War, and Conan Doyle had sent a presentation copy of *The White Company* as a token of his esteem. Shaw also knew Stead, and thought him a "complete ignoramus," though he did not say so at the time.

As he brooded over Shaw's insensitivity, Conan Doyle found himself "moved to write a remonstrance," matching Shaw's cool detachment with high emotion. His letter, headed "Mr. Shaw and the *Titanic*," was apparently written in some haste. "I have just been reading the article by Mr. Bernard Shaw upon the loss of the *Titanic*," Conan Doyle began. "It is written professedly in the interests of truth, and accuses everyone around him of lying. Yet I can never remember any production which contained so much that was false within the same compass. How a man could write with such looseness and levity of such an event at such a time passes all comprehension."

Having registered his dismay at Shaw's unseemly tone, Conan Doyle reviewed Shaw's charges of "outrageous romantic lying" and offered a point-by-point rebuttal. "What is the first demand of romance in a shipwreck?" Shaw had asked. "It is the cry of Women and Children first." In Shaw's view, however, this cry had not been heeded aboard the *Titanic*. As evidence, he gave the example of the notorious Lifeboat No. 1, which had a capacity of forty but was launched with only twelve people aboard—ten men and only two women.

Conan Doyle rose to the challenge: "Mr. Shaw wishes—in order to support his perverse thesis, that there was no heroism—to quote figures to show that the women were not given priority to escape. He picks out, therefore, one single boat, the smallest of all, which was launched and directed under peculiar circumstances, which are now matter for enquiry. Because there were ten men and two women in this boat, there was no heroism or chivalry; and all talk of it is affectation. Yet Mr. Shaw knows as well as I know that if he had taken the very next boat he would have been obliged to admit that there were 65 women out of 70 occupants, and that in nearly all the boats navigation was made difficult by want of men to do the rowing. Therefore, in order to give a false impression, he has deliberately singled out one boat; although he could not but be aware that it entirely misrepresented the general situation. Is this decent controversy, and has the writer any cause to accuse his contemporaries of misstatement?"

History bears Conan Doyle out on this point. Though many of the ship's lifeboats were launched with empty seats, women and children did receive priority. Of the women and children aboard the *Titanic*, three of every four survived. Of the men, four of every five were lost.

Unfortunately, not all of Shaw's charges could be answered so effectively. The second of his "romantic demands" centered on the conduct of Captain Smith. "Though all the men," he had written, "must be heroes, the Captain must be a super-hero, a magnificent seaman, cool, brave, delighting in death and danger, and a living guarantee that the wreck was nobody's fault, but, on the contrary, a triumph of British navigation."

Here again, Conan Doyle had a ready defense. It was wrong, Conan Doyle asserted, to suggest that the public's sympathy for the captain had taken the shape of condoning his navigation. "Now everyone—including Mr. Bernard Shaw—knows perfectly well that no defence has ever been made of the risk which was run, and that the sympathy was at the spectacle of an old and honoured sailor who has made one terrible mistake, and who deliberately gave his life in reparation, discarding his lifebelt, working to the last for those whom he had unwillingly injured, and finally swimming with a child to a boat into which he himself refused to enter. This is the fact, and Mr. Shaw's assertion that the wreck was hailed as a 'triumph of British navigation' only shows—which surely needed no showing—that a phrase stands for more than truth with Mr. Shaw."

As always, Conan Doyle's sincerity and eloquence do him credit. Unhappily, he chose to bolster his arguments by embracing the "heartbreaking rubbish" that had provoked Shaw's outburst. Conan Doyle took comfort in these tales of nobility amid the wreckage. It will never be known whether Captain Smith actually did swim through the waters to save a helpless infant. Conan Doyle chose to believe that he did. Shaw dismissed such claims as "disgusting and dishonourable nonsense."

This essential difference between the two men grew more pronounced as Conan Doyle turned his attention to the ship's officers. Shaw had written, as the third of his romantic demands, that the officers "must be calm, proud, steady, unmoved in the intervals of shooting the terrified foreigners." This was a low blow, a backhanded allusion to an unsubstantiated report that officers opened fire on third-class passengers when they threatened to storm the lifeboats. The very suggestion, Conan Doyle asserted, was a "poisonous" one, since no evidence had come to hand that anyone had been shot. Rather, a single officer was said to have discharged his revolver over the heads of a panicky crowd.

Oddly, Shaw had not seized this opening to address the high mortality rate among third-class passengers aboard the *Titanic*, possibly because the full particulars were not yet known. Instead, he focused on the somewhat dubious example of an officer named Harold Lowe, who was said to have told the much-maligned J. Bruce Ismay, the White Star executive, to go to hell. Lowe's outburst was understandable, Shaw allowed, but hardly a sterling example of heroism.

Conan Doyle disagreed. "I could not imagine a finer example of an officer doing his duty than that a subordinate should dare to speak thus to the managing director of the Line when he thought he was impeding his life-saving work," Conan Doyle wrote. "The sixth officer went down with the Captain, so I presume that even Mr. Shaw could not ask him to do more." Actually, Lowe was one of only four officers to survive the sinking, but Conan Doyle's confusion on this point is hardly surprising, as some early reports claimed that all of the officers had perished.

Conan Doyle reserved his sharpest words for the fourth and final entry in Shaw's list of romantic demands. "Everybody must face death without a tremor," Shaw had written, "and the band . . . must play 'Nearer my God to Thee' as an accompaniment."

Then as now, the conduct of the *Titanic*'s band was seen as one of the most stirring features of the tragedy. Shortly after the collision, the band was ordered to play lively ragtime tunes to help calm the passengers and avert panic. Even when it became apparent that the ship was sinking, the musicians continued to play until they could no longer keep their footing on the sloping deck. Legend holds that their last number was "Nearer my God to Thee," as Shaw stated, but the survivors offered no consensus on this point. Though the musicians were widely hailed for their serene bravery, Shaw saw evidence of further dishonor. The ragtime music, he insisted, created a false impression of normality, and prevented many who might have been saved from seeking the lifeboats until it was too late.

Here, Conan Doyle felt, Shaw had scored an unforgivable foul. Whatever his motives, Shaw had made light of the very concept of chivalry, something that Conan Doyle held to be sacred. "Mr. Shaw tries to defile the beautiful incident of the band by alleging that it was the result of orders issued to avert panic," he wrote. "But if it were, how does that detract either from the wisdom of the orders or from the heroism of the musicians? It was right to avert panic, and it was wonderful that men could be found to do it in such a way."

Indeed, in Conan Doyle's view, such gallantry would have brought credit to the likes of Sir Nigel Loring and Rodney Stone. The question of whether the gentlemen of the press had exaggerated—or even fabricated—their accounts of this bravery did not concern him. An epic calamity demanded epic heroes. In summing up his response to Shaw, Conan Doyle made this clear in no uncertain terms: "As to the general accusation that the occasion has been used for the glorification of British qualities, we should indeed be a lost people if we did not honour courage and discipline when we see it in the highest form. That our sympathies extend beyond ourselves is shown by the fact that the conduct of the American male passengers, and very particularly of the much-abused millionaires, has been as warmly eulogised as any single feature of the whole wonderful epic. But surely it is a pitiful sight to see a man of undoubted genius using his gifts in order to misrepresent and decry his own people, regardless of the fact that his words must add to the grief of those who have already had more than enough to bear."

Not everyone would describe the sinking of the *Titanic* as a "wonderful epic," but Conan Doyle's impassioned defense of the ship's crew caught the public mood perfectly. If Shaw had been content to let the matter rest, Conan Doyle might be seen to have held the day. Two days later, however, a withering response appeared.

In his first article, Shaw had railed against the faceless men of the press. Now he concentrated his venom solely on Conan Doyle. "I hope," he began, "to persuade my friend Sir Arthur Conan Doyle, now that he has got his romantic and warm-hearted protest off his chest, to read my article again three or four times, and give you his second thoughts on the matter; for it really is not possible for any sane man to disagree with a single word that I have written."

Shaw went on to reiterate the "inept romances" and "stories of sensational cowardice" circulating in the newspapers, dwelling at length on Conan Doyle's admiration for Harold Lowe, the young officer who had told his superior to go to hell. "Sir Arthur accuses me of lying," Shaw wrote, "and I must say he gives me no great encouragement to tell the truth. But he proceeds to tell, against himself, what I take to be the most thundering lie ever sent to a printer by a human author. He first says that 'I quoted as if it were a crime' the words used by the officer who told Mr. Ismay to go to hell. I did not. I said the outburst was very natural, though not in my opinion admirable or heroic. If I am wrong, then I claim to be a hero myself."

Conan Doyle, Shaw went on to say, had stated that he could imagine no finer example of an officer doing his duty. "Yes you could, Sir Arthur," Shaw retorted, "and many a page of heroic romance from your hand attests that you have often imagined much finer examples. Heroism has not quite come to that yet; nor has your imagination contracted or your brain softened to the bathos of seeing sublimity in a worried officer telling even a managing director (godlike being!) to go to hell. I would not hear your enemy libel you so. But now that you have chivalrously libelled yourself, don't lecture me for reckless mendacity; for you have captured the record in the amazing sentence I have just quoted."

Conan Doyle's defense of Captain Smith drew an even sharper response: "The Captain of the *Titanic* did not, as Sir Arthur thinks, make 'a terrible mistake.' He made no mistake. He knew perfectly well that ice is the only risk that is considered really deadly in his line of work, and, knowing it, he chanced it and lost the hazard. Sentimental idiots, with a break in the voice, tell me that 'he went down to the depths'; I tell them, with the impatient contempt that they deserve, that so did the cat."

Shaw acknowledged that his harsh words might cause pain to some, but circumstances, he felt, left him no choice. "I should not have run the risk of adding to the distress of Captain Smith's family by adding one word to facts that speak only too plainly for themselves if others had been equally considerate," Shaw insisted. "But if vociferous journalists will persist in glorifying the barrister whose clients are hanged, the physician whose patients die, the general who loses battles, and the captain whose ship goes to the bottom, such false coin must be nailed to the counter at any cost."

Wisely, Conan Doyle decided to end the matter there. No doubt he wished to respond to some of Shaw's more pointed barbs, but he must have understood that there was no point in going another round with so intractable a foe. He made a brief and dignified statement to bring the exchange to a close. "Without continuing a controversy which must be sterile," he wrote, "I would touch on only one point in Mr. Shaw's reply to my letter. He says that I accused him of lying. I have been guilty of no such breach of the amenities of the discussion. The worst I say or think of Mr. Shaw is that his many brilliant gifts do not include the power of weighing evidence; nor has he that quality—call it good taste, humanity, or what you will—which prevents a man from needlessly hurting the feelings of others."

In the end, the exchange said little about the *Titanic*, but revealed a great deal about Shaw and Conan Doyle. For Shaw, the word "romance" could only apply in a pejorative sense. Again and again, he used phrases such as "romantic lying," "inept romances," and "romantic insanity" to describe the actions of the press. Conan Doyle's entire point of view had been dismissed as "romantic and warm-hearted." For Conan Doyle, no other response was possible. He saw the tragedy as a "wonderful epic," like one of his own historical romances, and in this way was able to confer a solemn dignity on the victims. "The big blank spaces in the map are all being filled in," he had declared wistfully in *The Lost World*, "and there's no room for romance anywhere."

For all the strength of their convictions, each man had used the facts selectively to bolster his argument, and neither was above engaging in a bit of rhetorical fan-dancing. Conan Doyle appeared wounded by the very suggestion that he had called Shaw a liar, perhaps forgetting his earlier statement that he could recall no "production which contained so much that was false within the same compass." Shaw, for his part, attacked the press for glorifying the *Titanic* crew with half-truths, but his own winking allusion to "shooting the terrified foreigners" had brought him down to their level.

Conan Doyle never forgot the bitterness of the exchange, but it pleased him to report that it did nothing to modify the "kindly personal relations" he and Shaw enjoyed. Later that year they would share a platform to address the topic of religious persecution in Ireland. "[W]ith it all," Conan Doyle wrote, "Shaw is a genial creature to meet, and I am prepared to believe that there is a human kindly side to his nature though it has not been presented to the public. It took a good man to write 'Saint Joan.' "

In the whole of the tragedy, no single incident touched Conan Doyle more deeply than the drama of the ship's musicians, not one of whom survived. Conan Doyle, the veteran tuba player, decided to commemorate their sacrifice with a poem called "Ragtime," probably inspired by "The Birken'ead Drill," Rudyard Kipling's tribute to the British troopship that sank off South Africa in 1852. Like the *Titanic*, the *Birkenhead*'s lifeboats could not hold all her passengers. The soldiers and sailors gallantly saw to the safety of the women and children onboard, then stood in silent formation on the decks as the ship went down.

Conan Doyle's poetic gifts were modest beside Kipling's, but no one—with the possible exception of Shaw—could fault the sentiment behind his verses, which concluded with a heartfelt tribute:

There's a glowing hell beneath us where the shattered boilers roar,
The ship is listing and awash, the boats will hold no more!
There's nothing more that you can do, and nothing you can mend,
Only keep the ragtime playing to the end.

Don't forget the time, boys! Eyes upon the score!
Never heed the wavelets sobbing down the floor!
Play it as you played it when with eager feet
A hundred pairs of dancers were stamping to the beat.

Stamping to the ragtime down the lamp-lit deck,
With shine of glossy linen and with gleam of snowy neck,
They've other thoughts to think tonight, and other things to do,
But the tinkle of the ragtime may help to see them through.

Shut off, shut off the ragtime! The lights are falling low!
The deck is buckling under us! She's sinking by the bow!
One hymn of hope from dying hands on dying ears to fall—
Gently the music fades away—and so, God rest us all!

21

England on Her Knees

"The Press, Watson, is a most valuable institution, if you only know how to use it."

—SHERLOCK HOLMES IN "THE SIX NAPOLEONS"

In May of 1914, Conan Doyle set sail for America aboard the White Star liner *Olympic*, sister ship of the *Titanic*. Two years had elapsed since his quarrel with George Bernard Shaw, and if he felt any qualms about the *Olympic*'s captain or his crew, he managed to conceal them as he waved cheerfully from the departure deck.

Twenty years had passed since Conan Doyle's first visit to New York, and his reappearance sparked some fanciful speculation in the press. "Sherlock Holmes as a citizen of New York in the near future is one of the delightful possibilities suggested by Sir Arthur Conan Doyle," reported the *New York Times*. "It seems that Sir Arthur finds New York a not unworthy field for the exercise of the great detective's abilities—and we may be reasonably certain that if the American metropolis is large enough and wicked enough for Holmes, it will surely furnish an agreeable residence for the indefatigable Dr. Watson."

Actually, the great detective had nothing to do with the visit. The Canadian government had invited Conan Doyle on a goodwill tour of its national parks. Conan Doyle may have hesitated to leave Britain at such a politically volatile time, but he could not resist the chance to see the North American wilderness he had read about as a boy. Lady Conan Doyle accompanied him on the trip, leaving their children—including their daughter Jean, born two years earlier—in the care of a nanny.

The Conan Doyles planned to spend six days at New York's Plaza Hotel before making their way to Canada by train. Upon landing in New York, Conan Doyle found that much had changed since his 1894 visit. "I am amazed, fairly paralyzed at the sight of New York," he told the *New York Times*. "It seems as though someone had gone over the city with a watering pot and these stupendous buildings had grown up overnight as a result. When I was here twenty years ago, the World Building was your skyscraper. Today it is lost—a mere pedestal. New York is a wonderful city, as America is a wonderful country, with a big future."

William J. Burns, founder of the William J. Burns National Detective Agency, was there to greet the Conan Doyles at the dock, and played host for much of the visit. Known for his investigations into land fraud and political corruption, Burns enjoyed a reputation as "the Sherlock Holmes of America." Conan Doyle had received him at Windlesham the previous year and spent a pleasant evening pumping him for details of his days as a Pinkerton detective. Burns had, Conan Doyle wrote, "the easy and polished manners of a diplomat over something else that can be polished—granite."

The detective laid on a full itinerary. Conan Doyle lunched with Mayor Ardolph Kline, dined with publisher George H. Doran, toured the Sing Sing prison facilities, and took in a baseball game between the New York Yankees and the Philadelphia Athletics. He enjoyed the ball game, but Conan Doyle—who, at age fifty-five, still played in an amateur cricket league—expressed some reservations about professional sports. "[I]t means that the largest purse has the best team," he wrote, "and there is no necessary relation between the player and the place he plays for."

Conan Doyle drew "wild huzzahs" at the Pilgrim Club, an organization dedicated to Anglo-American friendship, which held a luncheon in his honor. "I stand here as a pilgrim," he told the gathering.

"In the old days, the kit of a pilgrim consisted mainly of a staff and an empty wallet. In my case, I have a good substitute for a staff in the shape of a good, stout English umbrella. As to my wallet, Mr. Lloyd George has taken care to see that it is empty. 'England expects every man to do his duty' was a slogan of other times. In this day, 'England expects every man to pay his duty.' "

Two days later, a visit to Coney Island found the author mixing easily with a "motley crowd of ballyhoos, frankfurter men and noisy sightseers," according to the *New York Times*. "Conan Doyle Like Big Boy at Coney," declared the newspaper's headline; "Laughs at Everything," observed the subhead. Cheering crowds greeted his arrival, and a brass band struck up "God Save the King" as he entered the Steeplechase Pavilion. An enthusiastic Conan Doyle rode the "seemingly perilous" Whip Ride, had his fortune told, and visited the "ridiculous Crazy Village" fun house, managing to keep his equilibrium amid the tilting walls and sliding floors. He emerged "somewhat disheveled, but unrestrainedly merry."

"Coney Island doesn't give one time to think," he told reporters, "but I certainly had a good time."

On reflection, he might have wished for less fun and more time to think, as his frequent press interviews would soon cause him considerable embarrassment. On his earlier visit, Conan Doyle managed to discharge his obligations to the press with one grueling press conference, facing his interviewers "like a rat among terriers." Now, with reporters dogging him at every stop, he offered an unguarded comment about the suffrage movement, a cause for which he had no sympathy. "People are getting tired of all this window smashing, house burning and picture mutilating," he told an attentive press. If the militant suffragettes continued in this vein, he warned, they would surely be lynched by an angry public.

On the strength of such comments, Conan Doyle is generally thought to have been something of a dinosaur on the issue of women's rights. Though he never wavered in his opposition to the suffrage movement, his true sentiments were far more complex—and not nearly so belligerent—as his off-the-cuff remarks suggested. Despite his work on behalf of divorce law reform, Conan Doyle's stand on women's rights had changed little since his days as a parliamentary candidate. A woman could expect the right to vote, he believed, only if she paid her own taxes. In fairness, this was not quite so narrow-minded as it appeared. He had seen by the example of his own mother that a woman could hold her own in a man's world, and he saw no reason why women should not enter professional life.

In the main, however, he wished to preserve the accepted social order of the previous century. It must be remembered that his own childhood had been anything but conventional. He had overcome a great deal of hardship to embrace the values of that time, and clung to them all the more tenaciously because of it. Sherlock Holmes once referred affectionately to Dr. Watson as "the one fixed point in a changing age." On this one point, the same must be said of Conan Doyle. For him, the suffragettes represented social chaos, not equality for women.

Conan Doyle's outspokenness on the subject excited much interest. Back home in England he had sulphuric acid poured through his letterbox as a response to his opinions. Now, as he read an exaggerated version of his comments in the New York press, he felt obliged to offer an immediate retraction. "I am in a wretched humor," he told a press conference, "all of it due to American journalism." He went on to describe his horror at opening the newspapers to find himself "headlined as desiring to lynch" the female suffragettes. "I must correct that or I shall not dare to return to England," he told the reporters. "I have many very good friends among the militants and among them who favor the militant movement. Now, what I did say to your reporters was that I was afraid the time was close at hand when some very drastic action would be taken. That I very much feared that the people would take the law into their own hands, and that the result would be nothing short of lynching. That would be a terrible outcome—I can conceive of nothing more horrible, except that I myself should subscribe to such an action!"

In still another interview, this one chronicling a visit to Sing Sing prison, Conan Doyle amplified his sentiments toward the press.

After sitting in the facility's cane-bottomed electric chair for a moment, Conan Doyle allowed himself to be locked away in a seven- by four-foot cell to experience the sensation of prison confinement. "It was the most restful time I have had since I arrived in New York," he declared, "for it was the only chance I had to get away from the reporters."

After the rigors of New York, Canada provided a welcome relief. The president of the Grand Trunk Railroad placed his "gloriously comfortable" private railroad car at the disposal of the Conan Doyles, complete with a parlor, dining room, and modern plumbing.

The tour had been designed as an exercise in goodwill between Canada and Britain, and Conan Doyle threw himself into it with his usual enthusiasm. He gave speeches, toured government facilities, and admired the natural beauty of the Jasper and Algonquin national parks. He posed for photographs with a baseball bat in hand, nearly decapitating the photographer when he knocked out a solid line drive. He marveled at the clear, unspoiled lakes and tried his hand at fishing with no particular success, though Jean managed to hook an eight-pound trout.

"Canada is like an expanding flower," he wrote, "wherever you look you see some fresh petal unrolling." Unlike New York, the vast open spaces of Canada seemed to him to be aglow with the "iridescence of romance." Grain elevators struck him as "not unlike the columns of Luxor," and his first glimpse of the Rocky Mountains brought the frontier tales of Mayne Reid, a boyhood favorite, flooding back. "What deeds have I not done among Redskins and trappers and grizzlies within their wilds!" he wrote. "And here they were at last glimmering bright in the rising morning sun. At least, I have seen my dream mountains. Most boys never do."

As he sailed for home in June, Conan Doyle would later recall, he had "little perception of how near we were to the greatest event of the world's history." In fact, Conan Doyle saw the coming of war with greater clarity than most. Three years earlier he had participated in a goodwill automobile rally called the Prince Henry Tour, an amateur competition that pitted fifty German drivers against some forty British drivers from the Royal Automobile Club. Organized by the German prince to coincide with the coronation of

George V, the three-week event was designed to strengthen Anglo-German relations, though ultimately it served only to expose the growing rift between the two countries.

Conan Doyle had looked forward to the event. He was an eager motorist, and his car-flipping, turnip-battering episodes were now a thing of the past. With Jean as navigator, he took his own 16-horse-power Dietrich-Lorraine landaulet to Hamburg for the start of the rally. The 2,500-mile course wound through Cologne to Bremerhaven, then crossed by steamer to Southampton, moving as far north as Edinburgh before the finish in London. The ninety drivers covered as much as 150 miles each day as they proceeded from checkpoint to checkpoint. Conan Doyle did his best to keep pace, even when it required climbing out to push his car up a steep hill.

Each car carried a military observer from the opposing country. The stiff and overly formal Count Carmer, Rittmeister of the Breslau Cuirassiers, rode along with the Conan Doyles, growing slightly more genial as the rally wore on. Other competitors fared less well. Conan Doyle was shocked by the warlike attitudes of the other German observers and overheard many remarks about the inevitability of war. The British drivers, for their part, had to be restrained from settling disputes with their fists. "The only thing I want to do with these people is to fight them," declared one British colonel. By the time Britain claimed victory in London, carrying away an ivory trophy inscribed with the word "Peace," Conan Doyle had come to regard the episode as a "clumsy bit of stage management," designed to distract attention from German naval activity in Morocco. "I came away with sinister forebodings," he recalled.

Publicly, he continued to espouse friendship with Germany. In a letter to the *Times* of London, he acknowledged the warm hospitality of his hosts in Germany. An endless line of friendly Germans had cheered the British motorists as they drove past, he wrote, sending a "true message of good will" to Britain. "The only *contretemps*," he added, "arose from ignorance of the fact that even a small bunch of flowers received in the face when you are travelling at high speed may become a dangerous missile."

It was typical of Conan Doyle to express his thanks in a public forum, despite his private misgivings. Even in later years, after the war had exacted a devastating personal toll, he could not look back on the Prince Henry Tour without recalling the kindness of a German officer who left flowers for Jean each morning.

Even so, as he became convinced that war was coming, Conan Doyle's attention turned toward military readiness. As early as 1906, he had written to the *Times* about organizing the motorists of Britain into a rapid response unit, ready at the first word of a coastal invasion to convey local riflemen to "the danger point." In 1910, he sent a letter to the *Daily Express* to weigh the merits of replacing mounted cavalry with bicycle regiments. After the Prince Henry Tour he began to study German war literature, notably the works of General von Bernhardi, whose hawkish *Germany and the Next War* filled him with dread. Conan Doyle responded with a lengthy article called "England and the Next War," published in the *Fortnightly Review* in 1913, in which he described powerful new forms of warfare that had never been tested in the hands of "competent" men. "These new factors are the submarine and the airship," Conan Doyle wrote, expressing a view that had not been widely discussed at the time. "The latter, save as a means of acquiring information, does not seem to be formidable—or not sufficiently formidable to alter the whole conditions of the campaign. But it is different with the submarines. No blockade, so far as I can see, can hold these vessels in harbour, and no skill or bravery can counteract their attack when once they are within striking distance."

Merchant vessels as well as military craft would be vulnerable to submarine attack, he continued, raising the fearsome prospect of Britain reduced to starvation if her food supplies were cut off. The only solution, as Conan Doyle saw it, lay in the building of a Channel Tunnel. He had studied the idea for some time and estimated that it would take three years to build and cost the British taxpayer five million pounds. In peacetime, the tunnel would encourage continental travel and bring thousands of tourists to Britain who might be deterred by sea travel. In time of war, the tunnel would insure the free movement of troops and supplies to the European mainland, and remove the threat of a total blockade.

Conan Doyle never claimed to have originated the idea of a Channel Tunnel, but he happily used his influence to bring it to the attention of the public. The idea provoked a lively debate in the newspaper letter columns, with more than one correspondent writing to ask what would happen if an enemy should seize the tunnel. Conan Doyle responded that an invading force would have to win and hold both ends of the tunnel. "Such a contingency is, I hold, beyond all bounds of common sense," he declared. Suppose, other correspondents wondered, Britain should find herself at war with France? Again, Conan Doyle found the prospect unlikely, but allowed that the tunnel could easily be sealed in such an event. As the debate stretched on, he came to resent each day that passed without any concrete action on the matter. "I wonder what our descendants will think of the whole business," he wrote, "probably what we think of the men who opposed the Suez Canal."

Frustrated to find his proposals "subordinated to party politics," Conan Doyle took his case to the general public. Six years earlier, in "The Bruce-Partington Plans," a "certain gracious lady" bestowed an emerald tie-pin on Sherlock Holmes for his role in recovering a stolen submarine blueprint. Now, with Britain on the brink of war, Conan Doyle renewed the theme with a cautionary tale called "Danger! Being the Log of Captain John Sirius." Written in February 1914, "Danger!" was published in *The Strand* shortly after his return from Canada. Set in the near future, "Danger!" finds Britain embroiled in a frontier dispute with a relatively weak European ally, artfully disguised as "Norland." As Norland's king contemplates surrender, Captain Sirius, who commands Norland's modest fleet of eight submarines, proposes a plan to paralyze British merchant shipping. "Sire," the captain tells his despairing king, "I will stake my life that if you will follow my advice you will, within a month or six weeks at the most, bring proud England to her knees."

The captain's plan, not surprisingly, is to choke off Britain's supply lines. Though Britain soon annihilates Norland's surface fleet, the eight submarines under Sirius's command slip past her torpedo boats and launch a series of devastating attacks on supply vessels headed for England. Soon Britain is gripped in a nationwide famine, and Norland's submarines have penetrated as far as the mouth of the Thames. "It is an amazing thing that the English, who have the reputation of being a practical nation, never saw the danger to which they were exposed," Captain Sirius observes. "Their ruin could not have been more complete or more rapid if they had not possessed an ironclad or a regiment."

"Danger!" is perhaps the most remarkable piece of propaganda Conan Doyle ever wrote. With its loving descriptions of the submarines and their armaments, the story not only anticipates the modern military thriller but also reveals the degree to which Conan Doyle had immersed himself in technical literature. As for the plot, it soon ran aground on the shoals of political diatribe. "Ah, Johnny, Johnny Bull," Captain Sirius intones as he sets off on his grim mission, "you are going to have your lesson, and I am to be your master. It is I who have been chosen to teach you that one cannot live under artificial conditions and yet act as if they were natural ones. More foresight, Johnny, and less party politics—that is my lesson to you."

Subtlety, it seems, was not Conan Doyle's primary concern. The story, he would later say, was intended not to entertain but to "direct public attention to the great danger which threatened this country."

To accompany the story's publication in *The Strand*, Conan Doyle and Greenhough Smith solicited the opinions of a dozen prominent naval experts. In his autobiography, Conan Doyle had sharp words for these commentators, many of whom were retired admirals: "I am afraid that the printed results, which I will not be so cruel as to quote, showed that it was as well they *were* retired, since they had no sense of the possibilities of the naval warfare of the future."

The assessment was unjust. One commentator found the story "eminently probable," and another declared that "the only *safe* defense against an attack in the near future as depicted lies in the establishment of national granaries or Channel Tunnels." Nearly all of the twelve commentators agreed with the assessment of Mr. Arnold White, a naval historian, who declared that "Sir Arthur Conan Doyle has placed his finger on the neuralgic nerve-centre of the British Empire—i.e., the precarious arrival of our food supply."

"Four-fifths of our daily bread and a large portion of our other food is sea-borne," added Mr. Douglas Owen, a lecturer on naval subjects. "By some it may be thought that for a popular writer to employ his talents in the creation of general alarm is to make ill use of them. If so, I think they will, on reflection, agree with those who hold, on the contrary, that a far-seeing citizen who places before his slumbering countrymen a graphic and awakening picture of a danger hanging over them is rendering them the highest service."

Others mentioned the nation's "lasting obligation" to Conan Doyle, and the "great national service" he had performed, but it was not enough for him. Impatient for immediate action, Conan Doyle fixed his attention on the few notes of dissent. Admiral C. C. Penrose Fitzgerald, while admitting that the debate was "all to the good," disagreed with Conan Doyle's assessment of the danger. "I do not myself think," Fitzgerald wrote, "that any civilized nation will torpedo unarmed and defenceless merchant ships."

"I do not think that territorial waters will be violated, or neutral vessels sunk," said Admiral William Hannam Henderson, taking up the theme. "Such will be absolutely prohibited, and will only recoil on the heads of the perpetrators."

If opinions were divided on the threat from submarines, the idea of a national food stockpile drew universal support. "The moral of the story is, of course, that we should have vast stores of grain in this country," wrote Admiral Sir William Kennedy, "in which opinion I cordially concur." As to Conan Doyle's insistence on a Channel tunnel, Kennedy, like many others, had grave reservations. "God made us an island," he declared, "by all means let us remain so."

By this time, however, the idea of a tunnel had gained independent momentum. A House of Commons debate on the matter was scheduled for June 29, 1914. As fate would have it, Archduke Francis Ferdinand of Austria was assassinated in Sarajevo one day earlier, rendering the debate moot. The official declaration of war followed six days later.

Conan Doyle's warning about the perils of submarine warfare had been dismissed as a Jules Verne fantasy by one naval expert. Within a year, as German *Unterseebooten*, or U-boats, began to prey on merchant ships, the story no longer seemed so improbable. Worse yet, reports from Germany made it appear that Alfred von Tirpitz, Grand Admiral of the German navy, had been more attentive than the British government. On February 18, 1915, the London *Times* carried a report of *Die Blockade Englands*, culled from German newspapers under the byline of "a neutral observer."

"Every German's heart welled with pride and delight," the story ran, "as he read the official *communiqué* announcing 'that on and after February 18 every British merchant ship entering British water would be destroyed.' "

When asked how this destruction would be carried out, several "well-informed Germans" pointed to Conan Doyle's story. "We had the idea ready-made for us in England," one source was reported to have said. "Conan Doyle suggested the outlines of a plan which every German has hoped would be used. His story, 'Danger,' will tell you far better than I can what we intend to do."

"This was said to me with all seriousness," the correspondent added, "and I heard Conan Doyle's story referred to repeatedly in defence of the blockade."

Horrified, Conan Doyle now found himself in the most awkward position of his career. Whatever his private feelings, he clearly understood that this was no time for finger-pointing. By the same token, any further elaboration of the dangers of submarine attack would only add to the public's distress and reinforce the image of himself as the architect of Germany's master plan.

Eager to respond quickly and forcefully, Conan Doyle made an immediate statement to the press. His remarks, which appeared under the headline "Doyle Doesn't Fear Submarine Raids," were designed to downplay the German report. "I need hardly say that it is very painful for me to think that anything I have written should be turned against my own country," he said. "The object of the story was to warn the public of a possible danger which I saw overhanging this country and to show it how to avoid that danger.

"In the story I place the incidents of the submarine blockade some years hence," he continued. "It was a story of the future, and my reason was that after studying the subject, I concluded that the submarine at present was not capable of the results which I depicted. But it is still my opinion that if this war had been delayed for five years, and if the submarine during that time had gone on improving as rapidly as it had done in the past, England would have been placed in a most serious position, exactly as outlined in the story. I am quite sure, in the present circumstances, that although we may possibly lose more ships, the German blockade can have no serious effect on the war."

Germany's efficient fleet of diesel-powered submarines did, of course, have a serious effect on the war, and one can only imagine Conan Doyle's thoughts at the sinking of the *Lusitania* in May 1915. What Conan Doyle had not anticipated, however, was the development of depth charges, underwater listening devices, and submarine attack vessels to counter the German threat. Looking back on "Danger!" at the close of the war, Conan Doyle was glad to admit that he had underestimated the energy and ingenuity of Britain's response. "The great silent battle which has been fought beneath the waves has ended in the repulse of an armada far more dangerous than that of Spain," he wrote.

Given the scope and complexity of Germany's naval agenda, it seems extremely odd that her commanders should have found time to tip their hats to Conan Doyle. The Imperial Naval Office had managed its strategy quite competently up to that point, and it is difficult to imagine von Tirpitz and his staff sending their U-boat commanders out to sea with copies of *The Strand* in their dispatch kits. As an exercise in demoralizing propaganda, however, the episode made perfect sense. If Conan Doyle, one of Britain's most beloved public figures, could be seen to have aided the enemy, it would seem as if Sherlock Holmes himself had betrayed his country.

However unlikely, the notion of Conan Doyle as German strategist persisted for the duration of the war. In May 1917, according to the *New York Times*, Conan Doyle received an unwelcome tribute in the Reichstag, Germany's national legislative committee. "The only prophet of the present economic war," declared Admiral Eduard von Capelle, the German Secretary of the Navy, "was the novelist Conan Doyle."

Conan Doyle's own propaganda initiative was just beginning.

22

An Audible Voice

It was nine o'clock at night upon the second of August—the most terrible August in the history of the world.

—ARTHUR CONAN DOYLE, "HIS LAST BOW"

"I want your advice," Conan Doyle wrote to his brother Innes in the early days of the war. "Do you think it would be a good thing for me to apply for a Captaincy (very senior) in the new army?"

Innes Doyle, who had trained for a career in the army at Woolwich Academy, may well have wondered if his older brother was serious. At fifty-five, and with no official military background, Conan Doyle was not officer material. Still, he wanted desperately to do his bit, just as he had at the start of the Boer conflict. If he were to join up at his age, he explained to Innes, it might shame others into doing the same.

"I think I may say that my name is well known to the younger men of this country," he declared in a letter to the War Office, "and that if I were to take a commission at my age it would set an example which might be of help.

"I can drill a company," he continued, referring to a group of local volunteers. "I do so every evening. I have seen something of campaigning, having served as a surgeon in South Africa. I am fifty-five but I am very strong and hardy, and can make my voice audible at great distances, which is useful at drill."

The rejection of his application, despite the audibility of his voice, came as a blow. Conan Doyle watched with mounting frustration as all of the young men of the family went off to join up. Innes would rise to the rank of brigadier general. Kingsley, Conan Doyle's son by Louisa, interrupted a course of medical training to join the First Hampshire Regiment. They were joined by two of Conan Doyle's brothers-in-law, Malcolm Leckie and Leslie Oldham, and two of his nephews, Oscar Hornung and Alec Forbes. All of them had gone out to face the enemy in a way that Conan Doyle could not.

Denied active service, Conan Doyle would find other ways to make his voice heard. A plumber from the village had sent a polite note: "There is a feeling in Crowborough," it read, "that something should be done." Conan Doyle at once set about organizing a group of 120 civilian volunteers. "Many of the men are fine shots and all are exceedingly anxious to be serviceable," he reported to the London *Times*. "We have our own record of organisation, and I should be happy to send copies of our method to anyone who may desire to form other centres." If every town mobilized its own civil defense unit, Conan Doyle reasoned, Britain's Territorial Army would be freed for active service. The idea drew hundreds of responses, all dutifully answered by Conan Doyle and his secretary, but within weeks the War Office ordered the units to disband in favor of a centrally administered government scheme. In recognition of Conan Doyle's initiative, the first authorization to form a volunteer battalion went to his unit, now known as the Crowborough Company of the Sixth Royal Sussex Volunteer Regiment.

After refusing command of the new battalion, Crowborough's most famous resident entered service as Private Sir Arthur Conan Doyle, eager to demonstrate that all men were equal in the defense of their country. He referred to himself as "Ole Bill," after a somewhat woebegone cartoon figure, but took pride in keeping up with the younger men. He cheerfully marched fourteen miles a day in full gear, singing all the way. He patrolled the town, practiced his shooting, worked as a signaler, and pulled shifts in a machine-gun nest.

On one occasion, he stood in the rain for eight hours guarding a labor detail of German prisoners as they loaded carts with manure.

As the privations of war mounted, the family voluntarily reduced its food supply. Conan Doyle, who had summed up his Dickensian childhood as "bracing," brought the same ironclad optimism to these new conditions. "There was a pleasing uncertainty about all meals," he wrote. "There was always a sense of adventure and a wonder whether you would get something. It all made for appetite."

While her husband marched and drilled, Jean rented a house in Crowborough and established a reception center for Belgian refugees. Mary, Conan Doyle's daughter by Louisa, spent her days making artillery shells in a factory assembly line and her evenings cooking in an army canteen. At such a time, Conan Doyle felt, one needed to keep busy. Few of Crowborough's residents would have argued the point: on a calm day, the guns of Flanders could be heard 120 miles distant.

When three British battle cruisers went down in a single day, at a cost of some 1,400 lives, Conan Doyle took it upon himself to suggest a number of lifesaving ideas to the War Office. "A young German lieutenant with twenty men had caused us more loss than we suffered at Trafalgar," he wrote. "We can spare the ships. We can't spare the men."

As with his submarine warnings and his Channel tunnel agitations, Conan Doyle made canny use of his own celebrity. Each suggestion to the War Office corresponded with a letter to the press, in the hope that a public "ventilation" would spur the government to speedier action. A letter to the *Daily Mail* urged the development of an "inflatable rubber belt" to give sailors a chance of survival if their ships went down. For his trouble, Conan Doyle received a public "rap over the knuckles" from a retired commander named Jane, who resented the intrusion of an apparently ignorant landlubber. Within days, however, the government placed an order for a quarter of a million inflatable rubber collars, a forerunner of today's lifejacket. It is impossible to say whether Conan Doyle's proposal had any decisive influence, but newspaper reporters were quick to hand him the credit. "The Navy has to thank Sir Conan Doyle for the new life-saving apparatus," wrote the *Hampshire Telegraph*, mangling his title. "There is little doubt that this swimming collar will result in the saving of many lives, and the Admiralty are to be congratulated upon the promptitude with which they have adopted the suggestion of Sir Conan Doyle."

Delighted by the development, Conan Doyle could not resist thumbing his nose at Commander Jane. "Your naval correspondent," he wrote in the *Evening Standard and St. James's Gazette*, "took me to task in your columns recently for so unreasonable a demand as that our sailors should be provided with some means of escape from certain death when their ships founder. I had suggested an inflatable rubber belt. He will be interested to hear that an inflatable rubber collar has actually been adopted, and is, as I understand, being served out to every sailor."

He readily acknowledged, however, that the collars would be of little use in rough weather or frigid seas, and soon put forward a plan for inflatable lifeboats. "In the merchant service there must be boat provision for every passenger," he told the *Daily Chronicle*. "Is it not simple common sense, therefore, that in a warship, which is so much more likely to sink, and where the men are so invaluable to the country, the same law should hold good?" The navy objected on the grounds that battleships, unlike civilian craft, had more rigid standards of speed and function, and could not afford to be hampered by excess material. Nevertheless, a flotation platform soon came into use, which could be detached from a sinking ship to give the sailors a better chance of survival.

Conan Doyle also threw his weight behind a plan to issue body armor to frontline soldiers. He often receives credit for having originated this idea, which is perhaps natural enough given his well-documented interest in medieval knights. In truth, the notion was already in play at the start of the war, though none of its proponents were as outspoken or relentless as Conan Doyle. "It has always seemed to me extraordinary," he wrote in the *Times*, "that the innumerable cases where a Bible, a cigarette case, a watch, or some other chance article has saved a man's life have not set us scheming so as to do systematically what has so often been the result of a happy chance."

Given the fact that the British had not even worn helmets for nearly two hundred years, body armor proved to be a tough sell. Army officials objected on the grounds of excess weight and lack of mobility, despite Conan Doyle's insistence that only vital body centers needed protection. Conan Doyle went so far as to have a Crowborough blacksmith make up some examples of armor plating, which he duly tested in his own garden. He came away more convinced than ever, though no one had been wearing the metal shields when he fired upon them. David Lloyd George, who would become prime minister in 1916, assured him that the question was receiving "very special attention," but no action was ever taken. "Sir Arthur," he was told at the Ministry of Munitions, "there is no use your arguing here, for there is no one in the building who does not know you are right."

Some government officials came to regard Conan Doyle's endless flow of suggestions as meddlesome, but he had many supporters in high places. Not least of these was Winston Churchill, who wrote in October 1916 to thank Conan Doyle for his thoughts on attaching armor plating to military vehicles. "There are plenty of good ideas," Churchill wrote, "if only they can be backed with power and brought into relief."

Captain Willie Loder Symonds, the brother of Jean's bridesmaid Lily, fell into enemy hands in the first months of the war. Conan Doyle learned that he was being held at a prison camp in Magdeburg and resolved to thwart the German censors with a "secret correspondence." He had heard that British prisoners had to rely solely on German newspapers for information about the war. Poring over the pages of one of his own books, Conan Doyle used a needle to punch holes beneath letters so as to spell out the latest British news. He enclosed a letter apologizing for the book's slow beginning, but advised the captain that things picked up in chapter three—which was where the needle pricks began. A return message assured him that his meaning had been understood, and Conan Doyle continued the laborious cipher with several more books. After months of this effort, he learned that his subterfuge had been unnecessary. The Red Cross had been bringing British newspapers into German prison camps since the beginning of the war.

Busy as he was on the home front, Conan Doyle knew that his

greatest contribution would be made, as always, with his pen. Within a month of the formal declaration of war he issued a pamphlet called "To Arms!" in which he set out the justice of the British cause for the benefit of neutral readers in Denmark, Holland, and—most important of all—the United States. He mapped out a similar pamphlet for distribution to the German military, but even he had to admit that the idea was impractical.

Perhaps inevitably, he began in 1916 to write what he hoped would be a definitive history of the war. Published in six successive volumes under the title of *The British Campaign in France and Flanders*, the history drew on his correspondence with at least fifty generals, many of whom gave him access to their personal papers. Conan Doyle boasted of the "wonderfully good inside knowledge" coming from such men as General Douglas Haig, the commander in chief on the western front, and General Edward Bulfin, who had been a classmate at Stonyhurst. "My hand is fairly cramped with writing history," he told Innes. "I have had great luck."

More such luck came his way in 1916. Following the highly criticized retreat from Trentino in May, Italian authorities requested that an independent British observer be sent to inspect conditions at the front. Conan Doyle seized the opportunity to gather firsthand information for his history, and managed to expand the mission to include visits to the French and British fronts, on the pretext that it would give him a basis for comparison.

When Lord Newton of the Foreign Office told him that he would need a uniform of some sort, Conan Doyle proudly responded that he was a private in the Crowborough Company of the Sixth Royal Sussex Volunteer Regiment. With some delicacy, Lord Newton suggested that the uniform might not appear sufficiently grand, and might in fact draw fire from both armies. Conan Doyle allowed that as Deputy-Lieutenant of Surrey, an office conferred on him at the time of his knighthood, he had the right to wear a more exalted uniform when reviewing troops.

"I went straight off to my tailor," he wrote, "who rigged me up in a wondrous khaki garb which was something between that of a Colonel and a Brigadier, with silver roses instead of stars or crowns upon the shoulder-straps." The resulting uniform had an unnatural sparkle—rather like Lewis Waller's pristine costume in *Brigadier Gerard*—and though Conan Doyle was entitled to wear a Boer War medal, he admitted to feeling like "a mighty imposter" beneath his officer's peaked cap. As if to underscore the make-believe aspect of the enterprise, he had matching uniforms made up for his sons Denis and Adrian, who were seven and five years old.

Conan Doyle departed for France on a Royal Navy destroyer in the company of General Sir William Robertson, then the British chief of staff. Upon arrival, he was given a gas mask and shrapnel helmet and was told to remove his silly hat. He spent the next weeks dutifully slogging through the muddy trenches, drinking tea with soldiers, signing autographs, and eating the "challenging" army food. In France, he leapt at the chance to interview British commanders on the battlefield, and managed to catch up with both Innes and Kingsley. His uniform, he admitted, made him a "rare specimen," and attracted notice wherever he went. "A Deputy-Lieutenant may not be much in England," he reported, "but when translated into French—my French anyhow—it has an awe-inspiring effect."

Not everyone shared in the awe. At Argonne, a French general fixed Conan Doyle with a hard stare and demanded to know if Sherlock Holmes was serving in the English army. Taken aback, Conan Doyle stammered that the detective had grown too old for active service. The remark drew appreciative laughter from the general's aides, and Conan Doyle felt he had scrambled out of an embarrassing situation.

In Italy, Conan Doyle wanted to visit Monfalcone, recently captured from the enemy, but came under artillery fire on the way. "As I glanced up I saw three clouds immediately above my head," he wrote, "two of them white and the other of a rusty red. The air was full of flying metal, and the road, as we were told afterwards by an observer, was all churned up by it. The metal base of one of the shells was found plumb in the middle of the road just where our motor had been. It was our pace that saved us." Conan Doyle's hosts were distressed at having placed him in harm's way, but he waved off their apologies. "As a matter of fact it was I who owed them an apology," he recalled, "since they had enough risks in the way of business without taking others in order to gratify the whim of a visitor."

Returning to Windlesham at the end of his tour, Conan Doyle wrote up his experiences in a small book entitled *A Visit to Three Fronts*. Intended as a morale booster, the book was an unabashed tribute to the jaunty and courageous British fighting man. "I confess that as I looked at those brave English lads," he wrote, "and thought of what we owed to them and to their like who have passed on, I felt more emotional than befits a Briton in foreign parts." The experience inspired him to offer yet another suggestion to the War Office. The French troops, he noticed, wore badges to indicate a wound in battle. This, Conan Doyle felt, "gave a man some credit and therefore some consolation for his sufferings." He broached the subject with General Robertson, and shortly thereafter British soldiers began to receive wound stripes.

Conan Doyle got a second, more brutal taste of the war when the Australian High Command invited him to visit their position at Péronne, on the river Somme. Here he witnessed the most ferocious fighting he had ever seen at the Battle of St. Quentin, coming within a few hundred yards of the front line. Conan Doyle's cool under fire greatly impressed the Australian troops, but he was profoundly disturbed by the horrors he witnessed. "None of us will forget what we saw," he declared. "There was a tangle of mutilated horses, their necks rising and sinking. Beside them a man with his hand blown off was staggering away, the blood gushing from his upturned sleeve. He was moving round and holding the arm raised and hanging, as a dog holds an injured foot. Beside the horses lay a shattered man, drenched crimson from head to foot, with two great glazed eyes looking upwards through a mask of blood." The image, he said, would haunt him for the rest of his days.

Back in England, Conan Doyle returned to his ongoing history of the war, which he had come to regard as his magnum opus. He would allow no distractions. At one stage the government sounded him out about becoming director of the official propaganda department, but he preferred to remain a free agent. When David Lloyd George became prime minister at the end of 1916, Conan Doyle was approached by his confidential secretary and longtime mistress, Frances Stevenson, about writing an official biography. "It is much needed," Miss Stevenson noted in her diary, "specially in the States, whence we have repeated inquiries." Conan Doyle admired Lloyd George greatly, but he must have considered the task a trivial one in the circumstances. He gave a polite refusal on the grounds that he had never written a biography before and was "full up" with his wartime chronicle. Miss Stevenson regretted the decision, and believed privately that Conan Doyle had become a pawn of the War Office. He was "a nice old gentleman," she noted, but he had a "childlike idea" of the infallibility of Britain's military strategists. "I could see, moreover, that they are only giving him what they want him to know."

It was a criticism that would be repeated often in the coming years, though Conan Doyle now had access to the inner circle of power. In April of 1917, he had a private breakfast with the new prime minister at 10 Downing Street. Conan Doyle found the new leader to be entirely free of pretension; Lloyd George poured the tea while his guest piled bacon and eggs onto a pair of plates at the sideboard. Lloyd George had been following Conan Doyle's history with interest and pumped him for his views on various field commanders. Never one to miss an opportunity, Conan Doyle once again expounded his thoughts on body armor and was pleased to find the prime minister "very keen" on the idea. "I came away reassured," he wrote, "and feeling that a vigorous virile hand was at the helm."

Conan Doyle expected greater cooperation from the War Office under the new prime minister, but his frustrations continued. By the end of 1917, his history became "bowdlerized and blue-pencilled" by military censors. When at length he could publish freely, the public response left him deeply disappointed. One newspaper dismissed the enterprise as "History While You Wait," admitting only that Conan Doyle's writings would be useful "when real histories come to be written." Others decried his excessive fascination with troop movements and technical detail.

As with his chronicle of the Boer War, Conan Doyle had sacrificed historical perspective for contemporary reporting, though he no longer held any illusions about the romance of war. He described the ordeal of combat in blunt, unadorned language, and regretted bitterly that the entire conflict had been so "evidently preventable."

"I hate fine writing about the war," he once declared, "it needs no gloss." Be that as it may, the author's compassion for the soldiers could be felt in every line, giving the prose a heat seldom matched in his other works: "The sky had clouded, the days were mirk, the hanging Madonna had fallen from the cathedral of Albert, the troops were worn to shadow. The twilight of the gods seemed to have come."

For the rest of his life, Conan Doyle held out the hope that his history would eventually receive its due. "I would reckon it the greatest and most undeserved literary disappointment of my life," he wrote in his memoirs, "if I did not know that the end is not yet and that it may mirror those great times to those who are to come."

Modern historians have, in fact, been more kind, praising Conan Doyle's exhaustive research and painstaking accuracy. Most admit, however, that the author's patriotism gave him a narrow, uncritical viewpoint. As Frances Stevenson noted, Conan Doyle accepted what the British commanders told him with few qualms or criticisms, and was too loyal to assign blame for British defeats. He performed a valuable service for wartime Britain, but the finished product—all six volumes of it—suffered for his good intentions.

It would not be his only literary disappointment of the war. Toward the end of 1913, Conan Doyle had begun work on a surprising project—a second full-length Sherlock Holmes novel. "With luck," he told Greenhough Smith at the beginning of 1914, "I should finish before the end of March."

The editor would have been overjoyed. *The Hound of the Baskervilles* had been hugely profitable in 1901, and the first installments of the new novel, *The Valley of Fear,* gave every reason for optimism. Sherlock Holmes appeared to be at the top of his form as he investigated the puzzling murder of John Douglas, late of Birlstone Manor House. For the second half of the novel, however, Conan Doyle moved his detective offstage in favor of a lengthy flashback, just as he had done so many years earlier in *A Study in Scarlet*. The action now centered on a Pinkerton detective named Birdy

Edwards, and his efforts to infiltrate a group of American labor agitators known as the Scowrers.

As with *The Hound of the Baskervilles*, Conan Doyle had found an intriguing story and decided it might be suitable for Sherlock Holmes. This time, he drew his inspiration from the saga of the Molly Maguires, the Irish-American secret society that had operated in the mining communities of Pennsylvania from the mid-1860s to the late 1870s. Conan Doyle gathered the details from an account by the legendary Allan J. Pinkerton, called *The Molly Maguires and the Detectives*. The detective William J. Burns probably furnished additional background and plot suggestions.

Conan Doyle completed the manuscript in April 1914. By September, as his attention shifted to the war, he regretted the "bad luck" of saddling Greenhough Smith with so trivial a manuscript at a time of national crisis. Actually, the editor was glad to be able to offer such a plum to his readers, who were getting more than enough war coverage in the newspapers. As always, the issues containing the latest Sherlock Holmes adventure sold briskly.

Though *The Valley of Fear* is as gripping as any of Conan Doyle's adventure tales, readers were nonplussed when the setting transferred to Pennsylvania. "But of course," the author had told Greenhough Smith, "in this long stretch we abandon Holmes. That is necessary." The detective's fans didn't see it that way. With Sherlock Holmes absent for more than half the book, the novel came off as two novellas that had not been properly introduced. *The Valley of Fear* remains one of the detective's least popular outings.

Holmes would soon redeem himself. Conan Doyle had spent the entire war offering reassurance to the public and praise for the British government and fighting forces. In 1917, with morale sinking in the face of heavy losses, Conan Doyle gave his beleaguered readers what they most wanted from him. In September, the words "Sherlock Holmes outwits a German spy" appeared on the cover of *The Strand*. Inside was a story called "His Last Bow," subtitled "The War Service of Sherlock Holmes."

Set in 1914, shortly before the start of the war, the story opens in an English coastal village. A German spymaster named von Bork is reviewing his operations for the benefit of an appreciative German official. "They are not very hard to deceive, these Englanders," von Bork declares. "A more docile, simple folk could not be imagined." After more commentary on Britain's failings, the German spy is left alone to await the arrival of an American agent named Altamont, who has promised to bring the key to Britain's naval codes. Presently Altamont arrives and hands over the prized signals. When von Bork unwraps the parcel, however, he barely has time to register its strange contents—*The Practical Handbook of Bee Culture, with some Observations upon the Segregation of the Queen*—before a chloroformed sponge is clamped over his face.

When the German spy awakes, bound hand and foot, he finds Sherlock Holmes and Dr. Watson sharing a dusty bottle of Imperial Tokay on his veranda. For two years, the detective explains, he has posed as Altamont to infiltrate the German spy network, passing along bad intelligence to von Bork while informing on genuine agents. Fittingly, Dr. Watson has joined him for the coup de grâce, posing as a chauffeur to assist in springing the trap. "I feel twenty years younger, Holmes," says Watson, delighted that the game is afoot once more.

"His Last Bow" occupies a unique place in the Sherlock Holmes canon. It remains one of the best of all the stories, but it was also Conan Doyle's finest hour as Britain's unofficial minister of propaganda, lifting the country's spirits in a time of universal gloom. In "Danger!" Conan Doyle had warned that the country was ill-prepared for the coming conflict. Now, he offered comfort: Sherlock Holmes, he assured the public, was on the case.

The story's title made it clear that this would be the detective's last bow, and the elegiac tone suggested that Conan Doyle really meant it this time. "Stand with me here upon the terrace," Holmes tells the loyal Dr. Watson, "for it may be the last quiet talk that we shall ever have."

Conan Doyle chose to tell this story in the third person, something he had never done with a Holmes tale. It is significant, therefore, that as the final curtain rang down, Sherlock Holmes spoke as never before. "There's an east wind coming, Watson," Holmes declared, gazing out toward the sea, "such a wind as never blew on England yet. It will be cold and bitter, Watson, and a good many of us may wither before its blast. But it's God's own wind nonetheless, and a cleaner, better, stronger land will lie in the sunshine when the storm has cleared."

Never had the voice of Conan Doyle been so audible. This was what he had wanted to say all along; not only to the British public, but also to those members of his own family who had gone out to fight—his brother, his son, his brothers-in-law, and his two nephews.

It is well that he said it when he did. Not one of his loved ones would return.

23

The Flail of the Lord

I sought by love alone to go
Where God had writ an awful no

—SIR ROGER CASEMENT

On the evening of Thursday, April 20, 1916, a German U-boat surfaced in Tralee Bay off the west coast of Ireland. A pale, gaunt man made his way up through the manhole to the conning tower and peered out at the darkened coastline. His name was Sir Roger Casement, and within hours this Irish-born diplomat would be known throughout England as the "foulest traitor who ever drew breath."

It had been an agonizing voyage, fraught with delays and miscommunication. Casement, who suffered from seasickness, couldn't stomach the shipboard rations of canned ham and salmon and spent most of the journey in his bunk. Now, aided by two companions, he gingerly made his way into a cockleshell dingy. As the tiny boat pushed away from the submarine, the German captain gave a curt salute. Casement, he later testified, was "a truly noble man."

Thirteen months earlier, Casement had left for Berlin on an extraordinary and audacious mission. Hoping to turn the war with

Germany to Ireland's advantage, Casement set out to gain German support—and military backing—for the Irish independence movement. Toward that end, he sought to raise a brigade of Irish soldiers from Germany's prisoner-of-war camps, with the idea that the captured men would cheerfully switch allegiances to fight the English on Irish soil.

German authorities had initially welcomed Casement's proposals, but the mission ended in confusion and failure. Worse, Casement believed that leaders of the insurgent Irish Republican Brotherhood were counting on German support for their planned Easter Rising—just three days away. A message had been sent through the German embassy in Washington asking for a large shipment of German arms. To emphasize the Kaiser's loyalties, the Irish insurrectionists also requested that a U-boat be sent to Dublin's harbor.

Though Germany tentatively agreed to send twenty thousand rifles—which subsequently went astray—Casement knew that this consignment was too small, and that no other support would be forthcoming. He returned to Ireland to warn the volunteers and—if possible—to postpone the insurrection. "I am quite sure it is the most desperate piece of folly ever committed," he wrote of his decision to return, "but I go gladly . . . if those poor lads at home are to be in the fire, then my place is with them."

Now, rowing toward shore, Casement's spirits began to lift. "I was for one brief spell happy and smiling once more," he would tell his sister. "I was back in Ireland again."

A wave overturned the dingy as it neared the coastline. Casement and his companions managed to scramble back onboard, but by the time they reached the shore, Casement was too exhausted to continue.

While the others went for help, Casement waited near the remains of a Roman fort. A police constable, noticing the dingy bobbing offshore, found Casement wandering close by and took him into custody. Casement told the authorities he was an English author out for a stroll, which did not entirely explain his brine-soaked clothing or the German train ticket in his pocket. Close questioning exposed his true identity, and Casement was taken under guard to London's Scotland Yard.

Branded a traitor, and awaiting a trial that would likely end in a death sentence, Roger Casement had few friends in the world.

One of them, strangely enough, was Sir Arthur Conan Doyle.

Six years earlier, Conan Doyle had taken Roger Casement to see his play *The Speckled Band* in London. At the time, Casement was serving as His Majesty's consul-general in Rio de Janeiro, but Conan Doyle had been more interested in the Belgian Congo, where Casement had spent more than twenty years in various consular posts. Through Casement, Conan Doyle had developed "a burning indignation" over atrocities against Congolese natives under the administration of Belgium's King Leopold II. "We live in the presence of the greatest crime which has ever been committed in the history of the world," Conan Doyle wrote at the time, "and yet we who not only could stop it but who are bound by our sworn oath to stop it do nothing."

For most Britons, the problems of the Congo seemed as remote and impenetrable as the territory itself. Vast and difficult to navigate, the region had remained largely unexplored until late in the nineteenth century. Henry Stanley—of "Dr. Livingstone, I presume?" fame—set out from Zanzibar in 1874 to trace the Congo River from its source down to the Atlantic. The three-year journey, which found Stanley in constant peril from tropical fevers, cannibals, and crocodiles, created a sensation in Europe. As the territory opened up to European trade, Leopold II commissioned Stanley to undertake further explorations and to establish administrative centers throughout the Congo. Roger Casement went out to take part in 1884, at the age of twenty.

The following year, after Belgium's territorial claims were recognized at the Conference of Berlin, King Leopold established the Congo Free State under his personal rule. The Berlin conference had put forward the aims of enforcing free trade, suppressing slavery, and insuring the rights and religious freedoms of the Congolese natives. Under Leopold's reign, exactly the opposite came to pass. He exploited the region ruthlessly, particularly its valuable rubber plantations, and his agents resorted to torture and mutilation to enforce their control. "As I write, my study table is covered with photographs of these unhappy people," Conan Doyle would recount. "They bear the marks of the tortures they have endured. Some have their feet lopped off, some their hands."

Roger Casement, horrified by these conditions, issued dozens of damning reports to the British government, and even made an appearance before Leopold himself. When reforms failed to materialize, Casement enlisted an Irish journalist named Edmund Dene Morel to create a protest movement, called the Congo Reform Association. In the hope of publicizing their campaign, the two men contacted a number of prominent writers, including Joseph Conrad, Rudyard Kipling, and Arthur Conan Doyle.

Conrad, who had drawn at least some of his inspiration for *The Heart of Darkness* from Casement's experiences, respectfully declined to take action, saying that he was "only a wretched novelist." Kipling hesitated to speak out on the grounds that Germany might then "fold her protective wings round Belgium." Conan Doyle, in typical fashion, grabbed the rudder with both hands. As in the cases of George Edalji and Oscar Slater, the injustice of the situation aroused his crusading instincts. He met with Edmund Morel in the summer of 1909 and offered to write a book based on the journalist's findings. "I pitched all my voluminous scribblings at his head and he set himself to master every detail of a most complicated and protracted struggle," Morel wrote. "Then, when he had probed the whole thing to the bottom, he shut himself up in his study and worked like a demon, hardly giving himself time to shave, as he put it. He wrote the book right off in a week."

The Crime of the Congo appeared toward the end of 1909 and Conan Doyle would claim it as a personal record—a 45,000-word book in only eight days. Even apart from the speed of composition, *The Crime of the Congo* is unique among his works for its raw, intense prose, especially in its unflinching descriptions of the brutalities visited upon the Congolese natives, which drew considerable criticism at the time. Conan Doyle quoted at length from eyewitness accounts, many of which dealt with the ruthless manner in which the unwilling natives were commanded to harvest rubber plants: "It is collected by force; the soldiers drive the people into the bush; if they will not go they are shot down, their left hands being cut off and taken as trophies to the Commissary. The soldiers do not care whom they shoot down, and they most often shoot poor, helpless women and harmless children. These hands—the hands of men, women and children—are placed in rows before the Commissary, who counts them to see the soldiers have not wasted the cartridges."

Conan Doyle felt strongly that his hard-edged reporting and the graphic photographs that accompanied it were absolutely necessary. "There are times," he declared, "when violence is a duty." With his usual energy, he rounded out his crusade with a letter-writing campaign and a lecture tour, which took him from Plymouth to Edinburgh.

Conan Doyle's success in the Congo campaign is difficult to measure. He fulfilled his aim of calling attention to the crisis, and caught the ear of Theodore Roosevelt and Winston Churchill, but he was only the latest in a series of would-be reformers. It is reasonable to suppose that the death of King Leopold, which occurred just as *The Crime of the Congo* appeared, had a greater influence in bringing about the eventual reforms. Edmund Morel had no doubt over the role Conan Doyle had played, however, and offered extravagant praise for the author's ability to marshal public support. "Yet it was not his book—excellent as it was—nor his manly eloquence on the platform, nor the influence he wielded in rallying influential men to our cause, which helped us most," Morel wrote. "It was just the fact that he was—Conan Doyle; and that he was with us."

Conan Doyle, for his part, had been equally impressed with Casement and Morel. When he began writing *The Lost World* a short time later, he based the character of Lord John Roxton, the sportsman-adventurer, on Casement. "I was the flail of the Lord up in those parts, I may tell you," Roxton says, describing his private war on Peruvian slave traders. As Casement had by that time taken up his post in Peru and was investigating abuses of native labor by the Peruvian Amazon Company, the provenance was not hard to trace. By the same token, it did not take a Sherlock Holmes to uncover the similarities between Edward Dunn Malone, the Irish journalist who narrated *The Lost World*, and Edmund Dene Morel, the Irish journalist who alerted Conan Doyle to the Congo crisis.

Conan Doyle kept up a detailed correspondence with Casement for the next few years. Casement sent background information from Peru that found its way into *The Lost World*, and Conan Doyle offered warm congratulations when Casement received a knighthood in 1911. Like Conan Doyle, Casement felt some reservations about the honor, worrying that the distinction had become a political sop rather than an expression of genuine merit. Unlike Conan Doyle, however, Casement had political motivations of his own, feeling that this British honor would compromise his growing ambitions for Irish independence. Casement had long been uncomfortable with the contradiction between his status as a British diplomat and his anti-imperialist leanings, a tension that became apparent even on his consular stationery, which he had modified to include the harp of Ireland. "But there are many in Ireland will think of me as a traitor," Casement wrote of his knighthood, "and when I think of that country, and of them, I feel I am."

Conan Doyle's own views on the subject of Irish Home Rule had shifted in the years leading up to the war, which probably owed something to Casement's influence. He attended a public conference on the subject in 1912, where he heard persuasive arguments in favor of Irish autonomy from George Bernard Shaw and Clement Shorter, the founder of the journals *Tatler* and *Sphere*. Conan Doyle had twice stood for Parliament as a Unionist candidate, and in support of that party's platform he was on record as an opponent of Home Rule. Now, as he modified his position, he explained his change of heart to a Belfast newspaper: "It is true that I have twice contested Parliamentary seats as a Unionist, but on each occasion I very carefully defined my own position as regards Home Rule. That position, which I made stronger in 1906 than I did in 1900, was that Home Rule could only come with time, that it would only be safe with an altered economic condition and a gentler temper among the people, and above all after the local representative institutions already given had been adequately tested."

In Conan Doyle's view, these conditions had all been satisfied.

Home Rule, he reasoned, was certainly preferable to civil unrest, and he firmly believed that Ireland would always remain loyal to the British Empire in times of crisis.

In this, Conan Doyle's opinions differed sharply from those of Roger Casement, a fact that became more apparent as the conflict with Germany approached. In 1913, when Conan Doyle published his views on "Great Britain and the Next War" in the *Fortnightly Review*, he sent proofs of the article to Casement. If war broke out, Conan Doyle had written, Ireland's heritage and strategic interests would compel her to put nationalist issues aside. "The Empire is in no sense an English thing," he stated in a letter to the *Freeman's Journal*. "Scotch and Irish have combined in the building of it, and have an equal pride and interest in its immense future."

Casement took exactly the opposite view, believing that if war came, Ireland must seize the opportunity to gain its freedom from English rule. Accordingly, he wrote a response to Conan Doyle's article called "Ireland, Germany and the Next World War." He argued that if Britain should lose the coming war, it would not be in Germany's interest to "impoverish and depress" Ireland but rather to enhance its strength and importance as a "counterpoise" to any recovery of Britain's naval strength. A strong Ireland, he continued, would "open the seaways of the world" for Germany. Casement sent his article to the *Fortnightly Review* as a rebuttal to Conan Doyle's remarks, but the editors would agree to run it only if he signed his name. At the time, Casement's commitments to the Foreign Service prohibited him from doing so. Instead, he published the article in the *Irish Review*, under a pseudonym.

Casement soon retired from the Foreign Service, citing poor health, to devote himself fully to the cause of Irish independence. When the war came, he resolved to back his beliefs with action. "I am going, Please God!, to carry this fight much further than they think in Downing Street," he wrote, "to an arbitrament they dread very much." Casement met with leaders of the separatist Sinn Fein movement in Dublin, and traveled to New York in an attempt to rally additional support. By October 1914, he had decided that his goals could only be accomplished in Germany. British officials now had him under surveillance, so Casement shaved off his beard and washed his face in buttermilk in the belief that it would lighten his complexion. Then, using a borrowed American passport, he boarded a Norwegian ship bound for Germany.

In later years, there would be an attempt to paint Casement as a rogue agent, a misguided, ineffective fanatic who acted completely on his own. Initially, however, he had the backing of the Irish Republican Brotherhood. "Sir Roger Casement has authority to speak for and represent the Irish Revolutionary Party," wrote John Devoy, a leader of the movement. Moreover, within three weeks of Casement's arrival in Berlin, the German government issued an official statement of goodwill toward Ireland, authored by Casement himself: "The Imperial Government formally declares," it read in part, "that under no circumstances would Germany invade Ireland with a view to its conquest or the overthrow of any native institutions in that country."

Back in England, Conan Doyle read press reports of Casement's activities with disbelief and horror. For him, these actions confirmed something he had long suspected—Roger Casement had gone mad. "He was a man of fine character," Conan Doyle told the *Daily Chronicle* one month after Casement's arrival in Berlin, "and that he should in the full possession of his senses act as a traitor to the country which had employed and honoured him is inconceivable to anyone who knew him. . . . [I]n all our discussions I have never heard him say a word which was disloyal to Great Britain. He was a sick man, however, worn by tropical hardships, and he complained often of pains in his head. Last May I had letters from him from Ireland which seemed to me so wild that I expressed fears at the time as to the state of his nerves. I have no doubt that he is not in a normal state of mind, and that this unhappy escapade at Berlin is only an evidence of it."

If any further proof of Casement's mental state were needed, Conan Doyle declared, one need look no further than the German proclamation. "On the face of it," Conan Doyle said, "would any sane man accept an assurance about Ireland which had obviously been already broken about Belgium?"

Weighed against Conan Doyle's other activities at this time—his efforts to enlist, his wartime writings, his volunteer service—this sympathetic view toward Casement is hard to credit. In *A Visit to Three Fronts*, Conan Doyle wrote of conscientious objectors as "half-mad cranks whose absurd consciences prevented them from barring the way to the devil." In Conan Doyle's view, Roger Casement would be something considerably worse, a man who had in effect gone to the devil on his knees. Yet he found sympathy for the traitor where he had none for the objector.

It made a pointed contrast to his feelings for Edmund Dene Morel, Casement's partner in the Congo Reform Association. Morel was now active in a pacifist organization called the Union of Democratic Control, whose members urged an immediate end to the hostilities. Morel published a series of pamphlets arguing against reprisals for German air raids—a tactic Conan Doyle had denounced as "a policy of murder." Morel's actions led to charges of treason and a six-month jail term, but Conan Doyle would do nothing to help him. His views on the war, Conan Doyle said, had "destroyed the feelings which I had for him." (Morel later managed to work his way back into public life, and one can imagine Conan Doyle's annoyance when Morel succeeded where he himself had twice failed—in the general election of 1922, Morel won a seat in Parliament, defeating liberal candidate Winston Churchill.)

Roger Casement knew little of events in Britain. In Germany, his mission soon ran aground over his plan to raise an Irish brigade from among the prisoners held in German camps. A number of officials dismissed the notion as absurd, but Casement cited a precedent from the Boer War in which a force of captured Irishmen were persuaded to switch allegiances and fight against the English.

Casement's hopes for a recurrence would not be realized. When Irish prisoners were shuttled to a separate camp in Limburg, the commandant received a polite message from their officers declaring that they would not want any concessions that were not shared by other prisoners. In addition to being Irishmen, the message asserted, "we have the honour to be British soldiers." When Casement went to Limburg to address the prisoners directly, he was greeted by jeers and had to fend off attackers with his umbrella. In the end, Casement managed to rally only about fifty prisoners to his cause. The failure damaged his credibility with German officials, and by

April 1916 he was on his way back to Ireland without the support he had hoped to muster.

Following his arrest in Ireland, Casement faced a series of interrogators at Scotland Yard. "I accept all the consequences," he told them. "All I ask you is to believe I have done nothing dishonourable, which you will one day learn." As questioning continued on Easter Monday, however, news came from Dublin of an armed insurrection by the Irish Republican Brotherhood—the Easter Rising that Casement had hoped to postpone. German involvement was suspected at once. "Germany plotted it," declared John Redmond, leader of the Irish Party, "Germany organised it, Germany paid for it." Up to this point, it had been possible to regard Casement as a harmless, somewhat quixotic figure. Now, in the light of the Easter Rising, he was transformed into a modern Benedict Arnold. In the Commons that afternoon, the prime minister was asked to give assurances that Casement would be taken out and "shot forthwith."

Conan Doyle must have agonized over the situation. In his eyes, Casement was the most loathsome of traitors, and his crimes seemed even worse when measured against his previous service to Britain. In addition, Conan Doyle must have felt a sense of personal betrayal. He had extended his friendship to Casement, given his time and energy to the Congo campaign, and paid tribute in *The Lost World*. "You have done so much good in your life," Conan Doyle wrote to Casement only four years earlier, "that no shadow should in justice come near you." By every conceivable measure, Casement had betrayed the feelings of honor, loyalty, and truthfulness that Conan Doyle held so dear. With the public calling for Casement's head, a less assured man might have backed away from his earlier statement of sympathy. Instead, Conan Doyle began a campaign to spare Casement's life.

As with George Edalji and Oscar Slater, the plight of Roger Casement stirred Conan Doyle's passions and set him on a crusade for justice. Once launched, these crusades were not easily derailed. In this case, however, the entire weight of Conan Doyle's reasoning rested on a fairly dubious foundation—Casement's supposed insanity.

Conan Doyle knew by the example of his own father that insanity was not a term to be bandied about lightly. He had been exposed to psychiatric patients during his medical training, and had a better understanding than most men of his time what it meant to be mentally ill. "What a satire an asylum is upon the majesty of man," he had written in a story called "A Medical Document," "and no less upon the ethereal nature of the soul."

Yet he had no hesitation in pronouncing Casement insane—at least to the extent that he could not be held wholly responsible for his actions in Germany. Conan Doyle's certainty on this point bears some examination. He was not a man who admitted his mistakes lightly, nor did he have much use for opinions that did not correspond with his own. In the months leading up to the war, Casement had elaborated his views on a possible Irish-German alliance in clear and cogent terms. To him, collaboration with Germany was preferable to British rule. These views seemed so radical to Conan Doyle, and differed so sharply from his own, that it seemed impossible that a man such as Casement could hold them. "When you have eliminated the impossible," Sherlock Holmes often said, "whatever remains, however improbable, must be the truth." For Conan Doyle, then, the only remaining explanation, however improbable, was that Casement was insane. Once he had reached this conclusion, his conscience demanded that he argue for leniency.

Many who saw Casement in London agreed with Conan Doyle's assessment. The prisoner had been transferred to a vermin-infested cell in the Tower of London to await trial. He still wore the brine-stained clothing in which he'd been captured, but his suspenders had been taken away after a suicide attempt, leaving him to hold up his trousers by hand. Visitors reported that he seemed "wild-eyed" and had difficulty remembering words and names.

When it was decided that Casement would have a civil trial rather than a military tribunal, he was transferred to Brixton prison and given a change of clothing. His trial on the charge of high treason opened at the Old Bailey on June 26. It lasted three days and it took the jury less than an hour to return a guilty verdict. In trials such as this one, the convicted prisoner had the right to address the court from the dock before sentencing. Casement spoke at great length, addressing his remarks "not to this Court, but to my own countrymen."

"I am being tried," Casement said in part, "not by my peers of the live present, but by the peers of the dead past; not by the civilization of the twentieth century, but by the brutality of the fourteenth; not even by a statute framed in the language of an enemy land—so antiquated is the law that must be sought today to slay an Irishman, whose offence is that he puts Ireland first."

Were these the words of a madman? One commentator was to compare Casement's eloquence favorably with that of Plutarch. Another believed that his words would be read and remembered by the Irish for generations to come. The judges, however, were unmoved. The extreme sentence of the law was to be enforced—death by hanging.

Conan Doyle immediately drafted a petition to the prime minister, asking that Casement's life be spared. He fully acknowledged Casement's guilt and the justice of the sentence but asked for the opportunity to set out some reasons why the execution should not be carried out. First, Conan Doyle reiterated his earlier sentiments about Casement's "pains in the head," calling attention to the "violent change" in Casement's attitude toward Great Britain. Casement had been exposed to severe strain during his long career of public service, Conan Doyle stated, and had also endured several tropical fevers. Furthermore, his investigations into the abuses in both the Congo and Peru had been of a "peculiarly nerve-trying character." For these reasons, Conan Doyle concluded, "some allowance may be made in his case for an abnormal physical and mental state."

More important, he continued, Casement's execution would prove "helpful to German policy, by accentuating the differences between us and some of our fellow subjects in Ireland." It would be used, "however unjustly," as a weapon against Britain in the United States and other neutral countries. A magnanimous response, on the other hand, would heal some of the wounds in Ireland and make a favorable impression abroad. By way of an object lesson, Conan Doyle pointed out that the United States had shown clemency to the officers of the Confederacy at the conclusion of the Civil War. This "policy of mercy," he maintained, "was attended by such happy results that a breach which seemed to be irreparable has now been happily healed over."

It was a careful, well-modulated document that wisely kept clear of the emotions excited by the trial. Conan Doyle simply made his case and warned of the consequences of hanging Casement. "A brave race can forget the victims of the field of battle, but never those of the scaffold," he had written in his Boer War history. "The making of political martyrs is the last insanity of statesmanship."

With the help of Clement Shorter, Conan Doyle circulated the petition among a small circle of influential citizens, gathering the signatures of scientists, politicians, and literary figures such as G. K. Chesterton, John Galsworthy, John Masefield, and Jerome K. Jerome. George Bernard Shaw withheld his signature, on the grounds that others might refuse if they saw his name on the document, and composed his own petition instead. H. G. Wells and Rudyard Kipling refused to sign either one.

It is often reported that Conan Doyle contributed £700 to Casement's legal defense, which would have been nearly half of the entire amount required. Such generosity would have been very much in character, since he had freely subsidized the legal expenses in other cases, but in this instance there seems to have been some confusion over names. An Irish-American lawyer by the name of Michael Francis Doyle, who came from America to assist in the case, appears to be the actual source of the donation usually ascribed to Conan Doyle.

If the American backing gave Casement any thoughts of a reprieve, however, his hopes were quickly extinguished. Soon after Casement's capture, police discovered a trunk filled with personal journals in his Dublin lodgings. These journals, according to the head of Scotland Yard's Criminal Investigation Department, contained material so shocking that it could never be printed "in any age, in any language." Casement, it emerged, was a homosexual. This was not exactly a closely guarded secret, especially after Casement brought a young Norwegian sailor along to Germany as his "servant," but the discovery of the so-called black diaries gave Casement's prosecutors a tool with which to head off the campaign for a stay of execution. The king, the archbishop of Canterbury, the pope, and the president of the United States were all made aware of the contents of the diaries. Copies were circulated in Parliament. No one who saw them, according to the *News of the World*, would "ever mention Casement's name again without loathing and contempt."

Being a traitor had been fairly serious. Chronicling one's homosexuality, it seemed, was a true hanging offense. Many who had signed the petitions for a reprieve now withdrew their support. At a stroke, said the editor of *The Nation*, the diaries "entirely killed any English sympathy there might have been for Casement." This campaign appears to have met with the approval of the government. When the American ambassador to London informed Prime Minister Asquith that he had seen a copy of the diaries, he was told, "Excellent; and you need not be particular about keeping it to yourself."

Conan Doyle stuck to his guns. When Foreign Office officials revealed the existence of the diaries to him, he would not withdraw his petition. "They told me that his record for sexual offenses was bad," he wrote to Clement Shorter, "and had a diary of his in proof of it. I had, of course, heard this before, but as no possible sexual offense could be as bad as suborning soldiers from their duty, I was not diverted from my purpose." It is tempting to conclude that Conan Doyle's views on homosexuality were more advanced than those of his peers, but in truth he saw Casement's diaries as further evidence of insanity, just as he had in the case of Oscar Wilde.

Not surprisingly, Casement preferred to think of himself as an Irish patriot rather than a lunatic or a degenerate. For this reason, Casement expressed resentment at Conan Doyle's intervention—referring to him with sarcastic derision as "my friend." Conan Doyle shrugged off this show of contempt. As with Oscar Slater, he drew a clear line between the justice of the case and the personality of the man.

Conan Doyle had accurately predicted that Casement's sentence would bring protests from America at the worst possible time, since President Wilson was still maintaining a policy of neutrality in the war. The American newspaper editor William Randolph Hearst used his influence to urge clemency for Casement—comparing him to

America's own revolutionary war heroes—and grumblings were heard on the floor of the Senate.

The foreign pressure came too late. Sir Roger Casement was executed at Pentonville Prison on August 3, 1916. "He marched to the scaffold," wrote Father Carey, the prison chaplain, "with the dignity of a prince."

"I hope I shall not weep," Casement himself had written a few days before, "but if I do it shall be nature's tribute wrung from me—one who has never hurt a human being—and whose heart was always compassionate and pitiful for the grief of others."

To the end of his life, Conan Doyle would maintain that Casement had been "a fine man afflicted with mania." In his autobiography, he would remember the "noble work" Casement had done in the Congo and Peru, and express regret over his "tragic end." It was not a popular view. The government had been placed in the unfortunate position of hanging a British knight, knowing full well that the execution would create an Irish martyr. Conan Doyle's articulate protests aggravated an already sensitive situation. It was one thing for an iconoclast like Shaw to embarrass his government, but quite another for a pillar of the establishment such as Conan Doyle. This single act, set among Conan Doyle's extraordinary record of service during the war years, is thought to have cost him a seat in the House of Lords.

Once again, Conan Doyle put his principles ahead of personal expedience. There were many who felt as he did; all but a few kept a discreet silence. Conan Doyle's conscience did not allow for discreet silences, nor did he submit easily to the will of others. Early in the war, while trying to enlist for active duty, Conan Doyle admitted as much to his brother. "I should love the work," he told Innes, "and would try to be subordinate—which is my failing."

It was also his greatest strength. In many ways, the Roger Casement affair had been a trial run. By the time Casement went to the gallows, Conan Doyle was preparing to embark on the last and greatest of his public crusades—spiritualism. The "psychic question," which had been gathering force from his earliest days in Southsea, now emerged as the most important thing in his life, and he was to become its most eloquent spokesman. "It is the thing," he would write, "for which every preceding phase, my gradual religious development, my books, which gave me an introduction to the public, my modest fortune, which enables me to devote myself to unlucrative work, my platform work, which helps me to convey the message, and my physical strength, which is still sufficient to stand arduous tours and to fill the largest halls for an hour and a half with my voice, have each and all been an unconscious preparation. For thirty years I have trained myself exactly for the role without the least inward suspicion of whither I was tending."

It was to be—as Dr. Watson remarked of the giant rat of Sumatra—a tale for which the world was not yet prepared.

24

Is Conan Doyle Mad?

Remember he believes it himself. Of that you may be assured. A more honest man never lived.

—MRS. CHALLENGER IN *THE LOST WORLD*

German bombers had struck London only a few days earlier, and near-blackout conditions were in force as Conan Doyle rose to give his lecture on October 25, 1917. Many years had passed since his first attempts at public speaking in Southsea, when his agitation would cause the bench to shake. After many hundreds of literary lectures and campaign stump speeches, Conan Doyle had developed into a polished orator. Nonetheless, he must have felt some of his old nervousness that night in London. Of all the speeches he had ever given, this was perhaps the bravest. The occasion was a meeting of the London Spiritualist Alliance, chaired by Sir Oliver Lodge, in the salon of the British Artists' Gallery in Pall Mall. After decades of experimentation and equivocation, Conan Doyle was now prepared to declare himself publicly as a dedicated spiritualist. He had crossed the Rubicon.

"The subject of psychical research," he told his audience, "is one upon which I have thought more, and been slower to form my opinion about, than upon any other subject whatever. Every now and then as one jogs along through life some small incident occurs to one which very forcibly brings home the fact that time passes and that first one's youth and then one's middle age is slipping away. Such an incident occurred to me the other day. There is a column in that excellent little paper, *Light,* which is devoted to what occurred on the corresponding date a generation—that is, thirty years—ago. As I read over this column recently I had quite a start as I saw my own name, and read the reprint of a letter which I had written in 1887, detailing some interesting spiritual experience which had occurred to me in a séance. This will confirm my statement that my interest in the subject is one of some standing, and I may fairly claim since it is only within the last year or so that I have finally announced that I was satisfied with the evidence, that I have not been hasty in forming my opinion."

That said, Conan Doyle went on to review the slow stages of his progress toward belief—his wide reading, his early experiments in Southsea, his long-standing membership in the Society for Psychical Research, and his correspondence with men such as Lodge and Sir William Barrett. He spoke for over an hour, giving a capsule history of the spiritualist movement from the Fox sisters to the present and discussing the manner in which this "new revelation" might be reconciled with conventional religion.

Like religion, Conan Doyle concluded, spiritual knowledge required belief rather than evidence. "When an inquirer has convinced himself of the truth of the phenomena, there is no real need to pursue the matter further," he insisted. "The real object of the investigation is to give us assurance in the future and spiritual strength in the present, to give us a clear perception of the fleeting nature of matter and reveal the eternal values beyond all the shows of time and sense—the things which are indeed lasting, going on and ever on through the ages in a glorious and majestic progression."

It was crucial to Conan Doyle that his views be taken as the culmination of a lifetime's deliberation. When his lecture came to be published, it was billed as "The Latest Pronouncement of Sir Arthur Conan Doyle after Thirty Years of Psychical Research." In many ways, however, his public declaration had come about quite abruptly. Only one year previously, in the *International Psychic Gazette,* he expressed regret that he could not offer a more tangible form of comfort to the families of soldiers lost in the war: "I fear I can say nothing worth saying. Time only is the healer."

This had certainly changed by the time of his address to the London Spiritualist Alliance, and he confirmed his beliefs one week later in the pages of *Light*. "[D]eath," he stated, "makes no abrupt change in the process of development, nor does it make an impassable chasm between those who are on either side of it. No trait of the form and no peculiarity of the mind are changed by death but all are continued in that spiritual body which is the counterpart of the earthly one at its best, and still contains within it that core of spirit which is the very essence of the man."

Readers of *The Strand* were also made aware of Conan Doyle's beliefs that year. "It is treacherous and difficult ground," he wrote, "where fraud lurks and self-deception is possible and falsehood from the other side is not unknown. There are setbacks and disappointments for every investigator. But if one picks one's path one can win through and reach the reward beyond—a reward which includes great spiritual peace, an absence of fear in death, and an abiding consolation in the death of those whom we love. It is, I repeat, this religious teaching which is the great gift that has been granted in our time."

No doubt there were members of *The Strand*'s editorial board who questioned the wisdom of publishing such statements. At this stage, however, Greenhough Smith could hardly refuse anything to his star author. For more than a quarter of a century, Conan Doyle's name on the magazine's cover was guaranteed to boost circulation. In years to come, however, as Conan Doyle turned out a steady flow of articles with titles such as "The Absolute Proof" and "The Evidence for Fairies," Smith's loyalty would be sorely tested.

Conan Doyle recognized only too well that many readers would scoff at his assertions, and he tried to anticipate some of their objections. "Theories of fraud or of delusion will not meet the evidence," he insisted in *Light*. "It is absolute lunacy or it is a revolution in religious thought."

Conan Doyle's son Kingsley and brother Innes were still alive when he made these statements, but the family had already suffered many losses. Jean's brother Malcolm was killed at Mons in the early days of the war. Oscar Hornung, Willie and Connie's son, died in battle the following year, as did Lottie's husband, Captain Leslie Oldham. These family tragedies would certainly have left Conan Doyle more inclined toward belief, but at that stage he was not prepared to accept spiritualism without some form of proof.

He soon found all the evidence he needed beneath his own roof. According to *The New Revelation*, a book he published in 1918, the ultimate confirmation of spirit phenomena came toward the end of 1915. "[S]ince the War," he wrote, "I have had some very exceptional opportunities of confirming all the views which I had already formed as to the truth of the general facts upon which my views are founded. These opportunities came through the fact that a lady who lived with us, a Mrs L.S., developed the power of automatic writing."

"Mrs. L.S." was Jean's closest friend, Lily Loder-Symonds. Very little is known of her—even her marital status is not entirely clear—except that she had been one of Jean's bridesmaids in 1907. Since then she had suffered poor health and other reversals of fortune, with the result that she now lived at Windlesham as a companion to Jean, ostensibly to help look after the children. As her health declined and more of her time was spent in bed, Lily came to exhibit a talent for automatic, or "trance'" writing. As with other forms of spirit communication, such as table-tipping and the Ouija board, this was thought to be a method by which a "sensitive," such as Lily, could act as a conduit for messages from the spirit world. In many cases, the medium would sit with a pen poised over a sheet of paper and then fall into a form of delirium while the message flowed forth. At other times, the sensitive remained conscious, watching with a kind of detached fascination as the pen moved over the pages, apparently of its own volition.

Conan Doyle knew enough of the workings of the subconscious mind to be deeply skeptical of automatic writing. "Of all forms of mediumship," he wrote, "this seems to me to be the one which should be tested most rigidly, as it lends itself very easily not so much to deception as to self-deception, which is a more subtle and dangerous thing. Is the lady herself writing, or is there, as she avers, a power that controls her, even as the chronicler of the Jews in the Bible averred that he was controlled. In the case of L.S. there is no denying that some messages proved to be not true, specially in the matter of time they were quite unreliable. But on the other hand, the numbers which did come true were far beyond what any guessing or coincidence could account for."

In Conan Doyle's view, no amount of guesswork could account for the message Lily produced in May 1915, when the morning papers announced the sinking of the *Lusitania*. The tragedy was deeply felt at Windlesham, as Charles Frohman, the producer of William Gillette's Sherlock Holmes play, had been onboard. "It is terrible, terrible," came a message through Lily's hand, "and will have a great influence on the War."

Few would argue that the destruction of a passenger ship, with a loss of some 1,200 lives, was a terrible event. At the time, however, it could not have been obvious that the attack on the *Lusitania* would help to draw the United States into the war. Conan Doyle believed that it required psychic knowledge to predict such an outcome.

One must ask whether this incident was really as convincing as he claimed. There is no denying that Lily's message accurately predicted a "great influence" on the war. It should be recalled, however, that Conan Doyle's story "Danger!"—published the previous year—had warned of precisely this sort of submarine attack and had produced a great deal of public debate over the vulnerability of merchant shipping. Lily, like everyone else who passed through Conan Doyle's orbit at that time, would certainly have been aware of his views. As a member of the household, she often listened in when Conan Doyle read his latest manuscripts aloud to Jean. It seems possible, therefore, that the story of Captain Sirius, rather than spirit inspiration, inspired a connection between the war and the *Lusitania*.

Similarly, Conan Doyle wrote in *The New Revelation*, another example of Lily's automatic writing had "foretold the arrival of an important telegram upon a certain day, and even gave the name of the deliverer of it—a most unlikely person." This incident is more difficult to prove or disprove, since he provides so little detail. The prediction certainly sounds intriguing, but Conan Doyle went on to say that other, presumably similar messages were quite often wrong. "The lapses," he wrote, "were notable. It was like getting a good message through a very imperfect telephone." Nevertheless, "no one could doubt the reality of her inspiration." Anyone who has ever received an unexpected phone call and uttered the words "we were just talking about you" might argue the point.

For Conan Doyle, however, Lily's apparent successes counted for more than her failures. Moreover, he felt enormous sympathy for her circumstances, which gave an added poignancy to many of her messages. Three of her brothers had been killed at the Battle of Ypres in 1915, and much of her automatic writing took the form of communication from them. Often these messages contained insight into military life and descriptions of battle scenes, but Conan Doyle expressed some skepticism over these details. He realized that Lily might have gleaned this information from the newspapers, or from his own writings. At the same time, he understood how her powerful desire to contact her brothers might take the form of self-delusion. Then one day Lily appeared to establish contact with Malcolm Leckie, Jean's dead brother, who had always been a particular favorite of Conan Doyle's. The message referred to a private conversation between Malcolm and Conan Doyle that had occurred some years earlier. If any single incident can be said to have crowned Conan Doyle's progress from acolyte to missionary, this would be it. He believed that no one else could possibly have known of this conversation. The message, therefore, was "evidential."

Again, one must take a hard look at this assertion. Few private conversations remain private. Without Conan Doyle's knowledge, his exchange with Malcolm Leckie may well have been overheard, or shared with others by Malcolm himself. Conan Doyle may have referred to the matter at some earlier stage and forgotten about it by the time of Lily's message. As in so many instances of this kind, he volunteered no detail that might invite further investigation. Even if he had, the assertion would be impossible to verify. It must be said, in any case, that he had a habit of describing such revelations as "unknowable" or "evidential" when in fact there were other, entirely plausible explanations. In time, perhaps, he might have come to think differently of Lily's frequent messages, especially if they had continued for any length of time. As it happened, they did not. Lily's health grew steadily worse, and she died in January 1916. Her early death imparted a sanctity to her mediumship. If at first Conan Doyle regarded her automatic writing as a parlor game of sorts, it now became the pure and unassailable testimony of a dying woman. He came to regard her as having been a "high soul upon earth."

A sad affirmation of Conan Doyle's flowering beliefs came from his friend Sir Oliver Lodge. In September 1915, Lodge's son, Raymond, was lost in the trenches. Up to this point, Lodge had been rather more cautious than Conan Doyle in his spirit inquiries. Now, struggling with his grief, he consulted a well-known medium named Mrs. Osborne Leonard. Like most mediums of the time, Mrs. Leonard communicated with the other side through a spirit control, an unseen presence who spoke through her. If one believed in such things, these spirit guides served as the point of contact between this world and the next. To the skeptics, such manifestations amounted to nothing more mysterious than the medium talking in a disguised voice.

Mrs. Leonard's control was said to be a young Indian girl named Feda. Within days of the death of his son, Lodge and his wife began receiving messages through Mrs. Leonard and Feda. These messages, Lodge believed, contained information about his son that Mrs. Leonard could not possibly have learned through any normal means. Lodge listened in wonder as Raymond—communicating through Feda—recounted his new life on the other side, a place he called "Summerland." This world, as Raymond described it, offered many of the familiar comforts of home—including, if one desired, whiskey and cigars. "[T]here are laboratories over here," one of Raymond's messages declared, "and they manufacture all sorts of things in them. Not like you do, out of solid matter, but out of essences, and ethers, and gases."

Lodge and his wife found great solace in these messages. With so many families in Britain suffering from similar bereavements, he felt an obligation to share his experiences. He published a book called *Raymond: Or Life and Death, with Examples of the Evidence for Survival of Memory and Affection after Death*. The book's success—it went through twelve printings in three years—showed that many in Britain were receptive to the idea of a spirit world where their departed loved ones carried on much as before. Lodge's reputation as a scientist, and the objective tone he adopted through much of the book, lent credence to his views. "If we can establish the survival of any single ordinary individual," he wrote, "we have established it for all." It was a message Britain wanted to hear.

As might be expected, the book took a hammering from skeptical critics, most of whom found great sport in the idea of an afterlife featuring whiskey and cigars. Conan Doyle rallied to his friend's defense. "This has tickled the critics to such an extent," he wrote, "that one would really think to read the comments that it was the only statement in a book which contains 400 closely-printed pages. Raymond may be right or wrong, but the only thing which the incident proves to me is the unflinching courage and honesty of the man who chronicled it, knowing well the handle that he was giving to his enemies."

For Conan Doyle, Lodge's experiences seemed to confirm the evidence he had received through Lily Loder-Symonds. "Many thanks to you for having written such a book," he wrote in a letter to Lodge, "and to Raymond for having inspired it." He went on to say that he would shortly be visiting a clairvoyant in London. "If you should be in touch with Raymond," he continued, "it would be interesting if you tried to put him on to me."

Clearly Conan Doyle believed that Lodge was fighting the good fight, and it was a cause he now felt ready to join. "I might have drifted on for my whole life as a psychical researcher, showing a sympathetic, but more or less dilettante attitude towards the whole subject," he wrote in *The New Revelation*. "But the War came, and when the War came it brought earnestness into all our souls and made us look more closely at our own beliefs and reassess their values. In the presence of an agonized world, hearing every day of the deaths of the flower of our race in the first promise of their unsullied youth, seeing around one the wives and mothers who had no clear conception whither their loved one had gone to, I seemed suddenly to see that this subject with which I had so long dallied was not merely a study of a force outside the rules of science, but that it was really something tremendous, a breaking down of the walls between two worlds, a direct undeniable message from beyond, a call of hope and of guidance to the human race at the time of its deepest affliction."

With this dawning sense of purpose, however, there also came a lowering of the critical standards he once brought to the psychic realm. "The objective side of it ceased to interest," he wrote, "for having made up one's mind that it was true there was an end of the matter. The religious side of it was clearly of infinitely greater importance. The telephone bell is in itself a very childish affair, but it may be the signal for a very vital message."

To his detriment, Conan Doyle often equated the idea of mediumship with such things as telephone bells and door knockers. He invited his readers to trust the message without regard to the messenger. Long ago in Southsea, General Drayson had warned him that the next world, like this one, had its pranksters and "naughty boys," whose unworthiness must not divert one from the psychic path. Conan Doyle now repeated Drayson's words in his own lectures. He was aware, he insisted, that there were charlatans who posed as mediums to prey on the hopes of the bereaved. He also conceded that on occasion a genuine medium might resort to deceit and trickery, but in these instances the deceptions were well meant—the mediums simply did not wish to disappoint the heartbroken mother or widow who longed for a hopeful sign. "We must not argue," he wrote, "that because a man once forges, therefore he never signed an honest cheque in his life."

Needless to say, not everyone shared Conan Doyle's willingness to suspend disbelief. At first, the news of his conversion was treated, for the most part, with a measure of respect and tolerance. The *Times* of London gave a dignified summary of his remarks to the London Spiritualist Alliance under the heading of "The Spirit Life." The writer Max Pemberton, reporting in the *Weekly Dispatch*, assured his readers that Conan Doyle was no zealot. "For many years I have watched Sir Arthur's voyaging upon these strange seas and have wondered into what port they would carry him," Pemberton wrote. He himself had shared in a few of Conan Doyle's table-tipping experiments many years earlier and had been impressed by the novelist's cautious approach. Now, having heard the results of his friend's long deliberation, he declared the lecture to have been "a profound confession of faith from a man who believes that a new revelation has been given to mankind."

Inevitably, Conan Doyle's pronouncements soon brought letters of protest from leading clergymen. At a conference of the Catholic Young Men's Society of Great Britain, a Father Bernard Vaughan denounced spiritualism as a menace, and accused Lodge and Conan Doyle of having "lost their mental poise," possibly under the sway of demonic force. "I would rather be in prison for the rest of my life," Father Vaughan insisted, "than carry on the work that is being done by these two gentlemen."

Initially, Conan Doyle did not believe that spiritualism would supplant the more established forms of religion. Instead, he asserted, spiritualism would "set right grave misunderstandings which have always offended the reason of every thoughtful man [and] also confirm and make absolutely certain the fact of life after death, the base of all religion."

In October 1919, Conan Doyle's lectures brought an angry challenge from the Reverend J. A. Magee at a congress of church leaders held in Leicester. Conan Doyle and his kind, according to Magee, threatened to lower the moral, mental, and spiritual standard of the country by urging unfit and unsupportable views on the populace. Incensed, Conan Doyle traveled to the city and offered a rebuttal entitled "Our Reply to the Cleric." "We come forward as allies," he stated. "And anyone who knows our literature—unfortunately these gentlemen at the Church Congress are ignorant of it—know we have proved that life goes on after physical death, carrying with it a reasonable evolution of the human soul. That being so, if these people were not blind they would say to us: 'Come in and help us to fight the materialism of the world.' "

His hopes for a peaceable coexistence would be short-lived, and it could not have quieted his critic's fears when he asserted that at least some clergymen were themselves "amongst the strongest mediums which we possess at this time."

That same month, under the heading of "Credulity Hard to

Understand," the *New York Times* offered a blunt and unflattering assessment of Conan Doyle's new crusade. "Admirers of Sir Arthur Conan Doyle as a writer of detective stories—a company about as numerous as readers of the English language—have reason for a peculiar grief because of the strange, the pathetic, thoroughness with which he has accepted as realities the 'spiritualistic' interpretation of the phenomena of trance speaking and writing. There is little of the mysterious and nothing of the other world in these phenomena for modern psychologists, and yet this well-educated and intelligent man—with not a little of the scientific and the philosophic, too, in his mental furnishings—talks much as did the followers of the Fox sisters fifty years ago."

With the publication of *The New Revelation* in 1918 and *The Vital Message* the following year, Conan Doyle came under more frequent attacks in the press. Hundreds of similar spiritualist tracts were appearing at this time, but Conan Doyle's fame separated his books from the rest of the pack—exactly as he intended. If his literary prestige brought new converts into the fold, it also made him the natural target for much of the scorn being heaped on the movement. The London *Times* in reviewing *The New Revelation* expressed an opinion shared by many when it accused the author of an "incredible naiveté." "We may respect Sir Arthur's sincerity," the reviewer continued, "and his serious desire to put to the highest uses a new development which he believes to be 'the greatest in the history of mankind,' but we would recommend him to follow his own counsel—'Above all, read the literature of this subject'—only we would add, read the literature on both sides." *The Nation* took the same tone: "The book leaves one with a rather poor opinion of the doctor's critical abilities."

James Douglas, in his weekly book column for London's *Sunday Express*, offered perhaps the most judicious assessment of Conan Doyle's new convictions, though his headline—"Is Conan Doyle Mad?"—suggested otherwise. Douglas admitted, in approaching one of Conan Doyle's psychic volumes, to a feeling of "benign contempt" of the author's opinions. "One does not trouble to analyse the ravings of a madman," he wrote. "One shrugs one's shoulders, laughs, and forgets." Reading Conan Doyle's arguments for the first time, however, Douglas found himself in a quandary. "He had plenty of vigorous common sense," the journalist allowed. "If ever there was a well-balanced mind in a well-balanced body, it is his." Moreover, Douglas acknowledged, Conan Doyle's talents as a novelist and historian, and his pioneering insight into such matters as submarine warfare, could not be cast aside lightly. "It is not easy to reconcile these facts with the hypothesis that he is stark, staring mad on the subject of the dead," Douglas admitted. "He has established his right to be heard, and we may be wrong in refusing to hear him. There may be oceans of fraud and folly in spiritualism, but there may be a grain of truth in it."

In years to come, as Conan Doyle's opinions grew even more extreme, this tolerant attitude became difficult to sustain. Oliver Lodge and his other colleagues in the spiritualist movement favored a cautious approach in spreading their message, so as not to invite ridicule. Conan Doyle, by contrast, resembled nothing so much as Gloucester Dick, the bare-knuckle brawler from his own *House of Temperley*, attempting to batter the public into submission with repeated blows to the head. He traveled the country and lectured tirelessly. He attended one séance after another, invariably giving a ringing endorsement of each medium's authenticity. He sent a barrage of letters to the press, pronouncing on each new spirit manifestation. He quickly became, as the popular press dubbed him, "the Saint Paul of Spiritualism."

Many years earlier in Davos, when Conan Doyle read the text of Arthur Balfour's presidential address to the S.P.R., he would have come across this passage: "I have often thought that when, on looking back over the history of human speculation, we find some individual who has anticipated the discoveries of a later age, but has neither himself been able to develop these discoveries nor yet to interest his contemporaries in them, we are very apt to bestow on him an undue meed of honour. 'Here,' we say, 'was a man before his time. Here was a man of whom his age was not worthy.' Yet such men do very little indeed for the progress of the world of which at first sight they would appear to be amongst the most distinguished citizens. There is no use in being before your age after such a fashion as this. If neither you nor those to whom you speak can make use of the message that you thus prematurely deliver, so far as the development of the world is concerned, you might as well have not lived at all."

But for the war, Conan Doyle might have settled for Balfour's "undue meed of honour." Now, as the nation mourned its dead, he resolved to bring the entire world around to his way of thinking. A single episode from those early years of lecturing illustrates the depth of his conviction. En route to Nottingham to deliver an address, he received a telegram informing him that his son Kingsley, weakened by injuries at the Somme, had died of influenza. The news left Conan Doyle staggered, but only momentarily. Mastering his emotions, he decided to carry on with his lecture. "My duty," he declared, "is to other sufferers."

"Had I not been a spiritualist," he told a friend afterward, "I could not have spoken that night. As it was, I was able to go straight on the platform and tell the meeting that I knew my son had survived the grave, and that there was no need to worry."

The modern reader may disagree with him, and perhaps think him foolish, but no one can doubt the strength and sincerity of his beliefs. Only four months later, the same epidemic of influenza would also claim his beloved brother Innes. Some two years later, the Ma'am would also pass away at the age of eighty-three, having outlived three of her children. "Thank God," Conan Doyle would write, "that I have since found that the gates are not shut, but only ajar, if one does show earnestness in the quest."

That earnestness lay at the heart of his faith. "[S]piritual truth does not come as a culprit to a bar," he later wrote, "but you must rather submit in a humble spirit to psychic conditions and so go forth, making most progress when on your knees." In other words, one must already believe in order to find proof. For many skeptics, this precondition of faith rendered Conan Doyle's testimony worthless. By his standard, anyone who came away from the séance room unconvinced had only themselves to blame. Any shadow of doubt, he argued, created a climate of hostility in which no spirit could appear. Even his most sympathetic readers found it difficult to suspend disbelief so entirely. Conan Doyle was unmoved. "It is not a question of proof," he often stated, "I *know* it to be true."

In this uncritical frame of mind, Conan Doyle now encountered one apparent proof after another. Then, on September 7, 1919, a lecture in Portsmouth led to a breakthrough he had long desired. Sharing the platform that night was a medium named Evan Powell, whom Conan Doyle described as "a colliery clerk and an amateur but a very powerful medium." Afterward, Powell agreed to hold a séance for Conan Doyle, Jean, and two others. It was the custom at the time to subject the medium to a rigorous search, and then tie him or her securely to a chair so as to rule out the possibility of deception. "We treated Powell as if he were a pro," Conan Doyle said, "stripping, searching and binding him with six separate lengths of string. We had to *cut* him loose afterward."

Nevertheless, when the lights were put out and the room plunged into darkness, Powell produced a remarkable manifestation. Afterward, Conan Doyle described it in a letter to Oliver Lodge:

> We had strong phenomena from the start, and the medium was always groaning, muttering, or talking, so that there was never a doubt where he was. Suddenly I heard a voice.
>
> "Jean, it is I."
>
> My wife cried, "It is Kingsley."
>
> I said, "Is that you, boy?"
>
> He said in a very intense whisper and a tone all his own, "Father!" and then after a pause, "Forgive me!"
>
> I said, "There was never anything to forgive. You were the best son a man ever had." A strong hand descended on my head which was slowly pressed forward, and I felt a kiss just above my brow.
>
> "Are you happy?" I cried.
>
> There was a pause and then very gently, "I am *so* happy."

Conan Doyle would repeat this description many times in the coming years. "I have had several communications since," he wrote many years later, "but none which moved me so much as this first one."

Much deception can be practiced on a willing subject in the darkened confines of a séance room. A confederate may move about freely, while any telltale sounds are masked by the groaning and muttering of the medium. The intense whisper of a spirit voice, no matter how passionate, does not invite positive identification. There is even such a thing as a "séance chair," long available in specialty catalogs, which features a collapsible armrest, so as to allow a medium to slip in and out of any inconvenient restraints.

Conan Doyle knew all of this and more, but he chose to believe anyway. For many years he had spoken of finding a greater meaning to his life, "some big purpose" for which he had been placed on earth. The Congo, George Edalji, divorce law reform, Oscar Slater, the Channel tunnel, civilian rifle ranges—there had been dozens of causes, and they all faded to insignificance when set against this. Years earlier, he had lost his Catholic faith, but the need for faith remained. At last, he believed.

"People ask me, not unnaturally, what is it which makes me so perfectly certain that this thing is true," he wrote in his autobiography. "That I am perfectly certain is surely demonstrated by the mere fact that I have abandoned my congenial and lucrative work, left my home for long periods at a time, and subjected myself to all sorts of inconveniences, losses and even insults, in order to get the facts home to the people. . . . I may say briefly that there is no physical sense which I possess which has not been separately assured. . . . I have seen my mother and my nephew, young Oscar Hornung, as plainly as I ever saw them in life—so plainly that I could almost have counted the wrinkles of the one and the freckles of the other. . . . All fine-drawn theories of the subconscious go to pieces before the plain statement of the intelligence, 'I am a spirit. I am Innes. I am your brother.' "

Many others felt as he did; all but a few kept quiet about it. Conan Doyle's sense of duty would not permit him to keep quiet. He had found solace in the face of devastating loss, and felt he must share it with others.

The task would absorb him for the rest of his life. If this makes him a madman, so be it.

25

Away with the Fairies

Her wings would scarcely carry her now, but in reply she alighted on his shoulder and gave his chin a loving bite. She whispered in his ear, "You silly ass."

—J. M. BARRIE, *PETER AND WENDY*

By December of 1920, readers of *The Strand* had grown accustomed to reading odd dispatches from Windlesham. The previous month, Conan Doyle had published a lengthy article about ectoplasm, defined as "the substance of spirit emanations and thought forms," which was accompanied by photographs of unsightly gelatinous material oozing from the nose and mouth of a medium. "The pictures are strange and repulsive," he admitted, "but many of Nature's processes seem so in our eyes." Earlier, he paid a glowing tribute to the Fox sisters as the "handmaidens of Spiritism," while a later article would speculate on the potential for posthumous collaboration with Oscar Wilde, Jack London, Charles Dickens, and Joseph Conrad.

Even so, nothing had prepared the readership for the revelation that awaited them in the pages of the Christmas issue. "Fairies Photographed" declared the headline. Though the article adopted a cautious tone, the implication was clear—Sir Arthur Conan Doyle, creator of Sherlock Holmes, now believed in fairies: "Should the incidents here narrated, and the photographs attached, hold their own against the criticism which they will excite, it is no exaggeration to say that they will mark an epoch in human thought."

This, for many people, was the last straw. Up to a point, even his skeptics had been willing to listen to Conan Doyle's exhortations with detached interest, and those who had not yet made up their minds on spiritualist matters came away impressed by his lucidity. Earlier that year, he had dealt with a highly publicized attack on his beliefs in a manner that even his critics had to admire. A man named Joseph McCabe, representing the Rationalist Press Organization, had let it be known that he regarded Conan Doyle as a well-intentioned fool. In an address entitled "Sir A. Conan Doyle's Ghosts," McCabe accused the author of using his influence to extend false hope to the families of the dead. He would like nothing better, McCabe declared, than to meet Conan Doyle in an open debate.

Conan Doyle accepted immediately, and the two men arranged to face off at London's Queen's Hall on March 11, 1920. Eager spectators flocked in from all over the country, paying inflated prices to scalpers to obtain tickets. Many believed that the confrontation would mark a defining moment of the spiritualist movement.

Joseph McCabe was an able speaker who felt he had a duty to expose the "overweening fraud" of spiritualism. Because he believed so completely in the strength of his position, he had not reckoned on the power of Conan Doyle's oratory. If his political adventures in Scotland taught him nothing else, Conan Doyle knew how to handle a hostile crowd. Over the years, he had cultivated a genial, avuncular manner that often took up where his facts left off. On one occasion, after knocking a bottle of water onto reporters during a lecture, he offered a memorable apology: "I may not have converted you, but at any rate I have baptized you."

Expectations ran high as the two men took the stage that evening. McCabe lost no time in coming to the point. The spiritualist movement, he declared, "was cradled in fraud. It was nurtured in fraud. It is based today to an alarming extent all over the world on fraudulent performances . . . but whether Sir Arthur Conan Doyle realizes the extent of that fraud I do not know." McCabe went on to attack the practices of such mediums as Eusapia Paladino, Daniel Dunglas Home, and Eva Carrière, all of whom Conan Doyle had ardently supported in his writings. Where Conan Doyle described their spirit manifestations as genuine, McCabe said he would substitute the phrase "not found out." He went on to attack Conan Doyle's insistence that dozens of scientists and scholars supported the spirit cause. "I courteously challenge him," McCabe declared, "to give me in his first speech tonight the names, not of fifty, but of ten, university professors of any distinction who have within the last thirty years endorsed or defended spiritualism."

The remark drew cheers from McCabe's supporters, but it proved to be a grave tactical error. Rising to reply, Conan Doyle began: "Mr. McCabe has shown that he has no respect for our intellectual position, but I cannot reciprocate. I have a very deep respect for the honest, earnest Materialist, if only because for very many years I was one myself." Turning to McCabe's challenge over the names of spiritualist supporters, Conan Doyle brandished a small notebook. "I have in this little book," he told the assembly, "the names of 160 people of high distinction, many of them of great eminence, including over forty Professors. He challenged me to name ten. I do not know why he limited me, but I have here the names of forty Professors." This drew calls from the audience to provide the names. Conan Doyle ticked off eight before continuing, "I beg you to remember that these 160 people whose names I submit to you are people who, to their own great loss, have announced themselves as Spiritualists. It never yet did a man any good to call himself a Spiritualist, I assure you, and we have had many martyrs among our people. These are folk who have taken real pains and care to get to the bottom of the subject."

From this point on, the debate belonged to Conan Doyle. In fairness to McCabe, Conan Doyle answered only one of his opponent's many charges, but he answered it in such high style that it swept the rest of McCabe's arguments aside, even though Conan Doyle's own remarks soon deteriorated into a pallid defense of Paladino, Home, and Eva Carrière. In hindsight, it is difficult to know why McCabe should have raised the matter of "professors of distinction." McCabe had read several of Conan Doyle's spiritualist works; he should have realized that his opponent liked nothing better than to list the names of prominent adherents to the cause.

The two men parted in an atmosphere of mutual respect. It is unlikely that anyone who came to the hall with a firm set of convictions was converted by either man's argument, but Conan Doyle had reinforced his reputation for plain speaking and common sense.

That reputation evaporated in December, when the first of Conan Doyle's pronouncements on fairies appeared in *The Strand*. Overnight, Conan Doyle became the spiritualist movement's greatest liability. "Poor Sherlock Holmes," ran one headline, "Hopelessly Crazy?"

The story began three years earlier, in the Yorkshire village of Cottingley, when sixteen-year-old Elsie Wright asked to borrow her father's new Midg camera so that she and her younger cousin, Frances Griffiths, might "take a picture of the fairies." Elsie's father, Arthur Wright, had long regarded his daughter's talk of fairies as a girlish fantasy, but he saw no harm in indulging her whim. The two girls took the camera and wandered off toward the stream at the back of their house, returning an hour later in high spirits. Arthur Wright was astonished when he developed the glass plate negative later that evening to see a strange image emerge: young Frances peering out over a quartet of tiny winged figures. Elsie, who had crowded into her father's makeshift darkroom with him, shouted excitedly to her cousin as the image began to emerge: "Oh, Frances, the fairies are on the plate!"

This photograph, and another that followed two months later, caused no great stir in the Wright household. The images were copied and circulated among friends as a novelty, but no one placed much store in their authenticity. Arthur Wright made his feelings plain to his daughter and her cousin. "You've been up to summat," he declared, in the manner of a true Yorkshireman.

Two years later, Elsie's mother became interested in the Theosophical movement, a Western reconstruction of Tibetan Buddhism made famous by Helena Blavatsky and Annie Besant. One night at a meeting of a local Theosophical Society, the subject of fairies happened to be raised. Mrs. Wright mentioned that her daughter had once taken a photograph of a fairy. Soon, copies were made available to members of the chapter. By February of 1920, the photographs had come to the attention of Edward L. Gardner, president of the Society's Blavatsky Lodge in London.

Edward Gardner was a forty-nine-year-old building contractor. In his spare time, he traveled the country giving lectures on Theosophy. A trim, dignified man who favored a tidy tweed suit and bow tie, Gardner earnestly believed in fairies, goblins, and pixies—creatures he regarded as a primitive link in the evolutionary chain. For him, the Cottingley photographs appeared to confirm his theories. He wrote at once to Mrs. Wright. "I am keenly interested in this side of our wonderful world life and am urging a better understanding of nature spirits and fairies," he explained. "It will assist greatly if I was able to show actual photographs of some of the orders." Soon, Gardner's lectures featured lantern slides of the two images from Cottingley.

By May, Conan Doyle had been made aware of the photographs. By an odd coincidence, he had just completed an article about fairies for *The Strand* when the images crossed his desk. In this article, which he eventually published as "The Evidence for Fairies," Conan Doyle cited the testimony of several witnesses of "unimpeachable honesty," including his own children, all of whom claimed to have encountered mysterious sprites of one sort or another. At this stage, before the Cottingley photographs convinced him otherwise, Conan Doyle did not insist on the existence of fairies, but he hoped that contemplation of the point would impart "an added charm to the silence of the woods and the wilderness of the moorland."

It seemed remarkable to Conan Doyle that the Cottingley photographs should come to hand just as he put the finishing touches on this article. In time, he came to regard the coincidence as providential. For the moment, he remained cautious. Hoping to learn more, he arranged to have lunch with Edward Gardner at the Grosvenor Hotel in London, and came away impressed. Gardner seemed to him to be quiet, well-balanced, and reserved—"not in the least of a wild and visionary type."

Conan Doyle's lecturing commitments prevented him from going to Yorkshire to meet Elsie and Frances. He had accepted an invitation to give a series of talks in Australia and New Zealand, which would take him away from England for nearly six months. In his absence, it was arranged that Gardner would do the legwork of the investigation. The first order of business, they agreed, would be a trip to Cottingley.

Up to this point, Arthur Wright had resisted the idea of allowing his daughter to attempt any more photographs. Gardner hoped that the interest of the celebrated Sir Arthur Conan Doyle would help to overcome these objections. For Gardner, this was a matter of some urgency. "[A]lmost certainly," he wrote in a letter to Conan Doyle, "the inevitable will shortly happen, one of them will 'fall in love' and then—hey presto!!"

By "hey presto," we must assume that Gardner believed that falling in love, and the attendant loss of childhood innocence, would dispel that rare and mysterious quality that enabled the girls to see and photograph fairies. "I was well aware," Conan Doyle later wrote, "that the processes of puberty are often fatal to psychic power." In any event, Conan Doyle promptly sent a letter to the Wright family, along with the gift of a book for Elsie. This overture had the desired effect. "I can assure you," Mr. Wright told Conan Doyle in a letter, "we do appreciate the honour you have done her." The following month, Gardner was invited to Cottingley.

Although matters were moving forward, Conan Doyle remained on guard against fraud. He showed the photographs to some of his spiritualist friends and received a decidedly mixed response. Oliver Lodge, in particular, smelled a rat and said so in no uncertain terms. Others expressed wonder that the woodland sprites appeared so fashion-conscious—their hairstyles and clothing seemed to reflect the very latest Parisian trends. Hoping to get answers, Gardner arranged to have the images tested by a photography expert named Harold Snelling, who had thirty years' worth of experience at a photographic studio in Illingworth. "What Snelling doesn't know about faked photography," Gardner was told, "isn't worth knowing."

In hindsight, it is clear that this confidence was misplaced, but Snelling's ringing endorsement offered much reassurance to Gardner and Conan Doyle: "These two negatives are entirely genuine and unfaked photographs of single exposure, open air work, show movement in all fairy figures, and there is no trace whatever of studio work involving card or paper models, dark backgrounds, painted figures, etc. In my opinion they are both straight, untouched figures."

To his credit, Conan Doyle sought confirmation. He borrowed the glass plate negatives and took them to the offices of Kodak in London. A pair of experts examined the plates and could find no evidence of a double exposure or other camera tricks. The Kodak experts went on to say, however, that they could undoubtedly produce a similar effect themselves and therefore could not endorse the images as genuine. "This, of course, was quite reasonable if the pictures are judged only as technical productions," Conan Doyle allowed, "but it rather savours of the old discredited anti-spiritualistic argument that because a trained conjurer can produce certain effects under his own conditions, therefore some woman or child who gets similar effects must get them by conjuring."

Any caution Conan Doyle might have shown over the Kodak verdict was soon eroded by Harold Snelling, the expert Gardner had consulted. Snelling refuted the Kodak experts' claim that such images might have been faked without darkroom tricks. If so, he claimed, he would have been able to spot it immediately. In other words, Snelling was not only prepared to swear that the photographic plate was clean, but also that the girls themselves had not staged any sort of fakery in front of the lens. The apparent movement of the tiny figures at the time of the exposure convinced him of this.

Conan Doyle needed no reassurance on this point. He refused to entertain any possibility of deception on the part of the two young girls, as the very idea offended his notions of chivalry. This attitude was typical of him, as his son Adrian once learned to his sorrow. Asked by his brother Denis if he found a certain woman attractive, Adrian replied, "No, she's ugly." The statement drew a slap across the face from his father, who informed him that "no woman is ugly." One hesitates to offer criticism of such a gallant sentiment, but it could be argued, in the age of the suffragette movement, that Conan Doyle's views were naive, if agreeably courtly. Where women were concerned, he was blind to the possibility of deception, or indeed any base motive. It was not a problem shared by Sherlock Holmes, who once declared that "the most winning woman I ever knew was hanged for poisoning three little children for their insurance money." A writer for *The Spectator* appeared to side with Holmes in the matter of the Cottingley photographs: "One must freely admit that the children who could produce such fakes would be very remarkable children, but the world, in point of fact, is full not only of very, but of very, very remarkable children."

While Conan Doyle carried on with his lecturing, Edward Gardner went to Yorkshire and found himself greatly impressed by the open and honest manner of the Wright family. At the end of his visit, he left a camera behind in the hope that Elsie might try to produce some more photographs. Three years had passed since the original pair were produced, so he held out no great hope of success.

In September, Conan Doyle received a jubilant letter. "[T]he wonderful thing has happened!" Gardner exulted. Elsie and Frances, it emerged, had produced three more photographs, along with an apology that bad weather had prevented them from taking more. Gardner once again submitted the negatives to Harold Snelling, who pronounced the new images entirely genuine.

In Melbourne, Conan Doyle responded with unrestrained enthusiasm. "Any doubts which had remained in my mind as to honesty were completely overcome," he later wrote, "for it was clear that these pictures . . . were altogether beyond the possibility of fake." He sent a grateful letter to Gardner, for it seemed to him that once the existence of fairies was established, skeptics would open their minds to other forms of psychic phenomena. "Good-bye, my dear Gardner," he concluded, "I am proud to have been associated with you in this epoch-making event."

Conan Doyle notified the world of this epoch in the December *Strand*, which presented the original pair of Cottingley photographs. In a letter to Oliver Lodge, he spelled out a strategy for convincing the doubters by holding the second series of images in reserve: "We will draw their fire with the first two, and then produce the other three, one of which is a fairy bower, showing them asleep in cocoons! It should mark an era." Enthusiastic photo captions were designed to assist in easing the readers over their initial incredulity. "The fairy is leaping up from leaves below and hovering for a moment," ran one, "it had done so three or four times." In March

1922 Conan Doyle published a book entitled *The Coming of the Fairies*, surely one of the most remarkable volumes ever written, which brought together all five photographs and other supporting evidence.

"It is hard for the mind to grasp," Conan Doyle wrote in *The Coming of the Fairies*, "what the ultimate results may be if we have actually proved the existence upon the surface of this planet of a population which may be as numerous as the human race, which pursues its own strange life in its own strange way, and which is only separated from ourselves by some difference of vibrations. We see objects within the limits which make up our colour spectrum, with infinite vibrations, unused by us, on either side of them. If we could conceive a race of beings which were constructed in material which threw out shorter or longer vibrations, they would be invisible unless we could tune ourselves up or tone them down." He went on to speculate as to the possibility of devising "psychic spectacles," which would enable everyone to see the fairies for themselves.

The public, to put it kindly, was bemused. One newspaper printed a doctored photograph showing Conan Doyle with fairies dancing in the foreground. Phrases such as "easily duped" and "sad spectacle" began to crop up. "What can he possibly be thinking?" asked one critic. Not all of the reviews were hostile. "An extremely interesting book," noted the *New York Times*, "and one, it is to be presumed, which will cause a great deal of argument pro and con. One does not necessarily have to believe in fairies to enjoy it."

This was a minority opinion. Before long, articles appeared that pointed out a suspicious similarity between the Cottingley fairies and the images in an advertisement for a brand of night light. A popular wisecrack suggested that at the crisis of the play *Peter Pan*, when Peter exhorts the audience to revive the dying Tinkerbell, the loudest shouts of "I do believe in fairies!" would be Conan Doyle's.

All but a few of his spiritualist allies deserted him. Conan Doyle had hoped that the episode would invite belief in spiritualism, but if anything it seemed to have the opposite result. By the time *The Coming of the Fairies* appeared, Conan Doyle felt obliged to shield the spiritualist movement from any further ridicule. "I would add that this whole subject of the objective existence of a subhuman form of life has nothing to do with the larger and far more vital question of spiritualism," he wrote in the book's preface. "I should be sorry if my arguments in favour of the latter should be in any way weakened by my exposition of this very strange episode, which has really no bearing upon the continued existence of the individual." Privately, he continued his efforts to rally support from other S.P.R. leaders. "The fairies still engage my attention," he told Oliver Lodge in 1922. "In August we get the girls together again and provide them with stereoscopic and also cinema cameras. No criticism which has come along as yet touches them in the slightest degree, tho' attempts at a press 'exposure' have been energetic."

In part, the energies of the press had been directed at ferreting out the identities of Frances and Elsie. In the initial *Strand* publications, Conan Doyle attempted to shield the girls from unwanted attention by writing of them as Alice and Iris Carpenter of Dalesby, West Riding. "I don't want you all to be worried by curiosity hunters," Conan Doyle wrote to Arthur Wright. As the piece was accompanied by photographs of the present-day Frances and Elsie posed by the stream in Cottingley, it did not take long for the press to penetrate this deception. Hounded by journalists, the Wright family came to regret the day that the photographs were made public.

In time, the flood of scorn would subside, but Conan Doyle never lost hope that his faith in the two girls would one day be borne out. In a second edition of *The Coming of the Fairies*, published in 1928, he reaffirmed his conviction: "The discovery by Columbus of a new terrestrial continent is a lesser achievement than the demonstration of a completely new order of life inhabiting the same planet as ourselves." In an addendum to his autobiography, written shortly before his death, he expressed a hope that the incident would "be recognized some day as opening a new vista of knowledge for the human race."

Needless to say, that new vista has yet to open, and the fairy episode has done more than any other to annihilate whatever reputation Conan Doyle might have had as a sober-minded investigator into the unknown. To the modern eye, these photographs are so palpably fake—like a young model gazing fondly at the Morton Salt girl—that any suggestion of truth seems preposterous. Conan

Doyle's defenders are quick to point out that photography was a relatively new science in 1920. In those days photographs did not lie, and few people understood what deceptions might be wrought with simple props. Even in these terms, Conan Doyle's credulity cannot be entirely explained away. He knew more than most men of his time about camera techniques, having been interested in photography since his student days. A camera and developing equipment were fixtures of his life in Southsea, and he contributed many essays to the *British Journal of Photography*. Any remaining doubts about the boundaries of photographic trickery would have been dispelled by the end of 1925, when the movie version of *The Lost World* appeared. The special effects designed by Willis O'Brien, who later brought his talents to *King Kong*, showed how dinosaurs could be brought to life on-screen. The fairies, by contrast, seemed a fairly modest achievement. Conan Doyle could easily have seen through them had he wished to do so.

One must ask, then, why a grown man should wish to believe in fairies. His faith in the innocence of Frances and Elise accounts for much of his gullibility, but Conan Doyle's actions in the Cottingley affair point to more than a gentleman's instincts. He had not even met the girls when he published his account in *The Strand*. For Conan Doyle, clearly, the Cottingley photographs came to represent far more than "an added charm to the silence of the woods."

There are two possible explanations. First, Conan Doyle had become deeply interested in the practice of spirit photography, a form of mediumship he defined as the "remarkable power of producing extra faces, figures or objects upon photographic plates." The process was simple: a subject would pose for a photograph taken by a so-called psychic sensitive. When developed, these images were likely to display some unexpected extra element—such as a ghostly form or a disembodied head—which was said to be the work of spirit forces. Often these blurry, half-formed manifestations resembled a departed relative or a prominent figure from history. Abraham Lincoln turned up regularly. Like the Cottingley photographs, the bulk of these images appear crude and unconvincing to modern eyes. Nonetheless, one can only imagine the reaction of a bereaved widow or heartsick mother as the face of a dead loved one loomed up in the shadows.

Conan Doyle displayed many such photographs in his spirit lectures. One in particular showed a crowd of mourners at the London Cenotaph on Armistice Day. The image, taken during two minutes of silent prayer, showed a great fog of spirit beings hovering above the crowd—the solemn and purposeful faces of fallen war heroes. The image invariably brought audience members to tears when it flashed on the overheard screen. Unfortunately, some of the faces were later identified as those of living football players.

Conan Doyle also placed great faith in the work of a spirit photographer named William Hope, a member of a group called the "Crewe Circle." He was horrified when Hope ran afoul of the investigator Harry Price, whose flamboyant style and high profile won him renown as the "Barnum of Psychic Research." In February 1922, Price laid a trap for Hope by introducing a set of glass negatives that had been secretly marked. When the resulting spirit photographs showed no sign of the markings, Price published an exposé and denounced Hope as a fraud. Conan Doyle rushed to the defense. He wrote to Price claiming that his own examination of the plates had turned up one of Price's markings—so faintly that it might easily have been missed. In light of this, he begged Price to reconsider his position. "At present," Conan Doyle insisted, "it makes an open sore in the movement." When Price refused to alter his views, Conan Doyle published his side of the affair in a short book called *The Case for Spirit Photography*, in which he presented Hope as an honest man who had suffered willful persecution.

Conan Doyle never gave up trying to bring Price around to a more receptive frame of mind, advising him to "concentrate upon positive things, rather than negative." Price respected Conan Doyle's great integrity, but thought him something of a fool in psychic matters. "Setting aside for the moment his extraordinary and most lovable personal qualities," Price wrote, "the chief qualification that he possessed for the role of investigator was his crusading zeal. Among all the notable persons attracted to Spiritualism, he was perhaps the most uncritical. His extreme credulity, indeed, was the despair of his colleagues, all of whom, however, held him in the highest respect for his complete honesty. Poor, dear, lovable, credulous Doyle! He was a giant in stature with the heart of a child."

The clash with Price may well have made Conan Doyle even more defensive over the Cottingley photographs. As his other examples of spirit photography were called into doubt, Conan Doyle would not have wanted to concede to any further charges of fakery. Price, for his part, regarded the fairy episode as a travesty and believed that Conan Doyle had made a mockery of serious psychic research.

A second, far more personal motivation may also have guided Conan Doyle's actions. His own childhood had been especially rich in fairy lore. Conan Doyle's Celtic heritage was rife with tales of fairy midwives, leprechauns, brownies, and other sprites. Though Chaucer spoke of their sad disappearance from the landscape, there were many in Conan Doyle's day for whom "the little people" remained an established fact—and no doubt many who continue to believe so today.

Conan Doyle's own family took a keen interest in fairies. His uncle Richard had been famous as an illustrator of children's books, many of which featured playful renderings of fairies. Conan Doyle's unhappy father also drew fairies, and there is ample reason to suppose that Charles Doyle continued to occupy his son's thoughts in the latter stages of his career. In "His Last Bow," the Sherlock Holmes tale that found the detective outwitting the German spymaster von Bork, Holmes posed as an Irish-American agent named Altamont—Charles Doyle's middle name. "It is one of my unfulfilled schemes," Conan Doyle wrote in his autobiography, "to have a Charles Doyle exhibition in London, for the critics would be surprised to find what a great and original artist he was—far the greatest, in my opinion, of the family." The scheme did not remain unfulfilled for long. In February 1924, Conan Doyle mounted just such an exhibition at London's Brook Galleries.

In a review of the exhibition, the critic William Bolitho remarked at length on Charles Doyle's fascination with fairies. "Charles Doyle reveled in this miniature world," Bolitho wrote, "his elves and fairies are Dresden figurines come to life and able ceaselessly to amuse themselves." This subject matter, he noted, opened a suggestive field for speculation: "Sir Arthur's own fairies, one realizes with a start, which have puzzled the world, and convinced part of it, are of the same race as these his father has drawn; identical in fancy, dress, psychology. One feels that the acute Sherlock, examining the evidence for fairies from his creator's own book, would have noticed this striking resemblance between the father's playful and the son's serious revelations."

Charles Doyle's sketchbook offers additional evidence of his fascination with such creatures. Its pages are filled with fairies, goblins, and elves who crouch under toadstools, play upon pipes, and whisper into the ears of innocent children. "This fairy knows a heep [*sic*] more than you do," one caption notes. Elsewhere, the artist refers to them by familiar names, and shows them sharing confidences with ducks and rescuing butterflies from hungry birds. On another page, Charles Doyle has scrawled: "I have known such a creature."

We are left to conclude that Charles Doyle, a man widely held to be insane, may well have believed in fairies. In some small measure, then, it is possible that his famous son regarded the Cottingley crusade as an act of redemption. If the existence of fairies could be proven, Charles Doyle could be seen as something of a visionary, rather than a broken-down drunkard. Perhaps he might then become—in memory at least—what his son had always wished him to be: "a man of sensitive genius, ill-suited to the harsh realities of our world."

For the rest of his life, Conan Doyle regarded the ability to see fairies as a rare and wonderful gift. Years later, Frances Way, née Griffiths, would tell a reporter of Conan Doyle's strong desire to produce such a photograph himself. There is no evidence that he ever tried, but the notion conjures a heartbreaking image of the burly writer, then in his sixties, peering into sylvan glades with a camera in hand, hoping to see fairies.

In June 1982, eighty-one-year-old Elsie Hill, née Wright, wrote to the managing director of Sotheby's auction house to offer for sale her own account of the events in Cottingley. At long last, she explained, she felt ready to provide the truth behind the "practical joke" that had confounded so many people, and hoped to realize some profit from the sale of artifacts connected with the episode. By this time, her cousin Frances, now seventy-five, had already made a confession to a psychic researcher named Joe Cooper, who would shortly publish his revelations in a book entitled *The Case of the Cottingley Fairies*. "From where I was," Frances had said, "I could see the hatpins holding up the figures. I've always marvelled that anybody ever took it seriously."

Elsie went on to offer further details to Geoffrey Crawley, editor of *The British Journal of Photography*. The entire affair, she explained, had been a schoolgirl game that got terribly out of hand when Conan Doyle and Edward Gardner became involved. As a friend of the family later declared: "The girls could hardly tell such important people they were wrong!"

According to Elsie, the two girls agreed to keep silent because they were "feeling sad" for Conan Doyle. "He had lost his son recently in the war," Elsie wrote in her letter to Sotheby's, "and I think the poor man was trying to comfort himself in these things, so I said to Frances, we are a lot younger than Conan Doyle and Mr. Gardner, so we will wait till they die of old age and then we will tell."

Edward Gardner lived to be one hundred years old, leaving the girls to maintain their silence well into their own declining years. Gardner continued to believe in the truth of the Cottingley fairies until the end of his days, publishing a book entitled *Fairies: The Cottingley Photographs and Their Sequel* in 1945. "It is not easy to convey the sense of integrity I felt at the end of the investigation," he wrote. "To share it properly one would have to meet the parents and the children as I did."

"The only theory which I would not discuss was the honesty of the children," Conan Doyle had told the readers of *The Strand*, "for that I considered to be well attested."

In this, both men were sadly, but perhaps honorably, mistaken. In a third and final article on the subject in *The Strand* in 1923, when a more circumspect man would have let the matter well enough alone, Conan Doyle put forward evidence he believed would establish the girls' credibility once and for all. He had come into possession of some private correspondence between Frances and a friend, in circumstances that did nothing to advance any public deception, showing that the girl regarded the appearance of fairies as a normal and not especially interesting occurrence. For this reason, there are those who feel even now that Elsie and Frances did, in fact, see fairies at the foot of the garden, even if the photographs themselves were fake. "Unlike Frances," Elsie wrote to Joe Cooper, "I much more prefer the role of being a solemn faced Yorkshire comedienne than being thought to be a solemn faced nut case."

No doubt Sherlock Holmes would have offered a curt dismissal of the entire affair: "Women are not to be trusted, Watson," he once declared. "Not even the best of them."

26

Pheneas Speaks

Although we may misbelieve mediums and
With doubt and suspicion our minds may be filled
Sherlock Holmes, we must grant, reappeared in the
Strand
A number of times after being killed.

—*THE GRAPHIC*

One day in the early months of 1921, Lady Jean Conan Doyle picked up a pencil, held it poised over a blank sheet of paper, and waited for psychic inspiration to come. She had seen her friend, the late Lily Loder-Symonds, perform acts of automatic writing many times. At first, Jean had regarded these demonstrations with suspicion and no little embarrassment. Over time, however, the content of the messages, coupled with her friend's obvious sincerity, broke down her resistance. It had been these messages, after all, which played such a large role in her husband's public advocacy of the spiritualist movement.

Now her husband had come under attack for his beliefs. The Cottingley episode had made him an object of derision and given fresh ammunition to the opponents of his crusade. One by one, each of the mediums he revered was being held up to damaging scrutiny by the likes of Harry Price and, in America, the magician Harry Houdini. Her husband showed no sign of any weakening of faith, but the strain of the constant struggle was beginning to tell. His broad shoulders often sagged with weary exasperation, and friends noted a deepening of the lines on his face, which could not be explained by age alone. He declared himself ready to sacrifice everything to take his message to the world. His greatest frustration lay in the resistance of those he sought to help. More than once, Jean had seen tears in her husband's eyes when the lights came up after a séance. "My God," he said on one occasion, "if only they could know!"

For some time, Jean sat motionless, staring down at the blank page before her. Then, slowly at first, the pencil began to move.

"It is now five years since the great gift of inspired writing first came to my wife," Conan Doyle wrote in 1926. "In her intense honesty and deep modesty, she somewhat retarded it at first by holding back her impulses in the fear lest they should come from her own subconscious self. Gradually, however, the unexpected nature of the messages, and the allusions to be found in them showed both her and me that there were forces at work which were outside herself."

At first, Jean's automatic writing took the form of messages from family members and friends who had "passed beyond the border." Jean's brother Malcolm, who had died at Mons, was among the first to make himself known: "Dear old chap," came the message. "It is good to be here." Conan Doyle's brother Innes also appeared: "I am so glad to be here. It is so grand to be in touch like this."

Even Conan Doyle's sister Annette, whose death more than thirty years earlier had long been a source of regret, transmitted a comforting message: "Tell the children that I love them all so much, and it is one of my most precious duties and joys looking after them, and helping dear Jean in her training."

Almost every one of the spirit contacts encouraged Conan Doyle to continue his lecturing efforts. "Spread the news," declared Malcolm Leckie. "The world needs it so."

Occasionally a stranger would make himself known in the family circle. "For God's sake, Sir Arthur," said one, "strike hard at these people—these dolts who do not believe. The world so needs this knowledge. If I had only known this on earth it would have so altered my life—the sun would have shown on my grey path had I known what lay before me."

Amid all these messages, which were to continue for the rest of Conan Doyle's life, one voice remained conspicuous by its absence. Louisa Conan Doyle, who had been dead for fifteen years when the messages began coming, never said a word.

On December 10, 1922, an influential spirit guide made himself known to Conan Doyle's family circle. "He is a very, very high soul," ran a message of introduction, "sent especially to work through you on the earth plane. He died thousands of years ago in the East, near Arabia. He was a leader among men. He wants me to say, dear one, that there is much work before you."

A moment later, the new presence announced himself: "Pheneas speaking."

From that point forward, Pheneas would act as the intermediary between Conan Doyle and the spirit world. In time, Pheneas revealed that he had been an Arab scribe of the city of Ur, the ancient Sumerian capital, and that he had lived some three thousand years before the time of Christ. Pheneas, too, encouraged Conan Doyle to continue with his work: "Go on as you are doing," Pheneas insisted. "Their unbelief will fall as a dark garment from them."

The reader must draw his or her own conclusions as to the value of such messages. It is curious, however, that nearly every communication told Conan Doyle precisely what he most wanted to hear. His friends and relatives were happily reunited in an idyllic afterlife. Contact between the dead and the living was not only possible, but would one day be a commonplace occurrence. Most gratifying of all, Conan Doyle's psychic crusade had met with enthusiasm on the spirit plane, and its value would soon be universally acknowledged among the living.

If one sets aside, for the moment, the possibility that these messages were genuine, several intriguing questions arise. Was this a conscious deception on Jean's part, a calculated effort to bolster her husband's flagging resolve? It is possible, of course, though the effort of sustaining such a deceit, over a period of nearly ten years, would be enormous. Moreover, she had regarded such messages with distaste when Lily Loder-Symonds first produced them. It seems improbable that she herself would have taken up the practice without some foundation of belief.

In discussing Lily's trance writing, Conan Doyle spoke of the "subtle and dangerous" power of the subconscious to deceive the conscious mind. His own wife, he freely admitted, had initially resisted the idea of automatic writing, for fear of falling victim to some form of self-delusion. These fears were assuaged to a great extent when Lily herself came through and chided Jean for ever having doubted her own psychic gifts. "Jean," ran the message, "you are awful at not believing. It is really wrong, old girl. It is *not* your subconscious self." Perhaps or perhaps not, but one is loath to accept the assurances of a spirit.

Not surprisingly, Conan Doyle needed no further urging to believe. He spoke often of the "purity" of his wife's mediumship and pointed out many "unknowable" details that could not have come from Jean's subconscious. "I cannot see how one can avoid all the snags of subconscious action," he wrote, "and the possible dramatisation of latent personalities, which would account for the writing itself. It is only by the information conveyed, its accuracy, and its remoteness from the normal mind of the medium that we can gain assurance." The appearance of Pheneas, to Conan Doyle's way of thinking, offered all the assurance he could have wished. "I am going this afternoon to the Euphrates," Pheneas declared in one session. "We did not call it that of old. We had an Arab word for that land which meant 'The Garden of Flowers.'" It is open to debate whether such facts were as unknowable as Conan Doyle supposed. A British Museum excavation of the city of Ur was under way at the time, under the leadership of Sir Leonard Woolley, and had uncovered a great deal about the culture of Early Mesopotamia. These findings were widely discussed in the popular press, even in the pages of *The Strand*. It is not impossible, therefore, that Jean might have gained insight into the background of Pheneas through earthly channels.

In some cases, researchers believe, a medium may appear genuinely ignorant of a particular fact or memory because the information has long since been banished from the active memory. In such cases, it is thought, the medium is motivated by such a powerful desire to succeed that it overwhelms the conscious processes. Jean, certainly, had a powerful motivation to provide such evidence. Whether this explains the pronouncements of Pheneas is a matter for conjecture.

If a willingness to believe lay behind the appearance of Pheneas, one must wonder over the fact that Conan Doyle himself demonstrated no particular mediumistic power. On only one occasion, during the war, did he claim any significant psychic experience. This occurred on the morning of April 4, 1917, when he awoke with the word "Piave"—the name of a river in Italy—ringing in his head. Some seven months later, convinced that this word represented a premonition of some kind, he wrote a brief statement and sent it in a sealed envelope to the secretary of the Society for Psychical Research, asking that it be opened only at his specific request. One year later, when the Piave River had become well known as the site of a decisive battle, the letter was opened and his premonition confirmed. "I claim that the only possible explanation," Conan Doyle wrote in the *Journal of the Society for Psychical Research*, "is that my friends on the other side, knowing how much I worried over the situation, were giving me comfort and knowledge."

Not everyone agreed with this interpretation. In the debate at Queen's Hall, Joseph McCabe ridiculed Conan Doyle's assertion that he could have imagined "few more unlikely things than that the war would be transferred to the Piave." Far from being unlikely, McCabe argued, the London *Times* of April 3—the day before Conan Doyle had his revelation—published a long article anticipating just such an event. Conan Doyle insisted that he had not read the *Times* article. That may be so, but at the time he was well immersed in writing his history of the war, so his claims of ignorance are not wholly convincing.

If the Piave revelation left room for doubt, Conan Doyle allowed no shadow of suspicion to fall on his wife. Jean's mediumship became the final plank of his psychic platform. Any skepticism of his beliefs now represented a slight on her integrity. This can hardly be seen as surprising, as he had taken the word of Elsie Wright and Frances Griffiths without ever having met them. Where his own wife was concerned, he would sooner have denied his own existence than allow contradiction of her testimony.

Conan Doyle, Jean, Mary, and the three younger children held regular séances at Windlesham beginning in 1921, in the room that had once been the children's nursery. In time, Pheneas began to deliver his messages through a form of "semi-trance inspirational talking." In these sessions, Conan Doyle reported, his wife "never completely lost consciousness, but her hold upon her own organism was slight. The eyes were tightly closed, and never opened until the power had left her." Later, Conan Doyle would collect the many examples of this mediumship together under the title of *Pheneas Speaks*.

Pheneas strongly urged Conan Doyle to continue traveling the world to spread the psychic message. In this, Conan Doyle needed little encouragement. His tour of Australia and New Zealand in 1920, though reckoned a success by its promoters, convinced him that much work remained to be done overseas. He drew large audiences and received a warm welcome from the spiritualist community, but dissenters made themselves known at every stop. This did not trouble him greatly. "If Spiritualism had been a popular cult in Australia," he wrote, "there would have been no object in my visit."

A "tragic intermezzo" had interrupted the return trip from Australia in early 1921. Word reached Conan Doyle in Paris that Willie Hornung had been stricken with influenza while visiting the Pyrenees. He started off immediately, but Hornung died on March 22, before Conan Doyle reached his bedside. It was the second family tragedy to strike during the Australian tour. Weeks earlier, in Melbourne, he had learned of his mother's death. There is reason to suppose that Conan Doyle's relationship with the Ma'am had been strained by his spiritualist efforts. Two or three years earlier, as her eyesight failed, Mary Doyle decided to leave Masongill. Conan Doyle offered to bring her to Crowborough, but she chose instead to move into a cottage near the Hornungs. Conan Doyle attempted to come to grips with this in *The Wanderings of a Spiritualist*, a book detailing his travels through Australia. "For my own psychic work she had, I fear, neither sympathy nor understanding," he wrote, "but she had an innate faith and spirituality which were so natural to her that she could not conceive the needs of others in that direction." This was artfully done, but it would perhaps be closer to the truth to say that the Ma'am regarded spiritualism as a load of rubbish.

Not surprisingly, the Ma'am and Willie Hornung soon returned to the family circle under the auspices of Jean's automatic writing, and both offered abject apologies for any doubts they expressed in life. "I am so glad to be here," came a message from Hornung. "Arthur, this is wonderful. If only I had known this on earth, how much I could have helped others."

The Ma'am took much the same tone: "I ought to have trusted your judgment, my own son."

By this time Conan Doyle had laid plans to continue the spiritualist crusade with a tour of America, and both Hornung and the Ma'am gave strong encouragement. "Dear ones," read a message from the Ma'am, "your tour in America will be a very great success. Strength, enormous strength, will be given to you, dear."

"Yes, rather," agreed Hornung. "The seed needs sowing in many places."

Conan Doyle had not been in America since before the war. On his previous two trips, the American lecture audiences had shown a warmth and enthusiasm that he hoped would make them amenable to the spirit message. "The ground is fertile there," he wrote to Oliver Lodge.

As with his tour of Australia, Conan Doyle brought Jean and the three younger children with him on the trip, along with the children's maid. On this and all future lecture tours, he paid the party's expenses out of his earnings, then handed over the surplus to spiritualist organizations. "I take not one shilling of the proceeds of my lectures," he insisted, "so that I have no material interest."

The family arrived in New York on April 9, 1922, aboard the White Star liner *Baltic*. At their hotel, Conan Doyle faced a crowd of reporters whose questions demonstrated no great sympathy for the purpose of the visit. "They perched themselves round our sitting-room as best they might," he recalled, "and I, seated in an arm-chair in the centre, was subjected to a fine raking fire which would have shot me to pieces had I been vulnerable." The press soon found a chink in his armor. Like his friend Oliver Lodge, Conan Doyle ran aground over his insistence that the spirit world offered many earthly delights—such as whiskey, cigars, and marital relations. The next day's headlines betrayed a certain irreverence: "High Jinks in the Beyond," read one. "Doyle Says They Play Golf in Heaven," announced another. In fact he had said no such thing, but the newspapers had elected to have some fun at his expense.

These gibes were not limited to the press. While Conan Doyle readied to deliver his lectures, the mayor of New York, John F. Hylan, publicly ridiculed him at a political event. According to the mayor, Conan Doyle had found "a new line of business, and from all reports the shekels are rolling in to him as fast as when he told how easy it was for the famous detective of fiction to get out of tight places." His Honor added that "Sir Arthur has told us nothing that has not long since been dismissed as 'wool gathering,' but the lure of the unknown is always fascinating and there will always be a large audience to listen to airy nothings. Mr. Doyle intends to spread them at so much per spread."

Others at the gathering were quick to take offense on Conan Doyle's behalf. Former Governor Al Smith suggested that the mayor might wish to consult Conan Doyle's spirits to gain an understanding of a current municipal issue, as "nobody on earth can explain it to him." William Prendergast, the public service commissioner, chided the mayor for his boorishness. "I have always been an admirer of Sir Arthur Conan Doyle," he declared. "Hospitality is due to this distinguished Britisher, even if here on a misguided mission."

Misguided or not, Conan Doyle delivered his first lecture at Carnegie Hall on April 12. Newspaper advertisements offered tickets that ranged in price from fifty cents to $3.50. The value in shekels was not indicated. The first night's audience numbered in the thousands and included many women who wore a gold star—indicating the loss of a son in the war. Conan Doyle's calm, reassuring voice filled the darkened hall as lantern slides of spirit phenomena flashed on a screen behind him. The sight of ectoplasm oozing from the mouth of the medium Eva Carrière was too much for the sensitive New York audience—hysterical screams and sobbing drowned out portions of the lecture, and fainting women had to be helped to the lobby. Those who were still conscious at the end were much moved by Conan Doyle's account of his own psychic encounters, especially those involving his mother. "I swear by all that's holy on earth," he declared, "I looked into her eyes."

At one point, it appeared as if the evening might feature its own demonstration of a spirit presence. A strange, shrill whistle could be heard as a late-arriving elderly gentleman was helped into his seat, much to the puzzlement of the gathering. "Persons on the stage said they heard this noise and wondered whether it was some manifestation of a spirit somewhere in the audience," reported the *New York Times*. "After three or four successive whistles, those seated around the newcomer saw that it was merely a note from a purely material plane." It seems the gentleman in question had a faulty hearing aid.

Apart from this interruption, Conan Doyle deemed the evening a success, although he had been nearly overwhelmed by the sweltering heat inside the hall, and mobbed by autograph hunters afterward. "I endeavoured to be patient and courteous," he wrote afterward, "but I admit that it was a strain."

In *Our American Adventure*, his subsequent chronicle of the tour, Conan Doyle declared that the press coverage of this first lecture had been "all that could be wished for by those who desired that this great subject should be ventilated in a fair and even sympathetic manner." In support of this, he quoted an account in the *New York Times*:

> The audience, which numbered 3,500 people, evidently saw a manifestation of the coming of a newer and finer religion that would clear out most of the weeds in the old religions and show the human race what God has written down in His eternal law.

If true, this certainly would have been all that he might have wished, but what the article actually said was:

> Sir Arthur Conan Doyle told about 3,500 persons that he saw manifestation of the coming of a new and finer religion which would "clear out most of the weeds in the old

religions" and show the human race "what God has written down as His eternal law."

All too often in these later years, Conan Doyle showed himself willing to play fast and loose with the facts. In ascribing his own views to the audience, and his own quotations to the writer of the article, Conan Doyle gave the impression that the coverage had been surpassingly favorable, when in fact it was merely tolerant. As with so many aspects of the spiritualist movement, his desire had gotten the better of him.

Even he could not have put a positive spin on a *New York Times* editorial entitled "Such a Man on Such a Mission!" It read in part: "[I]t is simply pathetic that a man like Sir Arthur—a man to whom in other years the English-reading world was indebted for no small amount of real pleasure—should now be devoting himself to the exploitation of such 'spiritualism' as this. . . . The emotions he excites by the description of visits from the audible and visible dead will be rather that of pity." A later article was even less kind: "With each of the interviews he gives, it becomes harder to be patient with him."

On April 15, three days after Conan Doyle's first lecture at Carnegie Hall, New York awoke to a different type of headline: "Wife Seeks Death to be a Spirit Guide—Newark Woman Kills Baby, Then Drinks Poison So She May Help Husband From Beyond." The woman in question, Maude Fancher, had been a devoted adherent of spiritualism. Troubled by financial worries and a kidney ailment, she had decided to end her life so as to hasten the happy journey into the afterlife. Before swallowing the poison, she first administered a fatal dose to her two-year-old son, Cecil. In her suicide note, she explained that she did not want to "leave him here to be raised by someone else." From the other world, she continued, she expected to be in a better position to help her husband in his troubles. "I will guide you from this day on," she wrote, "and my love will always be right with you."

The *New York Times* lost no time in connecting the tragedy to Conan Doyle's crusade. "Conan Doyle Defends Doctrines," declared a subhead on the front page. "The incident shows the great danger of the present want of knowledge concerning spiritual matters," he was quoted as saying. "We know from information from the beyond that suicide is a desperate and very grave offense, that the hand of Providence can not be forced and that the effect of a suicide is to separate the spirit of the offender from those whom he or she loves while they expiate the offense on the other side. If this poor woman had been better instructed she would never have ventured on such a deed."

It was hardly a compassionate statement, and his critics demanded a further explication. Two days later, a *Times* editorial headed "She Could Quote Sir Arthur" reviewed the unhappy situation. "It is decidedly embarrassing, though rather unfairly so, for Sir Arthur Conan Doyle that the woman over in Newark who poisoned herself and her baby should have written out in explanation of what she did an elaborate statement of her beliefs and hopes," the article stated. "Sir Arthur's defense from such accusations as may be made against him as a result of this pitiful occurrence will have to be that thousands of people have studied his views and have not thought of killing themselves or others."

Actually, the paper could have offered a better defense by reviewing its own coverage of the tour. An article in its April 11 edition—three days before Maude Fancher poisoned herself and her child—made Conan Doyle's views absolutely clear. The headline read: "Suicide Not an End of Ills, Says Doyle."

As in Australia, Conan Doyle took every opportunity to show his family the sights. In all, he gave seven lectures at Carnegie Hall, which left ample time for museums, a carriage ride in Central Park, and an aerial view of the city from the top of the Woolworth Building. Like many other visitors to the city, Conan Doyle had difficulties with taxicabs. After one ride, he realized he had forgotten his belongings in the backseat. Pedestrians on Fifth Avenue were elbowed aside as the sixty-three-year-old author sprinted past, waving his arms in a vain attempt to flag down the driver. When the cab turned onto a side street, Conan Doyle took a flying leap onto the running board, apparently causing some distress to the driver, who mistook the energetic approach for a robbery.

In addition to New York, the tour included stops in Boston, New Haven, Washington, D.C., Philadelphia, Chicago, and Atlantic City. Conan Doyle arranged for a special stop in Toledo, Ohio, so that he could visit the medium Ada Besinnet, who had greatly impressed him on four separate occasions in London.

The medium made the detour worthwhile, producing a message purporting to be from his son Kingsley. The communication informed Conan Doyle that "Oscar and Uncle Willie" were following his tour with great interest. This was a reference to Willie Hornung and his son—"of whose existence," Conan Doyle insisted, "or relation to my boy the medium had no possible means of knowing." To Conan Doyle, this seemed to be in the "highest degree evidential."

As it happens, Conan Doyle often professed amazement when a medium referred to his departed loved ones by the names used within the immediate family—such as Kingsley, Innes, Oscar, or Willie. His son, he pointed out, was actually named Alleyne, and Hornung's real name was Ernest. Kingsley and Willie were the more familiar names used within the family circle, a fact that would not have been readily apparent to an outsider. The phenomenon becomes less impressive when it is realized that Conan Doyle often used the family names in print—especially in the psychic press. That he continued to express astonishment at each recurrence is perhaps more an indication of his trusting nature—and his need to believe—than of the genuine character of the phenomenon.

In any case, Conan Doyle left Toledo well satisfied with Miss Besinnet's results. "It was one of the most remarkable experiences that I have ever had," he told the *Toledo News-Bee*. "She should be guarded and looked after very carefully, for she is very valuable."

Conan Doyle's regard for Miss Besinnet owed much to the fact that in London the previous year she had been the first to produce a visible manifestation of his mother. "At the end of a very wonderful sitting came my mother's face," he told a lecture audience in Toledo. "My wife and I could count the very wrinkles in her face and the gray hairs at the temples during the five or six seconds or more that the face was visible."

The following year, a lengthy article would appear in the magazine *Scientific American* that described the manner in which some mediums made use of paraffin masks in the séance room. These masks, which were sometimes dipped in phosphorus for a ghostly appearance, could be waved high over the heads of sitters on a long pole, or poked through the curtains of a medium's cabinet to give the impression of a disembodied face hovering in the darkness. When properly molded, these masks could have a striking effect upon a suggestible mind.

It is not possible to know whether Ada Besinnet resorted to parlor tricks of this type. Where his mother was concerned, however, Conan Doyle's impressions may not have been wholly objective. A subsequent séance in New York, which featured another encounter with the spirit of the Ma'am, brought him no end of misery. Dr. Leonard J. Hartman, a trustee of the First Spiritualist Church of New York, invited Conan Doyle to a séance conducted by William R. Thompson and his wife, Eva. Mrs. Thompson was thought to be a "materializing medium," with a "sensitive nature attuned to the finer harmonies of our etherealized dead." This sensitivity was thought to enable her to "bring those dead back to us, in materialized form, and even make them speak." All this was to take place while Mrs. Thompson herself remained hidden away in a cabinet, evidently deep in a trance.

In order to create a suitable atmosphere, the Thompsons insisted that each of the sitters adhere to a strict set of rules. They were told to sing hymns "industriously" throughout the proceedings. In addition, the lights were to remain extinguished, as even the slightest illumination might kill or otherwise injure the medium. Also, the sitters were warned against staring directly at the materialized spirits. "It's very bad form," they were told. Lastly, the spirits were to be given plenty of "elbow room."

When all present had agreed to these restrictions, Mrs. Thompson withdrew into a curtained enclosure and the room was plunged into darkness. After much singing of hymns, a ghostly form—barely visible in the darkness—emerged from the cabinet. Conan Doyle was said to be "overcome with emotion" as he recognized the spirit of his mother. According to Dr. Hartman, he reverently asked if he might be allowed to touch his mother's hand. After some consultation with Mr. Thompson, the spirit form offered the back of its hand. In some versions of the tale, Conan Doyle raised the hand to his lips. In others, he was so moved that he watered it with his tears. After a time, the figure withdrew into the cabinet.

When the séance concluded, according to Dr. Hartman, Conan Doyle declared himself greatly moved. "The chance to touch my mother's hand," he said, "and feel the substance there; the chance to see her force, was very precious to me."

Three days later, Mr. and Mrs. Thompson were arrested for fraud in a highly publicized police sting. A pair of undercover officers arranged a second séance in Dr. Hartman's home, and wrestled the spirit presence to the ground when it emerged from the cabinet. The spirit proved to be Mrs. Thompson in a set of iridescent robes. It seems the lusty singing of hymns was meant to cover any awkward noise associated with the costume change.

The New York papers raked Conan Doyle over the coals. A magazine called the *American Weekly* published a lengthy exposé entitled "How the Mediums 'Brought Back' Sir Conan Doyle's Dead 'Mother.' " It featured photographs of Mrs. Thompson and the robes she wore to impersonate spirits, along with an illustration of a reverent Conan Doyle bending to kiss the apparition's hand. "When I think now," wrote Dr. Hartman, "how the feeling of that son for that little old mother long dead was played upon by those charlatans I feel indignant clear through."

Perhaps, although it is difficult to regard Hartman as the injured party, as the police operation took place in his home, and the *American Weekly* article—which descended into low comedy at Conan Doyle's expense—appeared over his name. Conan Doyle vigorously defended himself, saying that he had not been fooled, but did not wish to offend his host by expressing his doubts openly. "Both my wife and I," he wrote in *Our American Adventure*, "were of the opinion that the proceedings were very suspicious and we came away deeply dissatisfied, for there were no test conditions and no way of checking such manifestations as we saw."

The incident would haunt Conan Doyle for the rest of his life. "I do not think that any punishment could be too severe for rogues of this kind," he remarked. "The rotten twigs must come off."

Possibly he should have grown suspicious at the moment he entered Dr. Hartman's parlor, as his host had invited an extra guest to fill out the séance circle. She was apparently a charming young woman, but her name would surely have put Sherlock Holmes on his guard.

It was Alice Moriarty.

27

The Ectoplasmic Man

His final device of offering five thousand pounds if the spirits of the dead would place the three first horses in the coming derby, and his demonstration that ectoplasm was in truth the froth of bottle porter artfully concealed by the medium, are newspaper stunts which are within the recollection of the reader.

—ARTHUR CONAN DOYLE, *THE LAND OF MIST*

"Who was the greatest medium-baiter of modern times?" Conan Doyle once asked. "Undoubtedly Houdini. Who was the greatest physical medium of modern times? There are some who would be inclined to give the same answer."

Harry Houdini, the "justly-celebrated self-liberator," first crossed Conan Doyle's path in March 1920. Houdini, in the midst of a tour of Britain, learned of Conan Doyle's interest in the Davenport Brothers, the American stage mediums of the previous century. The Davenports' act—and its exposure—had featured prominently in Houdini's book *The Unmasking of Robert-Houdin*, a copy of which he forwarded to Conan Doyle.

Conan Doyle wrote at once to thank Houdini for the book, but allowed as how he did not really believe that the Davenports had been exposed as frauds. "Every famous medium is said to have 'confessed,' " he wrote. "It is an old trick of the opposition's." He added a significant postscript: "Some of our people think that you have yourself some psychic power, but I feel it is art and practice."

Already, the battle lines had been drawn.

At first blush, it is difficult to imagine two men less alike than Harry Houdini, the brash American showman, and Sir Arthur Conan Doyle, the genial spiritualist. When they met, Houdini had already cultivated a reputation as the world's most outspoken anti-spiritualist crusader, which he came to regard as the most important work of his life. Houdini had been drawn into the spiritualist arena by a genuine desire to contact the spirit of his beloved mother, but with his knowledge of stagecraft he easily saw through the deceptions of the typical séance room. By rights, this should have made him the natural enemy of Conan Doyle, who had come to resent what he called the "Conjurer's Complex" of such magicians as P. T. Selbit and John Nevil Maskelyne, who insisted on explaining away psychic phenomena in terms of simple magic tricks.

Even physically, the two men presented a study in contrasts. Houdini, whom the press invariably described as "somewhat undersized," had angular features, blue eyes that often betrayed anger and impatience, and thick, black curly hair. Conan Doyle, in spite of his earlier course of muscular development, had grown somewhat portly in his advancing years. His hair had thinned and deep lines showed in his face, but the photographs of his later years usually find him beaming with the contentment of his happy home life. Side by side, Conan Doyle and Houdini looked uncannily like the Walrus and the Carpenter from *Alice in Wonderland*.

Below the surface there were compelling similarities. Both had drifted away from a strong religious background. As children, both had weak, absent fathers, and later compensated for the privations of childhood by showering wealth on their strong-willed mothers. A famous piece of Houdini lore has him returning from an early success with gold coins concealed in his clothing—"Shake me, Mama! I'm magic!" he is supposed to have said. The young Conan Doyle had done much the same thing on his return from the Arctic.

After corresponding through the early months of 1920, the two men arranged to meet in April when the Conan Doyles traveled to

Portsmouth to watch Houdini escape from packing crates and a straitjacket. Later that month, Houdini lunched at Windlesham and performed magic tricks for the children. On both occasions, the conversations were dominated by talk of spiritualism.

From the first, Houdini placed himself in an untenable position by pretending to be more open-minded on the subject than he actually was. Eager to cultivate a friendship with the famous author, Houdini dodged and parried when Conan Doyle sought his opinions on various mediums. "How people could imagine those men were conjurors is beyond me," Conan Doyle had said of the Davenports. Houdini's answer was a masterwork of ambiguity: "I can make the positive assertion that the Davenport Brothers were never exposed." This was true to the extent that their tricks had never been found out, but it was hardly the whole truth. Ten years earlier, Houdini had traveled some eight hundred miles to interview Ira Davenport, the surviving brother, and learn the secret of the "Davenport Rope Tie" that made their act possible. He knew perfectly well that the Davenports weren't genuine mediums—Ira had cheerfully admitted it. Still, when Conan Doyle attempted to pin him down, Houdini feinted: "Regarding the Davenport Brothers," he wrote in a letter, "I am afraid that I cannot say that all their work was accomplished by the spirits." This open-ended statement seemed to satisfy both men.

"Let me say," Conan Doyle was to write of Houdini, "that in a long life which has touched every side of humanity, Houdini is far and away the most curious and intriguing character whom I have ever encountered. I have met better men, and I have certainly met very many worse ones, but I have never met a man who had such strange contrasts in his nature, and whose actions and motives it was more difficult to foresee or to reconcile."

On the one hand, Conan Doyle recalled, he had known Houdini to round up five hundred barefoot children and have them all fitted with boots, while at the same time he grew indignant at being charged two shillings to have a suit pressed. Conan Doyle also professed himself to be astonished by Houdini's "obvious and childish" ego, as on the occasion when the escape artist introduced Theo Hardeen—a famous performer in his own right—simply as "the brother of the great Houdini."

Vanity aside, Conan Doyle admired that "essential masculine quality" of courage Houdini possessed to such a conspicuous degree. "Nobody has ever done, and nobody in all human probability will ever do, such reckless feats of daring. His whole life was one long succession of them, and when I say that amongst them was the leaping from one aeroplane to another, with handcuffed hands at the height of three thousand feet, one can form an idea of the extraordinary lengths that he would go."

It is worth noting that Houdini did not actually perform that stunt, which Conan Doyle would have seen in the Houdini movie entitled *The Grim Game*. The escape artist had been sidelined by a broken arm during the filming, and a stunt man had to perform the feat in his place—a fact Houdini kept closely guarded.

Houdini, for his part, regarded Conan Doyle as "just as nice and sweet as any mortal I have ever been near." He felt flattered by the famous author's attentions, and arranged to have their picture taken together at every opportunity. Whatever his reservations, Houdini genuinely believed that if anyone could show him a true psychic manifestation, it would be Conan Doyle. "[W]hatever one's views on the subject," he would write in *A Magician Among the Spirits*, "it is impossible not to respect the belief of this great author who has wholeheartedly and unflinchingly thrown his life and soul into the conversion of unbelievers. Sir Arthur *believes*. In his great mind there is *no* doubt."

Clearly Houdini respected Conan Doyle, but he could not bring himself to approach the matter in such an uncritical fashion. "You will note that I am still a skeptic," he told his new friend, "but a seeker after the Truth. I am willing to believe, if I can find a Medium who, as you suggest, will not resort to 'manipulation' when the Power does not 'arrive.' "

This did not entirely satisfy Conan Doyle, who recognized the deep suspicion behind Houdini's words. "It wants to be approached not in the spirit of a detective approaching a suspect," he cautioned him, "but in that of a humble, religious soul, yearning for help and comfort." For Conan Doyle, Houdini represented far more than an ordinary skeptical inquirer. He recognized that if he could bring

Houdini into the fold, he would have won an ally who could carry the message around the world.

For the moment, at least, Houdini seemed willing to play along. "I am very, very anxious to have a séance with any medium with whom you could gain me an audience," he insisted. "I promise to go there with my mind absolutely clear, and willing to believe. I will put no obstruction of any nature whatsoever in the medium's way, and will assist in all ways in my power to obtain results."

To some degree this was disingenuous on Houdini's part, and his critics have attacked him for taking advantage of Conan Doyle's kindness to gain audiences with mediums who might otherwise have turned him away. This is probably unjust, as Houdini never had any particular trouble finding his way into séance rooms and took a particular delight in wearing disguises when he went behind enemy lines. At the critical moment, he would whip off his wig and glasses and shout, "I am Houdini! And you are a fraud!"

No disguises were necessary when Houdini sat with Eva Carrière, who had impressed Conan Doyle in France, and Mrs. Wriedt, who claimed to produce the voices of departed family members. On both occasions Houdini came away unimpressed. Mrs. Wriedt had been so intimidated by Houdini that the hour-long séance passed without incident of any kind. Eva C. also sat motionless through several sittings, but subsequently managed to produce several "extrusions of ectoplasm" from her mouth, which had been examined beforehand. Houdini reported to Conan Doyle that he found the manifestations "highly interesting," but was "not prepared to say that they were supernormal."

Privately, he recorded that the demonstration had not impressed him in any way. Eva Carrière had a remarkable talent for producing strange objects from her otherwise empty mouth, but so did Houdini himself. The medium's effects reminded him of his own "Needles and Thread" trick, in which he swallowed a packet of loose needles and cotton thread, showed his mouth to be empty, and then pulled the cotton strand from his lips with the needles neatly threaded at regular intervals.

By now Conan Doyle had grown impatient with Houdini's equivocations. He invited Mrs. Wriedt to Windlesham and reported to Houdini that a spirit voice had been plainly heard. "Now, is that not final?" he asked. "What possible loophole is there in that for deception?" Houdini could not bring himself to accept Conan Doyle's assurances so readily. His confidence plummeted when Conan Doyle wrote an ecstatic letter describing the Cottingley photographs as "a revelation." For once, Houdini managed to maintain a discreet silence.

Baffled by Houdini's intransigence, Conan Doyle began to suspect an ulterior motive. Within two months of their first exchange of letters, when Houdini spoke of an investigation with the Society for Psychical Research, Conan Doyle asked, "Do they never think of investigating *you*?" Elsewhere, he expanded on the point: "My dear chap, why go round the world seeking a demonstration of the occult when you are giving one all the time? Mrs. Guppy could dematerialize and so could many folk in Holy Writ and I do honestly believe that you can also. My reason tells me that you have this wonderful power, for there is no alternative, tho' I have no doubt that, up to a point, your strength and skill avail you." To Conan Doyle's way of thinking, this explained everything. Handcuffs, straitjackets, and packing crates were no obstacle to a man who could dematerialize. Houdini would simply allow himself to be trammeled up in whatever constraint his audiences could devise, then reduce his body to ectoplasm and ooze free in the manner of a snail discarding its shell. Moreover, this theory accounted for Houdini's otherwise inexplicable hostility toward spiritualism. Houdini's psychic powers, Conan Doyle would later contend, obliged him to adopt this pretense of disbelief. "Is it not perfectly evident," he wrote, "that if he did not deny them his occupation would have been gone forever?"

Houdini took care to refute such notions. It was enough for him, as he declared with characteristic modesty, to be considered the world's greatest showman. "Sir Arthur thinks that I have great mediumistic powers and that some of my feats are done with the aid of spirits," he would write in *A Magician Among the Spirits*. "Everything I do is accomplished by material means, humanly possible, no matter how baffling it is to the layman."

The friendship reached its crisis during Conan Doyle's 1922 lecture tour of America. Houdini had invited the entire family to stay at his home on West 113th Street, but Conan Doyle declined, saying he needed to stay "semi public" to deal with the press. Nevertheless, Conan Doyle expressed great eagerness to see Houdini again—"your normal self, not in a tank or hanging by one toe from a skyscraper." Houdini and his wife, Bess, attended one of the Carnegie Hall lectures, and the Conan Doyles took in a showing of Houdini's latest film, *The Man from Beyond,* at the Times Square Theatre. As he watched the film, which touched on the subject of reincarnation, Conan Doyle was treated to the sight of Houdini reading from one of his own spiritualist books—*The Vital Message*—on-screen. Afterward, Conan Doyle was so pleased with the movie that he provided an open letter to help publicize it. "I have seen the Houdini picture *The Man from Beyond,*" he wrote in part, "and it is difficult to find words to adequately express my enjoyment and appreciation of it. I certainly have no hesitation in saying it is the very best sensational picture I have ever seen. It is a story striking in its novelty, picturized superbly and punctuated with thrills that fairly make the hair stand on end."

Conan Doyle gave endorsements rather freely during this tour. In Washington, D.C., the husband-and-wife team of Julius and Ada Zancig gave him a private demonstration of their mind-reading act. "[T]heir remarkable performance, as I saw it, was due to psychic causes," Conan Doyle stated, "and not to trickery." As Zancig was a member in good standing of the Society of American Magicians, and had often shared a bill with Houdini, Conan Doyle's faith would seem to have been misplaced. When notified that Zancig's secret had once appeared in a newspaper, Conan Doyle brushed the information aside. Perhaps, he reasoned, the Zancigs were reduced to artificial methods "when their powers are low."

At one stage, according to the legendary magician Milbourne Christopher, Houdini invited Conan Doyle to his home with the idea of giving him an object lesson. In his private study, Houdini displayed a large chalk slate hanging against a wall. He then gave Conan Doyle a free choice of four cork balls, cutting one of them open so it could be examined. The ball Conan Doyle selected was dropped into a container of white ink.

Houdini instructed Conan Doyle to write a secret message on a slip of paper. To insure that Houdini could not observe the message in any way, he told Conan Doyle to leave the house and walk as far away as he liked before writing anything down. Conan Doyle walked more than three blocks, paused to scribble a message, and then returned. On entering the library, Conan Doyle was handed a spoon and told to fish the cork ball out of the white ink. Next, Houdini directed him to carry the ink-soaked ball across the room and hold it up to the chalk slate. When Conan Doyle did so, the ball mysteriously adhered to the slate. Slowly, almost hesitantly, the cork ball rolled across the surface of the slate, leaving a trail of ink as it did so. As the ball rose and fell, animated by an unseen force, the ink trail spelled out a strange message. With becoming solemnity, Houdini asked Conan Doyle to read it aloud. The message was a biblical quotation: *"Mene, mene, tekel, upharsin"*—the exact words Conan Doyle had written on his folded slip of paper.

Needless to say, Conan Doyle was baffled, as anyone would have been. Houdini gave himself a moment to enjoy his friend's consternation, then offered a word of caution. "I did it by perfectly normal means," Houdini said. "I devised it to show you what can be done along these lines."

Predictably, Conan Doyle suspected Houdini of employing his supposed supernatural gifts. Houdini could easily have disillusioned him by revealing the secret of the effect, but his professional pride would not allow it. Conan Doyle would have done well to take Houdini at his word. The escape artist had purchased the slate-writing effect from a friend who had performed it in vaudeville for many years. In the seemingly innocuous setting of Houdini's private study, the effect became even more baffling. Suffice it to say that the walls of Houdini's study were not as solid as they appeared.

In June 1922, as the lecture tour drew to a close, Houdini extended an invitation to the Conan Doyles to attend the annual banquet of the Society of American Magicians. The affair was to be held in the grand ballroom of the McAlpin Hotel, and with Houdini as the master of ceremonies, the evening promised to be something more than the usual magicians' get-together. "You will meet some notable people," Houdini promised, "as some of the city officials and big business men will be there."

For Houdini, the banquet presented another opportunity to disabuse Conan Doyle of some of his spiritualist convictions, or at least to demonstrate some of the ways in which séance room effects could be achieved by earthly means. Accordingly, he arranged that the after-dinner entertainment would include a number of spirit exposés. Soon, Houdini would be doing this type of thing onstage. He would take particular delight in demonstrating a séance table technique for producing spirit messages: while volunteers held both of his hands, Houdini scrawled a message on a chalk slate, unseen by the volunteers, using his feet.

When Conan Doyle got wind of Houdini's plans, he declined the invitation. "I fear that the bogus Spiritual phenomena must prevent me from attending the banquet," he wrote. "I look upon this subject as sacred, and I think that God's gift to man has been intercepted and delayed by the constant pretence that all phenomena are really tricks, which I know they are not. I should be in a false position, for I must either be silent and seem to acquiesce, or else protest, which a guest should not do."

Houdini backpedaled. "I assure you," he wrote, "it was only with a view of letting you see mysterious effects and only for your special benefit that this was being put on; therefore I assure you as a gentleman that there will be nothing performed or said which will offend anyone. My motive was a sincere desire from the heart and an expression of good will." Houdini went on to repeat his assertion that "big men" would be present—a fact that held no attraction whatever for Conan Doyle—and mentioned that the famous magician Howard Thurston, himself "a firm believer in spiritualism," would also attend. Conan Doyle relented. "Of course we will come," he wrote. "All thanks."

On Friday night, June 2, the big men assembled as promised. The guest list amounted to a virtual dream team of magic, including Thurston, Adelaide Herrmann, Max Malini, Carl Heller, John Mulholland, The Great Raymond, Horace Goldin, and Theo Hardeen. Houdini had also reeled in the postmaster general of New York, the director of the New York Public Library, department store mogul Bernard Gimbel, and Alfred Ochs, publisher of the *New York Times*.

According to an account published in *Billboard*, Houdini showed himself to be a "tactful, affable and pleasant" toastmaster, three words not normally associated with him. After dinner, the banquet room was cleared with "marvelous celerity" and converted into a makeshift auditorium. Sixteen guests were called upon to entertain. Horace Goldin, who had not expected to perform, borrowed a pair of handkerchiefs and held the room spellbound for twelve minutes. Houdini, having shelved his spiritualist effects, trotted out a classic effect from his stage repertoire. "Mr. Houdini gave a perfectly amazing performance," Conan Doyle enthused, "in which having been packed into a bag, and the bag into a trunk, corded up and locked, he was out again after only a few seconds' concealment in a tent, while in his place his wife was found, equally bound, bagged and boxed, with my dress-coat on which I had put upon him before I tied his hands behind him." This was, of course, the legendary "Metamorphosis" substitution trunk mystery, the effect that had lifted Houdini out of the dime museums decades earlier. The sight of the diminutive Bess Houdini in Conan Doyle's evening coat, with the sleeves dragging nearly to the floor, gave the presentation an unexpectedly comic finish.

Conan Doyle himself participated in the after-dinner entertainment. As his contribution, he set up a projector and showed moving pictures of what appeared to be prehistoric animals. These were stop-action clay animations, created by special effects pioneer Willis O'Brien for use in the movie version of *The Lost World*, which was then in production. "It struck me that it would be very amusing if I could mystify the mystifiers," Conan Doyle wrote in *Our American Adventure*.

In order to bring his audience to the "tiptoe of expectation," Conan Doyle offered a pointedly ambiguous word of introduction. "These pictures are not occult," he said in part, "but they are psychic, because everything that emanates from the human spirit or human brain is psychic. It is not supernatural. Nothing is. It is preternatural in the sense that it is not known to our ordinary senses."

It is hard to imagine what the assembly made of these remarks. As the *New York Times* reported, the audience was left to draw its own conclusions as to whether the "sober-faced Englishman was making merry with them or was lifting the veil from mysteries penetrated only by those of his school." If Conan Doyle intended to create uncertainty over the origin of the film, he succeeded brilliantly, as the careful distinction between "supernatural" and "preternatural" phenomena may not have been quite as illuminating as he intended. Many of the guests that night were familiar with the Cottingley photographs and would have known that Conan Doyle had some peculiar ideas about "preternatural" images.

The next day, Conan Doyle wrote a letter to Houdini and made copies available to the press. Fearing that the episode might cast doubt on the origin of his lecture photographs, he admitted that his "cinema interlude" had derived from *The Lost World* footage, and emphasized his intent to fool the magicians. "I had to walk very warily in my speech," he noted, "so as to preserve the glamour and yet say nothing which I could not justify as literally true." He ended with a gracious nod to Houdini's own baffling display: "And now, Mr. Chairman, confidence begets confidence, and I want to know how you got out of that trunk."

Two weeks later, the uneasy relationship reached its turning point. Conan Doyle, planning a restful break at the Ambassador Hotel in Atlantic City, invited the Houdinis to join the family for a weekend. The two friends spent much of Saturday afternoon splashing in the hotel pool with Conan Doyle's children, where Houdini showed off his ability to stay submerged for more than two minutes.

On Sunday, as Houdini and Bess sat on the beach "skylarking," Conan Doyle appeared to suggest an experiment. Jean, he said, had offered to give Houdini a private demonstration of her talent for automatic writing. It was hoped that she might succeed in bringing through a message from Houdini's mother, which would provide the final confirmation he had long sought. Turning to Bess, Conan Doyle asked if she wouldn't mind remaining outside. The conditions would be more favorable, he explained, if Houdini came alone.

Houdini followed Conan Doyle back to his suite, where they pulled down the window shades against the bright sunlight. Jean sat at a table with a large block of writing paper and several pencils. The two men joined her, and laid their hands on the surface of the table.

Conan Doyle bowed his head to begin the séance with a prayer. "I had made up my mind that I would be as religious as it was within my power to be," Houdini recalled, "and not at any time did I scoff at the ceremony. I excluded all earthly thoughts and gave my whole soul to the séance. I was *willing* to believe, even *wanted* to believe."

Not entirely. The previous evening, Bess and Jean fell into conversation about Houdini's relationship with his mother. On the beach that morning, Bess shared the details with her husband, so that he would not be surprised if any of this information reappeared under the guise of psychic knowledge. Certainly Houdini had every right to be cautious, but at the same time, his claims of open-mindedness were not wholly justified.

After some moments, Conan Doyle would write, Jean was suddenly "seized by a Spirit." The psychic energies, she said, had taken hold more powerfully than ever before. Her body shook and her voice trembled as she called to the unseen presence to grant her a message. "Do you believe in God?" she asked. By way of response, her own hand pounded the table three times—signaling an affirmative answer. "Then I will make the sign of the cross," she said, scribbling unsteadily on the block of paper. Next she asked if the spirit was that of Houdini's mother, Cecilia Weiss. Again, her hand struck the table three times.

At that moment, Houdini later insisted, he focused all his energies on "feeling for the presence of my dearly beloved Mother." He longed to believe, he said, and his entire body tensed with anticipation. He watched as Jean gripped the pencil and began to write in a strange, lurching fashion, as though her hand could not keep pace with the flow of thoughts.

"It was a singular scene," Conan Doyle would write, "my wife with her hand flying wildly, beating the table while she scribbled at a furious rate, I sitting opposite and tearing sheet after sheet from the block as it was filled up, and tossing each across to Houdini, while he sat silent, looking grimmer and paler every moment."

The message began: "Oh, my darling, thank God, thank God, at last I'm through—I've tried, oh so often—now I am happy. Why, of course I want to talk to my boy—my own beloved boy—Friends, thank you, with all my heart for this."

The writing continued in this vein for fifteen pages. The spirit of Cecilia Weiss assured her son of her continuing love for him and of her great happiness in the spirit world. She told him that he would soon "get all the evidence he is so anxious for," and that she was busy "preparing so sweet a home for him" for the day when they would be reunited.

As the message poured forth, Conan Doyle broke in to ask if Houdini wished to pose a question, such as "Can my mother read my mind?" Later, there would be some disagreement as to whether this question had been spoken aloud or merely divined by the spirit. The answer came in forceful terms: "I *always* read my beloved son's mind—his dear mind—there is so much I want to say to him—but—I am almost overwhelmed by this joy of talking to him once more—it is almost too much to get through—the joy of it—thank you, thank you, friend, with all my heart for what you have done for me this day—God bless you, too, Sir Arthur, for what you are doing for us—for us, over here—who so need to get in touch with our beloved ones on the earth plane. . . ."

When the message finally ceased, Houdini found himself in an uncomfortable quandary. Ironically, the younger and less devout Conan Doyle had written of just such a dilemma many years earlier. In *The Parasite,* when a reluctant Austin Gilroy attends a séance at the home of a friend, he expresses himself in terms Houdini might have recognized. "I like none of these mystery-mongers," Gilroy declares, "but the amateur least of all. With the paid performer you pounce upon him and expose him the instant that you have seen through his trick. He is there to deceive you, and you are there to find him out. But what are you to do with the friend of your host's wife? Are you to turn on a light suddenly and expose her slapping a surreptitious banjo? Or are you to hurl cochineal over her evening frock when she steals round with her phosphorus bottle and her supernatural platitude? There would be a scene, and you would be looked upon as a brute."

In Atlantic City, the medium actually *was* the host's wife, and Houdini knew full well that he ran the risk of seeming a brute. Still, the message had left him torn and unhappy. He had no doubts whatever as to the sincerity of the Conan Doyles, but he could not bring himself to take the demonstration seriously. "I sat serene through it all," Houdini later wrote, "hoping and wishing that I might feel my mother's presence. There wasn't even a semblance of it."

In the message, the spirit of Cecilia Weiss had advised her son to "try and write" from his own home. Now, as he struggled to collect his thoughts, Houdini picked up a pencil and asked, "Is there any particular way in which I must hold this pencil when I want to write, or does it write automatically?" He then wrote the name "Powell" on the writing pad. In recalling this later, Houdini stated emphatically that he had not been under the influence of spirits when he did so: *"I wrote the name of 'Powell' entirely of my own volition."*

Conan Doyle was stunned. Dr. Ellis Powell, his "dear fighting partner in spiritualism," had recently died in London. Clearly, Conan Doyle insisted, Powell had managed to make contact through Houdini. "Truly Saul is among the prophets!" he announced.

Houdini shook his head. He had been thinking of Frederick Eugene Powell, a magician involved in the publicity for *The Man from Beyond*, with whom he had been corresponding lately concerning a dangerous surgical procedure. Conan Doyle waved this explanation aside. Ellis Powell, he insisted, was the one man he would have expected to hear from in these circumstances. Obviously, Houdini himself had been granted the gift of automatic writing.

For the moment, Houdini let the matter rest, saying nothing of his uncertainty over his mother's message. "I did not have the nerve to tell him," he admitted later. It would not have made any difference if he had. Both men emerged from the séance absolutely convinced that his own view had been confirmed. Conan Doyle insisted that Houdini had been "deeply moved" by what occurred. Later, he claimed, Houdini told him he had been "walking on air ever since."

Houdini withdrew and pondered the message. As he related the events to Bess, he could not overcome his doubts. Jean had marked the sign of the cross on the first page of the message, but Cecilia Weiss, the wife of an Orthodox rabbi, would never have transmitted a Christian symbol. Also, the message had come through in English, a language his mother did not speak. Furthermore, though the spirit presence claimed to be able to read her son's mind, it did not pick up a series of thoughts that Houdini tried to communicate during the séance. Finally, the weekend in Atlantic City happened to fall on Cecilia Weiss's birthday, a date of considerable importance to Houdini, but the spirit presence made no reference to this coincidence.

In time, when Houdini aired his misgivings, Conan Doyle had ready answers. He insisted that the sign of the cross had nothing to do with the spirit's earthly religion; his wife placed a cross at the top of all her messages to "guard against lower influences." As for the language barrier, only a "trance medium" could be expected to produce a message in the spirit's own tongue. A "normal inspirational medium," by contrast, made use of a "translating effect" that occurred simultaneously with the flow of thought. Conan Doyle also asserted that the spirit *had* successfully read Houdini's mind, and that Houdini admitted as much at the time. As for Cecilia Weiss's birthday, Conan Doyle said, such things no longer mattered in the spirit realm.

Soon enough, this debate would spill into the public arena, causing bitter recriminations on both sides. For the moment, as the Conan Doyles finished up their tour of America, Houdini kept up appearances in the hope of salvaging the friendship. He invited Conan Doyle and Jean to join him as he and Bess celebrated their wedding anniversary, and he waved from the dock as the family sailed for home on June 24.

Four months later, Houdini published an article in the *New York Sun* in which he expressed disenchantment with the spiritualist movement. "I have never heard or seen anything," he wrote, "that could convince me that there is a possibility of communication with the loved ones who have gone beyond." He had said much the same thing in a *New York Times* article that appeared during Conan Doyle's tour, but this new statement, coming on the heels of the séance in Atlantic City, struck Conan Doyle as a personal affront. Houdini's intransigence, in Conan Doyle's view, could only be taken as an insult to Jean. "I know by many examples the purity of my wife's mediumship," he insisted, "and I saw what you got and what the effect was upon you at the time." Angry as he was, Conan Doyle resolved to say no more on the subject, as he had "no fancy for sparring with a friend in public."

Conan Doyle returned to America the following year for a second lecture tour, taking the spirit message as far west as California. By this time, relations with Houdini had grown so strained that the press anticipated a major clash—"Sir Arthur Coming to Answer Houdini," read one headline. Their relationship now alternated between public criticism and private apologies. "I have had to handle you a little roughly in the *Oakland Tribune*," Conan Doyle wrote from Los Angeles. "I can't imagine why you say such wild things which have no basis in fact at all."

"I am commencing to believe that at last I am 'famous,' " Houdini wrote after a public salvo of his own. "Newspapers are misquoting me."

Their paths crossed in Denver, where Houdini had come to perform on an Orpheum circuit tour, but they could no longer find any common ground. "Our relations are certainly curious and are likely to become more so," Conan Doyle remarked, "for so long as you attack what I *know* from experience to be true, I have no alternative but to attack you in return. How long a private friendship can survive such an ordeal I do not know, but at least I did not create the situation."

The final blow came shortly after Conan Doyle's return to England. In *Our American Adventure*, there had been some attempt at a détente. "I may add that Houdini is not one of those shallow men who imagine they can explain away spiritual phenomena as parlour tricks," Conan Doyle had written, "but that he retains an open—and ever, I think, a more receptive—mind towards mysteries which are beyond his art." When it came time to write *Our Second American Adventure*, chronicling the 1923 tour, this pretense was dropped. Conan Doyle had praise for Houdini's skills as a magician but found him "most violent in his expressions of contempt and hostility" toward spiritualism.

Houdini's *A Magician Among the Spirits*, published in 1924, gave his side of the Atlantic City séance. "I have no desire to discredit

Spiritualism," he wrote. "I am willing to be convinced; my mind is open, but the proof must be such as to leave no vestige of doubt that what is claimed to be done is accomplished only through or by supernatural power. So far I have never on any occasion, in all the séances I have attended, seen anything which would lead me to credit . . . that it is possible to communicate with those who have passed out of this life. Therefore I do not agree with Sir Arthur."

From this point forward, Houdini and Conan Doyle communicated only through the letter columns of the press. Many of their exchanges centered on a contest sponsored by *Scientific American* magazine. To publicize its investigation into the paranormal, the magazine had offered "$2,500 for an authentic spirit photograph made under strict test conditions and $2,500 for the first physical manifestations of a psychic nature produced under scientific control." When Houdini was asked to serve on the investigating committee, Conan Doyle expressed outrage at the "capital error" of placing an enemy of spiritualism on such a body. "The Commission is, in my opinion, a farce," he wrote.

One of the first to apply for the *Scientific American* prize was Nino Pecararo, an Italian medium who had impressed Conan Doyle some months earlier. Although securely tied to a chair, Pecararo had caused a handbell to ring and a tambourine to float through the air. When Houdini tied Pecararo up, there were no manifestations.

Soon, however, the tables tilted the other way. An attractive young medium named Mina Crandon, known to the public as "Margery," had created a sensation in her native Boston. In the comfort of her Beacon Hill séance room, Margery produced a startling range of phenomena including bright lights, strange raps and whistles, messages in many languages, rose petals that seemed to fall from thin air, and megaphones that flew across the room. Margery's spirit control was her own deceased brother, Walter, a rough-talking fireman who had been crushed to death in a railway accident in 1911.

Before applying for the *Scientific American* prize, Margery traveled abroad and built up a consensus of favorable opinion from European experts. One of these, inevitably, was Conan Doyle, who stated "beyond all question" that her powers were genuine.

For Margery's *Scientific American* test, Houdini came up with the idea of building a wooden "control box." Margery was to sit inside a sturdy enclosure with her head protruding, in the manner of a steam cabinet. Holes at the sides of the box would allow her to reach through, but only to join hands with other sitters, so that her movements would remain under strict control. Margery agreed to these conditions, and for a time it appeared as if the device had curtailed her powers.

Soon, however, the challenge took an unexpected turn, as Conan Doyle related in a gleeful letter to Oliver Lodge. "There have been great doings at Boston," he wrote. "At the [séance], Houdini passed his hand through the hole in the box (under pretense of seeing if the medium was all right) and dropped inside a folded carpenter's ruler. At once Walter screamed out 'Houdini, you unutterable cad! What do you mean by dropping that ruler!' " In fact, what Walter had actually said was "Houdini, you God damned son of a bitch, get the hell out of here and never come back!" Conan Doyle cleaned up the language for Lodge's benefit, but pulled no punches about the consequences. "It should be the last of him as a Psychic Researcher," he gloated to Harry Price, "if he could ever have been called one."

Hoping to ensure this outcome, Conan Doyle wrote an article based on correspondence with Margery's husband. He protested that Margery had been the victim of a "very deadly plot" and expressed surprise that a distinguished body of American investigators should have tolerated Houdini's "outrageous" behavior. The escape artist, responding in the press, wondered how Conan Doyle could form such conclusions from a distance of 3,500 miles. In his view, the ruler had been planted to impugn his testimony, and he resented that anyone would take Walter's word over his. "Also, Sir Arthur is a bit senile," Houdini was quoted as saying, "and therefore easily bamboozled." The situation, he suggested, might well call for legal action.

The threat of a slander suit did nothing to silence Conan Doyle. A few months later he sounded off on the subject of "Houdinitis," a syndrome based on twin fallacies. "The first is that Spiritualism depends upon physical phenomena for its proofs," he wrote, while the "second is that manual dexterity bears some relation to brain capacity."

While the former friends traded insults, Margery's spirit control weighed in with a grim prediction. Houdini, said Walter, would be dead within a year.

Houdini managed to thwart Walter's prediction, but only just. He died on October 31, 1926, of complications following a blow to the stomach. Happily, Conan Doyle managed to recover his better nature on this sad occasion. "I greatly admired him," he told the *New York Times*, "and cannot understand how the end came for one so youthful." He wrote a long and heartfelt letter to Bess, assuring her that he would never again say an unkind thing about her husband. "Any man who wins the love and respect of a good woman must himself be a fine and honest man," he told her. "I am sorry that shadows grew up between us."

For all of this, now that Houdini could no longer dispute him, Conan Doyle allowed himself free reign in putting forward his beliefs about the escape artist's strange powers. The following year he published a two-part article in *The Strand* entitled "Houdini the Enigma." Describing an especially baffling packing crate escape, Conan Doyle once again advanced his dematerialization theory. "I contend that Houdini's performance was on an utterly different plane," he insisted, "and that it is an outrage against common sense to think otherwise." To the end of his life, Conan Doyle continued to hope that Houdini would manifest his spirit presence in some public forum, thus ending the debate for all time.

To date, Houdini—like the famous "dog in the night-time"—has been strangely silent.

28

A Packet of Salts and Three Bucketfuls of Water

The charlatan is always the pioneer. . . . The quack of yesterday is the professor of tomorrow.

—LIONEL DACRE IN "THE LEATHER FUNNEL"

Just before the release of Conan Doyle's autobiography in 1924, the publisher John Murray issued a small pamphlet entitled "Conan Doyle: Teller of Tales." It listed fifty-two of the Conan Doyle titles then available, including several multivolume collections. Potential readers were assured that "There's a Conan Doyle book for every taste." On the cover, a carefully trimmed photograph of the author's head stared out with a rather dazed expression, in the manner of one of his own spirit images.

The pamphlet made an effective promotion and paid fitting tribute to a varied and distinguished career. Inadvertently, it also highlighted a startling fact: Conan Doyle had not produced a novel since *The Valley of Fear* in 1915. There had been a vast quantity of writing done since then—including the six-volume history of World War I and seven spiritualist books—but his fiction had dwindled to the occasional short story.

The reason could be found in *Memories and Adventures*, his autobiography, which appeared after a successful serialization in *The*

Strand. In the final chapter, Conan Doyle made it clear that he had abandoned his "congenial and lucrative" work in favor of the psychic quest. "That is the work," he told his readers, "which will occupy, either by voice or pen, the remainder of my life."

Along with his voice and pen, Conan Doyle also gave freely of his checkbook. By his own estimate, he would subsidize the spiritualist movement to the tune of some £250,000 over these years. The figure is impossible to confirm, but there can be no doubt that the toll in lost earnings was enormous. The profit from his spiritualist books and lectures went to the cause. He often agreed to underwrite the books and pamphlets of other writers. For a time, he backed the spiritualist magazine *Light* out of his own pocket and contributed heavily to the running of the Marylebone Spiritualist Association. He was also generous with his time, serving as president of the London Spiritualist Alliance and the British College of Psychic Science. In 1925, he traveled to Paris to act as chairman of the International Spiritualistic Congress.

That same year, Conan Doyle opened a "central depot" of information called The Psychic Bookshop, dedicated to the dissemination of spiritualist materials. He chose a ruinously expensive site at 2 Victoria Street, mere steps from Westminster Abbey, hoping that the stately surroundings of the Houses of Parliament and the Westminster neighborhoods would prove mutually beneficial. The shop also contained a small museum, which displayed Conan Doyle's massive collection of spirit photographs, and a reference library culled from his own shelves. Conan Doyle's elder daughter, Mary, had a hand in running the shop, with her father and stepmother taking regular shifts at the register. Conan Doyle fussed over every detail of the operation, even issuing written instructions for the window displays. In time, the shop became the headquarters of the private Psychic Press, which published, among other things, *Pheneas Speaks*. Lest anyone be in doubt as to the proprietor's leanings, the telegraph address was listed as "Ectoplasm, Southwest."

"The venture will cost me £1500 a year but it may in time pay its own way," he told Lodge. "If not, I don't see how money can be better spent." Conan Doyle operated the shop at a heavy loss for four years, then announced that the "noble experiment" had failed, making it necessary to cut his losses. "The entire endeavour," noted Harry Price, "had been an unmitigated disaster."

Conan Doyle also had to offset some of the costs of his own two-volume study, *The History of Spiritualism,* after several editors declined the honor of publishing it. After a string of odd and commercially disappointing volumes such as *The Case for Spirit Photography,* the Conan Doyle name no longer held a guarantee of success. As it happened, *The History of Spiritualism* would stand apart from his many other contributions to the literature of the movement, and is perhaps the only one that retains interest for the modern reader. It offers a comprehensive survey of the movement from an insider's point of view, with careful documentation and a lucid, energetic prose style. "It will be a dignified and balanced book," he promised Oliver Lodge, "never extreme in statement." Whether he made good on that claim is open to debate, as Conan Doyle's enthusiasms and biases can be found on every page. He settles old scores with the likes of Frank Podmore and other "unreasoning critics," and expends much effort praising such mediums as the Davenports and Henry Slade, a "celebrated slate-writing medium," who had long since been discredited. For all of that, the book captures the urgent conviction of those who "followed the call."

A spiritualist researcher named Leslie Curnow contributed a great deal of material and wrote some of the chapters, which Conan Doyle freely admits in the book's preface. Conan Doyle wished to "conjoin" Curnow's name with his on the cover, but the publisher objected, fearing that this would extinguish any lingering commercial value.

"I should like to dedicate it to you, if I may," Conan Doyle told Lodge as the publication date approached, "for I think no one has shown greater courage in the matter than you." Lodge sent a grateful assent, but even he had begun to express misgivings about his friend's intemperate views. When Conan Doyle marshaled his forces to set up the Spiritualist Church in London, Lodge worried about a potential backlash. "I rather regret Doyle's decision," he wrote a friend. "But that I suppose is a natural outcome of his missionary activity. I suppose he regards himself as a sort of Wesley or Whitefield." This reference to the eighteenth-century evangelists underscores a view held by many: Conan Doyle had become too extreme for the times. Britain and the rest of the world had begun to throw off the gloom of the war years. As the Jazz Age made itself felt, the appeal of spiritualism dimmed. To some, Conan Doyle began to seem like a quaint artifact from a distant age—Sir Nigel Loring among the flappers.

Finding himself "almost alone in the polemical arena," Conan Doyle wrote to enlist the help of Arthur Balfour, the former prime minister, who had long kept his spiritualist sympathies silent. The statesman replied with a well-crafted evasion: "Surely my opinions upon this subject are already sufficiently well known."

Through it all, Conan Doyle received regular support through the Pheneas circle. "You see," one spirit told him, "we can make friends from this side." This was just as well, because over the final decade of his life Conan Doyle steadily alienated most of his earthbound friends. Jerome K. Jerome was the first to abandon ship, launching a public attack on the "puerile" events of the séance room and the "insipid logic" behind them. When *Pheneas Speaks* appeared, H. G. Wells published a withering review in the *Sunday Express*. "This Pheneas, I venture to think, is an imposter," Wells wrote, "wrought of self-deception, as pathetic as a rag doll which some lonely child has made for its own comfort."

Whenever possible, Conan Doyle struck back with equal force. When George Bernard Shaw wrote of using séance tricks to dupe his friends, he and Conan Doyle crossed swords yet again. "His argument," Conan Doyle wrote, "is that he himself has cheated at the séance table and has successfully deceived trusting friends, and that therefore all phenomena are suspect and worthless. To put this argument into concrete form, I have in the presence of witnesses unquestionably seen my mother since her death. But what I say must be false because Bernard Shaw cheated his friends. Was there ever a more absurd non sequitur than that?"

In those cases where Conan Doyle happened to outlive his friends, he allowed himself the final word in any lasting dispute. When Jerome K. Jerome died in 1927, a medium soon brought forward a message that Conan Doyle broadcast to the world: "Tell him from me that I know now that he was right and I was wrong. We never know our greatest mistakes at the time we make them. Make it clear to him that I am not dead." Conan Doyle's other skeptical friends undoubtedly hoped to survive him.

Conan Doyle's friendship with J. M. Barrie never descended into open conflict, but Barrie made it clear that he would not permit any discussion of psychic matters in his presence. Conan Doyle obliged, and they spent a pleasant enough evening together indulging in a favorite Barrie pastime—flicking moistened postage stamps at the ceiling on the backs of coins. Conan Doyle never lost his affection for his friend's work. In *Memories and Adventures*, he expressed the hope that a chance remark of long ago had helped to inspire *The Admirable Crichton*, one of Barrie's most memorable plays. It is more likely that Conan Doyle provided the stimulus for a lesser-known effort called *A Well-Remembered Voice*, which took a hearty swipe at the pieties of the spiritualist movement.

If the living community of writers occasionally shunned him, the dead ones appeared to welcome Conan Doyle with open arms—as he reported in the *Journal of the Society for Psychical Research*. Joseph Conrad sent a message that he would not be averse to seeing Conan Doyle finish up *Suspense*, his incomplete novel, and Charles Dickens indicated that if he made good with Conrad's request, *The Mystery of Edwin Drood* would be next. "I shall be honoured, Mr. Dickens," Conan Doyle told the spirit.

"Charles, if you please," came the reply. "We like friends to be friends."

Conan Doyle made no serious effort to fulfill these commissions, but by the end of 1924 his thoughts returned to his own career in fiction. Predictably, he approached the subject from a psychic perspective. Up to this point, his scattered attempts to blend fiction and the spirits had not been especially fruitful. Now, having reached his maturity as a spiritualist, Conan Doyle felt ready to try again. "I have for years had a big psychic novel in me," he told Greenhough Smith, "which shall deal realistically with every phase of the question, pro and con. I waited and knew it would come. Now it has come, with a full head of steam, and I can hardly hold on to my pen it goes so fast—about 12 or 15,000 words in three days."

By February of 1925, the novel was complete. "Thank God that book is done!" he wrote to Smith. "It was to me so important that I feared I might pass away before it was finished."

The Land of Mist, his first novel in ten years, began its *Strand* serialization in July. Many readers, weary of spirits and ectoplasm, undoubtedly approached this new offering with caution. The opening pages offered some reassurance. Professor George Edward Challenger, the familiar and well-loved hero of *The Lost World* and *The Poison Belt,* had returned for another adventure.

By the end of the first installment, however, the author's new enthusiasms made themselves felt. As the story opens, the reader learns that the journalist Edward Malone, now older and wiser, has undertaken to write an article on spiritualism in partnership with Enid Challenger, the professor's strong-willed daughter. Hearing this, Professor Challenger gives an angry snort—"Death ends all, Malone," he proclaims. "This soul-talk is the animism of savages. It is a superstition, a myth."

The reader learns that Professor Summerlee, Challenger's crusty foil in the earlier adventures, has died in Naples the previous year. When Summerlee manages to send a message from the other side, Malone and Enid Challenger find their minds opening to the new religion. Soon Lord John Roxton reappears, and he, too, falls under the sway of the spiritualist argument. At regular intervals, the trio of converts pause to derive benefit from the teachings of spiritualist leaders, some of whom are recognizable as Conan Doyle's real-life colleagues. Prominent among them is a Mr. Algernon Mailey. "His laugh was so infectious," the reader is told, "that the others were bound to laugh also. Certainly, with his athletic proportions, which had run a little to seed but were still notable, and with his virile voice and strong if homely face, he gave no impression of instability." The portrait is completed by a winking allusion to "vibrations"—a prominent term in the Cottingley episode—and by a familiar declaration that the spirit message is "infinitely the most important thing in the world." Apparently Conan Doyle could not resist giving himself a walk-on part.

Through it all, Professor Challenger refuses to bend in his

opposition, and will not even consider the psychic literature his daughter urges upon him. "Am I to study mathematics in order to confute the man who tells me that two and two are five?" he asks.

As might be expected, Challenger sees the error of his ways by the novel's end. His conversion comes as Enid falls into a trance and brings her father a momentous communication. Long ago, we discover, when the professor practiced as a physician, he administered an experimental drug to two patients, both of whom were found dead the following morning. "I believed that I had killed them," Challenger admits. "It has always been a dark background to my life." Now, these many years later, the two unfortunate patients return through Enid to offer spiritual salvation. The medications were blameless, Challenger is assured; their deaths had been the result of pneumonia.

The news leaves the professor staggered. After so many years, his "cloud of guilt" suddenly lifts. At the same time, he must accept the "incontrovertible evidence" of spiritualism. He knows his daughter to be "incapable of deceit," and since no living soul had known the sad fate of his former patients, no subconscious deception is possible. "It is incredible, inconceivable, grotesquely wonderful," says the chastened professor, "but it would seem to be true." The novel draws to a close as Challenger—now a "gentler, humbler, and more spiritual man"—declares his new faith to the world, and a happy crowd of spiritualists gather to celebrate the marriage of Malone and Enid.

Conan Doyle had originally wanted to call this novel *The Psychic Adventures of Edward Malone*. Cooler heads prevailed, fearing that such a title would scare away its potential audience. By the time the second installment appeared in the *The Strand*, however, there could be no hiding Conan Doyle's agenda. Twenty years earlier, in "The Abbey Grange," Sherlock Holmes offered a telling criticism of Watson's writings: "Your fatal habit of looking at everything from the point of view of a story instead of as a scientific exercise has ruined what might have been an instructive and even classical series of demonstrations." By that measure, Sherlock Holmes would have been absolutely besotted with *The Land of Mist*. The novel managed to be instructive and scientific without any regard whatever to storytelling. The skillful characterizations and witty situations of *The*

Lost World were nowhere to be found. Instead, a solemn procession of learned figures marched across the pages, spouting the author's propaganda. At times, Conan Doyle appeared to flaunt his disregard for the story: "The love-affair of Enid Challenger and Edward Malone is not of the slightest interest to the reader," he announced at one stage, "for the simple reason that it is not of the slightest interest to the writer." An appendix of spiritualist documentation completed the unhappy experience.

"This series of ill-linked stories of the supernatural may be good spiritualist propaganda," wrote a *New Statesman* reviewer, "but as an essay in imaginative fiction, in which guise it is presented, it is unworthy of so skilled a story-teller as Sir Arthur Conan Doyle." The *New York Times* agreed: "Unfortunately, yet perhaps inevitably, the characters of *The Land of Mist* are scarcely more than props for Sir Arthur's propaganda." The *Times* of London summed up the general chorus of negative reviews: "There is too much pill, too little sugar-coating."

Strangely, the Challenger of the earlier adventures had been far less intractable. In *The Lost World,* he showed an interest in telepathy. In *The Poison Belt,* he rejected Professor Summerlee's unspiritual philosophies: "No, Summerlee, I will have none of your materialism, for I, at least, am too great a thing to end in mere physical constituents, a packet of salts and three bucketfuls of water." But for *The Land of Mist,* Conan Doyle recast Challenger as a wooden skeptic, simply to throw him onto the bonfire of his belief. Challenger now believes, he told the reader—so should you.

The question naturally arises, where was Sherlock Holmes while Professor Challenger fought the good fight? With *The Land of Mist,* Conan Doyle showed himself willing to sacrifice his past triumphs at the altar of spiritualism. For him, this was a holy crusade. Fate had given him the most potent weapon any crusader could have wished, but he chose not to use it. Certainly the idea crossed his mind. As early as 1918, an interviewer asked him what Sherlock Holmes might have to say about his creator's new religion. "I suppose I am Sherlock Holmes, if anybody is," he answered, "and I say that the case for spiritualism is absolutely proved."

"I tell you, Watson, the thing is true."

The very idea brings a spasm of revulsion from the detective's admirers. The arguments are many: The conversion of Holmes, the ultimate rationalist, would not be credible. Conan Doyle recognized—and would not relinquish—his purchase on literary immortality. Such a story would oblige the author to drag Holmes into the present day. Conan Doyle's missionary work depended on the money that Holmes continued to provide.

There is merit in each of these objections. Conan Doyle, however, would have been the last person in the world to concede to any of them. He had set Challenger jumping through the hoops; he could easily have done the same with Holmes. In "His Last Bow," in which Holmes matched wits with a German spy, Conan Doyle felt perfectly comfortable using his detective as an instrument of propaganda. Why not do so again?

Conan Doyle clearly intended that "His Last Bow," published in 1917, should be the final adventure of Sherlock Holmes. As ever, the detective had refused to go quietly. A series of Sherlock Holmes films had sparked yet another surge of interest, just as the screen version of *The Lost World*, released in 1925, brought a new audience for Challenger. Beginning in 1921, Conan Doyle began periodically to produce new Holmes stories. That same year, the British Stoll Film Company made a series of fifteen two-reel Sherlock Holmes films, capped off by a full-length version of *The Hound of the Baskervilles*. The Stoll company would go on to film nearly fifty Holmes adventures, all starring Eille Norwood as the detective. Conan Doyle heartily approved of Norwood's performance. At a 1921 testimonial dinner, he enthused over the actor's "extraordinarily clever personation," adding that he had "never seen anything more masterly" than Norwood's performance in *The Hound*. To mark the occasion, a message arrived on behalf of Prime Minister Lloyd George. A new Holmes adventure, "The Mazarin Stone," had just appeared in *The Strand*, and the prime minister praised it as "one of the best Sherlock Holmes stories that he has read."

In this, the prime minister represented the minority. Of the twelve Sherlock Holmes stories written between 1921 and 1927, few could be called indispensable. At the low end were "The Mazarin Stone," "The Three Gables," and the irredeemable "Lion's Mane," all three of which betrayed the author's haste and indifference. Flashes of the old brilliance ran through the other stories, from the ingenious puzzle plot of "Thor Bridge," based on a suggestion from Greenhough Smith, to "The Creeping Man" and its oft-quoted telegram: "Come at once if convenient—if inconvenient come all the same." Sherlockians cherish the detective's rare burst of emotion when Watson sustains an injury from a villain's bullet:

> "You're not hurt, Watson? For God's sake, say that you are not hurt!"
>
> It was worth a wound—it was worth many wounds—to know the depth of loyalty and love which lay behind that cold mask. The clear, hard eyes were dimmed for a moment, and the firm lips were shaking. For the one and only time I caught a glimpse of a great heart as well as of a great brain. All my years of humble but single-minded service culminated in that moment of revelation.

Such moments were few and far between. Conan Doyle now reserved his best energies for the spiritualist movement, and Sherlock Holmes showed the effects. Most of the new stories were marred by jarring slang expressions, uncharacteristic and objectionable attitudes, and a Holmes who occasionally seemed to be mugging for the camera— "Good-bye, Susan. Paregoric is the stuff. . . ." No less a critic than T. S. Eliot spoke of the detective's "mental decay," and murmurs of ghostwriters and recycled manuscripts have been heard ever since.

By 1927, Conan Doyle would decide once and for all to send the detective into retirement. As he completed "Shoscombe Old Place" that year, he admitted his creative fatigue. "It's not of the first flight," he told Greenhough Smith, "and Sherlock, like his author, grows a little stiff in the joints, but it is the best I can do." There would be no more adventures. When the last stories were gathered into book form as *The Case-Book of Sherlock Holmes*, Conan Doyle added a dignified word of farewell: "I fear that Mr. Sherlock Holmes may have become like one of those popular tenors who, having outlived their time, are still tempted to make repeated farewell bows to their indulgent audiences. This must cease and he must go the way of all flesh, material or imaginary."

If the deerstalker appeared a bit battered by then, at least it had been a graceful exit, as opposed to a Challenger-style psychic awakening. For those seeking confirmation of the detective's earthbound frame of mind, Conan Doyle appeared to have provided it in "The Sussex Vampire," published in 1924. The story introduced a woman caught in the act of sucking blood from her child's neck—raising the specter of vampirism—but Holmes swiftly banished any suggestion of the supernatural. "This agency stands flat-footed upon the ground, and there it must remain," he tells Watson. "The world is big enough for us. No ghosts need apply." In the end, Holmes demonstrated that the mother's vampiric act had been an attempt to draw poison from a wound.

On this evidence, everything appeared secure in the world of Sherlock Holmes, and no séances seemed likely to erupt at Baker Street. Even the title deflated any pretense of the unknown, juxtaposing the mysteries of vampires with the less fanciful milieu of Sussex—an effect not unlike "The Werewolf of Trenton."

Conan Doyle aficionados usually point to this story, with evident relief, as proof that the author would never have countenanced Holmes as a spiritualist mouthpiece. It should be remembered, however, that Challenger was no less antagonistic at the start of *The Land of Mist*. For Challenger's conversion to be persuasive, he was required to begin the story in the enemy camp. There is no reason to suppose that Conan Doyle would not have taken a similar line with Holmes. The view expressed in "The Sussex Vampire" would only have made his reversal more effective.

"The Sussex Vampire" appeared in the same year in which Conan Doyle began writing *The Land of Mist*. At the very least, the timing suggests that he considered the possibility of using Holmes in his "big psychic novel." There were many good reasons to prefer Challenger, but if Conan Doyle wished to reach the widest possible audience, Holmes would have been the better choice. The author's decision, therefore, may point to something more than proprietary discretion.

A possible explanation emerges from the pages of *The Land of*

Mist. The character of Algernon Mailey, whose similarities to Conan Doyle have often been noted, is presented as a man who has gained fame in another arena. "Mailey the barrister?" asks Malone when the name is raised. "Mailey, the religious reformer," comes the reply. "That's how he will be known." Conan Doyle also wished to be known as a religious reformer, and not as a writer of detective stories. At times this seemed a forlorn hope, as he himself would remark in an interview some two months before his death. "To tell the truth," he would say on that occasion, "I am rather tired of hearing myself described as the author of Sherlock Holmes. Why not, for a change, the author of *Rodney Stone*, or *The White Company*, or of *The Lost World*? One would think I had written nothing but detective stories." A famous *Punch* caricature underscored the point. It showed a miserable-looking Conan Doyle literally shackled to a diminutive figure of Holmes. With his spirit quest, he aspired to break those shackles. He had spent years seeking "some big purpose" that matched his talents and ambition, finding it at last as a missionary of the "new revelation." His work on the spiritualist platform, he believed, marked the culmination of a life of service, and would secure his place in history. He could hardly be blamed, then, if he did not wish to share that platform with Sherlock Holmes.

In February 1925, even as he put the finishing touches on *The Land of Mist*, an urgent plea for help recalled Conan Doyle to the earthly plane. Sixteen years had passed since the imprisonment of Oscar Slater, the man Conan Doyle believed had been falsely convicted of the murder of Marion Gilchrist in Glasgow. In that time, Conan Doyle had made several attempts to reopen the case, but his efforts brought a stony silence from the Scottish authorities. "From time to time one hears some word of poor Slater from behind his prison walls," he wrote, "like the wail of some wayfarer who has fallen into a pit and implores aid from the passers-by."

In Peterhead Prison, on a remote stretch of Scottish coastline, Slater knew nothing of Conan Doyle's efforts on his behalf. Denied correspondence with the outside world, he engineered a desperate appeal. A fellow prisoner named William Gordon was due to be released. On a piece of waterproof paper from the prison bindery, Slater wrote an impassioned note. He then folded the coated paper into a tight bundle and persuaded Gordon to conceal it in his mouth. The ruse worked; Gordon submitted to a thorough search, but Slater's message was not discovered. On gaining his release, Gordon relayed the plea to Conan Doyle.

Conan Doyle could hardly ignore such a direct appeal. He sent a fresh barrage of letters to the secretary of state for Scotland, demanding that Slater's conviction be overturned. "Apart . . . from the original question of guilt or innocence," Conan Doyle wrote, "the man has now served 15 years, which is, as I understand, the usual limit of a life sentence in Scotland when the prisoner behaves well."

As it happened, Slater had not been a model prisoner. Indignant over his situation, he complained loudly about the deplorable conditions of the prison, and occasionally got into scuffles with other inmates. This had no bearing on the official reply to Conan Doyle's entreaties. He was notified that court officials found no justification for "advising any interference" in Slater's sentence.

Conan Doyle stepped up his effort, much as he had in the Roger Casement affair, with letters to influential friends and members of the press, along with public appearances where he aired Slater's grievances. Many others had taken up the case by this time, but no single supporter could rally public opinion as effectively as Conan Doyle, as Slater himself had recognized. With Conan Doyle putting his shoulder to the wheel, the campaign for Slater's release steadily gathered force over the next two years.

The turning point came in July 1927, with the appearance of a new book by William Park, a Glasgow journalist. Park, as Conan Doyle later described him, "had within him that slow-burning, but quenchless, fire of determination which marks the best type of Scotsman." He had spent years digging into the story, prompted by the disclosures of Lieutenant John Trench, the policeman whose forthright testimony had cost him his job. With Conan Doyle's help, Park gathered his findings under the title of *The Truth About Oscar Slater*. Conan Doyle contributed a crisp foreword and published the volume through his own Psychic Press.

Drawing on Lieutenant Trench's impressions, Park presented a graphic reconstruction of the murder. In his view—an opinion shared by many—Miss Gilchrist had known her killer and opened the door to him willingly on the night of her murder. Then, in the course of a quarrel over a document in her possession, the old woman had been pushed to the floor, striking her head on a coal box near the fireplace. Seeing that the injury was serious, the visitor faced an urgent dilemma. If Miss Gilchrist recovered and identified him to the police, he would be charged with a violent assault. If she subsequently died, the charge would be murder. Summoning his resolve, the visitor picked up a heavy chair and bludgeoned the old woman to death. Snatching up the incriminating document, he fled the scene—passing Miss Gilchrist's paid companion, Helen Lambie, in the corridor. According to Park, the murderer "slipped out unchallenged" because Miss Lambie knew him and had no reason to question his presence in the flat. Although libel laws prevented Park from naming the suspect, Conan Doyle and many others had known of his involvement for some time. It was Francis Charteris, the victim's nephew, now a professor at St. Andrews University.

Park's book touched off a press circulation war, with several newspapers vying to provide fresh revelations about the case. The *Empire News* registered a major coup when it published "Why I Believe I Blundered over Slater," which purported to be a statement from Helen Lambie, who had since immigrated to the United States. According to Miss Lambie, the police had disregarded her statement that she recognized the man fleeing the crime scene, and instead coached her to identify Slater. A rival newspaper, the *Daily News*, produced a second witness, who claimed that the police had offered her a £100 bribe to finger Slater.

On November 8, 1927, five days after the *Daily News* revelation, the secretary of state for Scotland issued a statement: "Oscar Slater has now completed more than eighteen and a half years of his life sentence, and I have felt justified in deciding to authorize his release on licence as soon as suitable arrangements can be made." The timing of this decision, coming as it did amid a public clamor for a retrial, was not lost on the press. By releasing Slater, the government hoped to preempt any further disclosures.

Six days later, Oscar Slater walked through the gates of Peterhead Prison a free man. Under his arm, he carried a brown paper parcel containing all of his worldly possessions. A special railway car carried him to Glasgow, where a large crowd awaited him, but Slater could not bring himself to address his supporters or answer questions from reporters. He was offered refuge in a private home, and at the sight of a clean bed and a hot water bottle, he burst into tears.

Conan Doyle sent a message to Slater in Scotland: "This is to say in my wife's name and my own how grieved we have been at the infamous justice which you have suffered at the hands of our officials. Your only poor consolation can be that your fate, if we can get people to realise the effects, may have the effect of safeguarding others in the future."

Slater, though not entirely comfortable with the written word, sent a heartfelt response. "Sir Conan Doyle," he wrote, "you breaker of my shackels [*sic*], you lover of truth for justice sake, I thank you from the bottom of my heart and the goodness you have shown me. My heart is full and almost breaking with love and gratitude for you and your dear wife Lady Conan Doyle and all the upright men and women, who for justice sake, (and that only) have helped me, me an outcast. . . ."

Although Slater was a free man, he had not been pardoned. Conan Doyle now led the calls for a retrial, in the hope of clearing Slater's name and winning compensation for his false imprisonment. He updated his "Case of Oscar Slater" pamphlet and sent a copy to every member of Parliament, including the Honorable John Charteris, the Conservative member for Dumfriesshire, the younger brother of the man widely held to be the true murderer of Marion Gilchrist.

A special act of Parliament was passed to enable the Scottish Court of Criminal Appeal to reopen the case. As Slater had no money for legal costs, his supporters raised a defense fund, bolstered by a £1,000 guarantee from Conan Doyle. At the last moment, when Slater discovered that he would not be permitted to give evidence, he announced that he would withdraw his appeal. Conan Doyle responded with white hot fury, as Slater appeared to be scorning the efforts of the many people who had expended time and money on his behalf. Conan Doyle was so angry, it has been said, that he declared himself ready to sign a petition to have Slater's original death sentence carried out. In time, others persuaded Slater of his error and the appeal proceeded as scheduled.

Conan Doyle went to Scotland for the proceedings, meeting Slater for the first time. In contrast to his admiration for George Edalji, Conan Doyle never regarded Slater as anything more than a petty criminal. When Slater sent a silver cigar cutter as a token of his gratitude, Conan Doyle returned it immediately. It was the miscarriage of justice, rather than the man himself, that had roused Conan Doyle's passions. Nevertheless, his account of the hearings, written for the *Sunday Pictorial*, demonstrated a keen sympathy for the plaintiff. "One terrible face stands out among all those others," he wrote of the courtroom. "It is not an ill-favoured face, nor is it a wicked one, but it is terrible nonetheless for the brooding sadness that is in it. It is firm and immobile and might be cut from that Peterhead granite which has helped to make it what it is. A sculptor would choose it as the very type of tragedy. You feel that this is no ordinary man but one who has been fashioned for some strange end. It is indeed the man whose misfortunes have echoed around the world. It is Slater."

After ten days of hearings, the original verdict was dismissed on a technicality. This was by no means the total vindication Slater's supporters had desired but a happy result nonetheless. Matters soon ran aground over the issue of compensation. The court awarded £6,000 to Slater, but left him responsible for the legal costs, which were settled with the funds contributed by Conan Doyle and others. Conan Doyle assumed that Slater would act quickly to reimburse his supporters. He did not. Slater argued that he should not have been held responsible for the court costs in the first place, and therefore could not be expected to pay them out of his settlement. At a stroke, Slater managed to alienate virtually every supporter he had. The money mattered little to Conan Doyle, but he bitterly resented Slater's intent to foist his debts on the people who had won his freedom. He also felt that William Park, whose book had been so instrumental in winning the release, deserved some form of compensation for his long years of labor on Slater's behalf.

Slater would not yield. "You seem to have taken leave of your senses," Conan Doyle told him. "If you are indeed quite responsible for your actions, then you are the most ungrateful as well as the most foolish person whom I have ever known." The two men eventually reached a compromise that found Slater contributing £250 to the costs. In Conan Doyle's view, Slater had simply reverted to type, an opinion Slater quite naturally resented for the rest of his life.

Slater retired quietly to the town of Ayr, on the western coast of Scotland, where he devoted much of his time to wood carving. He made many friends in the community, and even remarried in 1936, at the age of sixty-six. His death twelve years later brought a curious notice in the local newspaper. It read: "Oscar Slater Dead at 78, Reprieved Murderer, Friend of A. Conan Doyle."

29

The Case of the Missing Lady

Friends and relatives of Teresa Neele, late of South Africa, please communicate—Write Box R, The Times, E.C.4.

—PERSONAL AD IN THE LONDON *TIMES*, DECEMBER 11, 1926

It was in December of the year 1926 that all England was interested, and the publishing world dismayed, by the disappearance of Mrs. Agatha Christie, under most unusual and inexplicable circumstances.

Under the headline "The Missing Woman Novelist," the *Times* of London offered its readers the following summary of the case, taken directly from the official police report:

> Missing from her home, the Styles, Sunningdale, Berks., Mrs. Agatha May Clarisa Christie, wife of Colonel Christie, aged 35, height 5 ft., 7 in., hair reddish and shingled, eyes grey, complexion fair, well built, dressed in grey stockinet skirt, green jumper, grey and dark grey cardigan, small green velour hat, wearing a platinum ring with one pearl. No wedding ring. Had black handbag with her,

> containing probably £5 to £10. Left home in a Morris-Cowley car at 9:45 p.m. on Friday, leaving a note saying she was going for a drive. Next morning the car was found abandoned at Newlands Corner, Surrey.

For the next ten days, the "unavailing search" for Mrs. Christie would dominate Britain's newspapers. Not even the death of Claude Monet in Giverney, or the meeting of Winston Churchill and Benito Mussolini in France, could push the Christie story off the front pages.

Conan Doyle's name was also heavily featured in the press that month, though for less sinister reasons. The latest series of Sherlock Holmes stories was still running in *The Strand*, and each new story provoked a great deal of comment in the newspapers. "Those who were about fifteen years old when they first made the acquaintance of Sherlock Holmes, and when Dr. Watson first wrote about him, must be about fifty now," said the *Times*. "To whom else has it been given to share life so long with so persistent, though fictitious, a contemporary?"

While praising the longevity of Holmes, the newspaper mistakenly eulogized Dr. Watson, who had been absent from both "The Lion's Mane," published that December, and "The Blanched Soldier," which appeared the previous month. "Fame is a capricious bedlam," the *Times* declared, "but why is Holmes the only prolonger of his own life, the only survivor of his own biographer and obituarist, the only personage privileged to be his creator's never-failing resource?" No doubt there was much relief in the *Times* offices when Watson reappeared the following month in "The Retired Colourman."

While Conan Doyle enjoyed the accolades of a long career, Agatha Christie had only just begun to make her presence known. *The Murder of Roger Ackroyd,* a milestone of detective fiction, had appeared earlier that year to great acclaim. Mrs. Christie and her husband, the dashing Colonel Archibald Christie of the Royal Flying Corps, began to enjoy a new prosperity. Two years earlier they had moved thirty miles out of London to Sunningdale, where they purchased a large house and christened it the "Styles," a nod to the setting of her first novel, *The Mysterious Affair at Styles.*

As it happened, Mrs. Christie's first wave of commercial success coincided with a period of great personal unhappiness—just as it had with Conan Doyle. The death of her mother in the spring of 1926 threw Mrs. Christie into a deep depression. Matters grew worse in August when Colonel Christie revealed that he had fallen in love with a younger woman named Nancy Neele, a family acquaintance. Mrs. Christie resisted her husband's appeals for a divorce, and their relationship grew increasingly strained.

On the morning of Friday, December 3, a parlor maid overheard a bitter argument between the Christies at breakfast—though Colonel Christie would later deny it. Later that morning, the colonel drove off to spend the weekend with friends in nearby Godalming. Nancy Neele, his new love, was also expected to attend. It was even rumored that Colonel Christie intended to announce his engagement to Miss Neele at the gathering, despite his wife's refusal to grant a divorce.

With her six-year-old daughter Rosalind in tow, Mrs. Christie drove out to Dorking to have tea with her mother-in-law, Rosamund Hemsley. She appeared restless and distracted, though she put on a brave face for her daughter—even singing a few songs with the girl while waiting for the kettle to boil. Mrs. Hemsley attributed her daughter-in-law's moodiness to anxiety over her latest book, *The Blue Train Mystery,* which had brought on a serious case of writer's block. "These rotten plots," Mrs. Christie declared. "Oh, these rotten plots!" Later, Mrs. Hemsley asked why her daughter-in-law wasn't wearing her wedding ring. Mrs. Christie gave no answer. Instead, she sat very still for a moment, then burst into what Mrs. Hemsley called a "hysterical laugh." Upon leaving, Mrs. Christie spent several moments crouched behind the wheel of her car as if lost in contemplation, then she slowly drove away.

That night, Mrs. Christie left the Styles shortly before ten, leaving behind a small clutch of letters. The following morning, her "bottle-nosed" Morris-Cowley two-seater was found abandoned at Newlands Corner, about five miles from Godalming, where Colonel Christie was staying. The car had been driven off the road and abandoned with its lights still burning. A brown fur coat and small suitcase were found inside. The case, which had burst open, contained dresses, shoes, and an expired driver's license in the name of Agatha Christie. Nearby was a small body of water called the Silent Pool where, in one of Mrs. Christie's early novels, a body had been discovered.

Fearing the worst, the police launched a massive search of the area. Tracker dogs and spotter planes were brought in. A crew of divers dragged the Silent Pool. A "petrol-driven tractor" cleared away thick patches of undergrowth. Colonel Christie took an active part, even employing his wife's wire-haired terrier as a bloodhound. As the days dragged on with no progress, thousands of civilian volunteers joined in the search—including thirty-three-year-old Dorothy L. Sayers.

Strange, conflicting stories began to emerge. One man came forward to report that on the night in question he had encountered a stranded female motorist who was "strange in her manner." She wore no hat or coat, and her hair was "covered with hoar-frost." The man assisted her in restarting her Morris-Cowley, and she drove away in the general direction of Newlands Corner.

Colonel Christie's own mother threw coals on the fire with a confusing statement to a *Daily Mail* reporter. "I am inclined to think that my daughter-in-law planned her end and deliberately drove the car to where it was found," Mrs. Hemsley stated. If this appeared to suggest a premeditated suicide, however, she immediately contradicted herself: "She was devoted to her husband and child and would never willingly have left them. It is my opinion that in a fit of depression and not knowing where she was going or what she was doing, my daughter-in-law abandoned her car at Newlands Corner and wandered away over the Downs."

The question of premeditation was to vex more than one investigator. The noted crime novelist Edgar Wallace, speculating on the case in the *Daily Mail,* offered his own theory: "The disappearance seems to be a typical case of 'mental reprisal' on somebody who has hurt her. To put it vulgarly, her first intention seems to have been to 'spite' an unknown person who would be distressed by her disappearance. That she did not contemplate suicide seems evident from the fact that she deliberately created an atmosphere of suicide by abandonment of her car."

Wallace did not name the person against whom this mental reprisal might be directed, but the implication was clear. Initially, the public viewed Colonel Christie as the very model of the concerned, grieving husband. As the search dragged on, this perception began to change, fueled by lurid speculation in the press. One scenario had him receiving a phone call from his wife on the fateful night and rushing away from his dinner party to prevent her from causing a scene. As rumors of his affair with Nancy Neele began to circulate, Colonel Christie found himself transformed into a suspect in his wife's disappearance. Much conjecture centered on the letters Mrs. Christie left behind at the Styles. Though the contents were never disclosed, it was darkly hinted that the missing woman had feared for her safety. Colonel Christie had no illusions about the shifting attitude of the police. "They think I've murdered my wife," he complained to a colleague.

By the time Conan Doyle stepped in, Mrs. Christie had been missing for one week. Unlike Edgar Wallace, Conan Doyle could claim something of an official connection to the case. At the time of his knighthood in 1902, Conan Doyle had been given the honorary position of Deputy-Lieutenant of Surrey. Though he had shed the title as he transferred his energies to the spiritualist movement, the association may have provided a pretext for the chief constable of Surrey to seek his advice.

It was reasonable to hope that Conan Doyle, the creator of Sherlock Holmes, would approach the Christie disappearance with the same rigorous logic he brought to the cases of George Edalji and Oscar Slater. Instead, he decided to solve the problem by psychic means.

In fairness, this should not have come as a surprise to anyone who had been following Conan Doyle's "Uncharted Coast" writings in *The Strand*. In "A New Light on Old Crimes," published in 1920, Conan Doyle made it clear that he regarded psychic science as a powerful tool for clearing up unsolved mysteries. "It should be possible at every great police-centre to have the call upon the best clairvoyant or other medium that can be got, and to use them freely, for what they are worth. None are infallible. They have their off-days and their failures. No man should ever be convicted upon their evidence. But when it comes to suggesting clues and links, then it might be invaluable."

The Christie case, Conan Doyle believed, presented an ideal opportunity to showcase the clues and links one might glean from psychic investigation. Toward that end, he contacted Colonel Christie and obtained one of the missing woman's gloves. Next, he placed the glove in the hands of Horace Leaf, the man he considered to be the best psychic available. Conan Doyle thought so highly of Leaf that he occasionally sent the younger man out to lecture in his stead, and came to regard him as his "lieutenant" in the spiritualist crusade. "I knew him to be an exponent of the subject with an intellectual grasp of every aspect of it, and a pleasing platform manner and delivery," Conan Doyle wrote. "But above all he has what I lacked, those personal psychic powers which enabled him to give actual demonstrations."

Chief among Leaf's powers was a talent for psychometry, the ability to receive psychic impressions from a physical object. "The method is very simple," Leaf explained in his book *The Psychology and Development of Mediumship*. "An article worn or handled by an individual, held in the hand of the psychometrist or pressed against the forehead may call up in his mind thoughts, feelings, and even visions related to that individual."

In other words, Conan Doyle intended to use Horace Leaf as a kind of psychic bloodhound, after giving him the "scent" from Mrs. Christie's glove. "I gave him no clue at all as to what I wanted or to whom the article belonged," Conan Doyle said in a letter to the *Morning Post*. "He never saw it until I laid it on the table at the moment of consultation, and there was nothing to connect either it or me with the Christie case. The date was Sunday last. He at once got the name of Agatha."

In the absence of corroboration, we must take Conan Doyle at his word that he offered no clue as to the identity of the glove's owner. However, as Mrs. Christie's name had been on the front page of every newspaper for a full week, it is possible that Leaf reached his conclusion by other than psychic means.

It is also possible that Conan Doyle neglected to record intermediate steps that could have led Leaf to the name of "Agatha." Magicians who perform mind-reading effects sometimes employ a technique called "chaining," in which a string of canny, ambiguous questions is asked, phrased so as to invite response from the subject. A question such as "You're not married, are you?" will likely draw an affirmation or denial. If the answer is yes, the mind reader is able to say, "Ah! I thought so!" If not, an answer of "I didn't think so" is equally correct. In this manner, a skilled entertainer can pluck a seemingly impossible revelation from a series of benign questions. Once explained, as Dr. Watson often declared, the matter becomes absurdly simple.

It is not known whether Horace Leaf employed a similar technique, consciously or not, to produce the name of the owner of the glove. Having gotten that far, however, he could no longer have been in any doubt as to the identity of the owner. He might have stopped there and received full marks for an impressive psychometric display, but Leaf went on to offer a further series of impressions, with none of the misty ambivalence of a typical psychic reading. "There is trouble connected with this article," Leaf announced. "The person who owns it is half dazed and half purposeful. She is not dead, as many think. She is alive. You will hear of her, I think, next Wednesday."

At the time Mrs. Christie was widely presumed to be dead, especially by the Berkshire police, whose efforts were clearly aimed at retrieving a body, rather than at locating a missing person. Leaf's unambiguous declaration that she would be found alive appears very persuasive. From Conan Doyle's account, however, it is difficult to tell whether Leaf's impressions were quite as bold and precise as he suggests. "There was a good deal about character and motives which was outside my knowledge," Conan Doyle said in his letter to the *Post*. His reluctance to belabor the unhappy details of the Christies' marriage is entirely admirable, but it also tells us that he did not report the full content of Leaf's remarks, some of which may have been off the point.

One of those unrecorded remarks concerned an impression of water, which proved to be strangely accurate, though perhaps not in the way that Leaf or Conan Doyle imagined. An even more compelling clue might have been gleaned from the previous day's *Times*. While the front pages kept readers current on the search, a personal ad further back invited communication from friends and relatives of a woman named Teresa Neele, late of South Africa.

On Saturday, December 4—the morning after Mrs. Christie's disappearance—Teresa Neele had arrived by taxi at an elegant Edwardian spa called the Harrogate Hydropathic Hotel, in Yorkshire, with no luggage apart from a small bag. The other guests were led to believe that she had come to recover from the loss of a baby, which accounted for her melancholy appearance. Over the next few days, however, Mrs. Neele grew cheerier, acquired new clothing, and became more sociable. In the evenings, she danced the Charleston with the other guests to such hit tunes as "Don't Bring Lulu" and "Yes, We Have No Bananas," performed by the Happy Hydro Boys. On occasion, Mrs. Neele sang and played the piano in the lounge. She also tried her hand at billiards.

Bob Tappin, who played banjo with the Happy Hydro Boys, could not help noticing that Teresa Neele bore a strong resemblance to Agatha Christie. Other guests had noticed the similarity, and some had even pointed out the likeness to Mrs. Neele, who brushed the comments aside. Tappin waited a day or so, then took his suspicions to the police, who summoned Colonel Christie to Harrogate. "Fancy," said Teresa Neele at the sight of Colonel Christie, "my brother has just arrived."

The two withdrew into a private room as reporters converged on the hotel, clamoring for details. Later that evening, Colonel Christie offered a terse statement: "There is no question about the identity. It is my wife. She has suffered from the most complete loss of memory and I do not think she knows who she is." The following morning, while a decoy couple distracted the press, the Christies slipped into a waiting car at the hotel's side entrance.

While his wife recovered with friends, Colonel Christie expanded on the amnesia story. "My wife is extremely ill," he told the press. "Three years have dropped out of her life. She cannot recall anything that has happened during that period. The fact that she lives in Sunningdale has no significance for her, and she does not seem to realize that her home is at the Styles. As to what has happened since she left there her mind is a complete blank. She has not the slightest recollection of going to Newlands Corner or of proceeding eventually to Harrogate. . . . It is somewhat remarkable that she does not know she has a daughter. In this connexion, when she was shown a picture of herself and Rosalind, her little daughter, she asked who the child was, 'What is the child like?' and 'How old is she?' "

The explanation did not sit well with the press or the public. Further inquiries were brushed aside, though Mrs. Christie's doctors issued several bulletins concerning her health. Questions were raised in Parliament about the expense of the search, which some estimated to have amounted to £10,000, though the home secretary placed it at a considerably more modest £25. Colonel Christie indicated that he would pay the costs in either case, and renewed his pleas for solitude to allow his wife to recover.

Many questions and contradictions remain. No one can be certain how Mrs. Christie covered the three miles from Newlands Corner to the Guildford Railway Station, where she caught the milk train to London, on the night in question. It remains unclear what she hoped to accomplish by placing her personal ad in the *Times*. If her memory loss was genuine, it seems strange that her publisher, Sir Godfrey Collins, was heard to remark "She is in Harrogate, resting" on the morning after her disappearance. Stranger still, Harrod's of Knightsbridge forwarded a ring belonging to Mrs. Christie to Mrs. Neele in Harrogate. Mrs. Christie's brother-in-law also appears to have known that she was at a spa in Yorkshire, having received a letter to that effect from Mrs. Christie herself. The police followed up the lead, but the inquiry came to nothing since Teresa Neele, not Agatha Christie, had signed the hotel register.

Many theories were put forward. Some dismissed the entire episode as a publicity stunt. Others inclined to the view that Mrs. Christie hoped the drama would intimidate her husband into remaining in the marriage. Mrs. Christie's choice of the name Neele—the name of Colonel Christie's new love—cannot have been a coincidence. Another theory held that Mrs. Christie intended to frame her husband for murder, perhaps so that she herself could rescue him from the clutches of the law. This seemed outlandish, the theorists agreed, but no more so than the average plot of an Agatha

Christie novel. The contents of the letters Mrs. Christie wrote on the night of her disappearance have never come to light, but it is thought that one of them went to the local police, indicating that she feared for her life. Certainly the police came to take a dim view of Colonel Christie as the search dragged on. One journalist had no doubts on this point: "If she had intended suicide and if her body had been found in the Silent Pool, I have no doubt from what I knew of the police attitude that Colonel Christie would have been held on circumstantial evidence."

Conan Doyle, for his part, offered no opinion of Mrs. Christie's motives. For him, the case had been a triumph of psychometry. "The Christie case has afforded an excellent example of the use of psychometry as an aid to the detective," he wrote in his letter to the *Morning Post*. "It is, it must be admitted, a power which is elusive and uncertain, but occasionally it is remarkable in its efficiency. It is often used by the French and German police, but if it is ever employed by our own it must be *sub rosa*, for it is difficult for them to call upon the very powers which the law compels them to persecute."

Conan Doyle was indulging in a bit of rhetorical gamesmanship here. The French and German police were unlikely to contest this bland assertion, but the British police were quick to register annoyance. "We do not keep hopeless lunatics in the police forces of this country," declared one official.

Perhaps, but Conan Doyle, the canny propagandist, had already scored his point. He racked up further capital by appearing to disagree with one of Horace Leaf's psychic impressions. "[E]verything in the reading," he reported, "proved to be true. The only error was that he had an impression of water, though whether the idea of a Hydro was at the bottom of this feeling is at least arguable." This was exceedingly deft. Only a total pedant would deny a link between Leaf's impression of water and Mrs. Christie's discovery at a hydropathic spa, as Conan Doyle knew perfectly well. His apparent hesitation over the point invited the reader to affirm the association—and therefore take a step toward belief—while Conan Doyle himself maintained the appearance of critical scruple.

As it happened, Mrs. Christie had been located on a Tuesday, rather than a Wednesday, as Leaf had predicted. However, since Conan Doyle had recorded the phrasing as "You will hear of her, I think, next Wednesday," he could claim that the statement had been at least partly accurate—as the newspaper accounts did not appear until the following day.

No one knows what Agatha Christie thought of all this, though she soon threw off the ill effects of the Harrogate drama. In time she would agree to a divorce from Colonel Christie, who went on to marry Nancy Neele. She herself married Max Mallowan, an archaeologist, four years later. She would remain silent about her eleven-day disappearance for the rest of her life, but there can be no doubt that she had mixed feelings about the involvement of Conan Doyle in the affair. He would have been an intimidating figure to any budding crime writer, but especially to Agatha Christie, who had felt a heavy burden at the start of her career to create a fictional detective who was "not like Sherlock Holmes." In *A Study in Scarlet*, Sherlock Holmes made famously derogatory remarks about Dupin and Lecoq. In Agatha Christie's *Mrs. McGinty's Dead*, published in 1952, Holmes himself became the target of a similar diatribe: "I have my methods, Watson," a detective novelist remarks to Hercule Poirot. "If you'll excuse me calling you Watson. No offence intended. Interesting, by the way, how the technique of the idiot friend has hung on. Personally, I myself think the Sherlock Holmes stories grossly overrated."

"The doll and its maker are never identical," as Conan Doyle once remarked, so one hesitates to ascribe her character's views to Mrs. Christie. It is well known, however, that the Harrogate drama would remain a sensitive topic for the rest of her life. It cannot have pleased her to find Conan Doyle, the colossus of detective fiction, hovering at the edge of this highly personal, deeply painful episode.

In 1929, three years after the disappearance, an unusual Agatha Christie story appeared in her *Partners in Crime* collection. The action begins as a gentleman calls on Tommy and Tuppence Beresford, Mrs. Christie's husband and wife sleuths, for help in locating his missing fiancée. Tommy's appraisal of the new client has a familiar ring:

"Beyond the fact that it is urgent, that you came here in a taxi, and that you have lately been in the Arctic—or possibly the Antarctic, I know nothing."

Tommy, we discover, is writing "a little monograph" on the effects of the midnight sun and has taken to playing the violin—badly. At one stage, Tommy's impersonation of Sherlock Holmes grows so pronounced that Tuppence offers to get him a vial of cocaine.

As the story progresses, however, the initial suspicion of foul play proves unfounded. The missing fiancée, it emerges, has simply removed herself to a spa for slimming purposes. Crestfallen, Tommy expresses a hope that no record of the case will survive. "It has absolutely *no* distinctive features," he declares.

Did Agatha Christie intend a sly dig at Conan Doyle for his involvement in the affair? It is difficult to say, but the title of the story is highly suggestive. It was "The Case of the Missing Lady."

30

The End of the World

"I'm expecting the end of the world today, Austin."
"Yes, sir, what time, sir?"

—PROFESSOR CHALLENGER AND HIS BUTLER IN *THE POISON BELT*

In March 1927, Conan Doyle wrote to Oliver Lodge to discuss the end of the world. For five years, mediums from around the world had been forwarding dire warnings of a global apocalypse. They came from many sources, but the forecast was essentially the same. "The earth will rock and the seas run dry," ran one message. "A great calamity is about to happen to your earth," insisted another. "Thousands will perish by plagues and floods."

Conan Doyle had accumulated more than a hundred of these warnings by 1927. The urgent tone of the messages, along with an apparent increase in seismic activity worldwide, convinced him that the crisis was imminent. If nothing else, he believed, the sheer number of these grim portents could not be ignored. "It is impossible in my opinion not to take them seriously," he said of the messages, "for they represent in themselves a psychic phenomenon for which I know no parallel." Prominent among the soothsayers was Pheneas, Jean's spirit guide, who spoke of a coming "harvest time." Commenting on a powerful earthquake in Japan, Pheneas left little room for doubt: "We are loosening the rivets," he declared.

Conan Doyle believed that the cataclysm would take the form of earthquakes and tidal waves, a "terrific convulsion" that would sweep the globe in an instant. Entire countries would disappear, and the present form of civilization would end. The tide of death, it appeared, was to be selective. A great number of people—the "hopeless material"—would be culled, while members of the "Elect," who had accepted the message of spiritualism, would remain to govern over a new order. Conan Doyle theorized that some form of fatal gas would be released, to which members of the Elect would be rendered immune. For a brief time, the veil separating this world and the next would lift, so that earthly beings and spirits would stand face to face. After a short period of "utter chaos," an idyllic spiritualist utopia would emerge.

These prophecies, it would seem, grew out of a belief that the entire planet had become a modern Sodom and Gomorrah. In turning a deaf ear to the teachings of spiritualism, humanity had doomed itself to a painful period of cleansing and rebirth. Conan Doyle freely acknowledged the biblical aspects of this scenario and saw no contradiction in terms. He had long since come to regard spiritualism as the successor to traditional religious thought, absorbing some elements and discarding others. "Spiritualism," he insisted, "is the basis of the religion of the future."

Up to this stage, Conan Doyle had shown no great restraint in the psychic arena. Now, for perhaps the first time, he recognized the need for caution. He could imagine only too vividly how this new announcement would be greeted if he made it public. At the same time, for all the apparent consensus of psychic opinion, he felt some skepticism. "I repeat that I have no certainty over these events," he told Lodge. "We want no hysterical developments, nor do we wish to commit the spiritualistic movement to a prophecy which may not materialize."

In spite of his reservations, Conan Doyle felt a duty to circulate the forecasts among a small circle of enlightened friends, since he believed it would be the job of spiritualists to provide comfort and instruction if the crisis came. He drew up a small pamphlet entitled

"A Warning," but urged that it be handled with discretion. "Let those hear who have an ear to hear," he wrote, "but let it not be broadcast." Conan Doyle removed all references to the coming apocalypse from *Pheneas Speaks*, which appeared in 1927, and held them in reserve for a second volume—"which," he told Lodge, "will be much sterner stuff." This second volume never appeared.

Conan Doyle's colleagues were perplexed by this latest turn. "It won't do any good," Lodge wrote to a friend, "even if it should be true." Harry Price, writing in the *Journal for the American Society for Psychical Research*, would dismiss the matter in a smirking editorial: "The cataclysmic disaster of cosmic magnitude with which Doyle has been trying to make our flesh creep for the past two years still hangs fire and the dawn of 1927 finds us sleeping serenely in our beds, giving little heed to the devastating seismic catastrophe with which—says Sir Arthur—we are threatened by evil spirits on both sides of the veil. . . . We are now promised a new Armageddon for 1928!"

Price had been unjust, as the apocalyptic visions had not originated with Conan Doyle. One might argue over the source of Pheneas's predictions, but Conan Doyle could hardly have influenced each of the dozens of far-flung mediums who reported their results to him. His spiritualist fellows, seeing their influence fade, would not have been the first zealots to dangle the threat of extinction before an unresponsive world. Conan Doyle saw himself only as the "clearing house" of a strange concordance of psychic thought. He expressed sorrow, but no vindictiveness, toward the many millions who had failed to heed the psychic call and took no satisfaction that his message would be verified in such dramatic fashion.

Price aside, few who met the aging Conan Doyle would have cast him as a prophet of doom. He seemed instead a genial, contented figure, who spoke often of the "perfect happiness" of his family life. Each spring he hunted through the gardens at Windlesham for the first white snowdrop of the season, presenting it to Jean to mark the anniversary of their meeting. His younger daughter—nicknamed "Billie"—would remember him as an attentive and loving father, who would often make time to accompany her to the dentist or to Brownie meetings. In spite of his well-known distaste for the suffragettes, she recalled, he raised her to consider herself the equal of her two brothers. At the same time, according to her brother Adrian, their father would brook no violation of the family honor. As young men, Adrian would write, he and his brother Denis were given to occasional fits of recklessness. Conan Doyle would soon forgive the destruction of an expensive automobile or an accidental fire in the billiards room, but Adrian never forgot the "white blast of fury" that greeted an offense his father regarded as far more serious. Adrian, it seems, had been rude to the second housemaid.

Sports remained a favorite leisure activity. Although Conan Doyle had finally given up cricket, he golfed often at the nearby Crowborough Beacon Golf Club. On one occasion he returned home in his stockinged feet, having given his golf shoes to a passing tramp.

To the end of his life, he took a keen interest in new inventions and technological developments, and even posed with his radio and headphones for the cover of *Popular Wireless Weekly*. He remained enthralled with automobiles, though he now left the fast driving to his sons, and was taken on a high-speed circuit of the Brooklands racetrack at the age of seventy.

If the modern world fascinated him, modern art did not. Many of the new trends seemed strange and even offensive to him. As early as 1912, he had expressed despair over the direction of modern art, which had drifted so far from the familiar world of his famous uncles. "One should put one's shoulder to the door," he wrote, "and keep out insanity all one can." His tastes in literature, too, remained firmly rooted in the previous century. He repeatedly urged the work of authors such as Scott and Thackeray on young readers, while up-and-coming figures such as Hemingway, Eliot, and the members of the Bloomsbury group held no attraction. He would not have been the only reader who failed to apprehend the charms of *Ulysses*, first published in 1922, but at least one phrase would have struck a chord: "He had been meantime taking stock of the individual in front of him and Sherlockholmesing him up. . . ."

As he fell out of step with contemporary trends, Conan Doyle retreated into the imaginative realm of science fiction, though not always with the distinction of his younger days. Science fiction presented a clean slate on which to work out new ideas and enthusiasms, much as he had done with *The Lost World*. One of these fresh interests was the legend of Atlantis. In *The Wanderings of a Spiritualist*, the chronicle of his Australian lecture tour, Conan Doyle speculated at some length over the fate of the mythic island and traced its legend through the works of Plato and the ancient Egyptians. If the legends were true, he theorized that the destruction of Atlantis would have raised an enormous tidal wave, wiping out much of the world's population to make room for the present inhabitants. A similar fate, he hinted darkly, might lay in store for the modern world. "The great war," he suggested, "is a warning bell perhaps."

In 1927, Conan Doyle took up the theme in a cautionary novel called *The Maracot Deep*, which carried the subtitle "The Lost World Under the Sea." The story followed the adventures of a Professor Maracot and his companions, who set out to explore the ocean floor in a pressurized diving bell. When a giant lobsterlike creature attacks, sending the diving bell plunging into a mysterious trench, the adventurers are rescued by inhabitants of Atlantis. There, Maracot learns the sad fate of the Atlantean people, who have fallen into such a state of "moral degeneracy" as to be enslaved by an inferior race. This unhappy situation, the reader discovers, might have been averted if the Atlanteans had only heeded the warnings of a small minority of reformers, whose history is displayed for Maracot and his men on a luminous screen. "We saw them, grave and earnest men, reasoning and pleading with the people," Conan Doyle wrote, "but we saw them scorned and jeered at by those whom they were trying to save." Subtlety, it would seem, was in short supply beneath the sea.

For all of that, Conan Doyle handled the action scenes with his usual skill, and many reviewers compared the book favorably with Jules Verne's *Twenty Thousand Leagues Under the Sea*, which had been an obvious influence. Jules Verne was also much in evidence when Conan Doyle brought Professor Challenger back for a pair of brief curtain calls. In "The Disintegration Machine," Conan Doyle explored the potential of matter transmission—the ability to reduce an object to its component atoms and reassemble them elsewhere—an idea he had first considered in *The Mystery of Cloomber* some forty years earlier. This concept, now a science-fiction bromide, would have been startling to Conan Doyle's original readers, for whom the home radio set represented a fairly new technology. Challenger's other appearance, in a novella called *When the World Screamed*, found him drilling a tunnel deep into the earth's crust. The incursion produces a mighty roar of "Plutonic indignation" from deep within the earth, along with the eruption of every volcano on the surface—proving that the planet is, as Challenger had suspected, a living organism. "It has been the common ambition of mankind to set the whole world talking," wrote Conan Doyle in conclusion. "To set the whole world screaming was the privilege of Challenger alone."

Conan Doyle would have relegated these tales to that "different and humbler plane" that we recognize today as genre fiction. He never revised his view that Challenger—along with Sherlock Holmes and, to a lesser extent, Brigadier Gerard—had denied him his rightful place as the modern master of historical romance. In these latest efforts, however, he once again demonstrated the innovations of thought and style for which he is remembered today. He may have looked to Verne and H. G. Wells for raw material, just as he turned to Poe for the spark that became Sherlock Holmes, but the results showed the same pioneering spirit. Unfortunately, these last stories also show clearly that his mind was on other things. "Ideas and wit were there in abundance," as he once said of his friend James Barrie, but he did not carry them through to a satisfying conclusion. The plots fell short, and the characters appeared to be going through the motions.

In November 1928, Conan Doyle launched a five-month lecture tour of Africa, retracing some of the same ground he had covered during the Boer War, complete with a stop in Bloemfontein. Once again the family accompanied him, but the tour was not an especially happy one. Many local newspapers were hostile to the spiritualist crusade, and even he admitted that some audiences "listened with indulgence if not acquiescence." Lingering resentments from the war years brought further difficulties. Visiting a memorial to the casualties of British concentration camps, Conan Doyle employed a "warm expression" at a suggestion of British mistreatment. The press reported his outburst, with the result that a crowd of several hundred people gathered at his hotel threatening violence, only to be dispersed by police before Conan Doyle appeared. He wrote a letter of apology to the *Cape Times*, stating that he had misinterpreted the meaning of the monument's inscription.

At another stage of the tour, a critic of spiritualism baited him with charges of using Kingsley's death for propaganda purposes. Conan Doyle had to be restrained from administering a thrashing with his umbrella. The umbrella also came into play as Denis and Adrian ventured out on a big-game hunt. When beaters offered to drive a rhinoceros into the line of fire, Conan Doyle suggested that a surprise flick of his umbrella would distract the beast long enough for his sons to bag it. It seems the rhinoceros, who would have none of it, survived the encounter.

Visiting the grave of Cecil Rhodes in Rhodesia, now Zimbabwe, Jean yielded to one of her frequent psychic impulses and took down a communication from the late British imperialist. "This way I came and I went to my destiny, partly of happiness and partly of regret," the message ran. "But here one makes up for missed opportunities."

By the close of the tour, the heat and the long hours of travel had taken a toll on Conan Doyle. He began to experience dizzy spells and occasional jolts of pain in his chest. Where possible, he concealed his symptoms and soldiered on. As a medical man, however, he knew perfectly well that his campaigning days were coming to an end.

Back in England, he regained his strength in the relative isolation of the New Forest of Hampshire. Since 1925, the family had divided its time between Windlesham and a quiet retreat called Bignell House, near the town of Minstead. Conan Doyle had developed a lasting fondness for the area in his Southsea days, when he sequestered himself to a rustic cottage to write *The White Company*. As a gift to Jean, he purchased a small cottage that dated to the reign of George I and featured a greenhouse and a thatched Saxon barn. Conan Doyle had the property modified to join up the cottage and barn, and installed a heating system and water pump, driven by generators.

It would seem that Pheneas had a hand in the decision to buy the property. Quite probably the New Forest was thought to offer a comparatively safe haven in the coming global apocalypse. Be that as it may, it also afforded a much needed sanctuary for Conan Doyle, who could pursue his writing projects in peaceful solitude. It is often reported that the local villagers avoided Bignell House, regarding it as a hotbed of spiritualist activity. At one stage, it is said, even the postman declined to approach. Conan Doyle's younger daughter strenuously denied this notion. She recalled that the neighbors in Bignell Wood made the family feel welcome in the community, and that the cottage received many callers. Certainly the locals managed to overcome any inhibitions in August 1929, when sparks from the kitchen chimney ignited the thatched roof and set the entire house ablaze. While the family dashed into Conan Doyle's study to rescue his papers, neighbors gathered to do what they could. Later, Conan Doyle sent a grateful letter to the local newspaper, expressing gratitude to the villagers who dragged their furniture onto the lawn—"One or two, I regret to say, showed a disposition to remove the goods even further, but the greater number gave me invaluable assistance."

Little of the property remained standing by the end of the night. Privately, Conan Doyle came to suspect that the fire had been psychic in origin. Jean received a message shortly afterward that claimed a "bad psychic cloud" had infected parts of the property, and since Bignell House was to be used for "high purposes amid or before coming events," this negative force had to be purged. Psychic cloud or no, Conan Doyle hired builders to restore the property, but would not live to see it completed.

Two months after the fire, Conan Doyle embarked on another round of travels. "I am off next week to do Holland, Denmark, Stockholm and Oslo," he told Harry Price. "My ambition is to speak in each European non-Catholic capital before I pass." Although the schedule was lighter and the reception more cordial than it had been in Africa, his health buckled under the strain. In Copenhagen, he suffered a bout of agonizing chest pains, but refused to curtail his speaking schedule. In near constant pain, he carried on with his slate of lectures, often clinging to the podium for balance. Returning to England on the Channel ferry in November, he had to be carried ashore.

Doctors were summoned to confirm what Conan Doyle already knew. "I write this in bed," he told a friend in America, "as I have broken down badly, and have developed Angina Pectoris. So there is just a chance that I may talk it all over with Houdini himself before very long. I view the prospect with perfect equanimity. That is one thing that psychic knowledge does. It removes all fear of the future."

Against his doctors' orders, he struggled up to London to honor a speaking commitment at an Armistice Day spiritualist assembly. Riding to the Albert Hall in a cab, he suffered another attack. He leaned heavily on his sons as he staggered into the hall, and delivered his speech in a halting, weakened voice. Refusing to admit to his infirmity, he gave a second speech later in the day.

His doctors now ordered complete bed rest. A sickroom was established on the ground floor at Windlesham, as Conan Doyle now had difficulty climbing the stairs. As 1929 drew to a close, he tried as best he could to keep up with correspondence and business matters, often dictating to Major Wood, his secretary. A jotting at the bottom of one typewritten letter offers a glimpse of his slow progress: "I am still tied down—can do 100 yards—not more. No pain now." His diet was strictly monitored, and he had to content himself with a bunch of grapes at Christmas dinner.

In January 1930, as he paged through the *Journal of the Society for Psychical Research*, he roused himself for yet another letter-writing campaign. This time the target would be the Society itself, an organization he had come to regard with suspicion. The *Journal* had published a hostile review of a work called *Modern Psychic Mysteries*, by an investigator named Bozzano. This book described a series of séances held at Millesimo Castle, the home of the Marquis Scotto, an Italian nobleman of Conan Doyle's acquaintance. The offending review, by the society's librarian, Theodore Besterman, accused the marquis of failing to take any precautions against fraud and berated the author for having been duped by a series of routine deceptions.

For Conan Doyle, this represented the culmination of an alarming trend. The Society, he believed, had become far too critical of the mediums it examined, fostering an antagonistic attitude that could only inhibit, rather than promote, the development of spiritualist talent. "In certain directions the work of the society has been excellent," he had written in *The History of Spiritualism*, "but from the beginning it made the capital error of assuming a certain supercilious air towards spiritualism, which had the effect of alienating a number of men who could have been helpful in its councils, and, above all, of offending those mediums without whose willing cooperation the work of the society could not fail to be barren. At the present moment the society possesses an excellent séance room, but the difficulty is to persuade any medium to enter it."

Conan Doyle had never forgiven the Society's officers for refusing to censure Harry Price, the investigator who had exposed the deceits of spirit photographer William Hope. This latest affront, he feared, demonstrated a dangerous and inflexible policy. He lodged a formal complaint, protesting that the "insolence" and "insulting innuendos" of the Besterman review had been intolerable. When this failed to bring satisfaction, he penned a letter of resignation and circulated it among the members of the Society, calling on them to do the same. He had been a member for thirty-six years, but now, it appeared, even the world's foremost assembly of psychical researchers had grown too skeptical for his liking.

The officers of the Society, mindful of Conan Doyle's fragile health, sought a diplomatic resolution. When he rebuffed a private approach, an official response appeared. The purpose of the Society, it explained, had always been the critical and evenhanded investigation of psychic phenomena. The proof of this balanced policy could be seen in the membership roll, which included both skeptics and committed believers. If, the statement continued, the Millesimo Castle séances had conformed to a reasonable standard of scientific control, they would have received more serious attention: "It is, however, to be noted that sittings held in complete darkness, for the most part without control and without any searching of those present, sittings at which phenomena were produced which cannot be paralleled in the records of any sittings held under good conditions, are described by Sir Arthur as 'on the very highest possible level of psychical research.' Further comment is superfluous."

This left Conan Doyle no room to back down. In his resignation, he had stated that the affair "makes one ashamed that such stuff should be issued by an official of a Society which has any scientific standing." It was a feeble thrust, since the Society's insistence on scientific standards of proof appeared to be at the root of his protest. For years, Conan Doyle had presented his spirit convictions as a matter of religious faith, and declared them immune to any scientific proof or disproof. Now, in castigating the Society for falling short of scientific standards, he appeared to be playing both sides of the fence. All too often in those last years, he trotted out his own scientific credentials when it suited him, but retreated beneath the cloak of faith when it did not.

This churlishness showed itself only when he felt provoked. For the most part, he was content to tread more softly, as he did in a widely circulated Movietone newsreel of the time. Unlike George Bernard Shaw, who appeared stiff and dogmatic in his Movietone appearance, Conan Doyle looked relaxed and happy in his rose garden at Windlesham, chatting amiably and fluidly for some twenty minutes. Whereas Shaw had plunged straight into world politics, Conan Doyle warmed up his audience with a topic he knew would hook their attention: Sherlock Holmes. "The curious thing is how many people there are in the world who are perfectly convinced that he is a living human being," Conan Doyle told the camera. "I get letters addressed to him. I get letters asking for his autograph. I get letters addressed to his rather stupid friend, Watson. I've even had ladies writing to say that they'd be very glad to act as his housekeeper. One of them, when she'd heard that he had turned to the occupation of keeping bees, wrote saying that she was an expert at segregating the queen, whatever that may mean, and that she was evidently predestined to be the housekeeper of Sherlock Holmes."

He continued in this vein for some time, winning over his audience with his candid observations and engaging tone. After a time, the seasoned lecturer turned smoothly to "the psychic matter." Here, too, he kept his remarks light, trusting to his natural warmth and sincerity to carry the force of his message: "I suppose I've sat with more mediums, good and bad and indifferent, than perhaps any living being; anyhow a larger variety because I've traveled so much all over the world. . . . When I talk on this subject, I am not talking about what I believe, I'm not talking about what I think, I'm talking about what I know. There's an enormous difference, believe me, between believing a thing and knowing a thing. I'm talking about things that I've handled, I've seen, that I've heard with my own ears, and always, mind you, in the presence of witnesses."

He spoke for a few more minutes about his long study of the subject, and about all the "splendid young fellows" who had perished in the war, then concluded on a heartfelt note. "Certainly the results have justified me," he said. "I'm quite sure I could fill a room of my house with the letters that I have received from people telling me of the consolation which my writings on this subject—and my lectures on this subject—have given to them. How they have once more heard the sound of a vanished voice, and felt the touch of a vanished hand."

That said, he smiled warmly and stood up to take his leave. "Well, good-bye," he told his newsreel audience. Calling to the family dog, he strolled out of view. These few moments of film footage give some idea of the impact he must have had as a platform speaker. He radiated goodwill and decency; it seemed impossible that his views could be anything but plainspoken common sense. His detractors have occasionally cast him as a deluded and rancorous figure, cackling at the prospect of an imagined global cataclysm. If so, he managed to conceal it with uncommon skill. Seeing him on the screen, the spirits and fairies and nonsense fall away. One sees only good intentions.

Through the early months of 1930, he showed brief periods of improved health. He took advantage of his renewed energy to revise his autobiography, adding a chapter entitled "Up to Date," and to write a modest paragraph of introduction for *The Edge of the Unknown*, a collection of spiritualist essays.

On July 1, he went to the battlements for the last time. For some months he had been lobbying against an ancient piece of legislation called the Witchcraft Act, dating to the reign of James I, which had been revived as a means of prosecuting mediums. A steady flow of letters brought about a meeting with the home secretary, Mr. J. R. Clynes. Jean accompanied him to the Home Office and watched anxiously, clutching a vial of smelling salts, as her husband rose unsteadily to plead his case. Mr. Clynes appeared more concerned with his visitor's health than with the merits of his argument. "Pray sit down, Sir Arthur," he said, offering a glass of water. His voice faltering, Conan Doyle went ahead with his prepared statement, drumming his fingers against his chest as though to keep his heart beating.

He returned home badly weakened, but even now, there were some duties he could not entrust to others. One cold spring morning, his son later recalled, he rose from his sickroom and stole out into the garden, unseen by anyone in the house. A few moments later, the butler heard a crash in the hallway. He found Conan Doyle lying on the floor, gasping for breath.

One hand clutched his heart. The other held a single white snowdrop.

He told his family that he did not wish to die in bed. As the crisis neared, they helped him to a chair where he could look out at the Sussex countryside. He died there, surrounded by his family, on the morning of Monday, July 7, 1930. He was seventy-one years old. His last words were addressed to his wife. "You are wonderful," he said.

'The reader will judge that I have had many adventures," he had written a few days earlier. "The greatest and most glorious of all awaits me now."

Epilogue: A Well-Remembered Voice

"My dear Watson," said the well-remembered voice, "I owe you a thousand apologies. I had no idea that you would be so affected."

—SHERLOCK HOLMES IN "THE ADVENTURE OF THE EMPTY HOUSE"

Conan Doyle was laid to rest in the rose garden at Windlesham on July 11, 1930. "The funeral," reported the *Daily News Chronicle*, "was unlike any other; there were no tears, no anguish, and hardly anything that savoured of death." As Adrian told the reporters who flocked to Crowborough, "There is no mourning at Windlesham."

The mood at the graveside, while hardly festive, showed a notable moderation of feeling. Members of the spiritualist community arrived in bright colors and summery frocks. A few top hats and somber frock coats could also be seen, signaling that not everyone shared the family's convictions.

Brilliant floral displays lined the grave, many of which carried banner-messages from friends and admirers. Each member of the family was represented by a lavish wreath—even the family's Irish terrier, Paddy, whose offering bore a heartfelt sentiment: "To Master from the Dog who worshipped you."

Jean attended her husband's coffin in a subdued dress of gray chiffon, a compromise between her beliefs and her transparent sorrow. She listened with obvious approval as the Reverend C. Drayton Thomas, a spiritualist minister, described her husband as a visionary leader. "Sir Arthur will continue his work for the spreading of the great cause which soothes the anguished heart," Reverend Thomas declared, "and which is destined to change the whole outlook of human affairs." As the service concluded, Jean raised a red rose to her lips and threw it onto the coffin.

Messages of condolence flooded in. "A very great man has left us," wrote William Gillette, who had recently completed a farewell tour in the role of Sherlock Holmes, "but he has left us with the admirable and delightful literary work of his earlier years, and in later life had shown a tireless devotion to a cause that he considered of vital importance to humanity."

"I have always thought him one of the best men I have ever known," wrote James Barrie, "there can never have been a straighter nor a more honourable."

George Bernard Shaw, in a statement to the press, injected a characteristic note of pessimism. "I am very sorry to lose him," Shaw remarked, "but, after all, he has made good his escape from this miserable world."

Perhaps the most elegant tribute would come from Greenhough Smith in the pages of *The Strand*. "Doyle's work is done," the editor wrote, "and, in whatever sphere, it was well done." As a final testimonial, Smith arranged to reprint "A Scandal in Bohemia," the first and perhaps best of the Sherlock Holmes short stories. This done, he retired quietly later in the year.

Almost without exception, the press obituaries were headlined with the words "Creator of Sherlock Holmes." As the *Times* of London noted: "Conan Doyle, who became a teacher with a mission in later years, might not particularly desire, but had certainly earned, the grateful salute of the world to a teller of tales who gave, and continues to give, as much pleasure to his fellows as any writer of the age." The *Daily Herald* took much the same tone: "One might well express his passing in the phrase: 'Sir Arthur Conan Doyle is dead! Long live Sherlock Holmes!' " One New York paper, delivering the news on its front page, achieved an unintentionally comic effect: "Conan Doyle Dies of Sherlock Holmes Fame."

Within hours of the announcement, mediums reported the presence of a "brilliant new light" in the spirit world. Soon, spirit messages were pouring in at a fantastic rate. "Well," one psychic was told, "I have arrived in paradise." Another received a rebuke to church officials: "What do your bishops have to say now?" In New York, the itinerant spirit was reported to have exchanged pleasantries with a psychically oriented scrub woman. Matters soon reached a stage where a Bristol newspaper felt constrained to report: "No Message From Conan Doyle."

Faced with this torrent of alleged contacts, Jean issued a statement urging restraint. Her husband's spirit, she insisted, had not yet had time to summon the reserves of energy necessary to break through the veil. "When he has got anything for the world he will communicate with us first," she told the press. "These messages purporting to come from him already cannot be accepted."

Soon after the Albert Hall memorial service, where Estelle Roberts claimed to have contacted Conan Doyle's spirit, Jean began to receive regular messages through her own automatic writing. Within months, she and her children believed themselves to be in daily contact with his spirit, and these communications would continue for years to come. The messages offered advice and guidance in nearly every aspect of the family's affairs, from business matters to the purchase of automobiles. Some years hence, the spirit would advise Jean to seek medical attention. Ironically, though the living Conan Doyle had failed to detect his first wife's tuberculosis, the family credited him with diagnosing Jean's incipient cancer from beyond the grave.

Conan Doyle also began to appear regularly in spirit photographs, and showed himself to be a singularly obliging subject. As the Reverend Charles Tweedale developed one image, he noticed that a "cloudy band of ectoplasm" threatened to obscure his own self-portrait. Speaking aloud, he made a direct appeal to the spirit: "Will the manifesting personality please take care not to show up on my face?" The form migrated upward, and soon Tweedale had produced a ghostly image of Conan Doyle looming above his own head.

Of all the many posthumous sightings, easily the most ludicrous was reported by Harry Price. Earlier, in a memorial tribute, Price had harsh words for unscrupulous mediums who had taken advantage of Conan Doyle's ready friendship. "Too honest himself," Price wrote, "he could not imagine his too sympathetic credulity being imposed upon." Only three months later, however, Price published his own lengthy interview with Conan Doyle's spirit, conducted through the medium Eileen Garrett. "I feel myself the man I was on earth," Conan Doyle told his old adversary. "I find myself doing many of the things which I did there." Although Price allowed for the possibility of fraud, the exercise stands as a mercenary blot on his reputation.

Meanwhile, many of the mediums whom Conan Doyle had supported were falling from grace. Nino Pecararo, whose powers Conan Doyle had defended against the criticisms of Houdini, was soon hounded out of business by the magician Joseph Dunninger. "Spirit of Doyle's Son Merely Nino's Trick," reported the *New York Evening Journal*; "Nino Pecararo, Who Helped Conan Doyle's Faith in Mystic World, Admits Deceit," announced the *Herald Tribune*. For the next ten years, similar headlines would appear at regular intervals as one "reformed medium" after another attempted to convert exposure into financial gain.

Conan Doyle's own messages from the spirit world were also held up to criticism. "Now the late Sir Arthur was an admirable writer of English," noted one journalist. "If the post-death messages are exact copies of those messages, his knowledge of even the elementary rules of grammar must have suffered woefully since his death." If the powers of Sherlock Holmes had seemed to dim after his death at Reichenbach, many felt that Conan Doyle, too, had "never been the same man afterwards."

If Jean was troubled by these expressions of doubt, she gave no sign. For the rest of her life she would carry on her husband's work, even purchasing a special "motor van" to help spread leaflets and other psychic literature. In this way, she wrote, "I can look into my Beloved's dear face, when he meets me at the Gateway of Death, and say, 'I have tried to keep your Banner flying'—and we will part no more."

☾ ☾ ☾

Just a few days before his death, Conan Doyle had sat for an interview with a reporter named W. R. Titterton. Feeling weak and dizzy, Conan Doyle asked Titterton to sit beside him on the couch, so that he would not have to strain to make himself heard. "In every other way I'm the man I always was," he said, "but my heart's claiming some of my attention, and it is better not to tire my voice."

For the better part of an hour, Conan Doyle set out the foundations of his beliefs one last time, and patiently addressed the charges leveled at him by his critics. He concluded by urging his interviewer to visit a spiritualist church— "It will make you very happy," he said.

Afterward, Conan Doyle led his visitor to the door, pausing in the entryway to introduce him to Jean, Denis, and Adrian. There, the journalist dropped his professional reserve and admitted in gushing tones to a lifelong admiration of his host's novels and short stories. "I told them that I had read every one of Sir Arthur's stories," he wrote, "and knew many of them almost by heart." For some moments, he recalled his favorite passages for the family, and discussed some fondly remembered characters with Denis and Adrian. "I got through with honours," he recalled, "and my host was pleased, for I remembered the stories far better than he did." With a final word of thanks, Titterton took his leave and went back to London to file what would prove to be Conan Doyle's last interview.

"I am not certain," he wrote at the end of his piece, "but I rather think that throughout the interview we did not mention the name of Sherlock Holmes."

BIBLIOGRAPHY

Selected Works of Arthur Conan Doyle

FICTION:

The Adventures of Gerard; The Adventures of Sherlock Holmes; Beyond the City; The Case-Book of Sherlock Holmes; Danger! and Other Stories; The Doings of Raffles Haw; A Duet with an Occasional Chorus; The Exploits of Brigadier Gerard; The Firm of Girdlestone; The Great Shadow; The Green Flag and Other Stories of War and Sport; His Last Bow; The Hound of the Baskervilles; The Land of Mist; The Last Galley; The Lost World; The Man from Archangel; The Maracot Deep and Other Stories; The Memoirs of Sherlock Holmes; Micah Clarke; The Mystery of Cloomber; The Parasite; The Poison Belt; The Refugees: A Tale of Two Continents; The Return of Sherlock Holmes; Rodney Stone; Round the Fire Stories; Round the Red Lamp; The Sign of the Four; Sir Nigel; The Stark Munro Letters; A Study in Scarlet; The Tragedy of the Korosko; Uncle Bernac; The Valley of Fear; The White Company

NONFICTION AND SPIRITUALISM:
The British Campaign in France and Flanders; The Case for Spirit Photography; The Coming of the Fairies; The Edge of the Unknown; The Great Boer War; The History of Spiritualism; Memories and Adventures; The New Revelation; Our African Winter; Our American Adventure; Our Second American Adventure; Pheneas Speaks: Direct Spirit Communications in the Family Circle; Three of Them: A Reminiscence; Through The Magic Door; The Vital Message; The Wanderings of a Spiritualist

PAMPHLETS, PLAYS, AND POETRY:
Brigadier Gerard; "The Case of Oscar Slater"; *The Crime of the Congo; The Fires of Fate; The Guards Came Through; The House of Temperley; Jane Annie; Songs of Action; Songs of the Road; The Speckled Band; The Story of Mr. George Edalji; A Story of Waterloo;* "The War in South Africa: Its Causes and Conduct"

Other Sources

Baker, Michael. *The Doyle Diary.* London: Paddington Press, 1978.

Baring-Gould, William S. *The Annotated Sherlock Holmes.* London: John Murray, 1968.

Booth, Martin. *The Doctor, The Detective and Arthur Conan Doyle.* London: Hodder & Stoughton, 1997.

Brown, Ivor. *Conan Doyle.* London: Hamish Hamilton, 1972.

Carr, John Dickson. *The Life of Sir Arthur Conan Doyle.* London: John Murray, 1949.

Conan Doyle, Adrian. *The True Conan Doyle.* London: John Murray, 1945.

Cooper, Joe. *The Case of the Cottingley Fairies.* London: Robert Hale, 1990.

Coren, Michael. *Conan Doyle.* London: Bloomsbury, 1995.

Costello, Peter. *The Real World of Sherlock Holmes.* New York: Carroll & Graf, 1991.

Cox, Don Richard. *Arthur Conan Doyle.* New York: Frederick Ungar, 1985.

De Waal, Ronald Burt. *The World Bibliography of Sherlock Holmes and Dr. Watson.* New York: Bramhall House, 1974.

Edwards, Owen Dudley. *The Quest for Sherlock Holmes.* Edinburgh: Mainstream, 1983.

Ernst, Bernard M. L., and Hereward Carrington. *Houdini and Conan Doyle: The Story of a Strange Friendship.* New York: Albert & Charles Boni, 1932.

Gibson, John Michael, and Richard Lancelyn Green, eds. *Letters to the Press.* Iowa City: University of Iowa Press, 1986.

———. *The Unknown Conan Doyle: Essays on Photography.* London: Secker & Warburg, 1982.

———. *The Unknown Conan Doyle: Uncollected Stories.* New York: Doubleday, 1982.

Goldfarb, Clifford S. *The Great Shadow: Arthur Conan Doyle, Brigadier Gerard and Napoleon.* British Columbia: Calabash Press, 1997.

Green, Richard Lancelyn, ed. *Arthur Conan Doyle on Sherlock Holmes: Speeches at the Stoll Convention Dinner.* London: Favil Press, 1981.

———. *The Uncollected Sherlock Holmes.* London: Penguin Books, 1983.

Green, Richard Lancelyn, and John Michael Gibson. *A Bibliography of A. Conan Doyle.* Oxford, England: Clarendon Press, 1983.

Hall, Trevor H. *Sherlock Holmes and His Creator.* New York: St. Martin's Press, 1977.

———. *Sherlock Holmes: Ten Literary Studies.* New York: St. Martin's Press, 1969.

Hardwick, Michael, and Mollie Hardwick. *The Man Who Was Sherlock Holmes.* London: John Murray, 1964.

Harrison, Michael, ed. *Beyond Baker Street.* New York: Bobbs-Merrill, 1976.

Harrison, Michael. *The World of Sherlock Holmes.* New York: Dutton, 1975.

Higham, Charles. *The Adventures of Conan Doyle.* New York: W. W. Norton, 1976.

Holroyd, James Edward. *Baker Street By-ways.* London: George Allen & Unwin, 1959.

Jaffe, Jacqueline A. *Arthur Conan Doyle.* Boston: Twayne, G. K. Hall, 1987.

Jann, Rosemary, ed. *Detecting Social Order.* New York: Twayne's Masterwork Studies, 1995.

Jones, Kelvin I. *Conan Doyle and the Spirits.* Wellingborough, England: Aquarian Press, 1989.

Lachtman, Howard. *Sherlock Slept Here.* Santa Barbara, Calif.: Capra Press, 1985.

Lamond, John. *Arthur Conan Doyle: A Memoir.* London: John Murray, 1931.

Lellenberg, Jon L., ed. *The Quest for Sir Arthur Conan Doyle.* Carbondale: Southern Illinois University Press, 1987.

Liebow, Ely M. *Dr. Joe Bell: Model for Sherlock Holmes.* Bowling Green, Ohio: Bowling Green University Popular Press, 1982.

Nordon, Pierre. *Conan Doyle.* London: John Murray, 1966.

Orel, Harold, ed. *Critical Essays on Sir Arthur Conan Doyle.* New York: G. K. Hall, 1992.

———. *Sir Arthur Conan Doyle: Interviews and Recollections.* New York: St. Martin's Press, 1991.

Pearsall, Ronald. *Conan Doyle: A Biographical Solution.* London: Weidenfeld & Nicolson, 1977.

Pearson, Hesketh. *Conan Doyle: His Life and Art.* London: Methuen, 1943.

Pointer, Michael. *The Public Life of Sherlock Holmes.* London: David & Charles, 1975.

Redmond, Christopher. *Welcome to America, Mr. Sherlock Holmes.* Toronto: Simon & Pierre, 1987.

Roberts, S. C. *Holmes and Watson: A Miscellany.* Oxford, England: Oxford University Press, 1953.

Rodin, Alvin E., and Jack D. Key. *Medical Casebook of Doctor Arthur Conan Doyle.* Malabar, Fla.: Robert E. Krieger, 1984.

Rosenberg, Samuel. *Naked Is the Best Disguise.* London: Arlington Books, 1975.

Shreffler, Philip A., ed. *The Baker Street Reader.* Westport, Conn.: Greenwood Press, 1984.

———. *Sherlock Holmes by Gas Lamp.* New York: Fordham University Press, 1989.

Starrett, Vincent. *The Private Life of Sherlock Holmes.* London: George Allen & Unwin, 1961.

Stavert, Geoffrey. *A Study in Southsea.* Portsmouth, England: Milestone Publications, 1987.

Stone, Harry. *The Casebook of Sherlock Doyle.* Romford, England: Ian Henry Publications, 1991.

Symons, Julian. *Conan Doyle: Portrait of an Artist.* New York: Mysterious Press, 1987.

Tracy, Jack. *The Encyclopaedia Sherlockiana.* New York: Doubleday, 1977.

Tracy, Jack, with Jim Berkey. *Subcutaneously, My Dear Watson.* Bloomington, Ind.: James A. Rock, 1978.

Weller, Philip, with Christopher Roden. *The Life and Times of Sherlock Holmes.* New York: Crescent Books, 1992.

Weller, Philip, ed. *Recollections of Sir Arthur Conan Doyle.* Collected by Malcolm Payne. Hampshire, England: Sherlock Publications, 1993.

Related Materials

Barbanell, Sylvia. *Some Discern Spirits: The Mediumship of Estelle Roberts.* London: Psychic Press, 1944.

Barrie, James. *The Greenwood Hat.* London: Peter Davies, 1937.

Binyon, T. J. *Murder Will Out: The Detective in Fiction.* Oxford, England: Oxford University Press, 1990.

Brandon, Ruth. *The Spiritualists.* New York: Alfred A. Knopf, 1983.

Carrington, Hereward. *Modern Psychical Phenomena.* New York: Dodd, Mead, 1919.

Christie, Agatha. *Partners in Crime.* New York: Dodd, Mead, 1929.

Christopher, Milbourne. *Houdini: A Pictorial Life.* New York: Thomas Y. Crowell, 1976.

———. *Houdini: The Untold Story.* New York: Thomas Y. Crowell, 1969.

Cooke, Ivan, ed. *The Return of Arthur Conan Doyle.* Hampshire, England: White Eagle Publishing Trust, 1961.

Crookes, William. *Researches in the Phenomena of Spiritualism.* London: Psychic Book Club, 1953.

Ellman, Richard. *Oscar Wilde.* New York: Alfred A. Knopf, 1988.

Ford, Arthur. *Unknown But Known.* New York: Harper & Row, 1968.

Gardner, Edward L. *Fairies: The Cottingley Photographs and Their Sequel.* London: The Theosophical Publishing House, 1957.

Gill, Gillian. *Agatha Christie: The Woman and Her Mysteries.* New York: The Free Press, 1990.

Gresham, William Lindsay. *Houdini: The Man Who Walked Through Walls.* New York: Holt Rinehart Winston, 1959.

Hall, Trevor H. *The Strange Case of Edmund Gurney.* London: Duckworth, 1964.

Hill, C. W. *Edwardian Scotland.* Edinburgh: Scottish Academic Press, 1976.

Holroyd, Michael. *Bernard Shaw,* vol. 2. New York: Random House, 1989.

Home, Mme. Dunglas. *D. D. Home: His Life and Mission.* London: Kegan Paul, Trench, Trubner, 1921.

Houdini, Harry. *A Magician Among the Spirits.* New York: Harper & Bros., 1924.

———. *The Unmasking of Robert-Houdin.* New York: Publishers Printing, 1908.

Inglis, Brian. *Roger Casement.* London: Hodder and Stoughton, 1973.

Jerome, Jerome K. *My Life and Times.* New York: Harper and Bros., 1926.

Kee, Robert. *The Green Flag: The Turbulent History of the Irish National Movement.* New York: Delacorte Press, 1972.

Kellock, Harold. *Houdini: His Life Story.* New York: Harcourt, Brace, 1928.

King, W. D. *Henry Irving's Waterloo.* Berkeley: University of California Press, 1993.

Laurence, Dan H. *Bernard Shaw: Collected Letters 1911–1925.* New York: Viking, 1985.

Lodge, Sir Oliver. *Raymond: Or Life and Death.* New York: George H. Doran, 1916.

———. *Why I Believed in Personal Immortality.* London: Cassell, 1928.

McCabe, Joseph. *Is Spiritualism Based on Fraud?* London: Watts, 1920.

McClure, Samuel S. *My Autobiography.* London: John Murray, 1914.

Park, William. *The Truth About Oscar Slater.* London: The Psychic Press, 1927.

Pearsall, Ronald. *The Table-Rappers.* New York: St. Martin's Press, 1972.

Price, Harry. *Fifty Years of Psychical Research.* London: Longmans, Green, 1939.

———. *Leaves from a Psychist's Case-Book.* London: Victor Gollancz, 1933.

———. *Search for Truth: My Life in Psychical Research.* London: Collins, 1942.

Prince, Walter Franklin. *The Enchanted Boundary.* Boston: Boston Society for Psychic Research, 1930.

Randi, James. *Flim-Flam!* Buffalo: Prometheus Books, 1987.

Roberts, Estelle. *Forty Years a Medium.* New York: Avon Books, 1972.

Robyns, Gwen. *The Mystery of Agatha Christie.* New York: Doubleday, 1978.

Roughead, William. *Trial of Oscar Slater.* Edinburgh: William Hodge, 1929.

Sanders, Dennis, and Len Lovallo. *The Agatha Christie Companion.* New York: Delacorte Press, 1984.

Sidgwick, Henry et al. *Presidential Addresses to the Society for Psychical Research: 1882–1911.* Glasgow: Robert Maclehose, 1912.

Silverman, Kenneth. *Houdini: The Career of Ehrich Weiss.* New York: Harper Collins, 1996.

Stoker, Bram. *Personal Reminiscences of Henry Irving.* London: William Heinemann, 1907.

Symons, Julian. *Bloody Murder: From the Detective Story to the Crime Novel.* London: Faber and Faber, 1972.

Taylor, A. J. P., ed. *Lloyd George: A Diary by Frances Stevenson.* New York: Harper & Row, 1971.

Thurston, Fr. Herbert. *Modern Spiritualism.* London: Sheen & Ward, 1928.

Tietze, Thomas R. *Margery.* New York: Harper & Row, 1973.

Toughill, Thomas. *Oscar Slater: The Mystery Solved.* Edinburgh: Canongate Press, 1993.

Tweedale, Violet. *Phantoms of the Dawn.* London: John Long, 1938.

Watt, Francis. *The Book of Edinburgh Anecdote.* London: Foulis, 1913.

Whittington-Egan, Richard, and Molly Whittington-Egan, eds. *The Story of Mr. George Edalji.* London: Grey House Books, 1985.

Winks, Robin. *Modus Operandi: An Excursion into Detective Fiction.* Boston: David R. Godine, 1982.

Journals, Magazines, and Newspapers Consulted

ACD: The Journal of the Arthur Conan Doyle Society; The American Weekly; The Baker Street Journal; Boy's Own Paper; The Bristol Times & Mirror; The British Journal of Photography; Chambers's Journal; The Chronicle; Cornhill Magazine; The Edinburgh Evening Dispatch; The Express; The Glasgow Herald; The Hampshire Telegraph; The Idler; The Illustrated London News; John O'London's Weekly; The Ladies' Home Journal; Light; London Society; McClure's Magazine; The New York American; The New York Evening Journal; The New York Times; The New York Tribune; The New York World; The Observer; Pearson's Weekly; The Pharos; The Evening News (Portsmouth); *Quarterly Transactions of the British College of Psychic Science; Review of Reviews; The Saturday Evening Post; The Scotsman; The Sherlock Holmes Journal; The Journal of the Society for Psychical Research; The Spectator; The Spiritualist; The Strand; The Telegraph; Temple Bar; The Times; Two Worlds; The Yorkshire Evening News.*

ACKNOWLEDGMENTS

The author wishes to acknowledge the generous support of the U.S.–U.K. Fulbright Commission and Mr. Graham Greene of the Raymond Chandler estate.

I am also deeply indebted to the following people and institutions: Chrys Ray, Ben "Bullet Boy" Robinson, P. M. Meadows of the Cambridge University Manuscripts Department, Catherine Cooke of the Marylebone Library Sherlock Holmes Collection, Julian Symons, Alan Wesencraft of the Harry Price Collection, Julia Walworth of the Senate House Library, The British Society for Psychical Research, Joanne McMahon of the Eileen J. Garrett Library, The American Society for Psychical Research, Dr. John Corbett of Glasgow University, The Committee for the Scientific Investigation of Claims of the Paranormal, Selwyn Tillett of the Sir Arthur Sullivan Society, Sonny Wareham, Michael Ruhlman, Toby Linden, Mrs. Maurine Christopher and the Milbourne Christopher Collection, Eleanor and Frances, The Toronto Reference Library, Bob Loomis of The Association of International Magical Spectators, The Humanities Research Center of the University of Texas, The University of Edinburgh, The Oxford University Library, T. J. Binyon and the ever hospitable Senior Common Room of Wadham College, The Portsmouth City Council, The Library of Congress, Donald Maass, and Cynthia Vartan.

Thanks also for the gracious encouragement of Jon Lellenberg, Richard Lancelyn Green, Christopher and Barbara Roden, Peter Blau, R. Dixon Smith, Andrew Solberg, and John Baesch.

INDEX

Titles without author attribution are works by Conan Doyle.